Urban Society:
The Shame of Governance

Urban Society:
The Shame of Governance

edited by

Robert Grantham
Levon Chorbajian

University of Massachusetts Lowell

2011
Sloan Publishing
Cornwall-on-Hudson, NY 12520
http://www.sloanpublishing.com

Library of Congress Cataloging-in-Publication Data

Urban society : the shame of governance / edited by Robert Grantham, Levon Chorbajian.
-- 1st ed.
p. cm.
ISBN 978-1-59738-027-0
1. Sociology, Urban--United States. 2. Cities and towns--Growth. 3. Municipal govern-
ment--United States. I. Grantham, Robert. II. Chorbajian, Levon.
HT151.U683 2010
307.760973--dc22
2010026327

Cover photographs: Capitol, Jamie Blake; Wall Street, Michael Daddino (http://www.
flickr.com/photos/epicharmus/1481122250/); Broadway Avenue, Newburgh, NY, Bill
Webber.
Cover design: Amy Rosen, K&M Design

© 2011
Sloan Publishing, LLC
220 Maple Road
Cornwall-on-Hudson, NY 12520

Printed in the United States of America

10 9 8 7 6 5 4 3 2 1

ISBN 13: 978-1-59738-027-0
ISBN 10: 1-59738-027-X

Contents

Preface

In *Urban Society: The Shame of Governance* we feature studies that depict irresponsible actions, inactions, or neglect of cities by agencies of government, often working with the corporate community, including major real estate interests. However, we do not assume that there is a complete, one to one, correlation between irresponsible government actions and urban problems. In other words, we put this volume together with the understanding that while various acts of government contribute to social problems, such acts or failures are not the sole cause of urban malaise. There are other contributing factors. This acknowledgement allows us to avoid the trap of promoting specific initiatives intended to resolve urban problems when the effectiveness of such initiatives are likely to vary from city to city. Otherwise, we would be forced to provide an exhaustive city-by-city account of the successes and failures of specific programs.

Instead we recognize structural deficiencies linked to forces of governance that dampen access to resources, complicate claims to justice, and promote lop-sided socio-economic development. For example, federal grants in the 1980s under the Reagan Administration for a) mass transit, b) community and regional development, and c) education, training and social services were cut by 18, 39, and 33% respectively between 1980 and 1985. We argue that political commitment to a neoliberal agenda has influenced policy decisions in support of budgetary reductions of this magnitude, which, in turn, exacerbate existing urban problems. The studies that we include in this volume grapple with the fallout from the marriage of corporate interests and government policy under the umbrella of neoliberal ideology.

We are cautious, however, about making assessments regarding the merits of specific programs that were lost as a result of past or current policy decisions. Such precautions stem from our understanding that while it is often easy to identify problems of governance, individuals responsible for the implementation of policy are not infallible. So, as we note the unfortunate conditions tied to macro-structural forces of governance in this volume we also note that it would be naïve for anyone to assume that the implementation of social policies in cities are not sometimes hampered by ineptitude, corruption, inefficiency, power-struggles, and a lack of commitment of public officials, a pattern with variations from city-to city.

Acknowledgements

I thank my parents—Robert and Lillie Grantham—for their love and support, Sandra Barnes for her encouragement and insights, Elijah Anderson for his words of wisdom, Tony Santos for his odd (but appreciated) encouragement, and Lorrell Kilpatrick, Tom Krebs, Ted Brimeyer, Sharon Holtrop, Ambition Sandelmela, Tara Kazmi, Eric Gaydu,

Tom Andrews, and Harry Hanson for their continued moral support. Love to my aunts Yankee, Elma, Poochie, and Joyce and to my siblings Charis, Sonja, and Sekou.

—Robert Grantham

I thank my family, my wife Beverly and children Monty, Ruby, Garo, Seta, and Von for their inspiration and many forms of support including love and plenty of wit. I also thank Rose Najarian and Joyce Chorbajian for being great cousins for many years.

I have benefitted from the friendship and intellectual companionship of friends Corey Dolgon, Jerry Lembke, Markar Melkonian, Steve Rosenthal, Jim Russell, and Anoush Tertalian. Thanks so much!

—Levon Chorbajian

Jointly, Robert and Levon cannot say enough in praise of our editor Bill Webber of Sloan Publishing. Bill has been terrific with enthusiastic support, great advice, and hands-on help.

Introduction

While sociologists have studied many institutions over the years, no entity has so obsessed them like the city. Our focus is on cities in the United States from the 1970s to the present, a time span that has brought vast changes that have been shaped by reductions in government spending for large cities, tax-cuts for wealthier families and individuals, suburban growth, and a pro-business political climate. Many of the changes have been engineered by well financed and positioned forces in the corporate world and in government. Consequently, as a result of various political and economic forces, there have been winners and losers. For example, vast economic structural changes have led to an increase in urban families living below the poverty line. Working class and poor neighborhoods have been abolished and replaced with superhighways, convention centers, luxury condominiums, high rise office complexes, sports arenas, and upscale malls. Explanations for these changes have often led to claims of a need for urban renewal and development, resulting in gentrified areas. Most researchers readily describe gentrification as a process that displaces low income families from communities—communities that became the targets of economic developers. Urban renewal projects, however, are ubiquitous and commonly represented in the press as symbols of economic progress. Seldom do we read about the social fallout from these changes; and rarely about links between urban social dilemmas and government accountability.

For example, researchers argue that "newspapers allocate more space to sports than local government and urban issues. They pay more attention to sports 'box scores' than to 'keeping score' of how well public officials and government agencies carry out public policies, or of the economic and social conditions in urban neighborhoods."[1] Hence, the message we often receive about urban renewal and development is that change is not only necessary but essential for the welfare of the community. This argument is often validated by pro-growth advocates who envision and reap financial benefits from various projects. Sociologists point out that such pro-growth advocates adhere to growth machine theory arguments—arguments that often portray the promotion and validation of urban development strictly in terms of a value-free growth ideology, a claim that growth benefits everyone and is a collective good.[2] These so-called benefits are said to accrue from the development of new shops, tourist attractions, theme parks, and the like.

However, behind this comforting veneer or what some critics have referred to as the "disneyfication" of urban space,[3] there are other political, economic, and human stories to be told. In this volume, we feature studies that promote a different understanding--that a hybrid of political and economic dynamics has not necessarily resulted in a happy ending for urban residents. Large scale deindustrialization has led to a shortage of manufacturing jobs, high levels of unemployment and underemployment. People's neighborhoods and social networks have been destroyed, and people have even been dispersed throughout the city or out of it altogether. The flip side has been that tax dollars have been used in ways that further enrich real estate development and corporate interests. Human services and the

1

operation of basic institutional structures are now chronically underfunded, and this has led to large scale human crisis. Examples abound and can easily be found in media reports though the causes are only rarely intelligently considered or even ever addressed at all.[4] The result is a system we call the shame of governance caused by the neglect of public institutions and the use of government decision making authority to serve corporate interests and not human interests, i.e. profits first; people second, particularly urban residents.

Could it have been different? We think it could have. Corporate profits and the shame of governance were not the only options. Billionaire owners of sports teams could have been told to pay for their own new stadiums, and the public monies that went into them could have been invested in the construction and maintenance of affordable housing. Low or no interest loans could have been made available to building and small business owners to upgrade their investments in low income districts. Greater investments could have been made in urban public education, libraries, mass transit, and recreational facilities. Another alternative was provided by the commission report issued in the aftermath of the urban uprisings of the 1960s in places like Detroit and Newark and scores of other cities nationwide. That report called for massive expenditures in housing, education, and job training among other areas of social investment. Few of these expenditures were ever authorized at a time when federally funded urban renewal projects of the type we are critiquing here were in full swing.[5]

In this wide ranging introduction we consider a number of issues including the kinds of decisions that were made, why they were made, and their social consequences. We begin with a brief review of the literature on cities.

A Highly Condensed History of Urban Literature

Writers for close to 200 years have produced a lively, engaging, and often provocative literature on cities. Some of this writing has been produced by sociologists, and some valuable, even pathbreaking, contributions have been made by writers from other disciplines and professions.

In the 19th century, Karl Marx and Frederick Engels created a theory of history and an analysis of capitalism. The central focus of Marxist analysis was on class relations and the conflict between the working class which they called the proletariat and the class that owned the productive resources of society, the bourgeoisie. As a result Marx and Engels paid primary attention to the international class struggle, and social revolution within specific national states. They did not entirely, however, ignore cities. In fact there is a certain sense in which it can be said that Marx and Engels were intensely interested in cities, the social classes found in them, their actual conditions of life, and, not least, urban workers and the revolutionary potential they saw in them. This is strongly implied in *The Communist Manifesto* when they write of capital's need to replace the isolation of workers with their "radical combination" which we can take to mean their concentration in cities as wage laborers. The rise of industrial cities inevitably brings large numbers of workers into close proximity and provides them with a shared experience as exploited labor from which revolutionary movements are born. Marx and Engels also wrote two books with explicit urban themes. The first is Engels' study *The Condition of the Working Class in England in 1844* based on his ethnographic field work in Manchester and the second is Marx's *The Civil War in France*, his study of Paris Commune, the workers' rebellion and takeover of

Paris in the spring of 1871.[6] Also in the 19th century the social reformers Henry Mayhew and Charles Booth published important studies of the working class and poor in Britain.[7] Meanwhile in the U.S., the muckraking journalist Lincoln Steffens took aim at municipal corruption in *The Shame of the Cities*.[8]

In addition to Marx and Engels, other formative figures in the history of sociology made important contributions to our understanding of cities. W.E.B. Dubois' book on African-American Philadelphia still stands as a classic in the community and urban studies literature.[9] Max Weber's posthumously published study *The City* traces modern cities to a centuries-long evolution rooted in Christianity and especially its Protestant variant emerging from the Reformation.[10] In *The Metropolis and Mental Life* Georg Simmel argued that the Enlightenment freed people from the constraints of traditional society and allowed for the development of their individualism and independence. However, he saw a challenge to that independence in the modern metropolis itself, and called for "The resistance of the individuals to being leveled, swallowed up in the social-technological mechanism."[11]

Numerous writers attempted to capture the 19th century transition from traditional rural to urban society. One of these, Ferdinand Tönnies famously posed the ideal types he called *Gemeinschaft* (community) and *Gesellschaft* (society, association). In the former, people live in small communities and are embedded in strong social networks of friendship and kinship networks. In the latter urban settings, social interactions are seen as impersonal, superficial and fleeting, reflective of the absence of shared backgrounds, values, norms, and attitudes.[12]

Emile Durkheim framed a similar polarity based on solidarities he called mechanical and organic. Whereas Marx had celebrated the Paris Commune, it was Durkheim's nightmare, and his entire intellectual life may be seen as a quest for social order in the new, large industrial, capitalist cities. He associated cities with impersonality as well as freedom from traditional restraints such as religion. In one of Durkheim's major works, *Suicide*, he introduces the sociological concept of *anomie* or rootlessness which is caused by the absence of clear codes of behavior in urban settings. This concept of anomie became one of Durkheim's sociological explanations for suicide.[13] In *The Division of Labor* Durkheim sought to define the relationships that would unify societies much more urban than in the past and found it in the social bonds linking various sectors of society on which each individual was dependent for survival and well being.[14] Implicit in Durkheim's work is the notion that social welfare programs targeting lower income populations integrate potentially restive sectors of the population into society and forestall the growth of unstable and vulnerable social orders.[15]

In the U.S., the famous Chicago School coming out of the Department of Sociology at the University of Chicago in the 1920s and later was the scene of active research on the emergent Midwestern metropolis. As the second largest city in the U.S. at the time and the nation's most important interior city then and now, Chicago fascinated a generation and more of researchers interested in all facets of the new urban metropolis. Among the classics were Frederick Thrasher's *The Gang*,[16] Harvey Zorbaugh's *The Gold Coast and the Slum*,[17] and Paul Cressey's *The Taxi Dance Hall*.[18] Later, but still a part of this Chicago tradition, came Horace Clayton and St. Clair Drake's exquisite two volume study *Black Metropolis: A Study of Negro Life in a Northern City*.[19]

Cities have continued to have their draw and each decade seems to have produced its share of classics. From the 1940's we have William Whyte's study of Italian-American working class youths in Boston's North End, *Street Corner Society*.[20] In the 1950's David Riesman (*The Lonely Crowd*)[21] and C. Wright Mills (*White Collar*)[22] each tried his hand at coming to terms with fast paced changes in the first full post-World War II decade. Riesman posited a new emerging social psychology he called other-directedness while Mills took on the field of labor in what we now know as the service economy. While these widely read books were not about cities specifically, they did address social themes emanating from and concentrated in urban settings and their nearby environs.

In the 1960s Herbert Gans wrote The *Urban Villagers*[23], a book read by countless introductory and urban sociology students. Gans examined a neighborhood that was only a short distance from the setting of Whyte's *Street Corner Society*. Gans' focus was on the lives of working class Italian-Americans whose neighborhood became an early victim of urban renewal and gentrification. In the 1970's William Julius Wilson began writing a series of controversial books on the relationship of class and race in defining the lives of urban African-American populations.[24]

More recent decades have also brought with them the publication of lively case studies; among them Mitch Deneier's work on New York used book and magazine street venders[25], Katherine Newman's study of young African-American fast food workers[26], and Elijah Anderson's research on an African-American neighborhood in Philadelphia.[27] In *When a Heart Turns Rock Solid*, Timothy Black presents the lives of three Puerto Rican working class brothers set in and around Springfield, Massachusetts.[28]

We also owe a large debt to the pathbreaking work of social critic Mike Davis and geographer David Harvey. In his early work, *The City of Quartz* and *The Ecology of Fear*, Davis examined successive waves of class and racial exploitation as well as resistance in southern California.[29] David Harvey is perhaps the preeminent geographer of the late 20th century and early new millennium. His entire mid and late career writings have been concerned with issues of injustice, racism, and exploitation, and he has insisted that geography cannot remain objectively neutral in the face of urban poverty but rather must be socially engaged in combating it.[30] This volume introduces students to the work of both of these authors—Davis from *The Ecology of Fear* and Harvey from *A Brief History of Neoliberalism* along with two selections from William Julius Wilson.

Cities and the Industrial Revolution

The growth of cities in the western world is associated with the growth of industrial capitalism and European empire. This is part of a process that had already gained a foothold in the early second millennium when manufacturers began to hire labor, and trade and sell goods locally, and then in ever expanding arcs into North Africa, the Middle East and beyond. Trade, of course, was neither new nor unique to Europe, but European trade in this period was distinguished by a new emerging political economic form called capitalism. Already in the 12th century money had replaced barter as a form of exchange and small cities began to provide a physical context for the purchase of labor and resources for the manufacture of goods for sale. These sales, when profitable, were the source of additional capital for investment and growth. These changes were part of a long drawn out and violent process of change—violent because the newly emergent capitalist class clashed with the older, landed aristocracy and its ally, the Catholic Church. This led to many wars and came to a head in the French Revolution which spread from France to many parts of Europe and dealt the final death blow to European feudalism. In the Revolution's aftermath the capitalist class now not only possessed wealth, but it held, for the first time, the reins of power in its hands. This new class then used its control of the state to remake society in the image of its own needs as a class. The modern nation state with strong central governments and the power to tax became the major form of political organization. That state established schools to promote the literacy capitalism required to generate and maintain its accounting, inventory, sales and payroll records; funded polytechnic institutes to discover new ways of harnessing energy to machinery; made investments in roads, ports, bridges, and other infrastructure to facilitate trade and commerce; replaced mercantilism with laissez-faire economics; curbed the power of religion from the source of all knowledge to a much narrower institutional sphere; and accelerated the movement of people from rural areas into cities.[31] It is these momentous economic, social and political changes that gave rise to the large industrial cities of Europe and later the United States. London, the capital of the first industrializing nation, England, had 300,000 residents in Shakespeare's time, over half a million in 1700, nearly a million in 1800, and 6.5 million at the start of the 20th century. The growth of other European cities was not so spectacular as London's, but significant.[32]

Cities in the 19th century became centers of great wealth and great poverty, both emanating from the same, common source which was the economic exploitation of the many by the few. Those few were the capitalist class, the owners of the productive resources of society, and the many were the workers of the industrial capitalist nations and the residents of their far flung colonies. Those colonies were the result of Europe's ability to deploy its initially small but sufficient military superiority to conquer and subjugate the rest of the world and avail itself to cheap raw materials, cheap labor, and closed markets in which to sell goods and services at non-competitive prices. Though often glorified in school texts as "The Age of Discovery" this is actually a history of genocide and enslavement unrivaled in history. About this process of capital accumulation, Karl Marx and Frederick Engels famously said: "If money comes into the world with a congenital blood-stain on one cheek, capital comes dripping from head to foot, from every pore, with blood and dirt."[33] The larger European cities were the centers of capitalist political economies and were the locales for the administration, finance, and governance of national capitalist and international economies in addition to serving as manufacturing and shipping centers. Smaller cities, which were also growing in size, played regional, complementary, and specialized roles in these enterprises.

The Unites States plays an ironic and dual role in these developments, both as an exploited colony and the site of the American Revolution, the first anti-imperialist war in modern times, and then, after World War II as the world's most powerful imperial state. Already by the end of the U.S. Civil War, the United States was a significant industrial power and it can be argued by the end of World War I, the world's leading industrial power. In this process of economic development, U.S. cities grew just as English and continental cities had grown earlier. In the U.S. case these population increases came both from the large migrations of people from farms to cities and also from the large influx of European immigrants between the late 19th century and the 1920s by which time the demand for labor was satisfied and immigration was severely limited by law. The relevant legislation consisted of the Immigration Acts of 1921 and 1924 which imposed a quota system favoring European Anglo-Saxon and Nordic countries, a system that remained intact with minor revisions until the mid-1960s. Urban growth in the U.S. has been characterized by dramatically changing patterns of settlement. At various times in the nation's history relatively smallish cites by today's standards, such places as Charleston, South Carolina and New Orleans, have been among the five largest in the country. By 1900 the five largest cities were New York with a population of 3.4 million, followed by Chicago at 1.7 million, Philadelphia at 1.3 million, St. Louis at 580,000, and Boston at 560,000. This is the last half century interval, 1900, when the five largest cities were all in the Mid-Atlantic and industrial Midwest states. By 1950 Los Angeles had entered the top five, and the lineup consisted of New York at just shy of 8 million, followed by Chicago (3.6 million), Los Angeles (2 million), Philadelphia (2 million), and Detroit (1.8 million). The five largest cities according to the 2008 Census Bureau estimate are New York at 8.4 million followed by Los Angeles (3.8 million), Chicago (2.8 million), Houston (2.2 million), and Phoenix (1.6 million).

What we see since 1950 is a trend of population movement westward and southward from the northeast and industrial Midwest as well as movement from central core cities to suburbs nationwide. Of the ten largest cities in 1950 compared to today, New York has slightly gained in population while Los Angeles is the only one of the group to show strong, continuous growth. The remaining eight—Chicago, Philadelphia, Detroit, Baltimore, Cleveland, St. Louis, Washington, and Boston—have all lost significant population even though the size of their metropolitan areas has grown. Seven of the eight are northeast and industrial Midwestern cities while Washington is broadly speaking in the same geographical region though primarily administrative rather than industrial in nature. Of the ten largest cities in 2008, three are in California, three in Texas, and one in Arizona.[34]

Changes Affecting Cities: The Enabling Legislation and Several Case Histories

The major re-development of American cities after 1950 was the result of one of two major pieces of federal legislation: the 1949 Housing Act and the 1956 Highway Act. Adoption of the Housing Act was tied to the construction of affordable housing near military bases and factories, following the Depression in the 1930s. However, provisions of the legislation met with some serious disapproval. Critics of the Act point out that the legislation helped to undermine the availability of affordable housing. For example, provisions of the Act discouraged public housing suppliers from competing with the private housing market by (1) creating rent ceilings that were set at 20% lower than the lowest nearby private housing, (2) mandating the construction of affordable housing units with unappealing and austere physical designs, and (3) establishing low operating budgets for Public Housing Authorities (PHA).[35] Also, at the time of this legislation, racially segregated public housing units were a concern. Consequently, several progressive leaning legislators tried (unsuccessfully) to amend the Act in a manner that would promote better integrated communities.[36]

Additionally, other legislative efforts were adopted, specifically designed to deal with affordable housing concerns. Still, critics argue that the subsequent legislation amounted to an adoption of federal housing programs intended to accommodate the private sector. For example, Section 8 of the 1974 Housing and Community Development Act is described as a program that "provided housing vouchers for tenants to redeem with participating private sector landlords" and "provided incentives for private sector and non-profit real estate developers to construct low-income housing." Second, there is the HOPE VI program, established by the 1990 Cranston-Gonzalez National Affordable Housing Act. The program "provides funding for housing authorities to demolish severely distressed units, sells units to tenants, and creates partnerships with private sector developers and housing managers to reduce operating expenses." Finally, the Quality Housing and Work Responsibility Act "created legislation that enabled housing authorities to turn over management (and other provisions) of public units over to private managers."[37]

The original intent of the laws governing public housing, arguably, was to provide adequate and affordable housing for low income American families. However, the desire for political expedience, economic gain, and land control ultimately led to efforts to placate private interests while reducing the supply of affordable housing in urban areas. Today, lack of strict enforcement mechanisms, coupled with property acquisitions vis-à-vis various legal maneuvers, such as eminent domain, often result in the seizure of land. Unfortunately, however, the demolishing and clearing off of affected areas often occurs at the taxpayer's expense. In sum, conditions continue to exist today whereby land (in urban areas) becomes an auspicious target for commercial development projects, such as high rise office buildings, luxury condominiums, sports arenas, and five star hotels—all to accommodate affluent residents and to lure to cities what some researchers have referred to as the "visitor class."[38]

Transportation related concerns can also amount to structural level problems for urban residents, particularly with regard to necessary travel between home and employment. For some, public transportation is a strong option, in cities like Boston, New York, Chicago, and San Francisco. However, because of the distribution, access, and level of service in these cities—and especially in cities where mass transit is inadequate—owning a car as a means for work travel is essential. Consequently, researchers have examined the demographic make-up of cities and the availability of a car, as a means of transportation to and from work. According to one multi-city study of urban inequality, 86 percent of college and non-college graduates sampled report having access to a car as a mode of transportation for work. Considerations of race and other socio-economic characteristics reveal additional variations. For example, while 93 percent of whites responded to having access to a car, 76 percent of Hispanics and only 65 percent of Blacks reported having access to a car—for the purposes of traveling to work. Also, among high school drop-outs, the percentage of Hispanic and Black respondents (combined) was about a third less than white high school drop-outs who reported having access to a car. Finally, regarding a lack of transportation, of the low income adults in the study, 32 percent of welfare recipients reported *not having* access to a car, while 66 percent of combined welfare recipients and high school drop-outs reported *not having* an available car.[39]

The discussion above is an indication that public transportation is a crucial element in the lives of urban dwellers. It inspires us to review policy efforts that may have had an adverse effect on commitments to mass transit. In 1947 Congress authorized a 37,000-mile national highway network; then in 1956 adopted the Interstate Highway Act, while federal funds for highways went from $429 million in 1950 to $2.9 billion by 1960. The 1956 Highway Act, which created the Federal Highway Trust Fund, designated money for road construction projects that "leveled some older downtown neighborhoods and cut through the middle of others, in the process enabling highways to redesign racial space in cities like Atlanta and Miami by forcing massive relocations and by serving as barriers that separated black and white neighborhoods."[40] Today, researchers also call attention to the impact of the pro-automobile lobby on highway legislation—often at the expense of public transportation in urban areas. One recent study in 2004 suggests that links between the haphazard lifestyles of indigent populations and inadequate public transportation exist. Linda Burton and her co-authors have analyzed interview data of black, white, and Latino mothers in Chicago—amid shrinking fiscal commitments to mass transit—and found that low income mothers frequently have to adjust their daily routines, time obligations, and resource coordination efforts, while struggling to maintain access to transportation, to and from work.[41] While many may view this example through a personal responsibility lens, some social scientists associate these kinds of life adjustment requirements with unsatisfactory public infrastructures, spawned by an emphasis on privatization in the name of development.

Thus, a culmination of legislative patterns regarding urban housing and transportation has (over the years) contributed to unbalanced urban redevelopment patterns, with unfortunate consequences for working class populations in large cities. In the following discussion, we briefly describe examples of three different cities and their unbalanced redevelopment patterns[42]—New Haven, Denver and San Francisco. We then provide a review of the concept of neo-liberalism as it relates to urban areas.

New Haven, Connecticut

New Haven redevelopment, like much urban redevelopment elsewhere, can be described as radical in the physical changes it produced but narrow in the interests it served. From the beginning low income families and minorities were seen as obstacles to central business district expansion by virtue of the fact that they lived adjacent to downtown areas. Between 1956 and 1974 20% of New Haven's population was displaced through demolition and land clearance for development. In the instance of an African-American tenement area adjacent to downtown and the Yale University Medical School, 900 families were displaced along with 250 small commercial and manufacturing businesses to make room for an access road and parking for suburban shoppers. In another instance a factory employing 100 minority workers was demolished. These jobs were not replaced, nor was much of the low cost housing. In New Haven, as elsewhere, more low cost housing was destroyed than re-built. Nor is there evidence that more new employment was created through renewal than was destroyed through demolition. It was not until the 1960s that the African-American community in New Haven organized and began confrontational protests to air and redress grievances that some concessions were made. This too is part of a pattern repeated in other cities; namely, that poor and minority communities not part of the calculus of planning except as impediments to be removed can receive grudgingly provided and limited concessions through collective protest. But once again, in no instance is what they receive equal to what they lose.[43]

Denver, Colorado

In the case of Denver, it is now the leading city in the mountain states region and the headquarters for firms in financial and business services, petroleum and natural gas, and high tech, among others. Its downtown is similar to the downtowns of other similarly sized redeveloped cities with freeways, high rise office buildings, hotels, luxury condos, upscale rental apartments, convention centers, and sports arenas. Denver's redevelopment efforts were dominated by business/commercial interests from the first efforts in the mid-1950s.

The Denver Urban Renewal Authority was founded in 1958. It is a public/private agency whose members are appointed by the mayor. The appointees have consistently been drawn from large corporations in the city, and big merchant and real estate interests. DURA's website tells us that the agency works "…to assist in the redevelopment of blighted property and foster the sound growth and development of Denver." Denver's centerpiece redevelopment effort was the Skyline Project which cleared poorer areas adjacent to the central business district of residents and small, low rise businesses such as pawn shops, bars, and second hand stores that lowered real estate values. In the end more housing was destroyed than built, and most of the housing that was built was in the form of luxury condos and elderly housing. Very little low cost housing for families was ever constructed.[44]

San Francisco, California

San Francisco is often cited as the premier instance of the successful redevelopment of a declining manufacturing and port city transformed into a leading tourist and convention city, and the home of many major transnational corporations. It is also cited as a city where minorities and the poor have fared better than they have in many other places. The history of San Francisco's transformation, however, bears far more similarities to the development of other cities than such a sanguine characterization would indicate. San Francisco's initial urban renewal and planning organizations were private organizations, the regional Bay Area Commission and the city specific Blyth-Zellerbach Committee. Both of these brought together top business leaders to consider plans for the city's future. Eventually the San Francisco Planning and Urban Renewal Association (SPUR) and the San Francisco Redevelopment Authority (SFRA) played leading roles in several very large downtown redevelopment projects which displaced over ten thousand low income residents and hundreds of small businesses that employed thousands of people. From beginning to end both in government and in the redevelopment agencies the leadership consisted of top corporate leaders and professional experts hired to shepherd the corporate agenda to successful completion.

Their projects consistently promoted corporate objectives. The Bay Area Rapid Transit system (BART), for example, was neither designed nor built to link neighborhoods in the city but to ferry workers into and out of the city from the suburbs. The African-American Hunters Point neighborhood had no BART station, and one poorer area of the city was only able to obtain stations through collective protest. The SFRA functioned as a powerful and aggressive semi-autonomous agency dedicated to taking, leveling and rebuilding as much of the city's downtown and adjacent areas as possible. This was with the full endorsement of the city's economic elite which gave no consideration to those who lost their homes (some of them more than once), or to their neighborhoods and social networks. Through the mid-60s, poor and working class communities were not mobilized to resist. The 1964–1974 period was one of high mobilization and challenges to corporate redevelopment through court challenges and direct action, civil disobedience protests. One of the protest groups, Tenants and Owners in Opposition to Redevelopment (TOOR), won a major court case which forced the construction of over 2,500 affordable housing units that would not have otherwise been built. As in other cities, whatever concessions were extracted were won through battles in the courts or in the streets. Concessions were granted reluctantly, however, and strong measures on various fronts were taken to return to the *status quo ante* power hierarchy as soon as it could be managed and with as little damage to the elite agenda as possible.[45]

It is not claimed that no new jobs were created through redevelopment, but the majority of new jobs in the service and tourist industries consisted of low paying employment. Chester Hartman in his history of urban redevelopment in San Francisco claims that the giant Moscone Convention Center created fewer than 200 permanent full time jobs, most of them clerical jobs that would have been generated anyway through office construction elsewhere in the city. There are also the jobs that were eliminated through the destruction of small businesses to clear the land for the center.[46] This was a pretty typical outcome stemming from a pretty typical set of priorities which included removing lower income and minority populations from downtown areas and areas in close proximity to downtown areas, establishing clear-cut patterns of racial and class segregation, creating downtowns that would cater to tourists and conventioneers, and attracting national and regional corporate headquarters and a white collar, professional labor force living either in gentrified sectors of the city or commuting from suburbs. The cost of these transformations was borne by taxpayers through large federal government subsidies, tax increases, interest on bond issues, and other forms of financial transfers from public treasuries to private interests.[47]

Globalization, Neo-Liberalism, and the Shame of Governance

In this section we would like to explain what neoliberalism and the related concept of globalization are and how they connect to our concept of the shame of governance in U.S. cities. Processes of neoliberalism have been widely practiced in urban governance since the late 1970s. However, neoliberalism is not an entirely new concept. It is conceived generally as "a theory of political economic practices, which proposes that human well-being can best advanced by liberating individual entrepreneurial freedoms and skills within an institutional framework characterized by strong private property rights, free markets and free trade."[48] The roots of neoliberalism go back to the late 1940s when Austrian philosopher Friedrich von Hayek and others argued that "government should be used only sparingly and in very specific circumstances, rather than interfering within the marketplace."[49]This argument was predicated on classic liberalism, which asserts that the highest virtue of a society is the degree to which its individuals are allowed to pursue pleasure.[50] Opposing these ideas stands egalitarian liberalism, which accepts basic tenets of classic liberalism, but advocates for a more redistributive nation-state which would intervene whenever economic conditions threatened wider societal political freedoms.[51] Such threats express themselves in problematic or lopsided access to housing, education, health care, or employment, which mandates the careful study of cities whenever considering neoliberal arguments. We may shed further light on this matter by considering a local autonomy of cities context, which may help us to envision the undoing of good governance that has led, arguably, to a shame of governance.

Neoliberalism is often associated with the distinct but related concept of globalization. To help clarify the difference, neoliberalism usually refers to a set of policy prescriptions designed to create and administer the institutional arrangements which facilitate globalization: the physical movement of people, capital, and goods around the world. On the other hand, while in the process of creating institutional arrangements that facilitate globalization, a major critique of neoliberal policies is that they often help confound the local autonomy of cities, while deconstructing Keynesian[52] artifacts (public housing, public space), policies (redistributive welfare, food stamps), institutions (labor unions, National Labor Relations Board, U.S. Department of Housing and Urban Development), and agreements (Fordist labor pact, federal government redistribution to states and cities).[53] In other words, while neoliberal policies promote financial institutions like the International Monetary Fund (IMF), World Bank, and the World Trade Organization (WTO), it is clear that the social needs and local autonomy of cities have slid into the lower tier of considerations.

Traditionally, whenever we think about the local autonomy of cities, we consider their relationships with higher levels of government; in other words, an intergovernmental context. For example, how much discretion do cities have with their respective states? Political scientist Russell Hanson argues that the autonomy of cities rests on the discretion provided by their states regarding the structure and functions of governance, fiscal affairs, and personnel matters.[54] He argues that some cities enjoy more discretion than others regarding these matters. Other researchers study the local autonomy of cities in the context of regional dynamics and examine whether the push for local autonomy of communities is driven by self-interest or cooperation. In *City Making: Building Communities Without Walls*, Gerald Frug argues that states granted power to local governments and subsequent local laws have allowed cities "a sphere of local autonomy" in which "to pursue their own self-interest regardless of the impact on their neighbors."[55] Some scholars suggest that self-interest, in the name of local autonomy, may place some strains on urban governance.

Geographer Jason Hackworth argues that urban governance has shifted toward a neoliberal model, not necessarily because of an organic movement to the right and unavoidable choices, but because of purposeful and "ideological constraints" imposed on cities by finance capital. In this vein, he suggests that the local autonomy of cities has been threatened by the self-interest of financiers who have undermined the discretion of city officials in urban governance. For example, he examines the bond-rating market and argues that major players in the industry like Moody's, Fitch, and Standard & Poor's exercise almost exclusive power and influence over the ratings for municipal bonds (tantamount to a credit system), thus controlling cities' ability to finance major projects and forcing them to adopt more entrepreneurial principles. In the process, Hackworth argues that collusion between financiers, developers and sympathetic pro-corporate public officials contributes to undermining funding and legislation for public housing projects across U.S. cities. This credit rating process, however, has more than just fiscal considerations demonstrated by the fact that city officials in Detroit "embraced the virtues of fiscal conservatism since the early 1970s with less reluctance than Philadelphia or New York, which did not translate into favorable ratings" for Detroit.[56]

Internationally, there are several dimensions of neoliberal institutional arrangements that impact cities. One is to break down older, nationally based protectionist policies, for example, tariffs and other traditional financial and political policies, to allow for the easier movement of materials, people (workers), and goods along with financial assets from one nation state or region to another. A related dimension is to weaken or eliminate barriers to foreign investment in local economies and to orient production in these economies to export. Another is to impose policies on Third World nations which mandate reduced expenditures on education, public health, mass transit, pensions and other social welfare outlays along with public sector layoffs, regressive taxes, and higher interest rates. These policies enhance the ability of states to service debt to international lenders like the World Bank by shifting the costs to the general population while decreasing expenditures and services to that same population. Such policies include the rollback of even minimal legislation offering protections to children, workers, women, the elderly, and the destitute. The objective of these prescriptions is fourfold: 1) that the ability of foreign investors to invest in local economies is facilitated, 2) that government enterprises be sold to foreign investors and/or local elites at far below market prices, 3) that workers be available to labor at the lowest possible costs, and 4) that earnings on investments yield the highest possible levels of profitability.

Neoliberalism is grounded in the assumption that private market solutions to social problems are superior to government solutions and that, therefore, there should be a reduction of government regulation of the economy, a cutting back of government welfare benefits, and the privatization of government resources. This ideology has been actively applied to the governance of cities—as well as individual states and the nation—since about 1970. As it has been applied to cities, neoliberalism has taken a number of forms. These include cutbacks in government financing of public institutions such as schools leading to what is now often a state of chronic fiscal crisis. Another is in the form of new or higher costs to the public in, for example, transit fares, tuition in government institutions of higher education, museum and zoo entrance fees, trash collection fees, and high school user fees for athletic participation. A third is privatization of government services such as low cost housing, road maintenance, and cleaning and food services in public facilities such as schools and airports. A fourth is the withdrawal of the government altogether from the provision of certain kinds of services. For example, governments have all but ceased the construction of low cost housing. A fifth is found in the sub-market turnover of government assets to private corporations and investment interests. Such assets include buildings and land. And a sixth is a restructuring of taxes such that taxes on the working class and the poor are increased through the imposition of user fees, increased costs for government services, and a broad reliance on regressive taxation. Meanwhile subsidies and tax reductions to the wealthy and large corporate entities contribute to a fiscal crisis that justifies further decreases in public services and/or increased costs to partake of them. Finally, there is the reduction of government regulation of business practices which have implications for public safety and the integrity of the economy itself. These practices of withdrawing or cutting back on services or charging more for them is, in fact, the stated objective of neoliberal advocates—the reduction of the state sphere and the substitution of a reliance on what are called "market forces."

However to imagine neoliberalism entirely in terms of a shrinking state is to ignore its vital, core essence. The state shrinks only in its services and protections afforded to the working class and the poor. The state is a robust, activist, and partisan promoter of special interests. In the course of urban renewal and downtown economic redevelopment, for example, the state has provided funds, cleared land of homes and small businesses at government expense, turned over ready-to-go construction sites to private developers, co-opted or repressed community resistance where it has manifested itself, and provided tax breaks and other subsidies to wealthy development firms and corporations willing to remain in cities or willing to relocate to them. Big city governments have been anything but reclining, passive spectators while the action has shifted elsewhere. In fact, the neoliberal city could not have been constructed nor can it function without the active participation of the state.

It would be an error, therefore, to consider neoliberalism only in terms of smaller government. In the neoliberal regime the state, arguably, functions as a partisan, non-neutral political entity in the service of corporate interests, and this predates the application of the term neoliberalism with regard to cities in the mid to late 1970s. Indeed, the entire era of urban renewal and urban redevelopment going back to 1950 is characterized by direction and control by the corporate community marching forward hand-in-hand with the apparatus of government.[57]

While the government-corporate partnership is not new, it has, however, become much broader, deeper, and invasive since 1970. The ideology of the market has dominated educational, media, and public discourse, and it has guided public policy for several decades. Our term, the shame of governance, the subtitle of this book, is designed to capture the human consequences stemming from these policies. The ever more lopsidedness of state policies has increased levels of social neglect, crowded out alternative views, commercialized human needs, and increased the numbers of people whose class position bars them from market participation. A government that serves its people, all of them, has been the historical benchmark of a democratic society faithful to its principles. The triumph of neoliberalism has rendered this noble vision more of a quaint cliché when not altogether a taboo or unimaginable thought. The shame of governance refers to the many unmet needs of the poor and, to a mounting degree, middle-class Americans whose members in many cases have been forced to accept either declining living standards or increased work hours in the struggle to simply stay where they are.[58] Additionally, while there may be merits to pushing more openly for a hybrid of market-socialist economic approaches to governance; research presented in this volume hopefully inspires readers to consider a much broader conversation about what actually constitutes *good governance*.

The Readings

The book is divided into five sections. The four selections in the first section, "How We Got Here" document the neoliberal shift in national priorities that was made possible by the 1949 Housing Act and the 1956 Highway Act. These major pieces of federal legislation strengthened the ties between the various levels of municipal, state and federal government, and between governments and corporate elites. They also provided major government revenues that were expended for private, commercial gain while that fact was concealed to the degree possible behind a public rhetoric of progress, well-being, civic mindedness, and the common good. In this section we take a closer look at the historical background to these developments, and the consequences for those left behind, the specific impacts of several presidential administrations and the manufacture of public acquiescence to the far reaching changes that would engulf urban America. Overall, the first section sets the tone for the remainder of the book by introducing institutional inconsistencies that characterize the shame of governance.

In Section Two, "Institutional Imbalance and Crime," we present readings that examine the inconsistencies and injustices in the criminal justice system.[59] We note that some researchers have found a relationship between relative deprivation and crime linked to policy decisions made in the 1980s. Therefore we review studies that raise questions about how justice is meted out. For instance, are there any differences between how the criminal system deals with drug abuse suspects, and, if so, what are explanations for the disparate treatment? The answer to these questions ultimately forces us to dig deeper, looking at macro level processes that have strong implications for the institutional climate facing urban America. For example, how do interested parties from the private and public sector use the fear of crime as a social control strategy which is then used to justify the heavy handedness of the law imposed on segments of urban populations? Some researchers claim that the system has promoted both fear and a tough on crime posture in the U.S. which has led to wider efforts to profit from crime through mechanisms associated with prison operations.[60] A shame of governance perspective is appropriately applied here as we consider the idea that agencies of government work in concert with modes of profiteering from crime.

In "Institutional Imbalance and Spatial Arrangements" we trace lopsided economic and social development in urban areas to the unequal competition for access to space and control over it. Researchers show how lopsided development has been facilitated and driven by corporate needs leading to government policies that result in losses for less privileged and less well connected constituencies of people in urban areas. Therefore, whenever government action exacerbates inequities between cities and suburbs; or colludes with business elites in ways that result in the residential displacement of less well-off families; or invests in sports stadiums in response to the desires of private enterprises, despite the fiscal irresponsibility of such investments; or conspires to undermine public space for commercial development, we conclude that the government and/or its agencies have presided over an institutional imbalance that warrants our shame of governance critique.

Because of the unique demographic realities of urban areas, this line of inquiry is relevant for the "Institutional Implications: Race, Class, Education." Here we consider, for example, race and class dynamics relative to educational reforms that erode open access to public education and complicate neighborhood integration efforts, and also initiatives that deny minority and poor urban residents their "right to the city" following a natural disaster. We also consider whether cultural or structural deficiencies help best explain urban poverty.

We have considered government actions that harm the interests of urban residents. In this last section we look at the government's failure to act. A government agency like the Federal Communications Commission can take action to ban media practices that are detrimental to urban residents. The government can come to the aid of city dwellers who rely on a declining mass transit system for school and employment travel. It can also intervene on behalf of those whose health is threatened by the pollution of their communities. Finally, the state can provide access to proper health care. All of these issues fall under the rubric of what we have been calling the shame of governance. In this final section titled "Other Institutional Implications" we consider the areas of media, mass transit, the environment, and health from the perspective of prevailing policies and practices and ask whose interests are served by them.

Endnotes

[1]Peter Drier, "How the Media Compound Urban Problems," *Journal of Urban Affairs* 27, 2, (2005): 196.

[2]Parke Troutman, "A Growth Machine's Plan B: Legitimating Development When the Value-Free Growth Ideology Is under Fire," *Journal of Urban Affairs*, 26, 5, (2004): 611–622.

[3]Bart Eeckhout, "The "Disneyfication" of Times Square: Back to the Future?" *Research in Urban Sociology,* 6, (2001): 379–428.

[4]For example, in a single issue of the *Boston Globe* selected at random on March 10, 2010 we find articles on small city mayors clamoring for relief from high health care costs for their employees, the Superintendent of Schools for Boston announcing the "closing of a significant number of Boston schools over the next two years and further reductions in staff," a passionate public hearing over a proposal to consolidate and close some of the city's neighborhood branch libraries, and a complaint from the Boston Bar Association about lax security standards in courts caused by a succession of budget cuts.

[5]*Report of the National Advisory Commission on Civil Disorders* (New York: Dutton, 1968). Also, Robert Fogelson, *Violence as Protest: A Study of Riots and Ghettos* (New York: Doubleday & Company, 1971).

[6]Frederick Engels, *The Condition of the Working Class in England in 1844* (London: Allen and Unwin, 1952, orig. 1844) and Karl Marx, *The Civil War in France* (New York: International Publishers, 1945, orig. 1871).

[7]Henry Mayhew, *London Labour and the London Poor*, 4 vols. (New York: Dover Publications, 1968, orig. 1851–1862) and Charles Booth, *Life and Labour of the People of London*, 17 vols. (London: Macmillan & Co. Ltd., 1902–03, orig. 1887). These field work studies had their counterpart in the social realist tradition in literature. Charles Dickens' work, for example, often played off of the theme of naïve rural migrants coming to the big city and running afoul of urban opportunists. U.S. practitioners of social realism included Theodore Dreiser and Upton Sinclair. Sinclair's *The Jungle* was an influential expose of immigrant Chicago and its exploitation in the meatpacking industry. Upton Sinclair, *The Jungle* (New York: Doubleday, 1906).

[8]Lincoln Steffens, *The Shame of the Cities* (New York: McClure Phillips & Co., 1904).

[9]W.E.B. DuBois, *The Philadelphia Negro* (New York: Schocken Books, 1967, orig. 1899).

[10]Max Weber, *The City* (Glencoe, IL.: The Free Press, 1958, orig. 1921).

[11]Georg Simmel, *The Metropolis and Mental Life*. Reprinted in Kurt H. Wolff, ed., *The Sociology of Georg Simmel* (Glencoe, IL: The Free Press, 1964, orig. 1903). The vision of urban dystopia has a long tradition in film running from Fritz Lang's *Metropolis* and *M* through Charlie Chaplin's *Modern Times* to Ridley Scott's *Blade Runner* and beyond.

[12]Ferdinand Tönnies, *Community and Society* (New York: Harper Torchbooks, 1963, orig., 1903).

[13]Emile Durkheim, *Suicide* (Glencoe, IL: The Free Press, 1966, orig., 1897).

[14]Emile Durkheim, *The Division of Labor* (New York: The Free Press, 1949, orig., 1893).

[15]James Russell, *Double Standard: Social Policy in Europe and the United States* (New York: Rowman & Littlefield Publishers, 2006), pp. 30–33.

[16]Frederick Thrasher, *The Gang* (Chicago: University of Chicago Press, 1927).

[17]Harvey Zorbaugh, *The Gold Coast and the Slum: A Sociological Study of Chicago's Near North Side* (Chicago: University of Chicago Press, 1929).

[18]Paul Cressey, *The Taxi Dance Hall: A Sociological Study in Commercialized Recreation and City Life* (Chicago: University of Chicago Press, 1932).

[19]Horace Clayton and St. Clair Drake, *Black Metropolis: A Study of Negro Life in a Northern City* (New York: Harcourt Brace and Company, 1945).

[20]William Foote Whyte, *Street Corner Society* (Chicago: University of Chicago Press, 1943).

[21]David Riesman, *The Lonely Crowd* (New Haven: Yale University Press, 1953).

[22]C. Wright Mills, *White Collar* (New York: Oxford University Press, 1953).

[23]Herbert Gans, *The Urban Villagers* (Glencoe, Illinois: The Free Press of Glencoe, 1962).

[24]William Julius Wilson, *The Declining Significance of Race: Blacks and Changing American Institutions* (Chicago: University of Chicago Press, 1978); *The Truly Disadvantaged: The Inner City, the Underclass, and Public Policy* (Chicago: University of Chicago Press, 1990); *When Work Disappears: The World of the New Urban Poor* (New York: Vintage, 1997); *More than Just Race: Being Black and Poor in the Inner City* (New York: W.W. Norton & Company, 2009). For a thoroughgoing critique of Wilson's work see Steven J. Rosenthal, "How Liberal Ideology Assists the Growth of Fascism: A Critique of the Sociology of William Julius Wilson" *The Journal of Poverty* 3, 2, (1999): 67–87.

[25]Mitchell Deneier, *Sidewalk* (New York: Farrar, Straus & Giroux, 1999).

[26]Katherine Newman, *No Shame in My Game: The Working Poor in the Inner City* (New York: Knopf, 1999).

[27]Elijah Anderson, *Code of the Street: Decency, Violence and the Moral Life of the Inner City* (New York: W.W. Norton & Company, 1999). See Loïc Wacquant for a hard-hitting critique of Deneier, Newman, and Anderson and their hard hitting rebuttals. Loïc Wacquant, "Scrutinizing the Street: Poverty, Morality, and the Pitfalls of Urban Ethnography" *American Journal of Sociology*, 107, 6, (2002): 1468–1599.

[28]Timothy Black, *When a Heart Turns Rock Solid: The Lives of Three Puerto Rican Brothers On and Off the Streets* (New York: Pantheon, 2009).

[29]Mike Davis, *City of Quartz: Excavating the Future of Los Angeles* (New York: Vintage, 1992) and *The Ecology of Fear: Los Angeles and the Imagination of Disaster* (New York: Vintage, 1999). Davis' other urban themed books include *Magical Urbanism: Latinos Reinvent the U.S. City* (New York: Verso, 2001); *Dead Cities: and Other Tales* (New York: The New Press, 2002); *Planet of Slums* (New York: Verso, 2007); and *Evil Paradises: Dreamworlds of Neoliberalism* (New York: The New Press, 2008).

[30]Doug Harvey, *A Brief History of Neoliberalism* (New York: Oxford University Press, 2005). Among Harvey's other books are *The Condition of Post-Modernity* (Hoboken, NJ: Wiley-Blackwell, 1989); *Social Justice and the City,* revised edition (Athens: University of Georgia Press, 2009); *The Urban Experience* (Baltimore: Johns Hopkins University Press, 1989); *Spaces of Hope* (Berkeley: University of California Press, 2000); *Spaces of Capitalism: Towards a Critical Geography* (New York: Routledge, 2002); *The New Imperialism* (New York: Oxford University Press, 2003); and *Spaces of Global Capitalism: Towards a Theory of Uneven Geographical Development* (New York: Verso, 2006).

[31]Leo Huberman, *Man Makes Himself: The Story of the Wealth of Nations* (London: Victor Gollancz, 1937) and E.P. Thompson, *The Making of the English Working Class* (London: Victor Gollancz, 1963).

[32]Paris grew from 550,000 in 1800 to nearly 3 million in 1900, Rome from 150,000 in 1800 to 600,000 in 1900, and Berlin from 170,000 in 1800 to nearly 2 million in 1900. Matt Gottdiener and Ray Hutchison, eds., *The New Urban Sociology*, 3rd edition (Boulder: Westview Press, 2006), p. 37.

[33]Karl Marx and Frederick Engels, *Capital*, vol. I (Moscow: Progress Publishers, 1971), chapter 31. See also E.D. Morel, *The Black Man's Burden: The White Man in Africa from the Fifteenth Century to World War I* (New York: Monthly Review Press, 1969, orig. 1920), Walter Rodney, *How Europe Underdeveloped Africa* (Washington: Howard University Press, 1981), Adam Hochschild, *King Leopold's Ghost: A Story of Greed, Terror and*

Heroism in Colonial Africa (Boston: Houghton Miflin and Company, 1999), and Hans Konig, *Columbus: His Enterprise* (New York: Monthly Review Press, 1976).

[34]Gottdiener and Hutchison, p. 117. Detroit's steep decline is ably chronicled in Thomas J. Sugrue, *The Origins of the Urban Crisis: Race and Inequality in Post-War Detroit* (Princeton: Princeton University Press, 2005). Also see Lynda Ann Ewen, *Corporate Power and Urban Crisis in Detroit* (Princeton: Princeton University Press, 1978).

[35]Jason Hackworth, *The Neoliberal City: Governance, Ideology, and Development in American Urbanism* (Ithaca: Cornell University Press, 2007).

[36]Peter Dreier, John Mollenkopf and Todd Swanstron (2001), *Place Matters: Metropolitics for the Twenty-First Century* (Lawrence: University Press of Kansas, 2001).

[37]Ibid., p. 45, # 5.

[38]Peter Eisinger, "The Politics of Bread and Circuses, Building the City for the Visitor Class," *Urban Affairs Review* 35, 3, (2002): 316–333. Eisinger argues that re-organizing the city to accommodate affluent visitors strains bonds of trust between local leaders and local residents.

[39]See Alice O'Connor et al, *Urban Inequality* (New York: Russell Sage, 2003) for a full discussion of the comparative study.

[40]Howard Chudacoff and Judith Smith, *The Evolution of American Urban Society* (Englewood Cliffs, NJ: Prentice Hall 1994), pp. 255–287.

[41]Linda Burton et al, "Don't Have No Time: Daily Rhythms and the Organization of Time for Low-Income Families," *Family Relations* 53, 2, (2004): 168–178.

[42]Joe Feagin and Robert Parker, *Building American Cities* (Frederick, MD: Beard Books, 2002) for a discussion of uneven urban development.

[43]Norman Fainstein and and Susan Fainstein, *Restructuring the City: The Political Economy of Urban Development* (New York: Longmans, 1983), pp. 40–63.

[44]Ibid., 169–182.

[45]Chester Hartman, *City for Sale* (Berkeley: University of California Press, 2002), pp. 3–25, 392–396, and chapter 9, "Moscone Center Doings," pp. 191–212. See also "San Francisco: Urban Transformation and the Local State" in Fainstein and Fainstein.

[46]Hartman, "Moscone Center Doings," pp. 191–212.

[47]Fainstein and Fainstein, p. 253.

[48]Harvey, p. 2.

[49]Hackworth, p. 9.

[50]Ibid., p. 3.

[51]Harry Girvetz, *The Evolution of Liberalism* (New York: Collier, 1963).

[52]John Maynard Keynes (1883–1946), British economist whose theories influenced U.S. policy during the 1930s and later. He argued that markets can produce wealth, but also that government interventions in the form of corporate regulation and deficit spending were necessary in light of market failures.

[53]Neil Brenner and Nik Theodore, "Cities and Geographies of Actually Existing Neoliberalism," *Antipode*, 34, (2002): 349–379.

[54]Russell L. Hanson, "Intergovernmental Relations," *Politics in the American States*, edited by Virginia Gray and Herbert Jacobs (Washington: Congressional Quarterly, 1996).

[55]Gerald Frug, *City Making: Building Communities Without Building Walls* (Princeton: Princeton University Press, 1999). For a discussion of Frug's book see Victoria Basolo, "U.S. Regionalism and Rationality," *Urban Studies*, 40, 3, (2002): 447–462.

[56]Jason Hackworth, p. 37.

[57]This does not mean that corporate/government relations are conflict free or even that there are no structural factions within and between the corporate government spheres. It does mean that these are differences within an alliance that are resolved with relative ease. They are disagreements of a tactical nature and not ones over broader policy objectives.

[58]Lawrence Mishel, et al, *The State of Working America, 2008/2009* (Ithaca, New York: ILR Press, 2009), *passim*. See also K. Leicht and S.T. Fitzgerald, *Postindustrial Peasants: The Illusion of Middle Class Prosperity* (New York: Worth Publishers, 2007), pp. 1–15 and Robert Perrucci and Earl Wysong, *The New Class Society: Goodbye American Dream?* (New York: Rowman & Littlefield Publishers, 2008), pp. 17–69.

[59]Mainstream criminal justice predictably pays little to no attention to how the laws defining criminality come to be, or to the differential class and race enforcement of the law. See Jerome Miller, *Search and Destroy: African-American Males in the Criminal Justice System* (New York: Cambridge University Press, 1997), George Winslow, *Capital Crimes* (New York: Monthly Review Press, 1999), and Jeffrey Reiman, *The Rich Get Richer and the Poor Get Prison,* 8th edition (Allyn & Bacon, 2006).

[60]Christian Parenti, *Lockdown America: Police and Prisons in the Age of Crisis* (New York: Verso, 2008) and Daniel Burton-Rose and Paul Wright, *The Celling of America* (Monroe, Maine: Common Courage Press, 2002).

Section I:
How We Got Here

The field of urban sociology has taken many twists and turns over the past three decades, which has led some to question whether the field speaks as the central authority regarding the plight of cities.[1] Questions stem from whether quantitative or qualitative research most accurately captures the realities on the ground in cities; whether macro- or micro-level theoretical perspectives are better suited to understanding urban conditions in a critical fashion; or whether contributions from researchers from other disciplines also help us to understand cities better. This latter point is helpful, as it allows us to consider diverse points of view that move us forward toward our goal of understanding urban issues. Accordingly, we begin our examination of urban society by reviewing the work of scholars who have academic backgrounds in sociology, geography, political science, and history. Fortunately for us, the one thing in common about the selections in this first section (which sets the tone for the book) is that they all link a political economy perspective to urban conditions.

The *political economy perspective* is one of four approaches in urban studies which gained popularity among sociologists and other social scientists in the United States during the 1960s and 1970s. A second approach is represented by *socio-psychological perspectives*. These examine the mental and emotional stresses of city life on urban dwellers. A third, the *socio-cultural perspectives*, focus on interactions and social patterns that implicate certain values and norms, often argued to be the by-product of what Louis Wirth called an urban way of life.[2] In *urban ecological theories*, the fourth approach, cities are represented as living organisms. Cities, in other words, function as naturally growing phenomena, shaped by conditions related to overpopulation, density, spatial arrangements, technological advancements, competition, and overall societal growth.

The political economy approach to urban studies—seen as a necessary theoretical tool—addresses conceptual gaps in urban ecological perspectives. The gaps include, for example, an absence of any serious discussion about the role that the allocation of resources plays in the life of urban dwellers; and the absence of critical discussions relative to the salience of agency, which often has sociological consequences for city residents. The idea of agency, for example, allows for recognition and evaluation of decisions and actions taken by actors (or "agents") that influence and shape the life chances of those who rely on municipal goods and services. In other words, unlike ecological arguments, political economy scholars play down the idea that urban development is a result of neutral or natural competitive forces. Rather, political economy approaches examine social consequences of actions and decisions within capitalist societies that are often associated with, for example, *uneven* distribution of resources, policies that negatively affect labor patterns, skewed access to quality education, regressive taxation, unequal access to health care based on social class, location of hazardous environmental sites, questionable allocation of state and municipal services, reduced government spending, and the overall dynamics of class, status and power.

Historically, as a result of Franklin D. Roosevelt's New Deal legislation in the 1930s and Lyndon Johnson's Great Society programs in the 1960s, cities enjoyed a relationship with the federal government which resulted in greater funding opportunities for cities. It represented a political commitment which conveyed an acknowledgement that cities bear a larger proportion of the country's problems. These sentiments, however, would come to a halt in the mid-1970s, as the public became restless with government spending and a perceived lack of individual responsibility, particularly on the part of those living in the inner cities, which helped orchestrate a shift in the political landscape. In the first article of the section, sociologist William Julius Wilson—known for his work regarding the deindustrialization of large U.S. cities—broadly discusses the changing political landscape, where he ties various political forces to concentrated poverty in urban America. Here, from his recent book *More than Race* (2009), he provides an account of government institutions that characterize structural links to poverty in the inner cities, which help elaborate what urban sociologist Sandra Barnes recently describes as the "cost of being poor."[3] Overall, Wilson offers a critical analysis of United States policies that influence the lives of impoverished city residents. In the second article, Howard Chudacoff and Judith Smith provide a succinct historical overview of the urban crises that began to materialize in connection with a shift in priorities during the 1970s. They trace the plight of cities specifically from the Carter Administration to the Clinton Administration, arguing that cities experienced their biggest economic downfall during the Reagan Era. They briefly discuss how fiscal woes of cities complicate life for urban dwellers, relative to various social conditions. Next, in an original piece, Levon Chorbajian reviews what he calls an old debate, still germane. Chorbajian links political theory arguments about power and decision-making to the guns vs. butter debate and how the debate is relevant to the concerns of cities today.

Finally, in the last article of the section, David Harvey discusses how policies of neoliberalism have supplanted embedded liberalism[4] while helping to undermine the domestic agenda of cities in the United States. He argues that broad public consent for such policies is constructed vis-à-vis manipulation and collusion between public officials and business elites. In other words, Harvey insists that through the "construction of consent," many in society promote an uncritical acceptance of a market-driven logic which many studies have linked to negative social consequences. Acceptance of this logic was aided by the postmodernization of urban socio-economic life which began when people started treating markets as culture. Such treatments have led many urban sociologists to stress the need to more fully understand the interconnectedness between agency and social structures.[5] For example, how do we conceptualize the role that public officials and business elites have in shaping the framework of institutions like schools, banking, and housing, and how do these relationships impact urban dwellers in ways that question the integrity and responsibility of governance?

Endnotes

[1]Tim May and Beth Perry, "The Future of Urban Sociology" *Sociology, 39,* 2, 2005, pp. 343–370.

[2]Louis Wirth, "Urbanism as Way of Life" *American Journal of Sociology, 44*, 1938, pp. 1–24.

[3]Sandra Barnes, *The Cost of Being Poor: A Comparative Study of Life in Poor Urban Neighborhoods in Gary Indiana* (Albany: State University Press of New York, 2005).

[4]Harvey describes embedded liberalism as a form of political-economic organization, which refers to how market processes, and entrepreneurial and corporate activities were surrounded by a web of social and political constraints and a regulatory environment that sometimes restrained but in other instances led the way in economic and industrial strategy. David Harvey, *A Brief History of Neoliberalism* (New York: Oxford University Press, 2005), p. 11.

[5]Urban sociologists Kevin Fox Gotham and Sandra L. Barnes address the notion of agency and structure in their work. Gotham briefly discusses it in an early article where he describes the inter-connectedness between agency and structure as the "Lacuna of Postmodern Urban Analysis: Urban Sociology and the Postmodern Challenge" *Humboldt Journal of Social Relations,* 26 (1 & 2), 2001, pp. 57–79. Sandra Barnes discusses agency and structure in her book, *The Cost of Being Poor: A Comparative Study of Life in Poor Urban Neighborhoods in Gary, Indiana.* Barnes notes the structural links to poverty, while discussing the agency (or choices) made at the individual levels of analysis.

Forces Shaping Urban Poverty[*]

William Julius Wilson

Some people argued that Katrina demonstrated how foolhardy it is to rely on the government for protection rather than on oneself and control of one's own fate. However, it is unfair and indeed unwarranted to blame people with limited resources for being trapped in their neighborhoods and vulnerable to natural disasters. People who reside in these poor, ghetto neighborhoods include not only those on public assistance, but also the working poor, many of whom have never been on welfare.

The fact that many families in the inner city of New Orleans were trapped there during Katrina because they did not have access to automobiles and other means of transportation is a problem that is not unique to New Orleans. For example, research conducted in the Chicago inner-city ghetto areas revealed that only 19 percent of the residents have access to an automobile.[1] A person in these segregated and highly concentrated poverty areas could be very disciplined and responsible, working every day for minimum wages and barely making ends meet, in no position to buy and maintain an automobile; and by virtue of his or her low income, that person would be completely dependent on public transportation. No one in such a situation could quickly relocate his or her family to other areas.

If television cameras had focused on the urban poor in New Orleans, or on any inner-city ghetto before Katrina, I believe that the initial reaction to descriptions of poverty and poverty concentration would have been unsympathetic. Public opinion polls in the United States… routinely reflect the notion that people are poor and jobless because of their own shortcomings or inadequacies. In other words, few people would have reflected on how the larger forces in society—segregation, discrimination, a lack of economic opportunity, failing public schools—adversely affect the inner-city poor. However, because Katrina was clearly a natural disaster beyond the control of the inner-city poor, Americans were much more sympathetic. In a sense, Katrina turned out to be something of a cruel natural experiment, wherein better-off Americans could readily see the effects of racial isolation and chronic economic subordination.

Despite the lack of national public awareness of the problems of the urban poor prior to Katrina, social scientists have rightly devoted considerable attention to concentrated poverty because it magnifies the problems associated with poverty in general: joblessness, crime, delinquency, drug trafficking, broken families, and dysfunctional schools. Neigh-

[*]William Julius Wilson, *More than Race: Being Black and Poor in the Inner City* (New York: W. W. Norton, 2009). Reprinted with permission.

borhoods of highly concentrated poverty are seen as dangerous, and therefore they become isolated, socially and economically, as people go out of their way to avoid them.[2]

If social scientists are to effectively and comprehensively explain the experiences and social outcomes of inner-city residents to the larger public, they must consider not only how explicit racial structural forces directly contribute to inequality and concentrated poverty, but also how *political actions* and impersonal *economic forces* indirectly affect life in the inner city. Also important are the effects of national racial beliefs and cultural constraints that have emerged from years of racial isolation and chronic economic subordination.

The Role of Political Actions

Ever since 1934, with the establishment of the Federal Housing Administration (FHA), a program necessitated by the massive mortgage foreclosures during the Great Depression, the US government has sought to enable citizens to become home owners by underwriting mortgages. In the years following World War II, however, the federal government contributed to the early decay of inner-city neighborhoods by withholding mortgage capital and making it difficult for these areas to retain or attract families who were able to purchase their own homes. Spurred on by the massive foreclosures of the 1930s, the federal government began underwriting mortgages, but the FHA selectively administered the mortgage program by formalizing a process that excluded certain urban neighborhoods by using empirical data that suggested a likely loss of investment in these areas.

Redlining, as this practice came to be known, was assessed largely on racial composition. Although many neighborhoods with a considerable number of European immigrants were redlined, virtually all black neighborhoods were excluded. Home buyers hoping to purchase a home in a redlined neighborhood were universally denied mortgages, regardless of their financial qualifications. This practice severely restricted opportunities for building or even maintaining quality housing in the inner city, which in many ways set the stage for the urban blight that many Americans associate with black neighborhoods. This action was clearly motivated by racial bias, and it was not until the 1960s that the FHA discontinued mortgage restrictions based on the racial composition of the neighborhood.[3]

Subsequent policy decisions worked to trap blacks in these increasingly unattractive inner cities. Beginning in the 1950s, the suburbanization of the middle class, already under way with government-subsidized loans to veterans, was aided further by federal transportation and highway policies, which included the building of freeway networks through the hearts of many cities. Although these policies were seemingly nonracial, the line here between ostensibly nonracial and explicitly racial is gray. For example, we might ask whether such freeways would have also been constructed through wealthier white neighborhoods.

In any case, the freeways had a devastating impact on the neighborhoods of black Americans. These developments not only spurred relocation from the cities to the suburbs among better-off residents, but the freeways themselves "created barriers between the sections of the cities, walling off poor and minority neighborhoods from central business districts."[4] For instance, a number of studies revealed how Richard J. Daley, the former mayor of Chicago, used the Federal-Aid Highway Act of 1956 to route expressways through impoverished African American neighborhoods, resulting in even greater segregation and isolation.[5] A lasting legacy of that policy is the fourteen-lane Dan Ryan Expressway, which created a barrier between black and white neighborhoods.[6]

Another particularly egregious example of the deleterious effects of highway construction is Birmingham, Alabama's interstate highway system, which curved and twisted to bisect several black neighborhoods rather than taking a more direct route through some predominantly white neighborhoods. The highway system essentially followed the boundaries that had been established in 1926 as part of the city's racial zoning law, although these boundaries technically had been removed a few years before the highway construction began in 1956.[7] Other examples include the federal and state highway system in Atlanta, Georgia, which also separated white and black neighborhoods; and the construction of I–95 in Florida, which displaced many black residents in Miami's historically black Overtown neighborhood.[8]

Moreover, through its housing-market incentives, the federal government drew middle-class whites away from cities and into the suburbs.[9] Government policies such as mortgages for veterans and mortgage-interest tax exemptions for developers enabled the quick, cheap production of massive amounts of tract housing.[10] Although these policies appeared to be nonracial, they facilitated the exodus of white working and middle-class families from urban neighborhoods and thereby indirectly contributed to the growth of segregated neighborhoods with high concentrations of poverty.

A classic example of this effect of housing-market incentives is the mass-produced suburban Levittown neighborhoods that were first erected in New York, and later in Pennsylvania, New Jersey, and Puerto Rico, by Levitt & Sons. The homes in these neighborhoods were manufactured on a large scale, with an assemblyline model of production, and they were arranged in carefully engineered suburban neighborhoods that included many public amenities, such as shopping centers and space for public schools. These neighborhoods represented an ideal alternative for people seeking to escape cramped city apartments, and they were often touted as "utopian communities" that enabled people to live out the "suburban dream." Veterans were able to purchase a Levittown home for a few thousand dollars with no money down, financed with low-interest mortgages guaranteed by the Veterans Administration. However, initially the Levitts would not sell to African-Americans. The first black family moved into the New York Levittown neighborhood in 1957, having purchased a home from a white family,[11] and they endured harassment, hate mail, and threats for several months after moving in. Levittown, New York remains a predominantly white community today. Here, once again, we see a practice that denied African-Americans the opportunity to move from segregated inner-city neighborhoods.

Explicit racial policies in the suburbs reinforced this segregation by allowing suburbs to separate their financial resources and municipal budgets from cities. To be more specific, in the nineteenth and early twentieth centuries, strong municipal services in cities were very attractive to residents of small towns and suburbs; as a result, cities tended to annex suburbs and surrounding areas. But the relations between cities and suburbs in the United States began to change following the Great Depression; the century-long influx of poor migrants who required expensive services and paid relatively little in taxes could no longer be profitably absorbed by the city economy. Annexation largely ended in the mid-twentieth century as suburbs began to successfully resist incorporation. Suburban communities also drew tighter boundaries by implementing zoning laws, discriminatory land use controls, and site selection practices, which made it difficult for inner-city racial minorities to access these areas because they were effectively used to screen out residents on the basis of race.

As separate political jurisdictions, suburbs also exercised a great deal of autonomy through covenants and deed restrictions. In the face of mounting pressure for integration in the 1960s, "suburbs chose to diversify by race rather than class. They retained zoning and other restrictions that allowed only affluent blacks (and in some instances Jews) to enter, thereby intensifying the concentration and isolation of the urban poor."[12] Although these policies clearly had racial connotations, they also reflected class bias and helped reinforce a process already amply supported by federal government policies—namely, the exodus of white working-and middle-class families from urban neighborhoods and the growing segregation of low-income blacks in inner-city neighborhoods.

Federal public housing policy contributed to the gradual growth of segregated black ghettos as well. The federal public housing program's policies evolved in two stages that represented two distinct styles. The Wagner-Steagall Housing Act of 1937 initiated the first stage. Concerned that the construction of public housing might depress private rent levels, groups such as the US Building and Loan League and the National Association of Real Estate Boards successfully lobbied Congress to require, by law, that for each new unit of public housing, one "unsafe or unsanitary" unit of public housing be destroyed. As Mark Condon points out, "this policy increased employment in the urban construction market while insulating private rent levels by barring the expansion of the housing stock available to low-income families."[13]

The early years of the public housing program produced positive results. Initially, the program served mainly intact families temporarily displaced by the Depression or in need of housing after the end of World War II. For many of these families, public housing was the first step on the road toward economic recovery. Their stays in the projects were relatively brief because they were able to accumulate sufficient economic resources to move on to private housing. The economic mobility of these families "contributed to the sociological stability of the first public housing communities, and explains the program's initial success."[14]

Passage of the Housing Act of 1949 marked the beginning of the second policy stage. It instituted and funded the urban renewal program designed to eradicate urban slums and therefore was seemingly nonracial. However, the public housing that it created was now meant to collect the ghetto residents left homeless by the urban renewal bulldozers.[15] A new (lower) income ceiling for public housing residency was established by the federal public housing authority, and families with incomes above that ceiling were evicted. Thus, access to public housing was restricted to only the most economically disadvantaged segments of the population.

This change in federal housing policy coincided with the Second Great Migration of African-Americans from the rural South to the cities of the Northeast and Midwest, which lasted thirty years from 1940 to 1970. This mass movement of African-Americans was even larger and more sustained than the First Great Migration, which began at the turn of the twentieth century and ended during the Great Depression, and it had a more profound impact on the transformation of the inner city.

As the black urban population in the North grew and precipitated greater demands for housing, pressure mounted in white communities to keep blacks out. Suburban communities, with their restrictive covenants and special zoning laws, refused to permit the construction of public housing. And the federal government acquiesced to organized white inner-city groups that opposed the construction of public housing in their neighborhoods. Thus, public housing units were overwhelmingly concentrated in the overcrowded and deteriorating inner-city ghettos—the poorest and least powerful sections of the city and the metropolitan area. "This growing population of politically weak urban poor was unable to counteract the desires of vocal middle- and working-class whites for segregated housing,"[16] housing that would keep blacks out of white neighborhoods. In short, public housing became a federally funded institution that isolated families by race and class, resulting in high concentrations of poor black families in inner-city ghettos.[17]

In the last quarter of the twentieth century, new developments led to further changes in these neighborhoods. One of the most significant was the out-migration of middle-income blacks. Before the 1970s, African-American families had faced extremely strong barriers when they considered moving into white neighborhoods. Not only did many experience overt discrimination in the housing market, but some were victims of violent attacks. Although fair-housing audits continue to reveal the existence of discrimination in the housing market, the fair-housing legislation, including the Fair Housing Amendments Act of 1988, reduced the strengths of these barriers. And middle-income African-Americans increased their efforts to move from concentrated black poverty areas to more desirable neighborhoods in the metropolitan area, including white neighborhoods.[18]

This pattern represents an important change in the formation of neighborhoods. In earlier years, communities undergoing racial change from white to black had tended to experience an increase in population density, as a result of the black migration from the South. Because of the housing demand, particularly in the late stages or the succession from white to black, homes and apartments in these neighborhoods were often subdivided into smaller units.[19]

However, 1970 marked the end of the great migration wave of blacks from the South to northern urban areas, and two developments affected the course of population movement to the inner cities after that. Improvements in transportation made it easier for workers to live outside the central city, and industries gradually shifted to the suburbs because of the increased residential suburbanization of the labor force and the lower cost of production. Because of the suburbanization of employment and improvements in transportation, inner-city manufacturing jobs were no longer a strong factor pulling migrants to central cities.[20]

With the decline of industrial employment in the inner city, the influx of southern blacks to northern cities ceased and many poor black neighborhoods, especially those in the Midwest and Northeast, changed from densely packed areas of recently arrived migrants to communities gradually abandoned by the working and middle-classes.[21]

In addition, and more recently, a fundamental shift in the federal government's support for basic urban programs profoundly aggravated the problems of inner-city neighborhoods. Beginning in 1980, when Ronald Reagan became president, sharp spending cuts on direct aid to cities dramatically reduced budgets for general revenue sharing—unrestricted funds (money that can be used for any purpose)—urban mass transit, economic development assistance, urban development action grants, social service block grants, local public works, compensatory education, public service jobs, and job training. Many of these programs are designed to help disadvantaged individuals gain some traction in attaining financial security.[22] It is telling that the federal contribution was 17.5 percent of the total city budgets in 1977, but only 5.4 percent by 2000.[23]

...

In sum, federal government policies, even those that are not explicitly racial, have had a profound impact on inner-city neighborhoods. Some of these policies are clearly motivated by racial bias, such as the FHA's redlining of black neighborhoods in the 1940s and 1950s, as well as the federal government's decision to confine construction of public housing projects mainly to inner-city, poor, black neighborhoods. In other cases it seems that racial bias or concerns about race influenced but were not the sole inspiration for political decisions, such as the fiscal policies of the New Federalism, which resulted in drastic cuts in federal aid to cities whose populations had become more brown and black.

The point of conservative fiscal policy—no matter whose administration promulgated it (Reagan, George H. W. Bush, or George W. Bush)—was ostensibly to subject government to financial discipline. Nevertheless, the enactment of such policies creates financial constraints that make it difficult to generate the political support to effectively combat problems such as joblessness, drug trafficking, AIDS, family stress, and failing schools.

Endnotes

[1]William Julius Wilson, *When Work Disappears: The World of the New Urban Poor* (New York: Knopf, 1996).

[2]Paul Jargowsky, "Ghetto Poverty among Blacks in the 1980s," *Journal of Policy Analysis and Management, 13* (1994), 288–310.

[3]See the following chapters in *The "Underclass" Debate: Views from History*, ed. Michael B. Katz (Princeton, NJ: Princeton University Press, 1993); Michael B. Katz, "Reframing the "Underclass" Debate," 440–478; David W. Bartelt, "Housing the 'Underclass,'" 118–157; Thomas J. Sugrue, "The Structure of Urban Poverty: The Reorganization of Space and Work in Three Periods of American History," 85–117; and Robin D.G. Kelley, "The Black Poor and the Politics of Opposition in a New South City," 293–333.

[4]Katz, "Reframing the "Underclass" Debate," 462. See also Bartelt, "Housing the 'Underclass'"; Sugrue, "Structure of Urban Poverty'" and Martin Anderson, *The Federal Bulldozer: A Critical Analysis of Urban Renewal, 1949–1962* (Cambridge, MA: MIT Press, 1964).

[5]Raymond Mohl, "Planned Destruction: The Interstates and Central City Housing," in *From Tenements to Taylor Homes: In Search of an Urban Housing Policy in Twentieth Century America*, eds., John F. Bauman, Roger Biles, and Kristin Szylvian (University Park, PA: State University Press, 2000), 226–245; Adam Cohen and Elizabeth Taylor, *American Pharaoh: Mayor Richard J. Daley—His Battle for Chicago and Nation* (Boston: Little, Brown, 2000); Arnold R. Hirsch, *Making the Second Ghetto: Race and Housing in Chicago, 1940–1960* (Cambridge: Cambridge University Press, 1983).

[6]Cohen and Taylor, *American Pharaoh.*

[7]Charles E. Connerly, "From Racial Zoning to Community Empowerment: The Interstate Highway System and the African-American Community in Birmingham, Alabama," *Journal of Planning Education and Research 22* (1992), 99–114.

[8]Connerly, "From Racial Zoning"; Ronald H. Bayor, "Roads to Racial Segregation: Atlanta in the Twnetieth Century," *Journal of Urban History 15* (1988), 3–21.

[9]Katz, "Reframing the 'Underclass'Debate"; Kenneth T. Jackson, *Crabfrass Frontier: The Suburbanization of the United States* (New York: Oxford University Press, 1985);

and Ira Katznelson, *When Affirmative Action Was White: An Untold History of Racial Inequality in Twentieth-Century America* (New York: W. W. Norton, 2005).

[10]Robert J. Sampson and William Julius Wilson, "Toward a Theory of Race, Crime, and Urban Inequality," in *Crime and Inequality*, eds. John Hagan and Ruth Peterson (Stanford, CA: Stanford University Press, 1995), 37–54.

[11]Rosalyn Baxandall and Elizabeth Ewen, *Picture Windows: How the Suburbs Happened* (New York: Basic Books, 2000).

[12]Katz, "Reframing the 'Underclass' Debate," 461–62. On the history of suburbs in America, see Jackson, *Crabgrass Frontier*. For a good discussion of the effects of housing discrimination on the living conditions, education, and employment of urban minorities, see John Yinger, *Closed Doors, Opportunities Lost: The Continuing Costs of Housing Discrimination* (New York: Sage Foundation, 1995).

[13]Mark Condon, *Public Housing, Crime and the Urban Labor Market: A Study of Black Youth in Chicago*, Working Paper Series, no. H–91–3 (Cambridge, MA: Malcolm Wiener Center, John F. Kennedy School of Government, Harvard university, 1991).

[14]Ibid., 3.

[15]Ibid., 4.

[16]Ibid., 4.

[17]Sampson and Wilson, "Toward a Theory of Race." See also Bartelt, "Housing the 'Underclass'"; Kelley, "Black Poor and the Politics of Opposition"; Sugrue, "Structure of Urban Poverty'; Arnold R. Hirsch, *Making the Second Ghetto*; and John F. Bauman, Norman P. Hummon, and Edward K. Muller, "Public Housing Isolation, and the Urban Underclass," *Journal of Urban History 17* (1991), 264–92.

[18]Lincoln Quillian, "Migration Patterns and the Growth of High-Poverty Neighborhoods, 1970–1990," *American Journal of Sociology 105* (1999), 1–37.

[19]Ibid.

[20]Ibid.

[21]William Julius Wilson, *The Truly Disadvantaged: The Inner City, the Underclass, and Public Policy* (Chicago: University of Chicago Press, 1987); Wilson, *When Work Disappears*; Quillian, *Migration Patterns*.

[22]See Demetrios Caraley, "Washington Abandons the Cities," *Political Science Quarterly 107* (Spring 1992), 1–30.

[23]Bruce A. Wallin, *Budgeting for Basics: The Changing Landscape of City Finances*, Discussion paper prepared for the Brookings Institution Metropolitan Policy Program (Washington DC: Brookings Institution, August 2005).

Fate of American Cities[*]

Howard P. Chudacoff and Judith E. Smith

As the twentieth century entered its final quarter, several overlapping problems affected the fates of American cities. First, a slowdown of the national economy, the continuing effects of deindustrialization, and the dismantling of New Deal social programs dramatically increased the distance between rich and poor, and forcibly challenged city administrators to find sufficient revenues to meet their mounting needs. Second, the lack of a clear and consistent federal policy toward cities left municipalities to their own devices in dealing with problems that were basically national. Third, new immigrants reshaped urban ethnic and racial communities, unsettled prior political accommodations, and created new forms of urban culture.

Some urbanists have pointed to economic globalization as creating polarization between an emerging transnational capitalist class and its low-wage labor force, helping to explain the late twentieth century urban patterns of gentrification, immigrant enclave expansion, and the marginalization of the poor. Others point to national taxation, labor, and welfare policies as the culprits for a radically altered income distribution since the 1970s. Whatever the causes, cities were left without adequate resources to meet their needs, and political fragmentation prevented regional or metropolitan solutions. Suburbs also faced new fiscal constraints, especially after 1978 when widespread voter insistence on capping property taxes slashed local support for government services. Nonetheless, new as well as long-time urban residents continued to demand liveable cities and to devise creative solutions to improve the quality of urban life.

Fiscal Crisis and the Uncertainty of Federal Urban Policy

During the 1970s, urban administrations facing declining revenues tried to balance budgets and avoid tax increases by reducing expenses. But to meet service obligations such as road maintenance and education, and to honor union contracts, officials often had to overspend their budgets. They escaped deficits by borrowing from the city's cash flow, hoping to repay such loans from anticipated revenues due the following year. The next year, however, they found it necessary to borrow again and to postpone balancing accounts for another year. In this way, cities accumulated large internal debts. As expenses mounted and senti-

*Howard Chudacoff and Judith E. Smith, *The Evolution of American Urban Society* (Upper Saddle River, NJ: Pearson Education, 2005). Reprinted by permission of Pearson Education, Inc., Upper Saddle River, NJ.

ment against increasing taxes persisted, it became increasingly difficult for cities to repay and eliminate these loans. A sudden emergency could collapse the system and trigger fiscal crisis. In 1979, for example, cleanup from a massive snowfall cost Chicago an unanticipated $72 million. Once this bill was paid, however, the city lacked cash to meet normal obligations, including its payroll. Only an emergency loan and sharp tax hike forestalled major catastrophe.

The most publicized fiscal crisis occurred in New York City in 1974–75. During the optimistic expansion of the 1960s, the city borrowed heavily; when economic downturn came in the 1970s, New York's budget was badly overextended. The city had been financing services that elsewhere were provided by state, county, and special-district governments, and when the Nixon administration curtailed federal aid to the city, officials were forced into budget manipulation. Postponing payment on previous debts provided temporary respite. But in October 1974 and March 1975, a number of banks pulled the plug on the city's cash supply by refusing to underwrite its municipal bonds. In the end the banks agreed to loan more money, but at high interest rates.

Conventional explanations for New York's and other cities' fiscal problems blamed excessive wages paid to municipal employees and excessive welfare doles to malingering cheaters. But the causes ran much deeper. The core of New York's fiscal crisis was the loss of 542,000 jobs when offices, plants, and stores moved to the suburbs and the Sunbelt between 1969 and 1976. Losses of tax revenue inevitably ensued. Economists estimated that if those half-million jobs were still providing income for New Yorkers, the city would have received $1.5 billion in extra tax revenues and there would have been no fiscal crisis. The suburbs and Sunbelt took similar tolls on other cities. In the late 1960s and early 1970s, Philadelphia lost 17 percent of its jobs, and New Orleans lost 20 percent. Would Washington react to cities' needs by refining a federal urban policy? The subsequent years would provide a disappointing answer.

The federal-city relationship, which had originated during the New Deal in the 1930s and tightened during the Great Society of the 1960s, began to dissolve in 1974 with passage of the Housing and Community Development Block Grant Act. This measure, which initiated revenue sharing, was signed into law by President Gerald Ford, and it signaled a shift in federal attitudes, especially a retreat from the attack on poverty. Revenue sharing merged most federal grant programs into one program and provided for single block grants totaling $8.4 billion over three years. Instead of mandating spending on specific inner-city problems, these grants gave local officials more discretion over how to spend federal funds. Pledging that the act would avoid excessive federal regulation, Ford announced that cities would have greater certainty about the level of funding they could expect and that local officials could concentrate on broad programs of community betterment rather than applying for money for small-scale, individual projects. Revenue-sharing funds could be used for almost any purpose—public works, salaries, law enforcement, housing, job training. A formula based on population density, age of housing supply, and extent of poverty would determine the distribution of funds to ensure that needy cities received proportionately more than cities that were better off.

In practice, smaller communities, especially suburbs, benefited the most from revenue sharing. Federal grants enabled suburbs to undertake new projects such as roads and sewage treatment without raising taxes. But big city officials had to spend most of their grants to avoid severe budget cuts necessitated by loss of tax revenues and to sustain Great Society programs threatened by curtailment or impoundment of federal support and by soaring inflation. As a result, cities became increasingly dependent on federal money. The percentage of local budgets funded by Washington grew from 5.1 percent in 1970 to 12.9 percent in 1975. In 1967, federal aid accounted for only 1 percent of St. Louis's budget and 2.1 percent of Buffalo's. By 1978, federal aid accounted for 54.7 percent and 69.2 percent respectively. Government aid also made up one-fourth to one-half of operating revenues of Baltimore, Philadelphia, Phoenix, Cleveland, and Detroit. Cities had set themselves up for a new and different crisis if and when federal urban policy should shift or wither as it eventually did.

In 1976, Jimmy Carter, a rural Georgian, won the presidency by promising to help America's cities with a "comprehensive" urban program. His strategy won him a remarkably high percentage of the urban vote in 1976. Such support, however, carried with it high expectations. At first, the Carter administration fueled the appetites of America's cities. Several cabinet-level advisors spoke before the U.S. Conference of Mayors (USCM) and vowed that "no issue... will concern this administration more and concern the President more than the question of jobs and the question of cities." Secretary of Housing and Urban Development Patricia Roberts Harris announced, "the White House is now in the hands of a friend of the cities."

Big-city mayors, especially the increasing numbers of African-American mayors, intended to cash in on these promises. Kenneth Gibson, mayor of Newark and chairman of the USCM, heralded "the beginning of a new relationship," and the USCM proposed that $20 billion be spent for a "national urban investment program" to address such diverse problems as employment, health care, crime, welfare, housing, and transportation. Janet Frey Hayes, mayor of San Jose, California, spoke for most urban politicians when she announced, "We come not as beggars, but as elected officials to the places where 75 percent of the people are." After being ignored for almost a decade and courted during the Carter campaign, mayors shared a sense of entitlement.

Carter, however, diverged from urban and black interests over several ideological issues. Whereas mayors focused on getting increased federal spending in inner cities, Carter, believing that federal initiative alone could not save cities, supported fiscally conservative measures to spur private investment.

Consequently, Carter's programs would revolve around tax breaks and incentives that might help coax business and industry back into the cities. In addition, the President hoped to balance the federal budget and lower taxes, a combination that would require significant reductions in spending on social welfare.

When Carter proposed a broad urban policy, it reflected his retreat from federal urban spending. Instead of extensive government assistance, he offered "a New Partnership, involving all levels of government, the private sector, and neighborhood and voluntary organizations." The government would maintain popular programs such as Urban Development Action Grants, providing fiscal relief to cities in crisis, and initiating a $1 billion public works program. It hoped to bring private capital investment back to the cities by granting tax breaks to businesses that hired the long-term unemployed or set up shop in impoverished areas, and by creating an urban development bank that could give urban businesses loans they would be unable to secure on the open market. Finally, the urban policy invited more inter-government cooperation by encouraging state governments to get involved in renewal efforts, funding neighborhood development projects directly and creating an urban volunteer corps. Once the proposals went before Congress, urban and black leaders threw support to the President in a last-ditch attempt to salvage whatever federal commitments they could find. But Congress, tilting ever more toward suburban interests, balked at Carter's initiatives.

The defeat of Carter's urban policy in Congress was indicative of an emerging trend in national politics. It marked the end of an era of significant federal spending earmarked for cities and the beginning of collective urban belt-tightening. In 1979, the National League of Cities titled one of its themes "Making do with less," and Carter warned mayors against expecting new aid in the federal budget of that year. One of his advisors told the National Urban Coalition, "We cannot hope to devote the additional resources you and I would like to rebuilding our cities."

At least two factors contributed to this new attitude. First, Carter was fiscally conservative and generally averse to massive federal aid programs. Second, many middle-class Americans, reeling from the impacts of inflation and a stalled economy, were losing faith in governmental programs. Historian Bruce Schulman has labeled the 1970s as a period of southernization, when southern ideology of low taxes and limited public services began to direct national policy.

In November of 1979, Carter publicly marked the distance he had traveled from prior liberalism and from his original urban and black supporters by announcing a new policy of "urban conservatism," the goal of which was "to make sure that Federal Programs do not contribute to the economic deterioration of our cities." Almost as a response to such a plan, when the President visited riot-torn Miami in June 1980, a crowd in the Liberty City district threw bottles at his motorcade. Carter's retreat from engagement with urban problems was eloquently illustrated in the recommendation of his presidential commission that the urban mission of the federal government was to encourage inhabitants of inner cities of the Northeast and Midwest to relocate to the Sunbelt.

Ronald Reagan, George H.W. Bush, and Neglect as a Panacea

Although Ronald Reagan made a campaign stop in the South Bronx to criticize Jimmy Carter for his broken promises to urban neighborhoods, he won the presidency in 1980 without support from African-American and white urban voters. Believing in self-help and local responsibility for relieving poverty, Reagan put cuts in federal aid to cities and social programs that provided a safety net for the urban poor at the heart of his political beliefs. His supporters had been instrumental in the politics of middle-class tax revolt, white backlash, and distrust of big government, and "southernization" continued to privilege market solutions rather than federal intervention on behalf of social welfare and racial equality. Feeding on this energy, Reagan, focused on bolstering the suburban upper and middle class, claiming that the economic gains that would benefit these groups would eventually "trickle down" to the urban poor. By the time he left office in 1989, deepening divisions of social and economic stratification were apparent everywhere, but nowhere were they more visible than in cities.

Reagan's budgetary measures took a sharp toll on cities. In 1981 and 1982 he proposed deep cuts in welfare, food stamps, and child nutrition. In 1983 he proposed further cuts of $14 billion in welfare, food stamps, and child nutrition. An increasingly conservative and Republican Congress readily approved. In 1986, the President deferred funds earmarked for Urban Development Action Grants, the most successful urban policy of the Carter Administration, in preparation for his push to abandon the program entirely. In 1987, he canceled federal revenue sharing, which had disbursed $85 billion over its fourteen-year existence and touched more municipalities than any other legislation in history. Henry Maier, mayor of Milwaukee, described the process as "the sacking of urban America." A drastic shift had taken place. As one critic observed, with this last strike, the Reagan Administration had necessitated "a basic redefinition that there is no longer any essential Federal role with cities."

Reagan's aggressive budget slashing followed from his political and economic philosophy, which called for the downsizing of government in general. The president repeatedly referred to Washington as "big brother," and he theorized that only by reducing federal intervention in the marketplace could his government reinvigorate the American economy. If he could not justify cutting programs directly, he consolidated them under block grants and let states spend federal money however they saw fit. In 1982, Reagan announced that the Department of Housing and Urban Development (HUD) would no longer monitor Community Development Block Grants to ensure that federal funds were aiding moderate and low-income people, which had always been the intent of the program. Moreover, Reagan continually lowered taxes, though the government ran huge budget deficits every year. As far as the President was concerned, small government and the free market were the keys to economic success. In his June, 1982 formulation, he emphatically praised market rather than government intervention: "The Federal government," he stated, "cannot develop the flexible, broad range of policies and partnerships needed to rebuild and revitalize urban life. Neither can it guarantee a city's long-term prosperity. All too often the promise of such guarantees has created a crippling dependency rather than initiative and independence. It will now be the responsibility of local leadership, working closely with the private sector and the city's neighborhoods, to develop a strategy for the survival and prosperity of the country's cities."

Though Reagan eventually softened some of his admonishing tone, his message remained the same. In place of federal largesse, he offered his belief that a general economic recovery would reverberate through all levels of society and benefit poor people as well as the middle class. Through a series of tax cuts, he would give the middle class more spending power with the hope that this boost to the economy would stimulate urban development through market forces.

All Reagan had to offer as an urban policy was an initiative to establish "enterprise zones," a relatively inexpensive program that was supposed to promote private sector investment in the nation's most impoverished neighborhoods. Initially proposed in Congress by Republican Jack Kemp and Democrat Robert Garcia of New York, the program would cut taxes and minimize federal regulations (such as minimum wages, pollution control, and occupational safety) in inner-city areas selected by HUD as enterprise zones. The policy aimed to encourage businesses to enter depressed slums and create prosperous commercial districts in their place. Eventually, enterprise-zone legislation died in Congress, but by 1988 several states had created similar laws, though their impact was minimal.

After eight years of "Reaganomics," urban leaders were ready to call the experiment a failure. In response to Reagan's economic policies, cities had had to cut services and raise property taxes. By 1988, the prospects for the urban poor seemed especially dim. Street crime, homelessness, joblessness, hunger, and hopelessness had been persistent problems in most innercity neighborhoods for decades, but by 1988 urban leaders had to accept the fact that they lacked the political clout to pressure the federal government to solve these problems. According to the *New York Times*, Reagan had taught mayors two lessons: "to narrow their list of demands, and even then not to expect too much." Cities were left to search for new answers to old problems that no longer seemed to interest average people. Massive federal aid had not proved to be an urban panacea, but the Reagan administration had removed government's provision of a safety net and left a legacy of seeming disregard for poor people.

George H. W. Bush, Reagan's vice president, was elected to the presidency in 1988 by the same suburban constituency that had benefited his predecessor, and he showed few signs that he might alter Reagan's views regarding urban interests. Eight years earlier, Bush had labeled Reagan's supply-side economic theories as "voodoo economics." Once elected, his cabinet appointments, especially HUD Secretary Jack Kemp, appeared urban-friendly. Kemp even announced, "I'm going to be an activist. I'm going to be an advocate. I want to wage war on poverty." Mayors did not expect an all-out war on poverty, but they were encouraged by such aggressive rhetoric. Even the new vice president, Dan Quayle, seemed to mount the bandwagon, announcing his own commitment to combating drugs and crime and reducing the dropout rates at urban schools. African-American leaders were especially encouraged. After President Bush met with leading blacks on Martin Luther King Day, Detroit's Coleman Young observed, "In one day, he took a bigger step than his predecessor took in eight years."

When word spread late in 1989 that cities could expect a "peace dividend" resulting from the end of the Cold War, mayors believed their patience had paid off. However, the 1990 federal budget proved to be the first in a series of disappointments. It closely resembled the budgets Reagan had sent to Congress. New York's Mayor David Dinkins called it "mean-spirited." Bush's urban program, which focused on still-unfulfilled enterprise zones, languished in Congress without enthusiastic support, even from Bush himself. By the end of 1990, a *New York Times* poll revealed that 77 percent of Americans thought Bush was doing "not much" or "nothing at all" about urban problems.

The Persian Gulf crisis, which began when Iraq invaded Kuwait in the summer of 1990 and escalated into war in January of 1991, gave Bush an excuse to ignore domestic policy altogether. In addition, a recession, which gripped the country in 1991 allowed him to eschew new social spending even as cities and their inhabitants struggled to stay afloat. By mid–1991, most major cities again were being forced to deal with fiscal crisis, mostly by cutting services and raising taxes. In Philadelphia, four mayoral candidates, including the eventual victor, Ed Rendell, supported privatization of public services, and, once elected, Rendell raised taxes by $90 million. Meanwhile, the President proposed turning $15 billion in federal aid for health, education, welfare, housing, and law enforcement over to the states. Boston's mayor Raymond Flynn grumbled, "This isn't Federalism, this is fraud."

Leasing city services to private contractors offered several mayors a tempting way to effect cost-saving and efficiency. At the federal level, the U.S. Postal Service had been privatized, and numerous schemes for turning over management of public housing, toll roads, prisons, and airports to private companies circulated at state and local levels. By contracting out services, cities, could escape fast-rising employee wage, benefit, and pension costs and avoid having to purchase expensive equipment for tasks as varied as data processing and snow removal. The prospect of privatization could also force public workers to be more efficient. For example, the city of Phoenix required its own employees to bid against private firms for residential trash collecting. City workers initially lost these contracts but then streamlined their operation and won them back.

Estimates of savings to a city from privatization ranged up to 20 percent. Consequently, more and more cities began considering it. In the early 1970s, as a result of generous federal aid, Chicago, under the powerful Mayor Richard J. Daley, had over 44,000 people on the city payroll. By 1991, the payroll under his son, Mayor Richard M. Daley, had shrunk to 38,500, and the younger Daley was seeking ways to reduce it further. By contracting out jobs such as sewer cleaning, addiction treatment, towing away abandoned cars, and custodial service for city buildings, Daley hoped to prevent tax hikes and budget deficits.

But privatization did not meet with universal approval in Chicago and elsewhere. Public employee unions naturally objected, and racial minorities expressed fears that the private sector could not be prevented from discriminatory hiring practices as readily as the public sector could. Critics charged that Daley, Rendell and other mayors too easily could award contracts to friends and campaign contributors. Others lamented the enhanced possibilities for fraud when services were released from strict public supervision. Whatever its merits, privatization received encouragement from the administrations of Ronald Reagan and George Bush, and its momentum continued well into the 1990s.

Facing empty treasuries once more, several cities considered generating new revenues through legalized gambling. Since their inception, American cities have been centers for gambling, and though it was almost always illegal, urban leaders have alternated between tolerating some modicum of gambling and trying to eliminate it. In the post-World War II era, only the state of Nevada officially allowed gambling, and Las Vegas was the only city to base its growth on gambling and the tourism that accompanied it.

By the 1970s, however, fiscal shortfalls were tempting public officials to reconsider the jobs and tax revenues gambling could create. Several states revived lotteries, which during the colonial period had been used to raise revenue. Then, states and cities began to contemplate sponsoring casino gambling. In 1978, casino gaming became legal in Atlantic City, New Jersey, and a boom in hotel building and entertainment occurred there though not without the destruction of low-rent neighborhoods and an increase in crime. By the 1990s, other cities were moving toward legalized gambling as well. Several cities on or near waterways, such as Chicago, St. Louis, and Biloxi, benefited from gambling places, but the increased number of casinos spawned fears that there would be diminishing returns from an excess of casinos relative to the gambling population and that the economic returns hid problematic costs. Some economists estimated that for every job that legalized gambling created two were lost because consumers who lost money gambling would cut back on spending in other areas such as buying clothes or getting haircuts. Mayors, it seemed, would have to look elsewhere for a quick fix to the needs for tax revenues and unemployment relief.

If George H. W. Bush was susceptible to criticism on urban issues before the Los Angeles uprising in late April and early May of 1992, he was directly vulnerable afterward. Exposing deep-seated tensions from racism and police brutality against minority communities, the uprising's immediate spark was the acquittal of four police officers who had been videotaped violently subduing an African-American man, Rodney King, during an arrest. Abetted by youth gangs, some enraged blacks and Latinos destroyed whole city blocks in South Central Los Angeles and spread violence and fear into surrounding communities, including Hollywood. In all, more than thirty-five people were killed, most of whom were shot by the police, and $2 billion worth of property was destroyed. Like the uprisings of the 1960s, the 1992 violence renewed concern about abject poverty and anger among racial minorities in all cities as well as in Los Angeles. The conditions of economic marginalization, inadequacy of social welfare expenditures, and racial discrimination had in many ways worsened in the 1990s with the flight of capital, collapse of the welfare state, and racist backlash, but the 1990s riots also expressed complex inter-ethnic and racial tensions, as well as alienation from civic culture, among people of color.

Bush's immediate response to the rioting was to attack Great Society programs on which Reagan had effectively laid blame for most urban problems. This tactic only angered his opponents more. "It's just amazing," said presidential candidate Bill Clinton. "Republicans have had the White House for twenty of the last twenty-four years, and they have to go all the way back to the '60s to find somebody to blame." The *New York Times* was more blunt. "As if, after Los Angeles, there were any doubt; America's cities need help. So far, President Bush mainly offers them gratuitous insult." The riots jarred Americans who had mostly been content to reap the rewards of economic prosperity and to stand by as minorities and poor people suffered. According to one pollster, 61 percent of Americans now thought the nation was spending too little on inner cities, compared to just 35 percent four years earlier during the height of the Reagan Revolution.

Less than two weeks after the rioting, the President and Congress seemed on the way to forging an emergency aid package. Democrats in Congress were willing to give the President enterprise zones, public school choice, and privatization of public housing. In return, Bush would support several spending initiatives. Before the plan could pass, however, Washington again yielded to partisan squabbling. The President refused to sign any bill that included a tax increase, while Congressional Democrats held out for more spending. Meanwhile, Republicans held fast on fiscal policies. California Congressman Bill Lowery, a staunch conservative, accused Bush of "send[ing] the message that urban terrorism brings Federal largesse."

The window of opportunity had not opened very far. After some debate over how to approach issues raised by the uprising, the Bush Administration decided on middle-of-the-road themes of law and order. In May of 1992, Vice President Quayle delivered a speech in Los Angeles, essentially blaming the rioting on the immorality of its participants. Said Quayle, "I believe the lawless anarchy which we saw is directly related to the breakdown of family structure, personal responsibility, and social order." On June 18, the President and Congress agreed on a watered-down $1.3 billion aid package and promised to address urban policy needs more comprehensively at a later date. By the end of 1992, Congress had passed an urban aid and tax bill, but according to the *New York Times*, the policy was disingenuous. "Want a challenge?" an editorial asked, "Try to find urban aid in the urban aid bills just passed by… Congress." In the end Congress and the President could only accomplish a political standoff. Despite all the rhetoric, little actually was done to help cities, and even the measures that were passed were destined to have no lasting effect. George H. W. Bush may have paid dearly for his lack of firm response, for the legislative failures enhanced his image as a President without domestic sensitivities, an image that contributed to his defeat by Bill Clinton in 1992.

The Clinton Years: Further Neglect

Looking more liberal than Reagan or Bush, Clinton gave mayors cause to assume he would direct his attention to urban America. But like his predecessors, he was not forced by political winds to do so. He made few attempts to reach out to urban voters, and he borrowed much of his urban policy—law and order, home ownership, welfare reform, and enterprise zones—from Reagan. Though urban America enjoyed relative prosperity during Clinton's administrations, there was no guarantee that its fortunes would remain bright.

When Clinton was elected in 1992, the urban establishment did not know how to react. Some mayors were excited by the election of a Democrat. Yet Clinton was from a mostly rural state, had no experience with urban affairs, and had ignored cities during his campaign. He had no urban agenda to speak of, but he did address urban-related issues of health care, the AIDs epidemic, and welfare reform. The USCM decided to test the President early, presenting him with a $27 billion list of seven thousand ready-to-go projects during his first week in office. Several weeks later, Clinton promised a "fairly sizable increase" in block grants to cities.

In May of 1993, however, mayors got their first taste of what Clinton's urban policy would be like. He announced a plan to establish 110 "empowerment zones," his name for enterprise zones. The whole program would cost only $8 billion over five years. Later that month, he explained his Community Banking and Credit Fund, which would subsidize Community Development Banks, and called for $382 million in funding, substantially less than he had led mayors to expect. It was clear that Clinton had only modest plans for cities. His philosophy resembled Carter's, but he was not burdened by the inertia of massive federal spending on cities. He could concentrate on economic development without having to appease racial minorities with social spending programs. Consequently, his urban policy closely resembled those of his conservative predecessors. Half a year after Clinton took office, Louisville Mayor Jerry Abramson had resigned himself to four more years of executive inactivity. "There was a real question of whether it was humanly possible for any individual to reach our expectations," he said.

In the fall of 1996, Clinton signed a massive welfare reform bill that possibly served as his most influential urban policy. In reality, however, it was not his policy at all. Although Clinton talked frequently about welfare reform, he chose to sign a bill sponsored mostly by conservatives that had stirred aggressive liberal opposition in Congress. The legislation dismantled the 62-year-old welfare system and turned it over to state governments, imposing only the barest minimum of guidelines. Most big-city mayors opposed the legislation, arguing that it would cause suffering among poor mothers and their children.

Based on the premise that previous welfare measures fostered dependency, the new decentralized system focused on getting welfare recipients off relief and into the workplace. It relied on two principles. The first held that limited benefits would prevent welfare from becoming a way of life. The other assumed that uneducated single mothers needed support in order to find jobs and achieve stability. The policy flowing from these principles created new work rules, penalties, and time limits for welfare payments but also expanded certain services. For example, the Wisconsin welfare system required its recipients to work thirty hours a week in order to collect benefits. Recipients who broke the rules were cut off. In addition, no one could receive benefits for longer than five years. At the same time, however, the state made a more concerted effort to find work for welfare recipients and created public service jobs for those who could not find work. Other states pursued different paths to reach the same goals.

Though a booming national economy facilitated a decline in welfare rolls, even in hard-hit inner cities, many experts criticized the plan. Some argued that the focus on work of any sort would confine welfare recipients to dead-end jobs with no hope of receiving the training to move up the occupational ladder. Others feared the penalties were too strict and the rules too hard to follow. As of June, 1997, 20,000 people had already lost benefits for failing to comply with the work rules; many of them were welfare mothers who were dropped from the rolls because their time limit ran out.

Political scientist James Jennings found that welfare reform's focus on individual workforce participation had a negative impact on poor black and Latino neighborhoods, because it discouraged civic participation and burdened community-based organizations with monitoring individual compliance with regulations rather than focusing on comprehensive economic and social organizing and revitalization.

On June 23, 1997, President Clinton addressed the USCM and outlined what he called his first urban agenda. Most elements of the plan, such as giving police officers discounts on HUD-owned houses in the inner city and reducing closing costs for first-time homeowners, focused on long-time themes of law and order and promoting homeownership. Other aspects of the agenda already had been developed as part of the President's budget agreement with Congress. Conspicuously absent was any kind of social spending. Rather, Clinton focused on modest methods to promote economic development. Even with Clinton's low-key approach to urban policy, however, cities began to share in the general health of the economy. Urban crime and unemployment were down in the late 1990s, and several big cities were achieving unparalleled fiscal stability. The seventy-two urban empowerment zones supported by the federal government had generated almost $4 billion in private investment, a 200 percent return on the federal program of $2 billion. Whether or not this trend could be attributed to Clinton's efforts, the economic recovery did not seem to be leaving poor urban dwellers as completely desperate as they had been under Reagan and Bush. What might happen when the economic boom leveled off remained uncertain.

The Social Costs of Widening Income Inequality and Urban Neglect

Dense concentrations of poor people in urban neighborhoods magnified the problems related to poverty: joblessness, crime, delinquency, drug use and trafficing, family break-up, and poor school performance. The rise in poverty concentration began in the early 1970s in cities, because of declining incomes of the poor and the exodus of middle income families leaving inner-city neighborhoods. Mixed-income neighborhoods turned into high-poverty neighborhoods, marking them as dangerous. Once this transition took place, these neighborhoods became socially and economically isolated as people tried to avoid them at all costs. Sensational journalism, fiction, and film all played their parts in popularizing high-concentration poverty areas as urban wastelands.

As a source of fear and a matter that evaded easy analysis, crime has always plagued American cities. In actuality, crime rates—the number of serious crimes per 100,000 people—fell from 1980 to the late 1990s. But the absolute numbers of robberies, assaults, and homicides increased. Two related agents intensified the sense of danger in urban society: the widespread ownership of guns and the uncontrollable use and trafficking of illegal drugs.

The temporary escape from pain promised by drugs tempted all parts of American society, including the suburbs. But in the mid–1980s, the rapid spread of crack cocaine brought severe consequences to some poverty-concentrated neighborhoods. Easily addictive, crack became an entrepreneurial bonanza, attracting youths and their gangs into dealing and provoking violent conflicts over the huge profits involved in its sale. The money and competition also prompted dealers to acquire guns, some of which had extraordinary firepower, and to use them indiscriminately. The drug epidemic amplified the AIDS epidemic. Passed to victims through infected intravenous needles as well as through infected body fluids exchanged during sexual contact, AIDS became a major urban public health concern.

The despair of homelessness also increasingly marked the urban landscape. The decline in affordable housing resulted from demolition and gentrification in downtown neighborhoods as well as from government retrenchment. In 1970, there were a few more cheap apartments than needy renters: 6.2 million renters and 6.5 million apartments. But by 1995, there were 10 million needy renters and just 6 million low-rent apartments. By 1998, for example, as many as 16,000 homeless individuals wandered the streets of San Francisco on any given day, attracted by the city's mild climate and tradition of social consciousness. More than a third of those lacking permanent housing were mentally ill people, released from homes and hospitals by the Reagan administration's cuts in federal aid and by a trend toward removing people from institutions. Increasingly, the homeless population consisted of families, especially those headed by women, unable to derive sufficient income and cast adrift by cuts in housing subsidies. The burden of the shortage of affordable housing and the resulting homelessness fell heavily on children, who composed 40 percent of the poor by the year 2000, a proportion even higher in African-American, Latino, and new Asian immigrant populations.

Gentrification's role in the decline of affordable housing has sometimes implicated a group that have themselves been recipients of discrimination: middle-class homosexuals. Because gay communities tended to form in downtown neighborhoods and to participate in the process of revitalization, this process has sometimes resulted in sharp conflict with long-time poorer residents whose access to housing has been diminished. These tensions sometimes have taken on a racial inflection when the communities affected have included African-Americans, Latinos, or other people of color. Gay men and lesbians have often been the opening wedge in neighborhood gentrification, followed later by other young urban professionals whose presence helped to push out all but the wealthiest gay residents. Boston's South End, Brooklyn's Park Slope, Philadelphia's Rittenhouse Square, and Washington, D.C.'s Dupont Circle have exemplified neighborhoods where these transitions, with their attendant tensions, have occurred. When this process has managed to preserve some affordable housing, such as in Brooklyn's Prospect Heights, the resulting neighborhoods can be home to residents of diverse racial, ethnic, class, and sexual identities.

The economic boom of the Clinton years reduced unemployment, and increased the earnings of low wage workers. In 1990, 15 percent of all poor people lived in high poverty neighborhoods, but ten years later, only 10 percent did. This decline, which resulted partly from the tearing down of high rise public housing which had been allowed to fall into dangerous ill repair, was most significant in midwestern and southern cities like Detroit, Chicago, and San Antonio. Poverty concentrations remained unchanged in older northeastern cities. At the same time, poor residents moved into the inner ring of older suburbs in Chicago, Detroit, Cleveland, and Dallas. Black people were still more likely to live in high poverty neighborhoods than other poor people, although the numbers fell from 30 percent in 1990 to 19 percent in 2000. Los Angeles was the only city to show an increase in the number of high poverty neighborhoods over this time period, but rising unemployment and individual poverty rates related to the abrupt economic decline after 2001 has caused other cities to follow the Los Angeles pattern.

Editors' Note: No footnotes were provided in the original. For a full bibliography related to this piece see pp. 310–311 of the Chudacoff and Smith text.

An Old Debate Still Germane and a Vital Connection Seldom Made[*]

Levon Chorbajian

An Old Debate Still Germane

The question of who runs the country's cities has been a subject of intense debate going back to the 1950s. This is an important question because cities do not simply evolve, but rather are made. That is to say whatever a city may be, compared to what it has been in the past, is the outcome of decisions made by people and organizations poised to shape urban areas. Because the organization and operation of a city is not inevitable, the question of who has the power to run cities takes on considerable importance. We might even say that the question of power, who has it and how it is used, is central to our understanding of cities.

When sociologists speak of power, they are referring to economic, political, and social resources that allow certain actors to define the field of debate and who may participate in it. Pluralist theories have been influential in the fields of sociology and political science and have served to obscure the workings of power in urban governance. We begin therefore with a presentation of the pluralist perspective and follow with the analyses of several of its critics.

The conventional answer to the question "Who Runs America's Cities?" is that cities are not run by any particular group of individuals or set of organizations. A related claim is that cities are run in ways that bring maximum benefits to the city as a whole. In this pluralist interpretation, there is a decision making and administrative structure in charge of cities. Some of these people are elected, others are appointed, and the rest staff the permanent bureaucratic structure of governance. While pluralists usually acknowledge that there are interest groups that petition government for decisions and policies that they promote, the idea that cities are governed by anything like a cohesive class-based set of interests which promote certain agendas at the expense of others is rejected.

This pluralist model of urban governance was articulated by political scientist Robert Dahl and others, and the focus of their research was on the decision-making process and its outcome. In other words, as their argument ran, we can determine who runs cities by asking

---

[*]Original contribution written for this volume.

how particular issues and controversies are resolved. If we can determine who wins, we can determine who rules. Dahl put it this way in his definition of power "as A's capacity for acting in such a manner as to control B's responses." Implicit in Dahl's work is the notion that power is widely dispersed in society rather than concentrated in the hands of the few. An individual or organizational ability to exercise power is dependent on the resources brought to the table and the particular issue at hand because each issue brings together a different mix of interests and players, and calls for a different set of assets such that power is spread out and not dominated by a single actor on all or most issues.[1]

There are several major critiques of this pluralistic model. Of those we will examine here, one is a theoretical argument made by Steven Lukes and several are empirical studies, including Floyd Hunter's seminal study of Atlanta, Georgia.

In *Power: A Radical View*, Steven Lukes delineates three dimensions of power.[2] The first corresponds to Dahl's definition of power and looks at the outcomes of specific decisions on issues where observable and conflicting interests are found. Lukes refers to this as one-dimensional power and views it as a limited conceptualization because power involves so much more than the ability to make and enforce decisions. Lukes points out that while there may be disagreement and conflict among those seeking decisions in their favor, the parties often do agree on which groups, organizations, and individuals are to be excluded from the process. He refers to this exclusion as the two-dimensional expression of power which pays close attention to non-decision making as well as decision making. Exclusion can be exercised on the basis of dominant definitions of what is a reasonable or unreasonable idea, or a reasonable or unreasonable person or organization. Such definitions can then be acted upon to exclude the unwanted along with their objectives, perspectives, and proposals. The actual techniques for exclusion include secrecy, closed meetings, strict adherence to Robert's Rules of Order and other class-based techniques for conducting meetings, misinformation, red tape, and the selective deployment of ridicule, coercion, or manipulation for the purpose of the marginalization of opponents (or, in selected cases, their cooptation through the dispensing of money and other rewards). For example, most elections are contested, but money plays a critical role in determining who the candidates are. When we also consider that election laws in the U.S. are hostile to third political parties and that legislative seats are determined by the outcome of single district, winner-take-all elections, it becomes abundantly clear that many views are excluded and never become part of the "choice" voters are given.[3]

In the first and second dimensions of power, issues are contested, and dominant groups win by being stronger at the point of decision or by excluding competing views, groups, and organizations they do not wish to have in the mix. Lukes' three-dimensional power bears similarities to Antonio Gramsci's famous concept of hegemony where there are no issues.[4] Through sufficient if not total control over school curricula and media content, advertising, the clever use of language, the much expanded display of the national flag and the public singing of patriotic anthems, the celebration of national holidays complete with fly-overs and other displays of military might, people's consciousness of their political and social worlds is shaped from childhood. As a result of this slow, subtle, long-term socialization into the status quo people typically do not have systemic grievances because they do not perceive reality as oppressive or anything other than the natural order of things. Thus the absence of observable conflict does not necessarily imply the social consensus that Dahl and the other pluralists claim, but instead a generalized acceptance of a socially constructed 'common sense' that reinforces fundamental social relations, including class relations.

Dahl based his pluralist theory of decision making on his study of urban renewal in New Haven, Connecticut in the 1950s.[5] Dahl's project was to challenge Floyd Hunter's earlier research on Atlanta, Georgia. Hunter's finding that urban politics were controlled by business elites who could effectively dictate to political leaders was ideologically unacceptable. Dahl and the other pluralists had always insisted that political decision making was a process with many actors, none of whom was consistently dominant in the multitude of decisions that had to be made in the course of governing a city or other political entity. The relevance of Lukes' work for understanding municipal governance is that it calls our attention to other ways of exercising power that highlight the influence of major institutions, and the wealth and networks that they command compared to the power of neighborhoods, the poor, small businesses, and other less well-resourced constituencies. This alternative perspective is reinforced by several empirical studies of urban decision making.

The first of these is Floyd Hunter's. Hunter examined the structure of governance in Atlanta in the early 1950s and published his findings in the book *Community Power Structure*.[6] In the 1940s Hunter had held a series of social service jobs, first as a social worker in Indianapolis. During World War II, he was employed in various cities organizing recreation canteens for soldiers. It was here that Hunter first dealt with the Chamber of Commerce and other local power structures and their personnel. These contacts would continue when Hunter moved to Atlanta where he became the director of a community center for underprivileged youth. In his administrative capacities Hunter described himself as working with the 'second echelon' of the power structure. Due to his anti-segregationist views and progressive politics, Hunter was fired from his job. He then undertook his famous research project.

Hunter's method was to compile a list of 175 Atlantans who were active in governmental, corporate, and civic activities. The list was submitted to 14 professionals who were knowledgeable about the inner workings of the city. Each was asked to make a list of the top ten leaders in Atlanta. From these responses Hunter compiled a smaller list of the 40 most frequently selected names. He eventually succeeded in interviewing 27 of the 40 of Atlanta's movers and shakers. Hunter supplemented these interviews with nearly three dozen additional interviews with African-American leaders, and fourteen planners and welfare workers. Hunter's intent was to see whether or not there was, behind the maze of civic and voluntary associations, and the formal institutions of government, a core of informal rulers who set the city's agenda and facilitated its enactment.

The picture that emerged from these interviews very much confirmed Hunter's hypothesis. He did not find a single power pyramid, but he found several interlocked and overlapping ones consisting of a small number of people who were corporate lawyers, major owners of prominent businesses, and the top executives of the largest banks and concerns such as Coca-Cola and Georgia Power & Light. These people lived in the same neighborhoods, belonged to the same clubs, and sat on one another's boards of directors. In discussions among these friends and close associates, goals, strategies, and policies were discussed and then refined by hired experts. When Hunter asked his interviewees what was the most important issue for them, nearly 90% answered growth and physical improvements related to growth. They got what they wanted. Between 1956 and 1966 15% of the city's population was forced to move to make way for highways, urban renewal, and downtown development projects. These projects greatly enhanced the land and property values of Atlanta's elite and the businesses they represented as well as the markets for the goods and services they provided.[7]

Hunter's findings were confirmed by Clarence Stone who conducted two additional studies of Atlanta's power structure in the 1970s and 1980s. Stone found that although certain members of Atlanta's power structure had retired or passed away, the same structure representing the same interests remained intact into the later decades. The new elite was made up of the same sorts of people uncovered by Hunter, in some cases the very same people. Their priorities were still urban growth and the rise in land values.[8] They were able to bring this about through the expansion and development of the central business district but at the expense of low-income African-American neighborhoods. For example, these downtown business elites were able to secure land for a stadium, a civic center, and the expansion of a central city university, all the while blocking repeated calls for affordable public housing from residents of poorer neighborhoods. The election of African-Americans to the positions of mayor and city councilors had little or no effect on this elite agenda, which we can take as a measure of its strength and solidity.[9]

Further evidence comes from the work of G. William Domhoff, best known for his development of elite theory at the level of national governance.[10] Domhoff has not been indifferent, however, to local decision making authority. In fact, he re-examined the data for New Haven that had been the basis for Dahl's claim of pluralist decision making. Domhoff's re-examination of archival materials, including Dahl's original interviews, plus new interviews Domhoff conducted himself, strongly suggested that New Haven's urban renewal projects would not have been possible without the cooperation of downtown landowners and real estate development interests, Yale University, and U.S. Senator Prescott Bush (Yale graduate and father and grandfather of presidents George H.W. Bush and George W. Bush).[11]

It seems clear on the basis of the evidence that the broad outlines of urban decision making are shaped by corporate elites who have disproportionate influence at the local, state, and federal levels of decision making. Voluntary associations, tenants' associations, housing advocates, and community organizations can have input and sometimes do but only after the parameters have already been set elsewhere. For example, low income renters and owners of small businesses had no hand in deciding that their homes and businesses would be bulldozed to make way for highways and convention centers. They could acquiesce or they could resist, but they could have no input by sitting at the table where those plans were hatched, discussed, refined, and finalized for implementation.

Another type of limiting parameter on the range of options available to middle and working-class urbanites is set by national spending priorities. We address this neglected issue in the next section.

A Vital Connection Seldom Made

The size of the U.S. military budget serves as a limiting factor on urban resources because of the shift it represents away from domestic social welfare spending. This connection is well-known and understood by independent experts but seriously under-publicized in the media and under-taught in K-12 education and in colleges and universities. In other words, it is a censored reality. Nearly all writers who focus on urban problems and issues prefer to act as though the fiscal crises of city after city and the many cutbacks in social spending that ensue have no connection to national spending priorities. Contrary to this mainstream interpretation, we wish to argue that they do have a close, intimate connection. This connection was forthrightly stated by none other than Dwight D. Eisenhower, 34th President of the United States and Supreme Commander of Allied Expeditionary Forces (1943-1945) when he said:

> Every gun that is made, every warship launched, every rocket fired signifies, in the final sense, a theft from those who hunger and are not fed, those who are cold and are not clothed. The world in arms is not spending money alone. It is spending the sweat of its laborers, the genius of its scientists, and the hopes of its children.[13]

It is not our position that military spending cannot stimulate economic growth, or that it fails to create jobs. Under certain circumstances, it can do both. Ours is the broader contention that militarism has been unhealthy for the nation as a whole and for cities in particular because it drains resources away from investment in the service of human needs.

The military spending history of the U.S. prior to World War II is that the nation would mobilize armies and armaments in time of war, and, largely, if not completely, demobilize when wars ended. This longstanding pattern ended with the advent of the Cold War after 1945. When President Harry Truman proposed a military budget approaching $15 billion (roughly $150 billion in today's dollars) in 1948, much of the nation was aghast. It seemed so high for a peacetime budget. The request and its allocation represented a major break from previous national history, and it gave birth to what has come to be known as the permanent war economy which means large and ever-growing military budgets whether the nation is at peace or war.

In military Keynesianism, weapons research, design, and manufacture are used to pump government funds into the economy. The two problems with this policy as a strategy for economic growth are, first, that weapons do not constitute any kind of social good in the sense that education, housing, and health care are. Weapons are not social goods that are used and consumed by the population. Rather the resources pumped into military production represent a political choice that prioritizes military spending over the investment in social goods. As a result quality education, health care, mass transit, affordable housing and other social goods became ever scarcer as the institutions that provide them become ever more inadequately funded. A major place that this takes place is in cities. The second problem with military Keynesianism is that military industries tend to be highly automated, and therefore fewer jobs are created per million dollars of investment compared to investments in social goods.

The issue of the social costs of war were openly debated in the 1960s. After the 1964 presidential election, President Lyndon Johnson greatly escalated the Vietnam War at the same time that he sponsored major liberal domestic spending initiatives known as the Great Society programs. The Great Society initiatives succeeded in cutting the national poverty rate in half. At the time, during the 60s, there was a national debate as to whether the country could fund both a major war and a large number of social change initiatives such as Medicare, Medicaid, and numerous anti-poverty and empowerment programs. In this guns and butter debate, as it was known, the question was can we fund a major war and the permanent war economy as well as serve the needs of people for quality education, access to health care, affordable housing, elder services, government subsidized day care, and state of the art infrastructure?

The guns and butter debate remains relevant today. For one thing, the dollar figures are far more staggering than in the late 1940s and even the late 1960s. Meanwhile the social needs remain great. The 2010 defense budget when signed into law was $680 billion. The formal military allocation, however, is always an understatement of true costs because there are significant military expenditures in other sectors of the federal budget including the Departments of Energy and State, the National Aeronautics and Space Administration (NASA), and others. For this reason some argue that the actual, current military budget runs between $900 million to over $1 trillion annually.[14] The U.S. military budget is now nearly as large as the military budgets of all other nations in the world combined, ten times greater than the next largest spender, China.

In their book *The Three Trillion Dollar War: The True Cost of the Iraq Conflict*, Nobel Prize winning economist Joseph Stiglitz and his co-author, Linda Bilmer, provide a careful analysis of the total cost of the Iraq War. They dismiss figures provided by the government as based on "bad budgeting and misleading accounting."[15]

By considering all aspects of the cost of the Iraq War, Stiglitz and Bilmer estimate a total cost of approximately $3 trillion. The number includes not only Department of Defense figures but also costs not found there. These include the estimated lifetime costs of care of the severely wounded and disabled, and those returning with mental disorders (they estimate 100,000 by January, 2008, including many with chronic conditions); the costs of recruiting and training troops; combat pay; hardship benefits; re-enlistment bonuses which can reach as high as $100,000; paying and servicing over 100,000 contractors; fees paid to security and military contracting firms such as Blackwater and Dynacorp; the cost of replenishing weapons; and maintaining, repairing, and replacing equipment. Since most of the war costs are incurred through increased debt, Stiglitz and Bilmer also include future interest on that debt as part of the cost of war. Stiglitz and Bilmer conclude that these expenses will be costing taxpayers for generations to come in the form of higher direct and indirect taxes or reduced social services.[16]

Centrally important to the argument being made here are Stiglitz and Bilmer's calculations of what could have been purchased if the money spent on the Iraq War had been spent domestically on people stateside. Generally, Stiglitz and Bilmer argue that investments in research and development, technology, and education would have made the U.S. a stronger nation. They also offer specific alternatives. One trillion dollars, a third of their estimated cost of the Iraq War, would pay for any one of

- 8 million new housing units,
- 15 million additional teachers,
- 120 million children in Head Start programs,
- 530 million children insured for health care, or
- a full four year scholarship to a state college or university for 43 million students.

Stiglitz and Bilmer's alternative expenditure calculations allow us to understand that the cost of the Iraq War comes at the expense of the nation, its cities, and the millions of people who live in them. Seen from this perspective it becomes clear that there is simply no reason for public transit systems to be cut back while fares are increased; no need for high school football players to be taxed (user fees) for the right to compete; no need for schools in poor and working class neighborhoods of cities to stand as a national disgrace; no need for teachers, firemen, police and other municipal workers to have their wages cut because of poor contracts forced upon them; no need for bright young men and women to have a college education priced out of their reach; and no need for preventable deadly failures in infrastructure that cost lives as they did in Minneapolis when an interstate highway bridge collapsed. There is simply no need....[18]

Conclusion

Prevailing patterns of quasi or un-democratic decision making at the local, state and federal levels of government have led to urban fiscal crises and the allocation of funds for urban redevelopment that have served certain class interests exceedingly well while others have been served badly in a pattern of uneven development. We have shed light on these issues by looking at how municipal governmental decisions are made and how federal government spending priorities affect the living standards and well-being of working-class people in all areas of the country but especially in cities.

Endnotes

[1]Robert Dahl, *A Preface to Democratic Theory* (Chicago: University of Chicago Press, 1956), p. 13.

[2]Steven Lukes, *Power: A Radical View* (London: Macmillan, 1974), pp. 10–24.

[3]Dan Clawson et al, *Dollars and Votes* (Philadelphia: Temple University Press, 1998), passim.

[4]Antonio Gramsci, *Selections from the Prison Notebooks* (New York: International Publishers, 1971).

[5]Robert Dahl, *Who Governs?: Democracy and Power in an American City* (New Haven: Yale University Press, 1961).

[6]Floyd Hunter, *Community Power Structure: A Study of Decision Makers* (Chapel Hill: University of North Carolina Press, 1953).

[7]Hunter, passim. G. William Domhoff, "Atlanta: Floyd Hunter Was Right" October, 2005, http://sociology.ucsc.edu/whorulesamerica/local/atlanta.html.

[8]John Logan and Harvey Molotch, *Urban Fortunes: The Political Economy of Place* (Berkeley: University of California Press, 2007, orig. 1980).

[9]Clarence Stone, *Economic Growth and Neighborhood Discontent: System Bias in the Urban Renewal Program of Atlanta* (Chapel Hill: University of North Carolina Press, 1976) and Clarence Stone, *Regime Politics* (Lawrence: University Press of Kansas, 1989).

[10]G. William Domhoff, *Who Rules America?* (Englewood Cliffs, NJ: Prentice-Hall, 1967); *The Higher Circles: The Governing Class in America* (New York: Random House, 1970); *The Powers That Be: The Processes of Ruling Class Dominance in America* (New York: Vintage, 1979); *The Power Elite and the State: How Policy is Made in America* (Hawthorne, NY: Aldine de Gruyter, 1990); *State Autonomy or Class Dominance?: Case Studies on Policy Making in America* (Hawthorne, NY: Aldine de Gruyter, 1996); *Who Rules America Now?* (Prospect Heights, IL: Waveland Press, 1997, orig. 1983); *Who Rules*

America?: Power and Politics in the Year 2000 (Palo Alto: Mayfield Publishing Company, 1997).

[11]G. William Domhoff, *Who Rules America Now?*, chapter 6, "Community Power Structures"; G. William Domhoff, *Who Really Rules?: New Haven and Community Power Reconsidered* (New Brunswick: Transaction, 1987); G. William Domhoff, "C. Wright Mills, Floyd Hunter, and Fifty Years of Power Structure Research," http://sociology.ucsc.edu/whorulesamerica/theory/mills_address.html. Also see Richard Gendron and G. William Domhoff, *The Leftmost City: Power and Progressive Politics in Santa Cruz* (Boulder: Westview Press, 2008), pp. 203–204 and passim.

[12]We are considering militarism as an alternative expenditure stream to human investment in cities. There is another sense in which militarism applies to cities and that is the actual militarization of urban governance itself. See Mike Davis, *The City of Quartz: Excavating the Future of Los Angeles* (New York: Vintage, 1992), chapter 4 and Mike Davis, *The Ecology of Fear: Los Angeles and the Imagination of Disaster* (New York: Vintage, 1999), chapter 7. Also, William Staples, *The Culture of Surveillance: Discipline and Social Control in the United States* (New York: Bedford/St. Martin's, 1998) and William Staples, *Everyday Surveillance: Vigilance and Visibility in Post-Modern Life* (New York: Rowman & Littlefield, 2000).

[13]Speech before the American Society of Newspaper Editors, April 16, 1953.

[14]*Budget of the United States Government Fiscal Year 2010*, Table S–12; www.gpoaccess.gov/usbudget/fy09/pdf/budget/defense/pdf; and Elisabeth Bumiller, "Pentagon Expected to Request More War Funding," *New York Times*, November 11, 2009. These figures are reported across the political spectrum. See conservative economist Robert Higgs, "The Trillion Dollar Defense Budget Is Already Here", March 15, 2007, online.

[15]Joseph Stiglitz and Linda Bilmer, *The Three Trillion Dollar War: The True Cost of the Iraq Conflict* (New York: W.W. Norton and Company, 2008), pp. xii and 22–23.

16. Stiglitz and Bilmer, chapter 1, "Is It Really Three Trillion?" and chapter 2, "The Costs to the Nation's Budget". See also Frances Fox Piven, *The War at Home: The Domestic Costs of Bush's Militarism* (New York: The New Press, 2006) and David Harvey, *A Brief History of Neoliberalism* (New York: Oxford University Press, 2007), pp. 39–63. On the reduction of social welfare programs that has already taken place see Frances Fox Piven and Richard Cloward, *The New Class War: Reagan's Attack on the Welfare State and Its Consequences* (New York: Pantheon, 1982); Frances Fox Piven and Richard Cloward, *The Breaking of the American Social Compact* (New York: The New Press, 2006); Robert Perrucci and Earl Wysong, *The New Class Society: Goodbye American Dream?* (New York: Rowman & Littlefield Publishers, 2008), pp. 76–84.

[17]Stiglitz and Bilmer, p. xv.

[18]See John Holusha and Kenneth Chang, "Engineers See Danger in Aging Infrastructure," *New York Times*, August 2, 2007. Whether or not such vast military expenditures are necessary to protect the nation from invasion or terrorist threats (the rationale given for them) is beyond the scope of this article. We do point out that there is a large literature which brings such assumptions into question. For example, General Smedley D. Butler, *War Is a Racket* (Los Angeles: Feral House, 2003, orig. 1935); Christopher Scheer et al, *The Five Biggest Lies Bush Told Us About Iraq* (New York: Seven Stories Press, 2004); Pratap Chatterjee, *Iraq, Inc.: A Profitable Occupation* (New York: Seven Stories Press, 2004); Felix Greene, *The Enemy: What Every American Should Know About Imperialism*

(New York: Random House, 1970); Ward Churchill, *On the Justice of Roosting Chickens: Reflections on the Consequences of U.S. Imperial Arrogance and Criminality* (Oakland, CA: AK Press, 2003); Michael Parenti, *Against Empire* (San Francisco: City Lights, 1995); Michael Parenti, *The Terrorism Trap: September 11 and Beyond* (San Francisco: City Lights, 2002); Michael Parenti, *Superpatriotism* (San Francisco: City Lights, 2004); Noam Chomsky, *Year 501: The Conquest Continues* (Boston: South End Press, 1999); Noam Chomsky, *Hegemony or Survival: America's Quest for Global Dominance* (New York: Metropolitan Books, 2003); Chalmers Johnson, *Blowback: The Costs and Consequences of American Empire* (New York: Metropolitan Books, 2000); Chalmers Johnson, *Sorrows of Empire: Militarism, Secrecy, and the End of the Republic* (New York: Metropolitan Books, 2004); Chalmers Johnson, *Nemesis: The Last Days of the American Republic* (New York: Metropolitan Books, 2007); James Petras and Henry Veltmeyer, *Globalization Unmasked: Imperialism in the 21st Century* (London: Zed Books, Ltd., 2001); James Petras, *Global Depression and Regional Wars* (Atlanta: Clarity Press, 2009); Jerry Kloby, *Inequality, Power, and Development*, 2nd edition (Amherst, NY: Humanity Books, 2004), chapter 7, "The Sociology of Development" and chapter 8, "The Cold War and U.S. Interventionism".

The Construction of Consent*

David Harvey

How was neoliberalization accomplished, and by whom? The answer in countries such as Chile and Argentina in the 1970s was as simple as it was swift, brutal, and sure: a military coup backed by the traditional upper classes (as well as by the US government), followed by the fierce repression of all solidarities created within the labour and urban social movements which had so threatened their power. But the neoliberal revolution usually attributed to Thatcher and Reagan after 1979 had to be accomplished by democratic means. For a shift of this magnitude to occur required the prior construction of political consent across a sufficiently large spectrum of the population to win elections. What Gramsci calls 'common sense' (defined as 'the sense held in common') typically grounds consent. Common sense is constructed out of longstanding practices of cultural socialization often rooted deep in regional or national traditions. It is not the same as the 'good sense' that can be constructed out of critical engagement with the issues of the day. Common sense can, therefore, be profoundly misleading, obfuscating or disguising real problems under cultural prejudices.[1] Cultural and traditional values (such as belief in God and country or views on the position of women in society) and fears (of communists, immigrants, strangers, or 'others') can be mobilized to mask other realities. Political slogans can be invoked that mask specific strategies beneath vague rhetorical devices. The word 'freedom' resonates so widely within the common-sense understanding of Americans that it becomes 'a button that elites can press to open the door to the masses' to justify almost anything.[2] Thus could Bush retrospectively justify the Iraq war. Gramsci therefore concluded that political questions become 'insoluble' when 'disguised as cultural ones'.[3] In seeking to understand the construction of political consent, we must learn to extract political meanings from their cultural integuments.

So how, then, was sufficient popular consent generated to legitimize the neoliberal turn? The channels through which this was done were diverse. Powerful ideological influences circulated through the corporations, the media, and the numerous institutions that constitute civil society—such as the universities, schools, churches, and professional associations. The 'long march' of neoliberal ideas through these institutions that Hayek had envisaged back in 1947, the organization of think-tanks (with corporate backing and funding), the capture of certain segments of the media, and the conversion of many intellectuals

*David Harvey, *A Brief History of Neoliberalism* (New York: Oxford University Press, 2007). Reprinted with permission.

to neoliberal ways of thinking, created a climate of opinion in support of neoliberalism as the exclusive guarantor of freedom. These movements were later consolidated through the capture of political parties and, ultimately, state power.

Appeals to traditions and cultural values bulked large in all of this. An open project around the restoration of economic power to a small elite would probably not gain much popular support. But a programmatic attempt to advance the cause of individual freedoms could appeal to a mass base and so disguise the drive to restore class power. Furthermore, once the state apparatus made the neoliberal turn it could use its powers of persuasion, co-optation, bribery, and threat to maintain the climate of consent necessary to perpetuate its power. This was Thatcher's and Reagan's particular forte....

How, then, did neoliberalism negotiate the turn to so comprehensively displace embedded liberalism? In some instances, the answer largely lies in the use of force (either military, as in Chile, or financial, as through the operations of the IMF in Mozambique or the Philippines). Coercion can produce a fatalistic, even abject, acceptance of the idea that there was and is, as Margaret Thatcher kept insisting, 'no alternative'. The active construction of consent has also varied from place to place. Furthermore, as numerous oppositional movements attest, consent has often wilted or failed in different places. But we must look beyond these infinitely varied ideological and cultural mechanisms—no matter how important they are—to the qualities of everyday experience in order to better identify the material grounding for the construction of consent. And it is at that level through the experience of daily life under capitalism in the 1970s that we begin to see how neoliberalism penetrated 'common-sense' understandings. The effect in many parts of the world has increasingly been to see it as a necessary, even wholly 'natural', way for the social order to be regulated.

Any political movement that holds individual freedoms to be sacrosanct is vulnerable to incorporation into the neoliberal fold. The worldwide political upheavals of 1968, for example, were strongly inflected with the desire for greater personal freedoms. This was certainly true for students, such as those animated by the Berkeley 'free speech' movement of the 1960s or who took to the streets in Paris, Berlin, and Bangkok and were so mercilessly shot down in Mexico City shortly before the 1968 Olympic Games. They demanded freedom from parental, educational, corporate, bureaucratic, and state constraints. But the '68 movement also had social justice as a primary political objective.

Values of individual freedom and social justice are not, however, necessarily compatible. Pursuit of social justice presupposes social solidarities and a willingness to submerge individual wants, needs, and desires in the cause of some more general struggle for, say, social equality or environmental justice. The objectives of social justice and individual freedom were uneasily fused in the movement of '68. The tension was most evident in the fraught relationship between the traditional left (organized labour and political parties espousing social solidarities) and the student movement desirous of individual liberties. The suspicion and hostility that separated these two fractions in France (e.g. the Communist Party and the student movement) during the events of 1968 is a case in point. While it is not impossible to bridge such differences, it is not hard to see how a wedge might be driven between them. Neoliberal rhetoric, with its foundational emphasis upon individual freedoms, has the power to split off libertarianism, identity politics, multiculturalism, and eventually narcissistic consumerism from the social forces ranged in pursuit of social justice through the conquest of state power. It has long proved extremely difficult within the US left, for example, to forge the collective discipline required for political action to achieve social justice without offending the desire of political actors for individual freedom and for full recognition and expression of particular identities. Neoliberalism did not create these distinctions, but it could easily exploit, if not foment, them.

In the early 1970s those seeking individual freedoms and social justice could make common cause in the face of what many saw as a common enemy. Powerful corporations in alliance with an interventionist state were seen to be running the world in individually oppressive and socially unjust ways. The Vietnam War was the most obvious catalyst for discontent, but the destructive activities of corporations and the state in relation to the environment, the push towards mindless consumerism, the failure to address social issues and respond adequately to diversity, as well as intense restrictions on individual possibilities and personal behaviours by state-mandated and 'traditional' controls were also widely resented. Civil rights were an issue, and questions of sexuality and of reproductive rights were very much in play. For almost everyone involved in the movement of '68, the intrusive state was the enemy and it had to be reformed. And on that, the neoliberals could easily agree. But capitalist corporations, business, and the market system were also seen as primary enemies requiring redress if not revolutionary transformation: hence the threat to capitalist class power. By capturing ideals of individual freedom and turning them against the interventionist and regulatory practices of the state, capitalist class interests could hope to protect and even restore their position. Neoliberalism was well suited to this ideological task. But it had to be backed up by a practical strategy that emphasized the liberty of consumer choice, not only with respect to particular products but also with respect to lifestyles, modes of expression, and a wide range of cultural practices. Neoliberalism required both politically and economically the construction of a neoliberal market-based populist culture of differentiated consumerism and individual libertarianism. As such it proved more than a little compatible with that impulse called 'postmodernism' which had long been lurking in the wings but could now emerge full-blown as both a cultural and an intellectual dominant. This was the challenge that corporations and class elites set out to finesse in the 1980s.

None of this was very clear at the time. Left movements failed to recognize or confront, let alone transcend, the inherent tension between the quest for individual freedoms and social justice. But the intuitive problem was, I suspect, clear enough to many in the upper class, even to those who had never read Hayek or even heard of neoliberal theory. Let me illustrate this idea by comparing the neoliberal turns in the US and Britain in the troubled years of the 1970s.

In the US case I begin with a confidential memo sent by Lewis Powell to the US Chamber of Commerce in August 1971. Powell, about to be elevated to the Supreme Court by Richard Nixon, argued that criticism of and opposition to the US free enterprise system had gone too far and that 'the time had come—indeed it is long overdue—for the wisdom, ingenuity and resources of American business to be marshaled against those who would destroy it'. Powell argued that individual action was insufficient. 'Strength', he wrote, 'lies in organization, in careful long-range planning and implementation, in consistency of action over an indefinite period of years, in the scale of financing available only through joint effort, and in the political power available only through united action and national organizations.' The National Chamber of Commerce, he argued, should lead an assault upon the major institutions—universities, schools, the media, publishing, the courts—in order to change how individuals think 'about the corporation, the law, culture, and the individual'. US businesses did not lack resources for such an effort, particularly when pooled.[4]

How directly influential this appeal to engage in class war was, is hard to tell. But we do know that the American Chamber of Commerce subsequently expanded its base from around 60,000 firms in 1972 to over a quarter of a million ten years later. Jointly with the National Association of Manufacturers (which moved to Washington in 1972) it amassed an immense campaign chest to lobby Congress and engage in research. The Business Roundtable, an organization of CEOs 'committed to the aggressive pursuit of political power for the corporation', was founded in 1972 and thereafter became the centrepiece of collective pro-business action. The corporations involved accounted for 'about one half of the GNP of the United States' during the 1970s, and they spent close to $900 million annually (a huge amount at that time) on political matters. Think-tanks, such as the Heritage Foundation, the Hoover Institute, the Center for the Study of American Business, and the American Enterprise Institute, were formed with corporate backing both to polemicize and, when necessary, as in the case of the National Bureau of Economic Research, to construct serious technical and empirical studies and political-philosophical arguments broadly in support of neoliberal policies. Nearly half the financing for the highly respected NBER came from the leading companies in the Fortune 500 list. Closely integrated with the academic community, the NBER was to have a very significant impact on thinking in the economics departments and business schools of the major research universities. With abundant finance furnished by wealthy individuals (such as the brewer Joseph Coors, who later became a member of Reagan's 'kitchen cabinet') and their foundations (for example Olin, Scaife, Smith Richardson, Pew Charitable Trust), a flood of tracts and books, with Nozick's *Anarchy State and Utopia* perhaps the most widely read and appreciated, emerged espousing neoliberal values. A TV version of Milton Friedman's *Free to Choose* was funded with a grant from Scaife in 1977. 'Business was', Blyth concludes, 'learning to spend as a class.'[5]

In singling out the universities for particular attention, Powell pointed up an opportunity as well as an issue, for these were indeed centres of anti-corporate and anti-state sentiment (the students at Santa Barbara had burned down the Bank of America building there and ceremonially buried a car in the sands). But many students were (and still are) affluent and privileged, or at least middle class, and in the US the values of individual freedom have long been celebrated (in music and popular culture) as primary. Neoliberal themes could here find fertile ground for propagation. Powell did not argue for extending state power. But business should 'assiduously cultivate' the state and when necessary use it 'aggressively and with determination'.[6] But exactly how was state power to be deployed to reshape common-sense understandings?

One line of response to the double crisis of capital accumulation and class power arose in the trenches of the 1970s. The New York City fiscal crisis was an iconic case. Capitalist restructuring and deindustrialization had for several years been eroding the economic base of the city, and rapid suburbanization had left much of the central city impoverished. The result was explosive social unrest on the part of marginalized populations during the 1960s, defining what came to be known as 'the urban crisis' (similar problems emerged in many US cities). The expansion of public employment and public provision—facilitated in part by generous federal funding—was seen as the solution. But, faced with fiscal difficulties, President Nixon simply declared the urban crisis over in the early 1970s. While this was news to many city dwellers, it signaled diminished federal aid. As the recession gathered pace the gap between revenues and outlays in the New York City budget (already large because of profligate borrowing over many years) increased. At first financial institutions were prepared to bridge the gap, but in 1975 a powerful cabal of investment bankers (led by Walter Wriston of Citibank) refused to roll over the debt and pushed the city into technical bankruptcy. The bail-out that followed entailed the construction of new institutions that took over the management of the city budget. They had first claim on city tax revenues in order to first pay off bondholders: whatever was left went for essential services. The effect was to curb the aspirations of the city's powerful municipal unions to implement wage freezes and cutbacks in public employment and social provision (education, public health, transport services), and to impose user fees (tuition was introduced into the CUNY university system for the first time). The final indignity was the requirement that municipal unions should invest their pension funds in city bonds. Unions then either moderated their demands or faced the prospect of losing their pension funds through city bankruptcy.[7]

This amounted to a coup by the financial institutions against the democratically elected government of New York City, and it was every bit as effective as the military coup that had earlier occurred in Chile. Wealth was redistributed to the upper classes in the midst of a fiscal crisis. The New York crisis was, Zevin argues, symptomatic of 'an emerging strategy of disinflation coupled with a regressive redistribution of income, wealth and power'. It was 'an early, perhaps decisive battle in a new war', the purpose of which was 'to show others that what is happening to New York could and in some cases will happen to them'[8]

Whether everyone involved in negotiating this fiscal compromise understood it as a strategy to restore class power is an open question. The need to maintain fiscal discipline is a matter of concern in its own right and does not, like monetarism more generally, necessarily entail regressive distributions. It is unlikely, for example, that Felix Rohatyn, merchant banker who brokered the deal between the city, the state, and the financial institutions, had the restoration of class power in mind. The only way he could 'save' the city was by satisfying the investment bankers while diminishing the standard of living of most New Yorkers. But the restoration of class power was certainly what investment bankers like Walter Wriston had in mind. He had, after all, equated all forms of government intervention in the US and Britain with communism. And it was almost certainly the aim of Ford's Secretary of the Treasury William Simon (later to become head of the ultra-conservative Olin Foundation). Watching the progress of events in Chile with approval, he strongly advised President Ford to refuse aid to the city ('Ford to City: Drop Dead' ran the headline in the *New York Daily News)*. The terms of any bail-out, he said, should be 'so punitive, the overall experience so painful, that no city, no political subdivision would ever be tempted to go down the same road'.[9]

While resistance to the austerity measures was widespread, it could only, according to Freeman, slow 'the counterrevolution from above, it could not stop it. Within a few years, many of the historic achievements of working-class New York were undone'. Much of the social infrastructure of the city was diminished and the physical infrastructure (for example the subway system) deteriorated markedly for lack of investment or even maintenance. Daily life in New York 'became grueling and the civic atmosphere turned mean'. The city government, the municipal labour movement, and working-class New Yorkers were effectively stripped 'of much of the power they had accumulated over the previous three decades'.[10] Demoralized, working-class New Yorkers reluctantly assented to the new realities.

But the New York investment bankers did not walk away from the city. They seized the opportunity to restructure it in ways that suited their agenda. The creation of a 'good business climate' was a priority. This meant using public resources to build appropriate infra-structures for business (particularly in telecommunications) coupled with subsidies and tax incentives for capitalist enterprises. Corporate welfare substituted for people welfare. The city's elite institutions were mobilized to sell the image of the city as a cultural centre and tourist destination (inventing the famous logo 'I Love New York'). The ruling elites moved, often fractiously, to support the opening up of the cultural field to all manner of diverse cos-mopolitan currents. The narcissistic exploitation of self, sexuality, and identity became the leitmotif of bourgeois urban culture. Artistic freedom and artistic license, promoted by the city's powerful cultural institutions, led, in effect, to the neoliberaliation of culture. 'Deliri-ous New York' (to use Rem Koolhaas's memorable phrase) erased the collective memory of democratic New York.[11] The city's elites acceded, though not without a struggle, to the demand for lifestyle diversification (including those attached to sexual preference and gen-der) and increasing consumer niche choices (in areas such as cultural production). New York became the epicentre of postmodern cultural and intellectual experimentation. Mean bankers reconstructed the city economy around financial activities, ancillary services such as legal services and the media (much revived by the financialization then occurring), and diversified consumerism (gentrification and neighbourhood 'restoration' playing a promi-nent and profitable role). City government was more and more construed as an entrepreneur-ial rather than a social democratic or even managerial entity. Inter-urban competition for investment capital transformed government into urban governance through public-private partnerships. City business was increasingly conducted behind closed doors, and the demo-cratic and representational content of local governance diminished.[12]

Working-class and ethnic-immigrant New York was thrust back into the shadows, to be ravaged by racism and a crack cocaine epidemic of epic proportions in the 1980s that left many young people either dead, incarcerated, or homeless, only to be bludgeoned again by the AIDS epidemic that carried over into the 1990s. Redistribution through criminal violence became one of the few serious options for the poor, and the authorities responded by criminalizing whole communities of impoverished and marginalized populations. The victims were blamed, and Giuliani was to claim fame by taking revenge on behalf of an increasingly affluent Manhattan bourgeoisie tired of having to confront the effects of such devastation on their own doorsteps.

The management of the New York fiscal crisis pioneered the way for neoliberal prac-tices both domestically under Reagan and internationally through the IMF in the 1980s. It established the principle that in the event of a conflict between the integrity of financial institutions and bondholders' returns, on the one hand, and the well-being of the citizens on the other, the former was to be privileged. It emphasized that the role of government was to create a good business climate rather than look to the needs and well-being of the popu-lation at large. The politics of the Reagan administration of the 1980s, Tabb concludes, became 'merely the New York scenario' of the 1970s 'writ large'.[13]

The translation of these local conclusions of the mid–1970s to the national level was fast-moving. Thomas Edsall (a journalist who covered Washington affairs for many years) published a prescient account in 1985:

> During the 1970s, business refined its ability to act as a class, submerging competitive instincts in favour of joint, cooperative action in the legislative arena. Rather than individual companies seeking only special favours ... the dominant theme in the political strategy of business became a shared interest

in the defeat of bills such as consumer protection and labour law reform, and in the enactment of favourable tax, regulatory and antitrust legislation.[14]

In order to realize this goal, businesses needed a political class instrument and a popular base. They therefore actively sought to capture the Republican Party as their own instrument. The formation of powerful political action committees to procure, as the old adage had it, 'the best government that money could buy' was an important step. The supposedly 'progressive' campaign finance laws of 1971 in effect legalized the financial corruption of politics. A crucial set of Supreme Court decisions began in 1976 when it was first established that the right of a corporation to make unlimited money contributions to political parties and political action committees was protected under the First Amendment guaranteeing the rights of individuals (in this instance corporations) to freedom of speech.[15] Political action committees (PACs) could thereafter ensure the financial domination of both political parties by corporate, moneyed, and professional association interests. Corporate PACs, which numbered eighty-nine in 1974, had burgeoned to 1,467 by 1982. While these were willing to fund powerful incumbents of both parties provided their interests were served, they also systematically leaned towards supporting rightwing challengers in the late 1970s. Reagan (then Governor of California) and William Simon (whom we have already encountered) went out of their way to urge the PACs to direct their efforts towards funding Republican candidates with right-wing sympathies.[16] The $5,000 limit on each PAC's contribution to any one individual forced PACs from different corporations and industries to work together, and that meant building alliances based on class rather than particular interests.

The willingness of the Republican Party to become the representative of 'its dominant class constituency' during this period contrasted, Edsall notes, with the 'ideologically ambivalent' attitude of the Democrats which grew out of 'the fact that its ties to various groups in society are diffuse, and none of these groups—women, blacks, labour, the elderly, hispanics, urban political organizations—stands clearly larger than the others'. The dependency of Democrats, furthermore, on 'big money' contributions rendered many of them highly vulnerable to direct influence from business interests.[17] While the Democratic Party had a popular base, it could not easily pursue an anti-capitalist or anti-corporate political line without totally severing its connections with powerful financial interests.

The Republican Party needed, however, a solid electoral base if it was to colonize power effectively. It was around this time that Republicans sought an alliance with the Christian right. The latter had not been politically active in the past, but the foundation of Jerry Falwell's 'moral majority' as a political movement in 1978 changed all of that. The Republican Party now had its Christian base. It also appealed to the cultural nationalism of the white working classes and their besieged sense of moral righteousness (besieged because this class lived under conditions of chronic economic insecurity and felt excluded from many of the benefits that were being distributed through affirmative action and other state programmes). This political base could be mobilized through the positives of religion and cultural nationalism and negatively through coded, if not blatant, racism, homophobia, and antifeminism. The problem was not capitalism and the neoliberalization of culture, but the 'liberals' who had used excessive state power to provide for special groups (blacks, women, environmentalists, etc.). A well-funded movement of neoconservative intellectuals (gathered around Irving Kristol and Norman Podhoretz and the journal *Commentary*), espousing morality and traditional values, gave credence to these theses. Supporting the neoliberal turn economically but not culturally, they excoriated the interventionist excesses of a so-called 'liberal elite'—thus greatly muddying what the term 'liberal' might mean. The effect was to divert attention from capitalism and corporate power as in any way having anything to do with either the economic or the cultural problems that unbridled commercialism and individualism were creating.

From then on the unholy alliance between big business and conservative Christians backed by the neoconservatives steadily consolidated, eventually eradicating all liberal elements (significant and influential in the 1960s) from the Republican Party, particularly after 1990, and turning it into the relatively homogeneous right-wing electoral force of present times.[18] Not for the first, nor, it is to be feared, for the last time in history has a social group been persuaded to vote against its material, economic, and class interests for cultural, nationalist, and religious reasons. In some cases, however, it is probably more appropriate to replace the word 'persuaded' with 'elected', since there is abundant evidence that the evangelical Christians (no more than 20 percent of the population) who make up the core of the 'moral majority' eagerly embraced the alliance with big business and the Republican Party as a means to further promote their evangelical and moral agenda. This was certainly the case with the shadowy and secretive organization of Christian conservatives that constituted the Council for National Policy, founded in 1981, 'to strategize how to turn the country to the right'.[19]

The Democratic Party, on the other hand, was fundamentally driven by the need to placate, if not succour, corporate and financial interests while at the same time making some gestures towards improving the material conditions of life for its popular base. During the Clinton presidency it ended up choosing the former over the latter and therefore fell directly into the neoliberal fold of policy prescription and implementation (as, for example, in the reform of welfare).[20] But, as in the case of Felix Rohatyn, it is doubtful if this was Clinton's agenda from the very beginning. Faced with the need to overcome a huge deficit and spark economic growth, his only feasible economic path was deficit reduction to achieve low interest rates. That meant either substantially higher taxation (which amounted to electoral suicide) or cutbacks in the budget. Going for the latter meant, as Yergin and Stanislaw put it, 'betraying their traditional constituencies in order to pamper the rich' or, as Joseph Stiglitz, once chair of Clinton's Council of Economic Advisors, later confessed, 'we did manage to tighten the belts of the poor as we loosened those on the rich'.[21] Social policy was in effect put in the care of the Wall Street bondholders (much as had happened in New York City earlier), with predictable consequences.

The political structure that emerged was quite simple. The Republican Party could mobilize massive financial resources and mobilize its popular base to vote against its material interests on cultural/religious grounds while the Democratic Party could not afford to attend to the material needs (for example for a national health-care system) of its traditional popular base for fear of offending capitalist class interests. Given the asymmetry, the political hegemony of the Republican Party became more sure.

Reagan's election in 1980 was only the first step in the long process of consolidating the political shift necessary to support Volcker's turn to monetarism and the prioritization of the fight against inflation. Reagan's policies, Edsall noted at the time, centred on 'an across the board drive to reduce the scope and content of federal regulation of industry, the environment, the workplace, health care, and the relationship between buyer and seller'.

Budget cuts and deregulation and 'the appointment of antiregulatory, industry-oriented agency personnel' to key positions were the main means.[22]

The National Labour Relations Board, established to regulate capital-labour relations in the workplace in the 1930s, was converted by Reagan's appointments into a vehicle for attacking and regulating the rights of labour at the very moment when business was being deregulated.[23] It took less than six months in 1983 to reverse nearly 40 percent the decisions made during the 1970s that had been, in the view of business, too favourable to labour. Reagan construed all regulation (except of labour) as bad. The Office of Management and Budget was mandated to do thorough cost-benefit analyses of all regulatory proposals (past and present). If it could not be shown that the benefits of regulation clearly exceeded the costs then the regulations should be scrapped. To top it all, elaborate revisions of the tax code—mainly depreciation on investments—allowed many corporations to get away without paying any taxes at all, while the reduction of the top tax rate for individuals from 78 to 28 per cent obviously reflected the intent to restore class power. Worst of all, public assets were freely passed over into the private domain. Many of the key breakthroughs in pharmaceutical research, for example, had been funded by the National Institute of Health in collaboration with the drug companies. But in 1978 the companies were allowed to take all the benefits of patent rights without returning anything to the state, assuring the industry of high and highly subsidized profits ever after.[24]

But all of this required that labour and labour organization be brought to heel to conform to the new social order. If New York pioneered this by disciplining powerful municipal unions in 1975–77, Reagan followed at the national level by bringing down the air traffic controllers in 1981 and making it clear to the trade unions that they were unwelcome as participants in the inner councils of government. The uneasy social compact that had ruled between corporate and union power during the 1960s was over. With unemployment surging to 10 per cent in the mid–1980s, the moment was propitious to attack all forms of organized labour and to cut back on its privileges as well as its power. Transfer of industrial activity from the unionized north-east and midwest to the non-unionized and 'right-to-work' states of the south, if not beyond to Mexico and South-East Asia, became standard practice (subsidized by favourable taxation for new investment and aided by the shift in emphasis from production to finance as the centrepiece of power of capitalist class power). Deindustrialization of formerly unionized core industrial regions (the so-called 'rust belt') disempowered labour. Corporations could threaten plant closures, and risk and usually win strikes when necessary (for example in the coal industry).

But here too it was not merely the use of the big stick that mattered, for there were a number of carrots that could be offered to labourers as individuals to break with collective action. The unions' rigid rules and bureaucratic structures made them vulnerable to attack. The lack of flexibility was often as much a disadvantage for individual labourers as it was for capital. The virtuous claims for flexible specialization in labour processes and for flexitime arrangements could become part of the neoliberal rhetoric that could be persuasive to individual labourers, particularly those who had been excluded from the monopoly benefits that strong unionization sometimes conferred. Greater freedom and liberty of action in the labour market could be touted as a virtue for capital and labour alike, and here, too, it was not hard to integrate neoliberal values into the 'common sense' of much of the workforce. How this active potentiality was converted into a highly exploitative system of flexible accumulation (all the benefits accruing from increasing in labour allocations in both space and time go to capital) is key to explaining why real wages, except for a brief period during the 1990s, stagnated or fell and benefits diminished. Neoliberal theory conveniently holds that unemployment is always voluntary. Labour, the argument goes, has a 'reserve price' below which it prefers not to work. Unemployment arises because the reserve price of labour is too high. Since that reserve price is partly set by welfare payments (and stories of 'welfare queens' driving Cadillacs abounded) then it stands to reason that the neoliberal reform carried out by Clinton of 'welfare as we know it' must be a crucial step towards the reduction of unemployment.

All of this demanded some rationale, and to this end the war of ideas did play an important role. The economic ideas marshaled in support of the neoliberal turn amounted, Blyth suggests, to a complex fusion of monetarism (Friedman), rational expectations (Robert Lucas), public choice (James Buchanan, and Gordon Tullock), and the less respectable but but by no means uninfluential 'supply-side' ideas of Arthur Lauffer, who went so far as to suggest that the incentive effects of tax cuts would so increase economic activity as to automatically increase tax revenues (Reagan was enamoured of this idea). The more acceptable commonality to these arguments was that government intervention was the problem rather than the solution, and that 'a stable monetary policy, plus radical tax cuts in the top brackets, would produce a healthier economy' by getting the incentives for entrepreneurial activity aligned correctly.[25] The business press, with the *Wall Street Journal* very much in the lead, took up these ideas, becoming an open advocate for neoliberalization as the necessary solution to all economic ills. Popular currency was given to these ideas by prolific writers such as George Gilder (supported by think-tank funds), and the business schools that arose in prestigious universities such as Stanford and Harvard, generously funded by corporations and foundations, became centres of neoliberal orthodoxy from the very moment they opened. Charting the spread of ideas is always difficult, but by 1990 or so most economics departments in the major research universities as well as the business schools were dominated by neoliberal modes of thought. The importance of this should not be underestimated. The US research universities were and are training grounds for many foreigners who take what they learn back to their countries of origin—the key figures in Chile's and Mexico's adaptation to neoliberalism were US-trained economists for example—as well as into international institutions such as the IMF, the World Bank, and the UN.

The conclusion is, I think, clear. 'During the 1970s, the political wing of the nation's corporate sector,' writes Edsall, 'staged one of the most remarkable campaigns in the pursuit of power in recent history.' By the early 1980s it 'had gained a level of influence and approaching the boom days of the 1920s.'[26] And by the year 2000 it had used that leverage to restore its share of the national wealth and income to levels also not seen since the 1920s.

Endnotes

[1] A. Gramsci, *Selections from the Prison Notebooks*, trans. Q. Hoare and G. Norwell Smith (London: Lawrence & Wishart, 1971), 321–343.

[2] J. Rapley, *Globalization and Inequality: Neoliberalism's Downward Spiral* (Boulder, CO: Lynne Reiner, 2004), 55.

[3] Gramsci, *Selections from the Prison Notebooks*, 149.

[4] J. Court, *Corporateering: How Corporate Power Steals Your Personal Freedom* (New York: J. P. Tarcher/Putnam, 2003), 33–8.

[5]M. Blyth, *Great Transformations: Economic Ideas and Institutional Change in the Twentieth Century* (Cambridge, Cambridge University Press, 2002), 155. The information in the preceeding paragraph comes from chs. 5 and 6 of Blyth's account, supported by T. Edsall, *The New Politics of Inequality* (New York: Norton, 1985), chs. 2 and 3.

[6]Court, *Corporateering*, 34.

[7]W. Tabb, *The Long Default: New York City and the Urban Fiscal Crisis* (New York: Monthly Review Press, 1982); J. Freeman, *Working Class New York: Life and Labor Since World War II* (New York: New Press, 2001).

[8] R. Zevin, 'New York City Crisis: First Act in a New Age of Reaction', in R. Alcalay and D. Mermelstein (eds.), *The Fiscal Crisis of American Cities: Essays on the Political Economy of Urban America with Special Reference to New York* (New York: Vintage Books, 1977), 11–29.

[9]Tabb, *The Long Default*, 28. For Walter Wriston see T. Frank, *One Market Under God: Extreme Capitalism, Market Populism and the End of Economic Democracy* (New York: Doubleday, 2000), 53–6.

[10]Freeman, *Working Class New York*.

[11]R. Koolhaas, *Delirious New York* (New York: Monacelli Press, 1994); M. Greenberg, 'The Limits of Branding: The World Trade Center, Fiscal Crisis and the Marketing of Recovery', *International Journal of Urban and Regional Research*, 27 (2003), 386–416.

[12]Tabb, *The Long Default*; On the subsequent 'selling' of New York see Greenberg, 'The Limits of Branding'; on urban entrepreneurialism more generally see D. Harvey, 'From Managerialism to Entrepreneurialism: The Transformation of Urban Governance in Late Capitalism', in id., *Spaces of Capital* (Edinburgh: Edinburgh University Press, 2001), ch. 16.

[13]Tabb, *The Long Default*, 15.

[14]Edsall, *The New Politics of Inequality*, 128.

[15]Court, *Corporateering*, 29–31, lists all the relevant legal decisions of the 1970s.

[16]The accounts of Edsall, *The New Politics of Inequality*, followed by Blyth, *Great Transformations*, are compelling.

[17]Edsall, *The New Politics of Inequality*, 235.

[18]T. Frank, *What's the Matter with Kansas: How Conservatives Won the Hearts of America* (New York: Metropolitan Books, 2004).

[19]D. Kirkpatrick, 'Club of the Most Powerful Gathers in Strictest Privacy', *New York Times*, 28 Aug. 2004, A10.

[20]See J. Stiglitz, *The Roaring Nineties* (New York: Norton, 2003).

[21]D. Yergin and J. Stanislaw, *Commanding Heights: The Battle for the World Economy* (New York: Simon & Schuster, 1998), 337; Stiglitz, *The Roaring Nineties*, 108.

[22]Edsall, *The New Politics of Inequality*, 217.

[23]Again, the account here rests heavily on Blyth, *Great Transformations*, and Edsall, *The New Politics of Inequality*.

[24]M. Angell, *The Truth About the Drug Companies: How They Deceive Us and What To Do About It* (New York: Random House, 2004).

[25]M. Blyth, *Great Transformations*; see also Frank, *One Market Under God,* particularly on the role of Gilder.

[26]Edsall, *The New Politics of Inequality*, 107.

Section II:
Institutional Imbalance[1]and Crime

One unavoidable concern when considering problematic urban conditions is the persistence of crime and deviance—often intensified by inequality, concentrated disadvantage, and lack of social organization.[2] Consequently, some researchers advocate for greater formal and informal social control strategies as one way to curb incidents of crime and deviance. In other words, many believe that controlling incidents of crime through heavy-handed tactics by the criminal justice system is the best way to deal with urban crime. Others contend, however, that such needs are complicated by a criminal justice system influenced by subjective criminalization of various populations, where an inconsistent application of the law frequently occurs.[3] For example, one question we might ask is, do unlawful offenses committed by affluent individuals lead to the same consequences as similar offenses committed by minority or impoverished individuals in society? In *The Rich Get Richer and the Poor Get Prison*, Jeffrey Reiman provides useful statistics which indicate that a more favorable treatment of wealthier individuals by the penal system in the U.S. does *in fact* occur.[4] As a result of Reiman's study, might social science scholars and the public in general ponder whether criminal justice practices help to build a form of institutional imbalance in the United States, one that advances different notions of justice? If so, does it amount to a *shame of governance*?

Other studies may lead us to consider similar questions that challenge the intentions of governmental institutions and/or its agencies. For example, one study by sociologists Steven Messner and Richard Rosenfeld examined the relationship between unemployment conditions and homicide rates in Western nations, which we argue may have inspired others to take a closer look at the relationships between government institutions and various types of crime in cities. In short, Messner and Rosenfeld found that whenever government or non-economic institutions fail to play an active role in dynamics that negatively impact labor conditions, then such inactions are often associated with an incapacity to curb homicide rates.[5] Thus, whenever institutions of government help to predict incidents of crime, it challenges social norms or expectations that we have about the role of government, especially when that role is conflated by a dominance of private enterprise. Other studies, which *also consider a normative nature of governance*, suggest that an inequitable distribution of public resources leads to higher violent crime rates in cities, and (positively) that welfare expenditures—as an example of non-economic institutions—help to weaken the effects that income inequality has on homicide rates in urban areas.[6]

The discussion above suggests to us that while researchers traditionally discuss links between concepts like poverty, income inequality, social disorganization, unemployment and crime in urban areas, there are also explanations—not as widely pursued—that advance what we call "government culpability narratives," which implicate an abrogation of duty of governance. In fact, some ask rhetorically about the disappearance of government.[7] Said differently, when urban sociologists lament crises in cities created by questionable economic, fiscal and political decisions made by public officials, to what extent might we suspect that some of these actions and decisions actually agitate existing problematic conditions, discourage comprehensive solutions, encourage uncritical and unsophisticated views regarding the rights of profiteers, or ignore altogether inconsistencies that flow from the criminal justice system?

We recognize the occurrences and realities of unintended consequences brought on by urban fiscal crises. However, this volume raises questions about whether the irresponsibility or neglect of institutions has contributed to undermining the resolve of U.S. urban residents while at the same time obscuring society's ability to eradicate the seeds of crime. Accordingly, in the first article of the section, we begin with Joel Dyer's examination of the prison system in the United States, where he argues that by virtue of improper support of prisons in America, groups may actually benefit from crime. In the introduction to *The Perpetual Prisoner Machine*, Dyer explains that an explosion of the prison population in the U.S. since the mid-1970s was facilitated by (1) a consolidation of the media, which made stereotyping of certain individuals through television programming easier and more profitable; (2) a rise in political consultants, increasing the usage of polling data to gauge public opinion regarding crime; and (3) the rise of the prison-industrial complex, which highlights a shame of governance through the diversion of tax dollars from social programs to repay private developers who have invested in prison construction.

In the second article of the section, from his book *Race to Incarcerate*, Marc Mauer argues that inner-city African-American communities in the United States were the targets of a so-called "War on Drugs." He provides useful statistics from the 1980s and 1990s regarding drug use, drug possession, and arrest and incarceration rates, while noting the differences between black and white populations. Mauer implicates a shame of governance as he is critical of Congress for establishing harsher punishments for crack vs. powder cocaine users. He points out that crack cocaine users tend to be poor and live disproportionally in minority communities of cities.

In the third article, Mike Davis discusses the social climate in Los Angeles following the 1992 riots. He argues that city residents were unable to avoid a climate of fear that was orchestrated by the police, media, and politicians. Davis points out inconsistencies which suggest that the fear of crime was used by public officials and private interests as a mechanism of social control, which masks the seeds of socio-economic despair. The final article of the section is from a chapter in *Streetwise: Race, Class, and Change in an Urban Community*, an ethnography of a Philadelphia community where sociologist Elijah Anderson writes about the relationship between black males and the police. From his research as a participant observer in a Philadelphia neighborhood, Anderson offers his first-hand account of controversial social control tactics by the police that work to construct and validate the treatment of black males as quintessential perpetrators of crime.

Endnotes

[1]Steven Messner and Richard Rosenfeld (2007) in *Crime and the American Dream* discuss an institutional imbalance as indicated whenever economic institutions dominate

non-economic institutions. We loosely borrow from their conception, but conceive of institutional imbalance in other ways as well, relative to blatant inconsistencies, neglect, or incompetence.

[2]Lauren Krivo and Ruth Peterson, "Extremely Disadvantaged Neighborhoods and Urban Crime" *Social Forces*, 75 2: 619–648, 1996.

[3]Travis Hirschi, *Causes of Delinquency* (Berkeley: University of California Press, 1969); Richard Quinney, *The Social Reality of Crime* (Boston: Little, Brown, 1970); William B. Chambliss and Milton Mankoff, *Whose Law? What Order? A Conflict Approach to Criminology* (New York: Wiley, 1976).

[4]Jeffrey H. Reiman, *The Rich Get Richer and the Poor Get Prison* (New York: Wiley, 1979).

[5]Steven B. Messner and Richard Rosenfeld, *Crime and the American Dream* (Belmont, CA: Wadsworth, 2007).

[6]Thomas D. Stucky, "Local Politics and Violent Crime in U.S. Cities" *Criminology* 41 4:1101–1136, 2003; Michael O. Maume and Mathew R Lee. *Criminology* 41 4:1137–1172, 2003.

[7]Robert Grantham, "Urban Crime: The Effects of Government and Social Disorganization Factors" *Dissertation Abstracts International: The Humanities and Social Sciences*, vol. 66, no. 10, 2006).

Profiting from Prisons?*

Joel Dyer

Trying to figure out what went wrong with the U.S. criminal-justice system at the end of the twentieth century is no simple task. It reminds me of when I was a kid sitting in my grandfather's barbershop in Purcell, Oklahoma. You looked in the mirror in front of you and saw your reflection in the one behind, and it created an infinite number of images forever diminishing in size—each image's existence dependent upon the one that came before. The harder you strained to see the beginning, the further away you realized it was. And so it is with the problems confronting America's justice system.

To understand all the misguided efforts that have shaped modern penology you would literally have to trace the shrinking images back to ancient kingdoms of Egypt and Babylonia, for it is there that we find the roots of the modern prison system and the beginnings of its demise. That being the case, I have narrowed the focus... to an examination of only the most recent backward step in the evolution of the criminal-justice system—a significant leap that, though less than three decades old, has had a more profound impact on American justice than anything that came before.

The United States now incarcerates between 1.8 and 2 million of its citizens in its prisons and jails on any given day, and over 5 million people are currently under the supervision of America's criminal-justice system. That's more prisoners than in any other country in the world, an estimated 500,000 more than Communist China and just a few more than Russia, which offers the United States its only real competition when it comes to imprisonment.[1] But perhaps the most telling comparison of penal systems can be found in the statistics kept in the archives of our own Department of Justice. Today's 2 million prisoners represent a prison and jail system ten times larger than that which existed in the United States a mere twenty-nine years ago.[2] This unprecedented rise in the number of prisoners in the U.S. prison system reflects the largest prison expansion the world has ever known.

By way of comparison, the United States now locks up about five to seven times as many people as most other industrialized nations—nations whose crime rates are often similar to ours, but which have chosen to deal with the majority of their nonviolent offenders outside of prison walls through drug rehabilitation programs, various forms of community service, and well-supervised probation and parole.[3] These alternatives to incarceration are both more effective when it comes to reform and cost billions less per year to implement.

---

*Joel Dyer, *The Perpetual Prisoner Machine: How America Profits from Crime* (Boulder, CO: Westview Press, 2000). Reprinted with permission.

Once again, a quick look at the Justice Department's archives tells us that U.S. authorities are well aware of these programs and their obvious advantages over our prevailing policy of prison as the first choice for dealing with nonviolent lawbreakers because at one time, prior to the current prison expansion, we used to practice them ourselves.

So why is it that only America has abandoned these alternative programs in favor of a policy of mass imprisonment? Proponents of growing the prison population point to an increase in crime as justification for this trend. But Census Bureau statistics reflect that crime rates have been relatively flat or falling for the last three decades, which would seem to indicate that another explanation for our liberal use of incarceration is needed.[4] I believe that a more likely motive for our having launched the largest prison expansion in history can be found in the corresponding "largest" increase in criminal-justice expenditures in history. Or, put another way, the motive behind the unprecedented growth in the U.S. prison population is the $150 billion being expended annually on criminal justice,[5] much of which eventually winds up in the bank accounts of the shareholders of some of America's best known and most respected corporations. Although this explanation is admittedly controversial, I believe that it is fully supported by the evidence.

…[T]he pages that follow will examine "how America profits from crime" and, I think more important, how this profiteering is impacting our culture. When I say "how America profits from crime" I do not mean "how much it profits" per se, though such facts and figures will receive some treatment. Still, if someone wants to read a detailed description of the dollars and cents being generated by the prison industry, there are certainly better sources than this text for such fiscal information.

The purpose… is to expose and examine a political and economic chain reaction that I believe is largely responsible for the majority of the growth in the prison and jail population during the last three decades. I have chosen to describe this chain reaction as a "prisoner machine" because as I began to research the impact caused by various techniques for profiting from crime, it became clear that each such method had become somewhat dependent upon the others for its success, not unlike the gears of a machine that must be meshed in order to turn. …[T]he machine is self-sustaining, meaning that it has the ability to create new prisoners by way of the prisoners it has already created.

The perpetual prisoner machine is an impressive and complicated mechanism that owes its incarnation to no single power. It was during the late 1970s and early 1980s that the original three components of the machine appeared on the scene as the result of three separate and initially unrelated occurrences: the accelerating consolidation of the media industry, the rise in influence of political consultants, and the emergence of an organized prison-industrial complex that is perhaps best described as a collection of interests whose financial well-being rises and falls with the size of the prison population. As a result, the media, our elected officials, and the corporations that compose the prison industry each developed a unique method for turning crime into some form of capital—individual techniques that were, in the beginning, not particularly dependent upon one another for their success.

Subsequent changes within our political system—primarily the increasing use of public opinion polling and the rapid increase in the cost of political campaigns—have affected the various components of the machine the way the lightning bolt affected Frankenstein's monster. They caused these previously separated components to mesh and begin to function as a single mechanism that is considerably more efficient and powerful than any of its gears were on their own,

There is no adequate way to describe the function of the machine in only a few para-graphs, but just to give you a general idea... I offer this limited explanation. In the 1980s, when the media corporations decided to dramatically increase their use of violent, crime-oriented content as a means of increasing ratings or pickup rates and thereby enhancing their profits, it created a by-product—an exaggerated apprehension of crime throughout the general population. According to behavioral scientists, the majority of Americans now base their worldview more on the mediated messages offered by television than upon their own firsthand observations. As a result, nearly 80 percent of the public now believes crime to be one of the biggest problem confronting America, despite the fact that most of us are safer now than we were in the 1970s.[6]

Unfortunately, the arrival of this media-created anxiety over crime coincided with the rise in influence of the poll-taking political consultants. In the 1980s and 1990s, it has become the norm for these politically powerful consultants to use their public-opinion polls and their access to campaign funds to ensure that their candidate-clients' platforms on particular issues, such as crime, are not in conflict with the opinion of the majority of targeted voters. This increase in the importance of polling, coupled with the existence of the public's exaggerated concern over crime, explains in large measure why the vast majority of politicians from both parties have now fully embraced the politically expedient "hard-on-crime" position. That's to say that our war on crime is not rooted in rising crime rates but is rather the result of the rise in the public's concern over crime, which has been wrought not by the criminals in the real world but by the images of the criminals who now break into our living rooms nightly through the window of television.

Although the anxiety over crime that is driving our nation in a hard-on-crime direction is not based in reality, the criminal-justice policies being derived as a result are more tan-gible. Mandatory sentencing, including the "three-strikes" laws and "truth in sentencing," are the weapons of the war on crime that have increased our prison population ten times over in recent years—an extraordinary increase that would not have been financially fea-sible without the participation of the third gear of the machine, the increasingly privatized and politically influential prison-industrial complex.

By the late 1980s, the prison expansion had begun to reach what should have been its economic limits. State after state had built countless new prisons, only to see them quickly filled by hard-on-crime sentencing measures. The majority of taxpaying voters were begin-ning to express their concern over ever-increasing corrections costs, as exemplified by the fact that they began to vote down many of the bond issues needed for new prison construc-tion. Considering that most states were under court order to reduce overcrowding, this refusal by voters to allow state governments to create bond debt for prisons should have spelled the end of the war on crime—but it wasn't to be. Private corporations and politi-cians who were benefiting from the expansion came up with an alternative plan. If state governments couldn't get their voters to approve the general-obligation bonds historically needed to construct new prisons or they simply wanted to save their general-obligation bond capacity for more popular projects, then American Express, Allstate, Merrill Lynch, GE, Shearson Lehman, Wackenhut Corrections Corporation, Corrections Corporation of America, and others would raise the construction money the states needed by underwriting lease-revenue (a.k.a. lease-payment) bonds that don't require voter approval or by actually building the prisons themselves and then charging the states to house their inmates in the privately owned facilities.

In the end, this market intrusion into the system means that politicians can simply *divert* tax dollars out of existing programs such as education, child welfare, mental-health care, housing, and substance-abuse programs to repay the market and its investors for having put up the money to construct the prison facilities. If finagled properly, this diversion of funds does not require voter approval. In many ways, it's as if the prison expansion is now being funded by way of a credit card issued by the prison-industrial complex—a high-interest credit card that the taxpayers have no control over when it comes to spending but are nonetheless still being required to pay for at the end of the month.

I'm sure that private industry's rescue of the war on crime seemed like a good idea to politicians at the time. After all, it allowed them to continue to exploit the hard-on-crime platform as a means of growing their political fortunes à la Willie Horton. But in reality, the prison-industrial complex's "plan B" has turned out to be all too similar to the credit-card debt that has destroyed the finances of many a consumer. Taxpayers are paying far more for the market's prison system than they would have paid if they had been willing to pass the prison bond issues at the ballot box in the first place. Although the new prisons being built by investors and corporations have been wildly profitable for the prison-industrial complex, they have failed to provide the relief from overcrowding sought by the states because they too have been filled by hard-on-crime sentencing guidelines as quickly as they have been constructed. After thirty years and over 1,000 new prisons and jails, the system is now more overcrowded than it was when the expansion began, with most jurisdictions now operating at 15 to 30 percent over capacity.[7]

As a result of investors and corporations being willing to fund the construction of prisons that the majority of voters have shown increasing hesitance to bankroll, the budgets of corrections departments all across America have exploded. In many states, corrections expenditures have increased by more than seven times just since 1980, and they are still rocketing upward by at least 7 and up to more than 10 percent per year in many jurisdictions.[8] Picking up this ever-growing tab for prisoners is where the "perpetual" aspect of the machine kicks in.

Because much of the funding for corrections is now coming at the expense of social programs that have been shown to deter people from criminal behavior in the first place, I believe it is entirely accurate to say that the more prisoners whose incarceration we pay for through this diversion of funds, the more future prisoners we create.

Based on conversations I have had with criminologists both here and abroad, it appears that most of the civilized world finds the U.S. decision to use prisons to fight crime—a decision that flies in the face of research that strongly suggests that incarceration rates have little or no influence over crime rates—to be quite illogical. This low opinion of our justice system stems from the understanding that living in poverty is the most important factor in determining who is most likely to wind up in prison. That being the case, it is nonsensical to take money away from programs that fight poverty or help people to rise above its influence to pay for more prison cells. This poorly thought out fiscal maneuvering is playing a crucial role in one of the most significant human migrations in our nation's history—a migration that has seen hundreds of thousands of low-income citizens uprooted from their urban communities and relocated into places with names like Chino, Leavenworth, San Quentin, and Jolliette.

For the most part, America's prison population is being harvested from our growing fields of urban poverty. Since these fields are disproportionately composed of minority citizens, so too is the new prison population. By 1992, one out of every three black men in the United States between the ages of twenty and twenty-nine was under the supervision of the criminal-justice system. In some cities such as Washington, D.C., and Baltimore, 50 percent of black men between the ages of eighteen and thirty-five are now under the watchful eye of the Justice Department. Seventy percent of those being sent to prison these days are black or Hispanic, even though statistics tell us that these minorities are not committing anywhere near 70 percent of America's crimes.[9]

For example, blacks compose only 13 percent of monthly drug users, yet they are arrested five times as often as whites on drug charges, and once arrested, they are twice as likely to receive a prison sentence as their white counterparts and, on average, that sentence will be 20 percent longer than one doled out to a white offender.[10] This multiple is the result of race-biased law-enforcement practices and court procedures, and it helps to explain why in many states, blacks are filling prisons at a rate of ten to one over whites. It is estimated that if this prison expansion continues for twenty more years in its current discriminatory manner, we will eventually find ourselves imprisoning over 6 million minority citizens.[11]

This is the effect of the perpetual prisoner machine on American society at the end of the twentieth century. In short, the machine has overpowered the forces that historically determined the size and composition of the prison population—namely, the crime rates, the overall health of the economy, and the progressive ideal of reform over punishment.

I should point out that I do not believe that our current prison expansion will continue for another twenty years at its same rate. The truth is, it can't. Such an expansion would eventually consume nearly every dollar of every state budget in the union. There would be no public education, no infrastructure, no anything except for prisons, and that simply isn't going to happen. So the real questions becomes: How far will this prison madness go? How long will the perpetual prisoner machine be allowed to run unimpeded? How many hundreds of billions of tax dollars will it divert into the bank accounts of the prison-industrial complex? How many millions of lives within our low-income communities will it devastate? And who, in the end, will turn it off?

I do not know the answers to these questions, but I can tell you this: The machine will never be disabled by those who built it—the media, the politicians, those who compose the prison-industrial complex, and, most important, the shareholders of the corporations involved. They simply have no incentive to do so. For them, crime has become a valuable commodity. And if we want to get rid of this machine, we will have to do it ourselves. There are ways to accomplish this task, and I truly believe that it is in the best interest of the majority of Americans to pull the plug sooner rather than later.

Endnotes

[1] E. F. Schumacher, *Small is Beautiful* (New York: HarperCollins, 1973), quoted in *The Oxford Dictionary of Phrase, Saying, and Quotation*, ed. Elizabeth Knowles (New York: Oxford Univeresity Press, 1997), p. 139.

[2] Daniel Burton-Rose, "Prison Profits," *Cleveland Free Times*, November 19, 1997; Angela Y. Davis, "Masked Racism: Reflections on the Prison Industrial Complex," *Colorlines*, Alternet, downloaded November 1998 from <http://www.igc.apc.org/an/>, or see Colorline's web site at <http://www.arc.org/CLArchive/past.html>; "Present Market

Share of Private Prison Corporations," January 1999, <http://web.crim.ufl.edu/pcp/census/1999/Market.html>.

[3]U.S. Department of Justice, Bureau of Justice Statistics, *Direct Expenditure by Criminal Justice Function, 1982–1992* (Washington, DC: U.S. Government Printing Office, 1999), http://www.ojp.usdoj.gov/bjs>; U.S. Department of Justice, Bureau of Justice Statistics, *Justice Employment and Expenditure Extracts, 1992*, table F (Washington, DC: U.S. Government Printing Office, 1999), p. 6, <http://www.ojp.usdoj.gov/bjs>; various interviews with individuals as the National Institute of Justice and the U.S. Department of Justice in 1999 regarding estimated rate of growth of criminal justice expenditures between 1992 and 1999. Most recent available statistics for criminal justice expenditures are for 1992. The $150-billion figure is an estimate based on the belief of individuals interviewed who said expenditures grew as rapidly between 1992 and 1999 as they did between 1982 and 1992.

[4]Kristin Bloomer, "America's Newest Growth Industry," *In These Times*, March 17, 1997, p. 14.

[5]Corrections Yellow Pages web site, accessed February 24, 1999, at <http://www.correctionsyellow.com>.

[6]Project South staff, *Crime, Injustice, and Genocide Quiz* (Atlanta: Project South National Office, October 1996), <http://www.projectsouth.org/html/crimequiz.html>.

[7]New York Times Syndicate, "Prison Products, Services Attract Merchants, Wardens," *Palm Beach Post*, August 25, 1996; this article used a $26-billion figure for prison product sales. Steven R. Donziger, ed., *The Real War on Crime: The Report of the National Criminal Justice Commission* (New York: HarperPerennial, 1996), p. 93; this source quotes literature from the American Jail Association Convention, which states that the local-jail market alone is $65 billion. The $100-billion figure is based on adding these two figures together and adjusting for growth to the prison and jail system in recent years as determined from interviews with various Justice Department employees. See also footnote 3, this chapter.

[8]*State Farm Road Atlas* (Bloomington, IN: State Farm Insurance Companies, 1998).

[9]U.S. Department of Justice, Bureau of Justice Statistics, *Changes in the Number of Criminal Justice Employees* (Wshington, DC: U.S. Government Printing Office, 1999), <http://www.ojp.usdoj.gov/bjs>; James Austin, "America's Growing Correctional-Industrial Complex," *Focus* (The National Council on Crime and Delinquency), December 1990, p. 4; James Moran, "Privatizing Criminal Justice," paper presented at Crime and Justice in the Americas Conference, Office of International Criminal Justice (Chicago), March 13, 1995, pp. 2–3, <http://www.acsp.uic.edu/iocj/pubs/cja/080315./html>.

[10]Interview with Eric Butterfield, editor of *Construction Report*, published by *Correctional Building News* on March 14, 1999. Original source for Butterfield material is *The Corrections Yearbook* (South Salem, NY: Criminal Justice Institute, 1998).

[11]Construction Report web site, visited February 24, 1999, <http://www.correctonalnews.com>; Deeann Glamser, "Towns Now Welcoming Prisons," *USA Today*, March 13, 1996.

War Against Drugs[*]

Marc Mauer

Sure, it's true we prosecute a high percentage of minorities for drugs. The simple fact is, if you have a population, minority or not, that is conducting most of their illegal business on the street, those cases are easy pickings for the police.

—Delaware Prosecutor Charles Butler[1]

Picture this scene in any middle-class suburb in the United States: students at the local high school, a "good" school with high graduation rates and college acceptances, have been getting into trouble. Nothing too serious, but some drug use, some underage drinking, and a few smashed cars here and there. Parents are cautioned by the principal to check with their kids for signs of trouble.

The parents of one 17-year-old boy had already been concerned about possible drug use, and examine their son's bedroom while he is at school. They discover what appears to be some drug residue and a substantial amount of cash hidden in a drawer. Confronting their son when he comes home, he admits he has been using cocaine and occasionally selling to some friends.

How do the parents respond? Do they call up the police, demand that their son be arrested for using and selling drugs, and receive a five-year mandatory minimum sentence for his behavior? The question is ludicrous, of course.

Instead, the parents do what any good middle-class family would do: they consult with their insurance provider and then secure the best treatment program they can find. The criminal justice system never even becomes an issue for them.

A few miles away, picture another family in a low-income section of the city. Their son, too, appears to be getting involved with drugs. Unfortunately for him, his parents have no health insurance, and there are few drug treatment programs available in the neighborhood. Finally, he is picked up one night on a street corner and charged with drug possession with the intent to sell.

Two families with substance abuse problems, two different responses. What does this tell us about the choices available to families and communities, and whether the criminal justice system need be the inevitable response to illegal behavior?

*Marc Mauer, *Race to Incarcerate* (New York: The New Press, 1999). Copyright © 1999 by The Sentencing Project. Reprinted by permission of The New Press. www.thenewpress.com

Since 1980, no policy has contributed more to the incarceration of African-Americans than the "war on drugs." To say this is not to deny the reality of drug abuse and the toll it has taken on African-American and other communities; but as a national policy, the drug war has exacerbated racial disparities in incarceration while failing to have any sustained impact on the drug problem.

Drug Use and Drug Arrests

With nondrug street crimes, such as burglary or larceny, the police operate in a reactive mode: citizens report a crime and the police investigate. With drug selling or possession, though, there is no direct "victim"; consequently, no reports are made to the police (except possibly those made by complaining neighbors). Drug law enforcement is far more discretionary than for other offenses. The police decide when and where they will seek to make drug arrests, and most important, what priority they will place on enforcing drug laws.

The drug war's impact on the African-American community can be mapped by looking at two overlapping trends. First, there has been an enormous increase in the number of drug arrests overall; second, African-Americans have constituted an increasing proportion of those arrests.

As seen in Figure 1–1, in 1980 there were 581,000 arrests for drug offenses, a number that nearly doubled to 1,090,000 by 1990. Although it appeared for a while that these trends

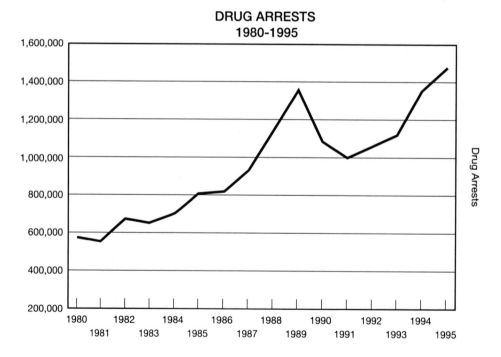

Figure 1–1 Drug Arrests, 1980–1995.

Source: FBI data provided to the author.

might be leveling off in the early 1990s with a decline in arrests, that trend was quickly reversed: a record 1,476,000 drug arrests were made by 1995.[2]

Did these arrests reflect rising rates of drug abuse nationally? No. In fact, the best data available show that the number of people using drugs had been declining since 1979, when 14.1 percent of the population reported using drugs in the past month. This proportion had halved to 6.7 percent by 1990, and it declined to 6.1 percent by 1995.[3] Since fewer people were using drugs, and presumably fewer selling as well, then all things being equal, one would have thought that drug arrests would have declined as well.

But all things are not equal when it comes to crime and politics. Instead, heightened political and media attention, and increased budgets for law enforcement all contributed to a greater use of police resources to target drug offenders. At the same time, police increasingly began to target low-income minority communities for drug law enforcement.

We can see this most clearly by analyzing arrest data prepared annually by the FBI. As seen in Figure 1–2, in 1980, African-Americans, who constitute 13 percent of the U.S. population, accounted for 21 percent of drug possession arrests nationally. This number rose to a high of 36 percent in 1992 before dropping somewhat to 33 percent by 1995. For juveniles, the figures are even more stark: although blacks represented 13 percent of juvenile drug possession arrests in 1980, this proportion climbed to 40 percent by 1991, before declining to 30 percent in 1995. In looking at these statistics, we might conclude that blacks began using drugs in greater numbers during the decade of the 1980s, thereby leading to

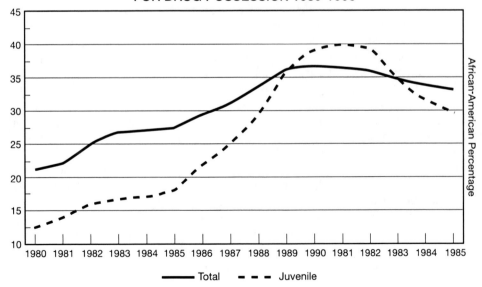

Figure 1–2   African-American Proportion of Arrests for Drug Possession, 1980–1995.
Source: FBI data provided to the author.

their being arrested more frequently. Certainly, a glance at television newscasts or weekly newsmagazines would have given us this impression.

In fact, no such dramatic rise can be detected. The best data available on drug use is compiled by the Substance Abuse and Mental Health Services Administration (SAMHSA) of the Department of Health and Human Services, which conducts a household survey annually to prepare estimates on the extent of drug use. Although these data cover 98 percent of the population, they have some limitations. Since this is by definition a household survey, anyone not living in a household will not be incorporated in the findings. Thus, prisoners, homeless persons not living in a shelter, and military personnel are not covered. Since minorities are disproportionately represented among these groups, they will therefore be underrepresented in the household survey. Nevertheless, the survey is generally regarded as the best portrait of the nation's drug-using population.

The SAMHSA surveys question individuals regarding drug use during the past month, past year, or ever in their lifetime. For our purposes, drug use during the past month is the most relevant piece of information, since frequent users are more likely to be arrested than infrequent ones.

Looking at the data for 1995, we find that while African-Americans were slightly more likely to be monthly drug users than whites and Hispanics (7.9 percent vs. 6.0 percent and 5.1 percent respectively), the much greater number of whites in the overall population resulted in their constituting the vast majority of drug users. Thus, the SAMHSA data indicate that whites represented 77 percent of current drug users, with African-Americans constituting 15 percent of users and Hispanics, 8 percent.[4] Even assuming that blacks may be somewhat undercounted in the household surveys, it is difficult to imagine that African-American drug use is of a magnitude that could explain blacks representing 15 percent of current drug users yet 33 percent of arrests for drug possession.

Some observers have speculated that the higher arrest rates for drug possession may reflect the type of drug that is being used—in essence, law enforcement is more likely to target cocaine users or crack cocaine users. Unfortunately, FBI arrest data do not distinguish between powder cocaine and crack cocaine. Arrest data for all cocaine possession offenses for 1995 show that African-Americans constituted 47 percent of all such arrests. Looking at data on cocaine use, though, we find that there are no dramatic differences in cocaine use by race or ethnicity. In 1995, 1.1 percent of blacks reported that they had used cocaine in the past month, compared to 0.7 percent of Hispanics and 0.6 percent of whites.[5] Overall, this translates into African-Americans representing 18 percent of all recent cocaine users.

For users of crack cocaine, the disproportionate use among blacks is considerably higher than for cocaine overall, but it doesn't explain the arrest disparities. Data for 1995 show that although crack use is quite low for all groups, African-Americans are six times as likely as whites to have used it in the past month and three times as likely as Hispanics (0.6 percent vs. 0.1 percent and 0.2 percent respectively).[6] Given the much greater proportion of whites in the overall population, though, these user rates translate into whites representing 54 percent of current crack users, blacks 34 percent and Hispanics 12 percent.

Are police arresting crack and cocaine users in general or preferentially going into black neighborhoods where some people are using these drugs? Conducting drug arrests in inner-city neighborhoods does have advantages for law enforcement. First, it is far easier to make arrests in such areas, since drug dealing is more likely to take place in open-air drug markets. In contrast, drug dealing in suburban neighborhoods almost invariably takes place behind closed doors and is therefore not readily identifiable to passing police. Second, because both drug use and dealing are more likely to take place openly, residents of African-American neighborhoods are more likely to complain about these behaviors and to ask for police intervention. Since law enforcement has long been accused of failing to respond to problems of minority neighborhoods in a timely manner, many police departments are now more focused on attempting to remedy this problem so they are likely to respond to complaints emanating from these neighborhoods.

Racial targeting by police may also have an effect on black neighborhoods that are not inner-city. Criminologists James Lynch and William Sabol analyzed data on incarceration rates, race, and class during the period 1979–91.[7] They identified inmates as either being "underclass" or "non-underclass" (working-class or middle-class) based on educational levels, employment history, and income. They concluded that the most significant increase in incarceration rates was for working class black drug offenders, whose rates increased sixfold, from 1.5 per 1,000 in 1979 to match that of underclass blacks at 9 per 1,000 by 1991. The trend for whites, on the other hand, was just the opposite; the underclass drug incarceration rate was double that of the non-underclass by 1991.

Lynch and Sabol suggest that two factors may explain these trends. First, law enforcement targeting of inner-city neighborhoods may initially sweep many underclass blacks into the criminal justice system. Second, due to residential racial segregation patterns, there may be a "spillover" effect whereby police increase the number of arrests in the working-class black neighborhoods that border underclass communities. They conclude that there has been

> an increased targeting of black working and middle class areas for discretionary drug enforcement and ultimately increased incarceration for drug offenses. The immunity that working and middle class status used to bring in the black community (and still does among whites) may have been lost. While the processes that produced these outcomes may not have been racially motivated in intent, they have resulted in racially disparate outcomes.[8]

Drug Sales and Arrests

Similar disproportionate arrest patterns can be seen for drug selling. In this area, the African-American proportion rose from 35 percent in 1980 to 49 percent by 1995.

It is at least theoretically possible that the proportion of black drug traffickers has risen substantially in recent years, and that the arrest percentages reflect actual law-breaking behavior. However, as we examine these disparities we find that statistics on drug users are fairly irrelevant, since one can be a drug seller without being a user.[9] One means of addressing this problem is to look at responses to parts of the SAMHSA surveys in which respondents are asked whether it is "fairly or very easy" to obtain drugs in your neighborhood. Overall, 43 percent of the population in 1996 responded affirmatively regarding cocaine and 39 percent regarding crack. These figures, which document the relative ease of obtaining drugs after fifteen years of massive increase in the law enforcement resources devoted to the drug war, should give pause to those committed to such policies.

While blacks were more likely than whites to report that it was easy to obtain these drugs (57 percent vs. 43 percent for cocaine, and 58 percent vs. 38 percent for crack), the differences are still nowhere near the order of magnitude that would explain the arrest disparities.[10] A report issued by the Wisconsin Policy Research Institute, a conservative think-tank, provides part of the explanation in describing differences in the white suburban drug markets and inner-city black and Hispanic neighborhoods of Milwaukee.[11] While drug dealing was prevalent in each of the communities, the inner-city sales tended to be neighborhood-based, often taking place on street corners. In contrast, the suburban distribution of cocaine and other drugs took place by word of mouth through contacts at work, bars, athletic leagues, and alternative cultural events such as "raves." Suburban sales locations were more hidden from law enforcement than were those in the inner-city neighborhoods, but they were "not very difficult to locate," in the words of the author.

A 1997 report of the National Institute of Justice lends support to the fact that whites are frequently involved in selling drugs. In an analysis of drug transactions in six cities, the researchers found that "respondents were most likely to report using a main source who was of their own racial or ethnic background."[12]

Finally, consider the patterns of daily life in urban areas. If it were true that the overwhelming number of drug dealers are black, we would see large numbers of drug-seeking whites streaming into Harlem, South Central Los Angeles, and the east side of Detroit day after day. While some do visit these neighborhoods, there are few reports of massive numbers doing so on a regular basis. As Barry McCaffrey, director of the White House Office of National Drug Control Policy, has stated, if your child bought drugs, "it was from a student of their own race generally."[13]

Sentencing for Drug Offenses

The overrepresentation of African-Americans in the criminal justice system has been exacerbated by changes in sentencing policy that coincided with the current drug war. Since 1975, every state has passed some type of mandatory sentencing law requiring incarceration for weapons offenses, habitual offenders, or other categories. These statutes have been applied most frequently to drug offenses, with two primary effects. First, they increase the proportion of arrested drug offenders who are sentenced to prison and, second, they increase the length of time that offenders serve in prison.

Data from the Bureau of Justice Statistics show that the chances of receiving a prison term after being arrested for a drug offense increased by 447 percent between 1980 and 1992.[14] A good portion of this increase was likely related to the requirement of mandatory sentencing, although no breakdown is available. Part of the increase may have also been a result of generally harsher attitudes toward drug offenders—that is, prosecutors and judges responding to a political climate increasingly punitive in its orientation toward drugs.

The impact of mandatory drug laws can be seen most dramatically in the federal court system. Drug offenders released from prison in 1990, many of whom had not been sentenced under mandatory provisions, had served an average of 30 months in prison. But offenders sentenced to prison in 1990—most of whom were subject to mandatory penalties were expected to serve more than twice that term, or an average of 66 months.[15] This fact, combined with a greatly increased number of federal drug prosecutions, has resulted in the proportion of federal prisoners who are drug offenders increasing from 25 percent in 1980 to 60 percent by 1995.

TABLE 1–1   State Prison Inmates by Race and Offense

	White				Black			
Offense	*1985*	*1995*	*% Increase*	*% Total Increase*	*1985*	*1995*	*% Increase*	*% Total Increase*
Total	224,900	471,100	109%	100%	211,100	490,100	132%	100%
Violent	111,900	214,800	92%	42%	124,800	228,600	83%	37%
Drug	21,200	86,100	306%	26%	16,600	134,000	707%	42%
Property	75,100	130,700	74%	23%	60,600	100,200	65%	14%
Public Order	14,900	39,000	162%	10%	7,600	25,000	229%	6%
Other	1,800	500	–72%	–1%	1,400	2,300	64%	0%

Source: Christopher J. Mumola and Allen J. Beck, "Prisoners in 1996," Bureau of Justice Statistics, June 1997.

At the state level, the longer prison terms brought about by mandatory sentencing laws have also had a significant impact on African-Americans. Between 1985 and 1995, the average time served in prison for drug offenses rose by 20 percent from 20 months to 24 months.[16] Overall, the number of drug offenders in prison increased by 478 percent during this period, compared to a rise of 119 percent for all offenses.

A substantial portion of this increase consists of African-Americans. This can be seen in Table 1–1. From 1985 to 1995, drug offenders constituted 42 percent of the rise in the black state prison population. Note here that drug offenders in this case refers to individuals convicted only of a drug offense and not, for example, a drug-related assault or robbery. For white offenders, by contrast, drug offenders represented 26 percent of the increase and violent offenders 42 percent. Overall, the number of white drug offenders increased by 306 percent in the ten-year period, while for blacks the increase was 707 percent.

The combined impact of law enforcement and sentencing policies on minorities is even more startling in some states. A 1997 study of drug law enforcement in Massachusetts found that blacks were 39 times more likely to be incarcerated for a drug offense than whites.[17] And the impact of drug policies on black women has been even more dramatic than for black men. In just the five-year period 1986–91, the number of black women incarcerated in state prison for a drug offense rose by 828 percent. Although the absolute numbers of women drug offenders in the system are considerably lower than for men, the trend is clearly disturbing.

Besides mandatory sentencing, other drug policies that may have been well intended have contributed to the alarming trends in black incarceration. One such policy is the set of drug laws that increase penalties for offenders who sell drugs near schools or public housing. Ostensibly, the goal is to establish "drug-free" zones that are safe for children and other residents. As a University of Chicago law professor reminds us:

> in Illinois, a fifteen-year-old first-time offender charged with selling a controlled substance within 1,000 feet of public housing is treated as an adult. In contrast, a fifteen-year-old first-time offender charged with selling a controlled substance from or near his home in the suburbs is treated as a juvenile. Counseling, treatment, and targeted programs are made available to the juvenile

suburbanite while the inner city youth most in need of social services enters the resource starved adult criminal justice system.[18]

Bobbie Marshall, an African-American who has used drugs since his teens, experienced the impact of this kind of law following his arrest for selling drugs within 1,000 feet of a school in Los Angeles. Because of his three prior convictions for selling small quantities of drugs to feed his habit, Marshall faced the possibility of life without parole under a federal statute. Marshall's attorneys documented that 89 of 90 persons arrested under a joint state/federal task force in the "schoolyard program" were either African-American or Hispanic.

By the time of Marshall's sentencing, he had in many ways turned his life around. He had become active in counseling gang members, helped keep the peace during the 1992 Los Angeles riots, and remained drug free. His efforts led to letters of support from ministers, a police commander, a congressman, and others. Although the prosecution eventually agreed to a nine-year term for Marshall, the sentencing judge imposed only half that term, arguing that Marshall's rehabilitation and value to the community were exceptional. Under the federal mandatory sentencing laws, though, the judge was overruled on appeal.

The most discussed reason for the racial disparity in drug sentencing in recent years has been the issue of sentencing for crack cocaine offenses. As crack made its entry into urban areas in the mid–1980s, reports began to surface about this new highly addictive and powerful drug. Cover stories appeared in *Newsweek*, *Time*, and periodicals around the country. Reports of "crack babies" born to addicted mothers were among the most frightening to surface. How could anyone fail to respond to this human tragedy? Only later did information surface that indicated that there were in fact no data on crack-addicted babies.

Testing cannot distinguish between prenatal exposure to crack cocaine and powder cocaine, so there is no way to know how many of these mothers had in fact used crack while pregnant. Further, the children of drug-abusing mothers who develop poorly may in fact be suffering from a combination of factors that often correlate with low-income drug abusing mothers, including poor nutrition, smoking, and lack of prenatal care. A study by researchers at the Albert Einstein Medical Center in Philadelphia tracked the development of more than 200 low-income inner-city children, half of whom had been exposed to cocaine in the womb and half not. The study found that both groups of children scored below average on IQ tests and other measures of cognitive development, but that there was no significant difference between the two groups.[19] Clearly, any type of substance abuse by pregnant women is unhealthy for both mother and child. In this instance, though, the image of "crack babies" had a significant impact on subsequent legislation.

Crack, of course, is a dangerous drug; its use has caused real destruction to many individuals and communities. The extent of this harm and any realistic assessment of possible responses, though, were hardly considered by Congress in its rush to adopt harsh "antidrug" penalties in 1986 and again in 1988. The mandatory sentencing laws passed by Congress provided for far harsher punishments for crack offenses than for powder cocaine crimes. Thus, the sale of 500 grams of cocaine powder resulted in a mandatory five-year prison term, while only 5 grams of crack was required to trigger the same mandatory penalty.

In addition to the other racial dynamics of the drug war, these laws have had a major impact on African-Americans. The vast majority of persons charged with crack trafficking offenses in the federal system—88 percent in 1992–93—have been African-American.[20] Federal prosecutors contend that these figures merely reflect the proportions of large-scale traffickers in crack who qualify for federal prosecution because of their substantial role in the drug trade. Data analyzed by the U.S. Sentencing Commission, though, casts doubt on this contention: in the Commission's analysis of crack defendants in 1992, only 5.5 percent of the defendants were classified as high-level dealers, while 63.7 percent were considered street-level dealers or couriers, and 30.8 percent mid-level dealers.[21]

Given the severity of crack penalties in the federal system, the prosecutorial decision regarding whether to charge a drug offense as a state or federal crime has potentially significant consequences for sentencing. The results of a *Los Angeles Times* analysis, which examined prosecutions for crack cocaine trafficking in the Los Angeles area from 1988 to 1994, are quite revealing.[22] During that period, not a single white offender was convicted of a crack offense in federal court, despite the fact that whites comprise a majority of crack users. During the same period, though, hundreds of white crack traffickers were prosecuted in state courts, often receiving sentences as much as eight years less than those received by offenders in federal courts. As is true nationally, the *Times* analysis revealed that many of the African-Americans charged in federal court were not necessarily drug kingpins, but rather low-level dealers or accomplices in the drug trade.

The folly of using expensive prison space for drug offenders, even traffickers, has been documented in research conducted on the federal prison population. One study examined costs and recidivism for low-level drug traffickers in the federal prison system before and after the imposition of mandatory prison terms.[23] It found that over half of the offenders sentenced to prison in 1992 were drug traffickers. Of these, 62 percent, or 9,000 offenders, were considered low-risk as defined by their limited criminal histories. The study then examined recidivism rates for a comparable group of 236 offenders released from prison in 1987, prior to the adoption of mandatory minimums and the federal sentencing guidelines. It found that only 19 percent of the low-risk drug traffickers were re-arrested during the three years after release, and that none of those arrested were charged with serious crimes of violence.

In contrast, the low-risk traffickers sentenced to prison in 1992 were expected to serve three years longer in prison than the 1987 release group (51 months vs. 17 months). The study concluded that the additional time spent in prison for the 9,000 offenders would cost taxpayers approximately $515 million.

Similar findings have been documented regarding the relatively minor roles and criminal histories of drug offenders in state prisons. A report published by the Urban Institute provided an analysis of the more than 150,000 drug offenders incarcerated in state prisons in 1991.[24] Almost 127,000 of these offenders, or 84 percent, had no history of a prior incarceration for a violent crime, and one half of the offenders had no prior incarcerations at all. One third of the drug offenders sentenced to state prison had been convicted of the less serious possession offenses—hardly a qualification for a high-level player in the drug trade.

The Urban Institute analysis further documents that the increased incarceration of drug offenders has contributed to a rise in the imprisonment of what has been termed "socially integrated offenders" in other words, there has been a rise in the proportion of inmates who have ties to legitimate institutions such as families, education, and labor markets. Between 1979 and 1991, for example, the number of state prison inmates with some college education rose from 10,000 to 44,000, and the number employed prior to their incarceration increased from 192,000 to 476,000.[25] The Urban Institute authors contend that the incarceration of socially integrated offenders "may be unnecessary because prior experience has shown that socially integrated people are less likely to re-offend. Such people can, therefore, be punished by means other than incarceration without putting the public at undue risk." Further, by reducing ties to legitimate institutions, incarceration may make these offenders "more prone to subsequent criminal involvement."[26]

Endnotes

[1]Barry Bearak, "Big Catch: Drug War's Little Fish," *Los Angeles Times*, May 6, 1990.

[2]All figures on drug arrests in this chapter taken from data provided by the FBI to the author.

[3]Substance Abuse and Mental Health Services Administration, *Preliminary Results from the 1996 Household Survey on Drug Abuse* (Washington, D.C.: Substance Abuse and Mental Health Services Administration, July 1997), p. 61.

[4]Substance Abuse and Mental Health Services Administration, *National Household Survey on Drug Abuse, Population Estimates 1995* (Washington, D.C.: Substance Abuse and Mental Health Services Administration, June 1996), pp. 18–19.

[5]Ibid., pp. 30–31.

[6]Ibid., pp. 36–37.

[7]James P. Lynch and William J. Sabol, "The Use of Coercive Social Control and Changes in the Race and Class Composition of U.S. Prison Populations," paper presented at the American Society of Criminology, Nov. 9, 1994.

[8]Ibid., p. 30.

[9]The SAMHSA surveys ask respondents if they have sold drugs, but most experts in the field do not consider these data nearly as reliable as the user figures.

[10]Substance Abuse and Mental Health Services Administration, "Preliminary Results from the 1996 Household Survey on Drug Abuse" (Washington, D.C.: Substance Abuse and Mental Health Services Administration, July 1997), Tables 314B and 315B.

[11]John M. Hagedorn, "The Business of Drug Dealing in Milwaukee," Wisconsin Policy Research Institute, June 1998.

[12]K. Jack Riley, *Crack, Powder Cocaine, and Heroin: Drug Purchase and Use Patterns in Six U.S. Cities*, National Institute of Justice, Dec. 1997, p. 1.

[13]Patricia Davis and Pierre Thomas, "In Affluent Suburbs, Young Users and Sellers Abound," *Washington Post*, Dec. 14, 1997, p. A20.

[14]Allen J. Beck and Darrell K. Gilliard, *Prisoners in 1994* (Washington, D.C.: Bureau of Justice Statistics, August 1995), p. 13.

[15]Douglas C. McDonald and Kenneth E. Carlson, *Federal Sentencing in Transition, 1986–90* (Washington, D.C.: Bureau of Justice Statistics, June 1992), p. 4.

[16]Christopher J. Mumola and Allen J. Beck, *Prisoners in 1996* (Washington, D.C.: Bureau of Justice Statistics, June 1997), p. 11.

[17]William N. Brownsberger, *Profile of Anti-Drug Law Enforcement in Urban Poverty Areas in Massachusetts*, Harvard Medical School, 1997, p. 21. The study also documented that Hispanics were 81 times more likely than whites to be incarcerated for a drug offense.

[18]Randolph N. Stone, "The Criminal Justice System: Unfair and Ineffective," paper presented at the Chicago Assembly on "Crime and Community Safety," November 19–20, 1992, pp. 2–3.

[19]Susan FitzGerald, "'Crack Baby' Fears May Have Been Overstated," *Washington Post Health*, Sept. 16, 1997.

[20]United States Sentencing Commission, *Cocaine and Federal Sentencing Policy* (Washington, D.C.: United State Sentencing Commission, February 1995), pp. 122–23.

[21]United States Sentencing Commission, p. 172.

[22]Dan Weikel, "War on Crack Targets Minorities over Whites," *Los Angeles Times,* May 21, 1995.

[23]Miles D. Harer, "Do Guideline Sentences for Low-Risk Traffickers Achieve Their Stated Purposes?" *Federal Sentencing Reporter* 7.1 (1994).

[24]James P. Lynch and William J. Sabol, *Did Getting Tough on Crime Pay?* (Washington, D.C.: Urban Institute, 1997).

[25]Ibid., p. 8

[26]Ibid., p. 7.

Criminal Justice Through Fear[*]

Mike Davis

In my 1990 book, *City of Quartz*, I explored various tendencies toward the militarization of the Southern California landscape. Events since the 1992 riots—including a four-year-long recession, a sharp decline in factory jobs, deep cuts in welfare and public employment, a backlash against immigrant workers, the failure of police reform, and an unprecedented exodus of middle-class families—have only reinforced spatial apartheid in greater Los Angeles....

Scanscape

Is there any need to explain *why* fear eats the soul of Los Angeles? Only the middle-class dread of progressive taxation exceeds the current obsession with personal safety and social insulation. In the face of intractable urban poverty and homelessness, and despite one of the greatest expansions in American business history, a bipartisan consensus insists that any and all budgets must be balanced and entitlements reduced. With no hope for further public investment in the remediation of underlying social conditions, we are forced instead to make increasing public and private investments in physical security. The rhetoric of urban reform persists, but the substance is extinct. "Rebuilding L.A." simply means padding the bunker.

As city life grows more feral, the various social milieux adopt security strategies and technologies according to their means.... To the extent that these security measures are reactions to urban unrest, it is possible to speak about a "riot tectonics" that episodically convulses and reshapes urban space. After the 1965 Watts rebellion, for instance, downtown Los Angeles's leading landowners organized a secretive "Committee of 25" to deal with perceived threats to redevelopment efforts.[1] Warned by the LAPD that a black "inundation" of the central city was imminent, the committee abandoned efforts to revitalize the city's aging financial and retail core. Instead, it persuaded city hall to subsidize the transplanting of banks and corporate front offices to a new financial district atop Bunker Hill, a few blocks to the west. The city's redevelopment agency, acting as a private planner, bailed out the committee's lost investments in the old business district by offering discounts far below real market value on parcels of land within the new core.

*Mike Davis, *City of Quartz* (Vancouver, WA: Vintage Books, 1990). Reprinted with permission.

The key to the success of this strategy, celebrated as Downtown's "renaissance," was the physical segregation of the new core and its land values behind a rampart of regraded palisades, concrete pillars, and freeway walls. Traditional pedestrian connections between Bunker Hill and the old core were removed, and foot traffic was elevated above the street on "pedways"... access to which was controlled by the security systems of individual skyscrapers. This radical privatization of Downtown public space, with its ominous racial overtones, occurred without significant public debate.

The 1992 riots vindicated the foresight of Fortress Downtown's designers. While windows were being smashed throughout the old business district, Bunker Hill lived up to its name. By flicking a few switches on their command consoles, the security staffs of the great bank towers were able to cut off all access to their expensive real estate. Bullet-proof steel doors rolled down over streetlevel entrances, escalators instantly froze, and electronic locks sealed off pedestrian passageways. As the *Los Angeles Business Journal* pointed out, the riot-tested success of corporate Downtown's defenses has only stimulated demand for new and higher levels of physical security.[2]

One consequence of this demand has been the continuing erosion of the boundary between architecture and law enforcement. The LAPD have become central players in the Downtown design process. No major project now breaks ground without their participation. Police representatives have exerted effective pressure against the provision of public toilets ("crime scenes" in their opinion) and the toleration of street vending ("lookouts for drug dealers"). The riots also provided suburban police departments with a pretext for enhancing their involvement in planning and design issues. In affluent Thousand Oaks, for example, the sheriff's liaison to the planning commission persuaded the city to outlaw alleys as a "crime prevention priority."[3]

Video monitoring of Downtown's redeveloped zones, meanwhile, has been extended to parking structures, private sidewalks, and plazas. This comprehensive surveillance constitutes a virtual *scanscape*—a space of protective visibility that increasingly defines where white-collar office workers and middle-class tourists feel safe downtown....

A premier platform for the new surveillance technology will be that anachronism of the nineteenth century: the skyscraper. Tall buildings are becoming increasingly sentient and packed with deadly firepower. The skyscraper with a mainframe brain in *Die Hard* (actually F. Scott Johnson's Fox-Pereira Tower in Century City) anticipates a new generation of architectural antiheroes as intelligent buildings alternately battle evil or become its pawns. The sensory systems of many of Los Angeles's new office towers already include panopticon vision, smell, sensitivity to temperature and humidity, motion detection, and, in a few cases, hearing. Some architects now predict that the day is coming when a building's own artificial intelligent computers will be able to automatically screen and identify its human population, and even respond to their emotional states, especially fear or panic. Without dispatching security personnel, the building itself will be able to manage crises both minor (like ordering street people out of the building or preventing them from using toilets) and major (like trapping burglars in an elevator).

The Invisible Riot

Friday, 5 May 1992. The armored personnel carrier squats on the corner like *un gran sapo feo*—a "big ugly toad"—according to nine-year-old Emerio. His parents talk anxiously, almost in a whisper, about the *desparecidos*: Raul from Tepic, big Mario, the younger Flores girl, and the cousin from Ahuachapan. Like all Salvadorans, they know about those who "disappear"; they remember the headless corpses and the man whose tongue had been pulled through the hole in his throat like a necktie. That is why they came here—to zip code 90057, Los Angeles, California.[4]

Their neighborhood, on the edge of MacArthur Park, is part of the large halo of older, high-density housing surrounding the scanscape of the fortified core. These tenement districts perform the classic functions of Burgess's "zone in transition": providing urban ports of entry for the city's poorest and most recent immigrants—in this case from Mexico, Guatemala, and El Salvador rather than Ireland and Bohemia—who work in Downtown hotels and garment factories. But the normally bustling streets are now eerily quiet. Emerio's parents are counting their friends and neighbors, Salvadoran and Mexican, who are suddenly gone.

Some are in the county jail on Bauchet Street, little more than brown grains of sand lost among the 17,000 other alleged *saqueadores* (looters) and *incendarios* (arsonists) detained after the most violent American civil disturbance since enraged Irish immigrants burned Manhattan in 1863. Those without papers are probably already back in Tijuana, broke and disconsolate, cut off from their families and new lives. Violating city policy, the police fed hundreds of hapless undocumented *saqueadores* to the INS for deportation before the ACLU or immigrant rights groups had even realized that they had been arrested.

For many days the television talked only of the "South Central riot," "Black rage," and the "Crips and Bloods." Truly, the Rodney King case was a watershed in national race relations, a test of the very meaning of the citizenship for which African-Americans have struggled for four hundred years. It was also the fuse on an explosive accumulation of local grievances among young blacks, ranging from Chief Gates's infamous mass detentions ("Operation Hammer") to the murder of 15-year old Latasha Harlins by a Korean grocer in 1991. But the 1992 upheaval was far more complex than the 1965 Watts rebellion, although some issues, especially police abuse, remained the same. While most of the news media remained trapped in the black-and-white world of 1965, the second Los Angeles riot burst emphatically into technicolor....

Despite the tabloid media's obsession with black violence, only 36 percent of the riot arrestees were African-American, while 52 percent had Spanish surnames and 10 percent were white. Moreover, the greatest density of riot-related "incidents" occurred north of the Santa Monica Freeway in predominantly Latino and Asian areas. Indeed, nearly as many suspects were booked by the LAPD's Ramparts station, which polices Emerio's neighborhood, as by all four stations which make up the department's South Bureau in South Central Los Angeles. Even the Hollywood station made twice as many arrests as the 77th Street station, which patrolled the supposed riot epicenter—where truck driver Reginald Denny was nearly beaten to death—at the intersection of Florence and Normandie Avenues.[5]

This invisible Mid-City riot, conflated by most news reports with events in majority-black areas,* was driven primarily by empty bellies and broken dreams, not by outrage over the acquittal of the cops who beat Rodney King. It was the culmination of a decade of declining economic opportunity and rising poverty followed by two years of recession that

---

* The "independent" press was as fixated as the mainstream on exclusively black-and-white images of the riots. The Institute for Alternative Journalism's *Inside the L.A. Riots*, for example, contains 70 dramatic photographs, only one of which clearly depicts a Latino (a small boy).[6]

tripled unemployment in Los Angeles's immigrant neighborhoods. Academic studies since the riot have shown that Mexican and Central American immigrants arriving after 1980 had less hope than their predecessors of finding stable, entry-level positions in a regional economy that had become supersaturated with unskilled labor. "Massively growing numbers of Mexican immigrants," according to UCLA sociologist Vilma Ortiz, "have been packed into a relatively narrow tier of occupations."[7] Already by 1980, starting wages for new arrivals had fallen by 13 percent compared to 1970, and in the decade that followed, the portion of the Los Angeles population falling below the poverty line grew by a full percentage point or more each year.[8]

Then, 1990: cutbacks in defense spending and the bursting of the Japanese financial bubble (source of massive "super-yen" investments in Los Angeles real estate during the 1980s) converged to plunge the Southern California economy into its worst recession since 1938. An incredible 27 percent of national job loss was concentrated in the Los Angeles metropolitan region. In Los Angeles county this translated into a catastrophic 30 percent decline in manufacturing employment that savaged light industry, where Mexican immigrants make up the majority of workers, as well as aerospace and military electronics.[9] The impact of the recession, moreover, was intensified by simultaneous cutbacks in AFDC and MediCal benefits as well as deep slashes in local school budgets. Tens of thousands of families lost their tenuous economic footholds, while the number of children living in poverty increased by a third during the course of the recession.[10]

For anyone who cared to pay attention there were dramatic social storm warnings in the months before the spring 1992 riots. Indeed, no image revealed the mixed origins of the upheaval more clearly than the photograph published in the *Los Angeles Times* three days before Christmas 1991. It showed part of the throng of 20,000 women and children, predominantly recent Latino immigrants, waiting outside skid row's Fred Jordan Mission for the handout of a chicken, a dozen corn tortillas, three small toys, and a blanket. According to the *Times*, "Eight blocks were cordoned off around 5th Street and Towne Avenue to accommodate the crush of people. Some in the five-hour line said they were willing to brave the gritty streets for what one woman described as her 'only possibility' for a Christmas dinner.[11] Human distress on so broad a scale had not been photographed in California since the famous depression-era documentaries of Margaret Bourke-White and Dorothea Lange.

Nineteen-thirties-type misery was no surprise, however, to food bank volunteers, who had been warning city officials about the ominous decline in emergency food resources, or to public health workers, who were reporting classic symptoms of malnutrition—anemia and stunted growth—in nearly a quarter of the poor children passing through a county screening program.[12] Other visible barometers of the crisis included the rapidly growing colonies of unemployed busboys, gardeners, and construction laborers living on the desolate flanks of Crown Hill across from Downtown or in the concrete bed of the Los Angeles River, where the homeless are forced to use sewage outflow for bathing and cooking.

Emerio's parents and their neighbors spoke of a gathering sense of desperation in early 1992, a perception of a future already looted of opportunity. The riot arrived like a magic dispensation. In Mid-City neighborhoods people were initially shocked by the violence, then mesmerized by the televised images of black and Latino crowds in South Central Los Angeles helping themselves to mountains of desirable goods without interference from the police. On the second day of unrest, 30 April, the authorities blundered twice: first by suspending school and releasing the kids into the street, second by announcing that the National Guard was on the way to help enforce a dusk-to-dawn curfew.

Thousands immediately interpreted this as a last call to participate in the general redistribution of wealth in progress. Looting exploded through the majority-immigrant neighborhoods of Mid-City, as well as Echo Park, Van Nuys, and Huntington Park. Although arsonists struck wantonly and almost at random, the looting crowds were governed by a visible moral economy. As one middle-aged lady explained to me, "Stealing is a sin, but this is more like a television game show where everyone wins." In contrast to the looters on Hollywood Boulevard who stole Madonna's underwear from Frederick's, the masses of Mid-City concentrated on the prosaic necessities of life like cockroach spray and Pampers.

> Since most of the liquor stores and markets in this area greatly overcharge the customers for poor quality merchandise, there is great resentment. My students told me that when some of them saw Viva Market, on Hoover and Olympic, being looted as they watched television, their parents immediately left the apartment only to return an hour later with food and other items. They didn't see this as a "riot," just an opportunity to get even with the "exploiters."

> There was no coordination or planning by the people north of the Santa Monica Freeway, other than that provided by the roadmap shown on television.... I do not think that Korean stores were attacked for exclusively ethnic reasons. If Korean-owned liquor stores were burned, Korean travel agencies and beauty-shops were not touched. The uprising was directed against the police and rip-off merchants in general. It was driven by economic desperation and class resentment, not race.[13]

The official reaction to this postmodern bread riot was the biggest multiagency law enforcement operation in history. For weeks afterward, elite LAPD Metro Squad units supported by the National Guard, swept through the tenements in search of stolen goods, while Border Patrolmen from as far away as Texas trawled the streets for undocumented residents. Meanwhile, thousands of *saqueadores*, many of them pathetic scavengers captured in the charred ruins the day after the looting, languished for weeks in the county jail, unable to meet absurdly high bails. One man, apprehended with a packet of sunflower seeds and two cartons of milk, was held on $15,000 bond. Some curfew violators received 30-day jail sentences, despite the fact that they were either homeless or spoke no English. Angry suburban politicians, meanwhile, outbid one another with demands to deport immigrants and strip their U.S.-born children of citizenship.

Free-Fire Zone

By mid-May 1992, the National Guard, together with the army and the marines, had withdrawn from the inner city neighborhoods of Los Angeles. Flags folded and rifles stacked, thousands of citizen-soldiers returned to their ordinary suburban lives. As the humvees and trucks moved out, another army, the Eighteenth Street gang, immediately resumed its occupation of Los Angeles's Mid-City area. Some members taunted departing guardsmen with the boastful chant that weary neighbors had been hearing for years: "Soy Eighteen with a bullet / I got my finger on the trigger / I'm gonna pull it."

By their own admission, the overwhelmed inner city detachments of the LAPD have been unable to keep track of all the bodies on the street, much less deal with common burglaries, car thefts, and gang-organized protection rackets.[14] … [T]he present-day occupants of the transition zone are left to fend for themselves. Lacking the resources or political clout of more affluent neighborhoods, they have turned to Mr. Smith and Mr. Wesson, whose names follow "protected by …" on handmade signs decorating humble homes all over South Central and Mid-City Los Angeles.

Slumlords, meanwhile, are conducting their own private reign of terror against drug dealers, petty criminals, and deadbeat tenants. Faced with "zero tolerance" laws authorizing the seizure or destruction of properties used for drug sales, they are hiring their own goon squads and armed mercenaries to "exterminate" crime on their premises. Shortly after the 1992 riots, *Times* reporter Richard Colvin accompanied one of these crews on a swashbuckling rampage through the Westlake, Venice, and Panorama City districts.

Led by a six-foot-three, 280-pound "soldier of fortune" named David Roybal, this security squad was renowned among landlords for its efficient brutality. Suspected drug dealers and their customers, along with rent-in-arrears tenants and other landlord irritants, were physically driven from buildings at gunpoint. Those who resisted or even complained were beaten without mercy. In a Panorama City raid a few years earlier, "Roybal and his crew collared so many residents and squatters for drugs that they converted a recreation room into a holding tank and handcuffed arrestees to a blood-spattered wall." The LAPD knew about this private jail but ignored residents' protests. An envious police officer told Colvin, "If we could do what these security guards do, we'd get rid of the crime problem, just like that."[15]

In addition to these rent-a-thugs, the inner ring has also spawned a vast cottage industry manufacturing wrought-iron bars and grates for home protection. An estimated 100,000 inner city homes, like cages in a human zoo, have "burglar bars" bolted over all their doors and windows. As in a George Romero movie, working-class families now lock themselves in every night from the zombified city outside.… Yet such security may be a cruel illusion. The Los Angeles Fire Department estimates that at least half of the city's barred homes lack the legally required quick-release mechanisms that allow residents to escape in an emergency. The result has been a recent epidemic of horrific fires in which entire trapped families have been immolated in their bungalows or apartments.[16]

The prison cell finds many other architectural resonances in the post-riot inner city. Even before the Rodney King uprising, most liquor and convenience stores, taking the lead from pawnshops, had completely caged in their cash register counters, sometimes with lifesize cardboard cutouts of policemen placed near the window. Even local greasy spoons had begun to exchange hamburgers for money through bulletproof acrylic turnstiles. Now the same design—call it the "Brinks" aesthetic—has been extended to social service offices and hospitals. In light of recent cutbacks in welfare programs and medical services, along with all-day waits in welfare lines or for emergency medical treatment,[17] the county has sought to protect employees from public rage through the comprehensive installation of metal detectors, video monitors, convex surveillance mirrors, panic buttons, chairs bolted to the floor, and "interview booths divided by thick, shatterproof glass partitions." Not surprisingly, advocates for the poor have denounced this paranoid environment in which welfare mothers are treated like dangerous inmates in a high-security prison.[18]

Schools also have become more like prisons. Even as per capita education spending has plummeted in many local school districts, scarce resources are being absorbed in fortifying school grounds and hiring more armed security police. Teenagers complain bitterly about overcrowded classrooms and demoralized teachers, about decaying campuses that have become little more than daytime detention centers for an abandoned generation. Many students are literally locked in during school hours, while new daytime curfew laws—the violation of which carries stiff penalties for parents—allow police to treat truancy as a criminal offense. In some Southern California communities, the police have direct access to computerized school records. In the Los Angeles Unified School District kids who become informers on fellow students' drug habits are rewarded with concert tickets, CDs, and new clothes, and if Mayor Riordan gets his way, the LAPD may even gain its very own high school: a 'junior police academy" magnet school that would be a national first.[19]

The school yard, meanwhile, has become a killing field. Scores of students since 1985 have been wounded or killed during school hours. As a result, high school students in Los Angeles are now checked for weapons by metal detectors as they enter school each morning. At Long Beach's Lindbergh Junior High School, frequently raked by gunfire, administrators built a 900-foot-long, 10-foot-high wall "to deflect bullets" fired from a neighboring public housing project. At a Santa Monica elementary school, little kids regularly practice "drive-by drills." Just as their parents once learned to cower under desks in case of a nuclear attack, so are today's students "taught to drop at a teacher's signal in case of another drive-by shooting and stay there until they receive an all-clear signal."[20]

Federally subsidized housing and public housing projects, for their part, are coming to resemble the "strategic hamlets" that were used to incarcerate the rural population of Vietnam. Although no Los Angeles housing project is yet as militarized as those in San Juan, Puerto Rico, where the National Guard was sent in by the governor, or as technologically sophisticated as Chicago's Cabrini-Green, where retinal scans (as in the opening sequence of *Blade Runner*) are used to check IDs, the housing authority police exercise absolute control over residents freedom of movement.[21]

In a city with the nation's worst housing shortage, project tenants, fearful of eviction, are reluctant to claim any constitutional protection against unlawful search or seizure. Like peasants in a rebel countryside, they are routinely stopped and searched without probable cause, while their homes are broken into without court warrants. In several projects, public access is restricted by guard posts, and residents must submit lists of frequent visitors. And, as in other big cities, federal "one strike and you're out" regulations allow managers to evict otherwise innocent tenants of federally subsidized housing for crimes committed by their relatives or guests: a policy of collective punishment similar to that long practiced by Israelis on the West Bank.*

Half-Moons of Repression

... In contemporary metropolitan Los Angeles, new species of enclaves are emerging in sympathy with the militarization of the landscape. For want of any generally accepted name, we might call them "social control districts." They merge the sanctions of the criminal or civil code with land-use planning to create what Michel Foucault would undoubtedly have recognized as a yet higher stage in the evolution of the "disciplinary order" of the

---

*In November 1997, three mothers from a housing project in Venice, aided by the ACLU, challenged the constitutionality of the "one strike" policy in a major lawsuit against the federal government.[22]

modern city. Growing like weeds in a constitutional no man's land, Southern California's social control districts can be distinguished according to their specific juridical modes of imposing spatial "discipline."

Abatement districts, currently enforced against graffiti and prostitution in signposted neighborhoods of Los Angeles and West Hollywood, extend the traditional police power over nuisance (the legal fount of all zoning) from noxious industry to noxious behavior. Financed by fines collected (on prostitution offenses) or special sales taxes levied (on spray paints, for example), they devote additional law enforcement resources to specific social problems. Going a step further, business leaders in Little Tokyo and Hollywood have proposed the establishment of self-taxing "improvement districts" which would be able to hire private security guards to supplement the police. Needless to say, this would further erode the already fuzzy boundary between public and private policing in Los Angeles.

Since the 1992 riots, moreover, the LAPD has buttressed abatement programs by interventions in the zoning process. Using computer software to identify hot spots of prostitution, petty crime, and drug use, the police now routinely veto building and operating permits for "crime magnet" businesses. "Most commanding officers don't want new bars in their area, or new liquor locations or new dance halls," a police spokesperson explained to the *Los Angeles Times*. "What you have is an increased police interest in using zoning laws as vehicles to stop these businesses when they have problems." The LAPD considers this a logical extension of "community-based policing," but some Latino community leaders have complained that it really constitutes discrimination against Spanish-speaking mom-and-pop businesses like meat markets and *tiendas* (corner grocery stores) that need liquor sales to break even. Drinkers simply shop at supermarkets instead.[23]

Enhancement districts, represented all over Southern California by the "drug-free zones" and "gun-free zones" surrounding public schools, add extra federal or state penalties ("enhancements") to crimes committed within a specified radius of public institutions. In other cases, new laws, targeted at specific groups and locations, criminalize otherwise legal behavior. As a condition of probation, for example, prostitutes are now given maps demarcating areas, including parts of Hollywood, South Central, and the San Fernando Valley, where they can be arrested simply for walking down the street. In Costa Mesa (Orange County) prostitutes are further humiliated by having their clothes confiscated after arrest. They are released from jail wearing flimsy white paper jumpsuits.[24]

From the circumscription of a group's otherwise legal behavior, it is a short step to *containment* districts designed to quarantine potentially epidemic social problems or, more usually, social types. In Southern California these undesirables run the gamut from that insect illegal immigrant, the Mediterranean fruit fly, to homeless people. Since the early 1980s, the city of Los Angeles has tried to prevent the spillover of cardboard "condos" into surrounding council districts or into the more upscale precincts of Downtown by keeping homeless people "contained" (the official term) within the 50-square-block area of skid row. In 1996, the city council formalized the status quo by declaring a portion of skid row's sidewalks an official "sleeping zone." As soup kitchens and skid row missions brace themselves for a new wave of homelessness in the wake of recent state and federal welfare reforms, the LAPD maintains its traditional policy of keeping street people herded within the boundaries of the nation's largest outdoor poorhouse.

Obverse to containment is the formal *exclusion* of pariah groups from public space or even the city limits. The tactics are sometimes ingenious. In Anaheim, for instance, a city-supported citizens' group ("Operation Steer Clear") dumped tons of steer manure in local parks in the hope that the stench would drive away drug dealers and gang members. "Anti-camping" ordinances, likewise, have been passed by a spate of Southland cities, including the "Peoples' Republic" of Santa Monica, with the goal of banishing the homeless from sight. Since such exclusion ordinances merely sweep a stigmatized social group onto the next community's doorstep, each city, in a chain reaction, adopts comparable legislation in order to avoid becoming the regional equivalent of a human landfill.

Similarly, Los Angeles and a score of smaller cities have used sweeping civil injunctions—whose constitutionality was upheld by the California Supreme Court in January 1997—to prevent gangs from congregating in parks or on street corners. Although one high-ranking LAPD official has complained that these "gang-free zones" merely push gang activity into adjoining neighborhoods, they are highly popular with vote-conscious district attorneys and city council members who love the image that the injunctions broadcast of decisive action and comprehensive deterrence.[25] In a typical example, a Los Angeles judge banned Eighteenth Street homeboys in one neighborhood from "associating in public view" in groups larger than two, even in their own front yards. He also imposed an 8 P.M. curfew on juvenile gang members and banned the use of cellular phones and pagers. In addition, his injunction prohibited Eighteenth Street members from whistling in public—a form of signaling, the city attorney alleged, used by lookouts for drug dealers.[26]

As civil libertarians have pointed out, the social control district strategy penalizes individuals, even in the absence of a criminal act, merely for group membership. "Status criminalization," moreover, feeds off middle-class fantasies about the nature of the dangerous classes. And fearful fantasies have been growing in hothouse fashion.

In the mid–1980s, for example, the ghost of Cotton Mather suddenly appeared in suburban Southern California. Allegations that local day care centers were actually covens of satanic perversion wrenched courtrooms back to the seventeenth century. In the course of the McMartin Preschool molestation trial—the longest and most expensive such ordeal in American history—children testified about molester-teachers who flew around on broomsticks and other manifestations of the Evil One.

The creation by the little city of San Dimas of the nation's first "child-molestation exclusion zone" was one legacy of the accompanying collective hysteria, which undoubtedly mined huge veins of displaced parental guilt. This Twin Peaks-like suburb in the eastern San Gabriel Valley was sign posted from stem to stern with the warning: "Hands Off Our Kids! We ID and Fingerprint Our Kids for Safety." It is unclear whether the armies of lurking pedophiles in the mountains above San Dimas were deterred by these warnings, but any post-Burgess mapping of urban space must acknowledge the power that bad dreams now wield over the public landscape.

The Neighbors Are Watching

The Neighborhood Watch program—comprising more than 5,500 crime surveillance block clubs—is the LAPD's most important contribution to urban policing.... [A] huge network of watchful neighbors provides a security system midway between the besieged, gun-toting homeowners of the transition zone and the private police forces of more affluent, gated suburbs. The brainchild of former police chief Ed Davis, the Neighborhood Watch concept has been emulated in hundreds of North American and European cities from Seattle to London. In the aftermath of the 1965–71 cycle of unrest in South Central and East Los Angeles, Davis envisaged the program as the anchor for a "basic car" policing strategy designed to rebuild community support for the LAPD. He wanted to reestablish a strong territorial identity between patrol units and individual neighborhoods. Although his successor Daryl Gates preferred the commando bravado of SWAT units to the public-relations-oriented basic car patrols, Neighborhood Watch continued to flourish throughout the 1980s.

According to LAPD spokesperson Sgt. Christopher West, "Neighborhood Watch clubs are intended to increase local solidarity and self-confidence in the face of crime. Spurred by their block captains, residents become vigilant in the protection of each other's property and well-being. Suspicious behavior is immediately reported and homeowners regularly meet with patrol officers to plan crime-prevention tactics." An off-duty cop in a Winchell's Donut Shop in Silver Lake was more picturesque. "Neighborhood Watch is like the wagon train in an old-fashioned cowboy movie. The neighbors are the settlers and the goal is to teach them to circle their wagons and fight off the Indians until the cavalry—the LAPD—can ride to their rescue."[27]

Needless to say, this Wild West analogy has its sinister side. Who, after all, gets to decide what behavior is "suspicious" or who looks like an "Indian?" The obvious danger in any program that conscripts thousands of citizens as police informers under the official slogan "Be on the Look Out for Strangers" is that it inevitably stigmatizes innocent groups. Inner city teenagers are especially vulnerable to flagrant stereotyping and harassment.

At one Neighborhood Watch meeting I attended in Echo Park, an elderly white woman asked a young policeman how to identify hardcore gang members. His answer was stupefyingly succinct: "Gang-bangers wear expensive athletic shoes and clean, starched tee-shirts." The woman nodded her appreciation of this "expert" advice, while others in the audience squirmed in their seats at the thought of the youth in the neighborhood who would eventually be stopped and searched simply because they were well groomed.

Critics also worry that Neighborhood Watch does double duty as a captive constituency for police interests. As Sgt. West acknowledged, "Block captains are appointed by patrol officers and the program does obviously tend to attract the most law-and-order conscious members of the community." These pro-police residents, moreover, tend to be unrepresentative of their neighborhoods. In poor, youthful Latino areas, Watch captains are frequently elderly, residual Anglos. In areas where renters are a majority, the Watch activists are typically homeowners or landlords. Although official regulations are supposed to keep the program apolitical, block captains have long been regarded as the LAPD's precinct workers. In a bitter 1986 election, for example, the police union routinely used Neighborhood Watch meetings to campaign for the recall of the liberal majority, led by Rose Bird, on the California Supreme Court.

The "community policing advisory boards" established in the wake of the Rodney King beating have been hardly more independent. Although a reform commission headed by Warren Christopher criticized the LAPD's refusal to respond to citizen complaints, it failed to provide for elected advisory boards. As with Watch groups, board members serve strictly at the pleasure of local police commanders. When the Venice advisory board endorsed a spring 1992 ballot measure crafted by the Christopher Commission but opposed by the police union, they were summarily fired by the captain in charge of the Pacific Division.[28]

Since the 1992 riots some Neighborhood Watch groups have, with police encouragement, engaged in forms of surveillance that verge on vigilantism. In the San Fernando Valley, for example, volunteers from the white, upper-income neighborhoods of Porter Ranch
and Granada Hills have been informally deputized as stealth auxiliaries in the police war
against black and Latino gang youth. Clad in black ninja gear, they "perch in the dark on
rooftops or crouch in vacant apartments, peering through shrouded windows," in hopes of
photographing or videotaping graffiti taggers and drug peddlers. In a twist on the Rodney
King affair, the videos are then used by the police as evidence in court.[29]

Several law-and-order pundits believe that Los Angeles needs to go even further and
like Israel "flood the streets... every bus, shop and public space" with armed auxiliaries
trained at police firing ranges and recruited from the respectable classes ("over forty and
with a clean criminal record").[30] As a first approximation to this ideal "vigilantopolis,"
the LAPD has turned a blind eye on openly aimed and menacing groups of homeowners
and businessmen. In the Mid-City area, the ethnic enclave of "Koreatown" bristles with
automatic weapons and informal militias composed of veterans of the Korean military who
promise "punishment in kind" in the event of another attack on their businesses. Similarly
in Hollywood, a member of the county Republican Central Committee claims that she has
organized a gun-toting posse "old West style" to render summary justice to looters in the
next riot:

> Civilians can deal with crime more easily because we are not hampered by
> constitutional restrictions like the police. We can slam and jam. People were
> nice in the last riot. Next time we will shoot looters first and ask questions later.
> A lot of blood will be spilled.[31]

The Gulag Rim

The road from Mecca follows the Southern Pacific tracks past Bombay Beach to Niland,
then turns due south through a green maze of marshes and irrigated fields. The bad future of
Southern California rises, with little melodrama, in the middle distance between the skel-
eton of last year's cotton crop and the aerial bombing range in the Chocolate Mountains.
From a mile away, the slate-gray structures resemble warehouses or perhaps a factory. An
unassuming road sign announces "Calipatria State Prison." This is the outer rim of Los
Angeles's ecology of fear....[32]

Calipatria, which opened in 1993, is a "level 4," maximum security prison that currently houses 10 percent of California's convicted murderers, 1,200 men. Yet the guard
booth at the main gate is unmanned, as are 10 of its 12 perimeter gun towers. If the startling absence of traditional surveillance looks negligent, it is deliberate policy. As Daniel
Paramo, the prison's energetic public relations officer, explains, "The warden doesn't trust
the human-error factor in the gun towers; he puts his faith, instead, in Southern California
Edison."[33]

Paramo is standing in front of an ominous 13-foot electric fence, sandwiched between
two ordinary chain-link fences. Each of the 15 individual strands of wire bristles with
5,000 volts of Parker Dam power—about 10 times the recognized lethal dosage. The elec-

trical contractors guarantee instantaneous death. (An admiring guard in the background mutters: "Yeah, toast....")

The original bill authorizing the high voltage "escape-proof" fence sailed through the legislature with barely a murmur. Cost-conscious politicians had few scruples about an electric bill that saved $2 million in labor costs each year. And when the warden quietly threw the main switch in November 1993, there was general satisfaction that the corrections system was moving ahead, with little controversy, toward its high-tech future. "But," Paramo adds ruefully, "we had neglected to factor the animal-rights people into the equation."

The prison is just east of the Salton Sea—a major wintering habitat for waterfowl and the gently purring high-voltage fence immediately became an erotic beacon to passing birds. Local bird-watchers soon found out about the body count ("a gull, two owls, a finch and a scissor-tailed flycatcher") and alerted the Audubon Society. By January, Calipatria's "death fence" was an international environmental scandal. When a CNN crew pulled into the prison parking lot, the Department of Corrections threw in the towel and hired an ornithologist to help them redesign the fence.

The result is the world's only bird-proof, ecologically responsible death fence. Paramo has some difficulty maintaining a straight face as he points out $150,000 in innovations: "a warning wire for curious rodents, anti-perching deflectors for wildfowl, and tiny passageways for burrowing owls." Calipatria has also built an attractive pond for visiting geese and ducks.

Although the prison system is now at peace with bird lovers, the imbroglio roused the powerful California Correctional Peace Officers' Association (CCPOA) to question management's right to "automate" the jobs of the 30 sharpshooters (three shifts per tower) replaced by the fence. To proceed with his plan to lethally electrify all the state's medium and maximum security prisons (23 of 29 facilities) in the coming years, Director of Corrections Joe Gomez may have to negotiate a compromise with the CCPOA that preserves more of the "featherbed" gun tower jobs.

Calipatria's four thousand inmates, most of them from the tough ghettos and barrios of Los Angeles County, shed few tears for either the ducks or the guards. Their lives are entirely absorbed in the daily struggle to survive soul-destroying claustrophobia and ever threatening racial violence. Like the rest of the system, Calipatria operates at almost double its design capacity. In the state's medium security facilities, squalid tiers of bunk beds have been crowded into converted auditoriums and day rooms much as in overflowing county jails. In "upscale" level–4 institutions like Calipatria, on the other hand, a second inmate has simply been shoehorned into each of the tiny, six-by-ten-foot one-man cells.

When "double-celling" was first introduced into the system a decade ago, it helped fuel a wave of inmate violence and suicide. Civil liberties advocates denounced the practice as "cruel and unusual punishment," but a federal judge upheld its constitutionality. Now inmates can routinely expect to spend decades or even lifetimes (40 percent of Calipatria's population are lifers) locked in unnatural, and often unbearable, intimacy with another person. The psychological stress is amplified by a shortage of prison jobs that condemns nearly half the inmate population to serve their sentences idly in their cells watching infinities of television. As behavioral psychologists have testified in court, rats confined in such circumstances invariably go berserk and eat each other.

The abolition of privacy, together with the suppression of inmate counterculture, are explicit objectives of "new generation" prisons like Calipatria. Each of its 20 housing units is designed like a two-story horseshoe with a guard station opposite. Yet another variation on Jeremy Bentham's celebrated eighteenth-century panopticon prison, this "270 plan" (referring to the guards' field of vision) is intended to ensure continuous surveillance of all inmate behavior. Official blurbs boast of a "more safe and humane incarceration" and an end to the "fear-hate syndrome" associated with prisons that tolerate zones of unsupervised inmate interaction.

In practice, however, panopticonism has been compromised by construction shortcuts and chronic understaffing. Although toilets sit nakedly in the middle of the recreational yards as symbols of institutional omniscience, there are still plenty of blind spots—behind tier stairs or in unsurveilled kitchen areas where—inmates can take revenge on staff or one another. As Paramo warns visitors when they sign the grim waiver acknowledging California's policy of refusing to negotiate for hostages, "The war is on."

For a quarter of a century, California prisons have institutionalized episodic violence between inmate guerrilla armies. The original order of battle, after the death of Black Panther leader George Jackson in 1971, allied the Black Guerilla Family and La Nuestra Familia (mainly Northern California Latinos) against the Aryan Brotherhood and the East L.A.-based Mexican Mafia (or EME). Today there are also rising Asian and Central American gangs, but the carnage has been centralized into a merciless struggle for power between blacks and the EME.

...

To deal with such explosions, California's higher level prisons have introduced new and extreme sanctions. Each institution, for example, now has its own internal SWAT unit—or Special Emergency Response Team—capable of countering outbreaks with staggering amounts of firepower and paramilitary expertise. These elite units have been widely praised for preventing inmate-upon-inmate slaughters like that in the New Mexico State Penitentiary in 1984. The price of such prevention, however, sems to be an extraordinary toleration of official violence. Over the last decade, trigger-happy guards have killed 38 inmates in California institutions (including three in Calipatria)—more than triple the *total* of the six other leading prison population states and the federal penitentiary system combined.[34]

Staff at Calipatria speak with measured awe of CCPOA president Don Novey, a former Folsom prison guard, who has made the Correctional Officers the most powerful union in the state. Under his leadership, the CCPOA has been transformed from a small, reactive craft union into the major player shaping criminal justice legislation and, thereby, the future of the California penal system. Part of the secret of Novey's success has been his willingness to pay the highest price for political allies. In 1990, for example, Novey contributed nearly $1 million to Pete Wilson's gubernatorial campaign, and CCPOA now operates the second most generous PAC in Sacramento.[35]

Novey has also leveraged CCPOA's influence through his sponsorship of the so-called victims' rights movement. Crime Victims United, for example, is a satellite PAC receiving 95 percent of its funding from CCPOA. Through such high-profile front groups, and in alliance with other law enforcement lobbies, Novey has been able to keep Sacramento in a permanent state of law-and-order hysteria. Legislators of both parties trample each other in the rush to put their names at the top of new, tougher anticrime measures, while ignoring the progressive imbalance between the number of felons sentenced to prison and the existing capacity of Department of Corrections facilities.[36]

This cynical competition has had staggering consequences. Rand Corporation researcher Joan Petersilia found that "more than 1,000 bills changing felony and misdemeanor statutes" had been enacted by the legislature between 1984 and 1992. Taken together, they are utterly incoherent as criminal justice policy, but wonderful as a stimulus to the kind of carceral Keynesianism that has tripled both the membership and the average salary of the CCPOA since 1980. While California's colleges and universities were shedding 8,000 jobs, the Department of Corrections hired 26,000 new employees to guard 112,000 new inmates. As a result, California is now the proud owner of the third largest penal system in the world (after China and the United States as a whole).[37]

A host of critics, including an official blue ribbon commission, have tried to wean the legislature from its reckless gulagism. They have produced study after study showing that superincarceration has had a negligible impact on the overall crime rate, and that a majority of new inmates are either nonviolent drug offenders (including parolees flunking mandatory urinalysis) or the mentally ill (28,000 inmates by official estimate). They have also repeatedly warned that a day of reckoning will come when the state will have to trade higher education, literally brick by brick, to continue to build prisons.[38]

Politicians do not dispute that this day is now close at hand. When one education leader in testimony before the legislature pointed to the inverse relationship between the college and prison budgets, state senator Frank Hill (R-Whittier) acidly retored: "If push came to shove, the average voter is going to be more supportive of prisons than of the University of California."[39] Although it costs taxpayers more than twice as much to send an 18-year-old to prison as to university, politicians reap greater rewards from lobbyists and conservative voters for building cells than for building classrooms.

It was not surprising, therefore, that the legislature instead of hitting the brakes went full throttle in 1994 with a "three strikes" law (subsequently enshrined in the state constitution by a referendum in 1994) which doubles sentences for second felonies and mandates 25 years to life for three-time losers.[40] As a direct result, Department of Corrections planners predict a 262 percent increase in the penal population (to 341,420) by 2005 (as contrasted to 22,500 inmates in 1980). Commenting on these projections, a spokesman for Governor Wilson simply shrugged his shoulders: "If these additional costs have to be absorbed, I guess we'll have to reduce other services. We'll have to change our priorities.[41]

It is sobering to recall that the Department of Corrections with 29 major "campuses" is already more expensive than the University of California system, and that young black men in Los Angeles and Oakland are twice as likely to end up in prison as in college. The three strikes law, moreover, is widening racial disparities in sentencing. According to data from Los Angeles County public defenders, African-Americans made up 57 percent of the early three strikes filings, although they are only 10 percent of the population. This is 17 times the rate of whites, although other studies have shown that white men commit at least 60 percent of rapes, robberies, and assaults.[42] The majority-suburban legislature, however, has been unfazed by studies demonstrating the profound racial inequities of recent criminal legislation.

Initial hopes that Cruz Bustamante—the Fresno Democrat who in 1997 became the first modern Latino Assembly Speaker—would restore some sanity to crime-and-punishment debates were quickly dashed when Bustamante tried to outflank Governor Wilson on the subject of capital punishment for minors. When Wilson suggested death sentences for criminals as young as 14 (the current minimum age is 18), Bustamante responded that he might "with a tear in my eye, cast a vote to execute 'hardened criminals' as young as 13." (Thanks to bipartisan legislation in 1996, 14-year-olds in California can already be tried as adults and receive life imprisonment for serious felonies.)[43]

To Tom Hayden—one of the few members of the legislature to publicly denounce the three strikes legislation—such bravado about executing children is more proof that California is sinking into a "moral quagmire... reminiscent of Vietnam." "State politics has been handcuffed by the law enforcement lobby. Voters have no real idea of what they are getting into. They have not been told the truth about the trade-off between schools and prisons, or the economic disaster that will inevitably result. We dehumanize criminals and the poor in exactly the same way we did with so-called gooks in Vietnam. We just put them in hell and turn up the heat.[44]

Endnotes

[1]Mike Davis, "The Infinite Game: Redeveloping Downtown L.A.," in Diane Ghirardo (ed.), *Out of Site: A Social Criticism of Architecture* (Seattle, 1991).

[2]Jim Hathcock, "Security Firms Overwhelmed by Sudden Demand for Riot Protection," *Los Angeles Business Journal* 27 July 1992.

[3]*LAT* 6 August 1993 (Ventura County edition).

[4]This is based on my first-hand reportage of the Los Angeles riot, "In L.A., Burning All Illusions," *Nation,* 1 June 1992. For an extended discussion of the riot's origins and immediate aftermath, see my "Who Killed Los Angeles?" *New Left Review* 197 (January-February 1993) and 199 (May-June 1993).

[5]Riot incident and arrest figures from William Webster, special advisor to the Board of Police Commissioners, *The City in Crisis: Appendices* (Los Angeles, 21 October 1992).

[6]Don Hazen, ed., *Inside the L.A. Riots: What Really Happened—and Why It Will Happen Again* (New York: Institute for Alternative Journalism, 1992).

[7]Vilma Ortiz, "The Mexican-Origin Population: Permanent Working Class or Emerging Middle Class?," in Roger Waldinger and Mehdi Bozorgmehr, eds., *Ethnic Los Angeles* (New York: Russell Sage, 1996), p. 257.

[8]The seminal study is Paul Ong, project director of the Research Group on the Los Angeles Economy, *The Widening Divide: Income Inequality and Poverty in Los Angeles,* report, Graduate School of Architecture and Urban Planning (UCLA, 1989), p. 101 and *passim*.

[9]Cf. Stephen Cohen, "L.A. Is the Hole in the Bucket," *LAT* 8 March 1993; Benjamin Cole, "Industrial Study Long on Problems, Short on Remedies," *Los Angeles Business Journal* 14 November 1994, p. 22; and DRI/McGraw Hill, *Gateway Cities Economic Strategy Initiative* (Downey, 1996), p. ii (executive summary).

[10]Jennifer Wolch and Heidi Sommer, *Los Angeles in an Era of Welfare Reform: Implications for Poor People and Community Well-Being* (Los Angeles: Human Services Network, 1997), pp. iv, 8, 11, 71.

[11]Photograph by Jim Mendenhall, *LAT* 22 December 1991.

[12]Wolch and Sommer, *Los Angeles,* p. 96.

[13]Letter from Mike Dreebin, 28 March 1993.

[14]Repeated LAPD attempts "to take back the park," involving horse patrols, barricades, and 80-officer sweeps, usually end up trawling dozens of harmless but illegal street vendors. The gangs and crack dealers return as soon as the police leave.

[15]*LAT* 19 October 1992.

[16]LAT 20 July 1986.

[17]In 1991, doctors at County-USC Medical Center told state officials that patients were dying because operating rooms were full and they were prematurely moved from ventilators. "We are being required to ration health care and at times to perform what amounts to passive euthanasia" (see *LAT* 18 December 1981).

[18]*LAT* 27 January 1994.

[19]*LAT* 9 February 1995.

[20]Cf. Mary Jordan, "I Will Not Fire Guns in School. I Will Not Fire Guns in School," *Washington Post National Weekly Edition* 5–11 July 1993; and Kathleen Lund-Seeden, "Schools Step Up Security," *Outlook* (Santa Monica), 24 March 1992.

[21]The Puerto Rican case—"the first time U.S. military units have been pressed into routine crime-fighting service with the police"—is an ominous precedent little appreciated on the mainland ("Puerto Rico Uses Troops to Occupy Housing Project," AP wire story, 2 October 1993).

[22]*LAT* 22 November 1997.

[23]*LAT* 26 September 1993.

[24]*LAT* 4 May 1994 and 11 October 1995.

[25]For the critical views of the LAPD deputy chief Michael Bostic, see *LAT* 23 November 1997.

[26]*LAT* 22 May 1997.

[27]What follows is based on interviews with the LAPD used in my article, "Vigilancia Policial Comunitaria: Ventajas y Desventajas," *La Opinion* (Los Angeles) 17 May 1992.

[28]*LAT* 15 April 1992.

[29]*LAT* 17 March and 2 June 1993.

[30]*LAT* 3 May 1993.

[31]Interview with E. Michael, July 1992.

[32]What follows is based on formal interviews of prison staff at Calipatria State Prison in November 1994. In January 1995 I also spoke to several families of inmates, as well as one (anonymous) guard.

[33]All statistics double-checked with Department of Corrections, "Institutional Population Characteristics" (Sacramento, August 1994).

[34]*LAT* 27 October 1994.

[35]Cf. *LAT* 6 February 1994; Joe Dominick, "Who's Guarding the Guards?" *Los Angeles Weekly* 2 September 1004; and Vincent Schiraldi, "The Undue Influence of California's Prison Guards' Union," *In Brief* (Center on Juvenile and Criminal Justice, San Francisco), October 1994.

[36]Ibid.

[37]Joan Petersilia, "Crime and Punishment in California," in James Steinberg et al. (eds.), *Urban America: Policy Choices for Los Angeles and the Nation* (Santa Monica, 1992).

[38]Blue Ribbon Commission on Inmate Population Management, *Final Report* (Sacramento, January 1990).

[39]San Francisco *Chronicle* 26 April 1993.

[40]Cf. *LAT* 1 March 1994.

[41]Cf. James Gomez, director of Department of Corrections, "Memorandum: Impact of 'Three Strikes' on Occupancy Level and Future Bed Needs," 4 March 1994; Department of Corrections, *Statewide Emergency Housing Information* (Sacramento, 6 January 1995); and Department of Corrections, 1996–2001 *Five-year Facilities Master Plan* (Sacramento, June 1996).

[42]Vincent Schiraldi and Michael Godfrey, "Racial Disparities in the Charging of Los Angeles County's Third "Strike" Cases," *In Brief*, October 1994.

[43]*LAT* 11 April 1997.

[44]Interview with Tom Hayden, January 1995.

Police and the Black Male*

Elijah Anderson

The police in the Village-Northton, as elsewhere, represent society's formal, legitimate means of social control.[1] Their role includes protecting law-abiding citizens from those who are not law-abiding by preventing crime and by apprehending likely criminals. Precisely how the police fulfill the public's expectations is strongly related to how they view the neighborhood and the people who live there. On the streets, color-coding often works to confuse race, age, class, gender, incivility, and criminality, and it expresses itself most concretely in the person of the anonymous black male. In doing their job, the police often become willing parties to this general colorcoding of the public environment and related distinctions, particularly those of skin color and gender, come to convey definite meanings. Although such coding may make the work of the police more manageable, it may also fit well with their own presuppositions regarding race and class relations, thus shaping officers' perceptions of crime "in the city." Moreover, the anonymous black male is usually an ambiguous figure who arouses the utmost caution and is generally considered dangerous until he proves he is not.

In July 1988, in the area just south of the Village, my own automobile was taken from its parking place on a main thoroughfare. Convinced that a thief had stolen the car, I quickly summoned the police. Within ten minutes of my calling 911 a police car arrived, driven by a middle-aged white officer. He motioned for me to get in. Because the front seat was cluttered with notebooks and papers. I opened the back door and got in on the right-hand side. I introduced myself to Officer John Riley, mentioning that I was a professor, mainly to help establish myself with him. He was courteous, commiserated with me, then asked for the basic information. What time did I park the car? Could a friend or relative have taken it? During our exchanges I said that my family and I were planning a trip to the Midwest the next day to attend a family reunion, and I could feel his empathy. He said he would call in the report right away, and since the case was "hot," meaning the theft had just occurred, there might be a good chance of getting the car back soon, if not that very night. He then reported the theft and put out a bulletin. Into his radio he said, "Be on the lookout for a maroon 1982 Oldsmobile four-door sedan, heading northwest on Warrington

*Elijah Anderson, *Streetwise: Race, Class, and Change in an Urban Community* (Chicago: The University of Chicago Press, 1990). Reprinted with permission.

Avenue." Every police car in the city, particularly those in the same district, was thus given a description of my car and would presumably be on the lookout for it. I was pleased with his attention to my misfortune.

As we sat in the patrol car, the officer interviewed me; and I took the opportunity to interview him as well. We spoke about policing the local area, about car thefts, and about the general crime rate. We discussed the characteristics of car thieves, robbers, muggers, and other antisocial persons in the area. I did not tell him I was a sociologist. I think he thought of himself as simply doing his job, treating me as just another victim of local crime—which I was indeed.

During this conversation the police officer seemed to be feeling me out, attempting to get a fix on me as a person, perhaps wondering where I stood politically. At one point we discussed jobs and crime and their relation to one another. Then the officer mentioned the way "he" had messed up this city and how the "big boys" had already gotten to "him." I took this as implicit criticism of the city's black mayor, so I deferred and listened intently, thinking I could learn something about his attitude concerning local city politics. But I also did not want to alienate this person who was trying to find my car. Hence I played along, pointing out that the mayor's stock had declined in the black community, that even many blacks were not satisfied with his performance.

After this conversational give and take, the officer seemed favorably impressed. He appeared genuinely sympathetic with my fear of missing my family reunion. More than once he suggested that I try to forget the theft for now, rent a Lincoln Town Car like his own, and drive to the reunion. I demurred, insisting that I wanted my own car back as soon as possible.

Through our conversation, he seemed to open up and trust me. Then he offered, "Listen, why don't we drive around and see if we can spot your car. Maybe some kids just took it for a joyride and ditched it." I was appreciative and encouraged him, but I stayed in the backseat, wondering where he would take me to look for my car. We headed north through the Village, across Bellwether, and into Northton. After driving up and down a number of the familiar streets of Northton, we headed for "the projects," about a mile northwest of the Village. When I asked why he had chosen to come here, he replied, "This is where they usually take them [cars]." It seemed he had a definite idea who he was talking about. They were the thieves, the robbers, the muggers, and generally the people who cause trouble. And they lived in Northton. As we proceeded, we passed numerous street corner groups of young black men, with some young women among them. Many were simply loitering. He knew some of them and greeted them in a familiar way as we slowly drove past. He would wave and say, "How y'all doin'" in what sounded like affected Black English. By showing this level of familiarity, he let me know he knew the community: it was to some degree his turf.

As we drove through the projects and the neighborhoods of Northton, ostensibly looking for my car, I felt strange—as though I was somehow identified with "the enemy"— though I was safe in the backseat. Also, when a young black man is sitting in a police car, most people perceive him to be in custody, in some kind of trouble, regardless of the real circumstances. This seems to go with the general definition of affairs in the neighborhood—that to be black and male, particularly when young, is to be suspect; that the young man must prove he is law-abiding. Even though I was sitting in the backseat, so that many onlookers might know the officer considered me "safe" or a victim to be aided, this reality goes strongly against the common sense of the community: a young black male is a suspect until he proves he is not. The burden of proof is not easily lifted.

After riding around Northton for about twenty minutes, we met another police car. The driver, who was white, middle-aged, and alone, had stopped at the corner, preparing to make a right-hand turn. My driver turned left onto the same street, and both stopped with the two cars facing in opposite directions. As they exchanged pleasantries, the second policeman kept looking at me with puzzlement. Black male alone in rear seat. Officer Riley felt the need to explain me and said, "Oh, somebody stole his car, and we're out looking for it. It's a maroon '82 Delta 88. The other policeman nodded. The two continued to make small talk, but the second officer could not keep his eyes off me. I felt that if I made a false move he would come after me. In essence the policeman played his role, and I played mine; notwithstanding that I was a victim of crime, my color and gender seemed to outweigh other claims.

Such roles are expected by the young black men of the neighborhood, who have a clear sense of who they are and what they mean to the police. It is from this knowledge that they infer how to act, and how the police will act, believing both must behave according to an elaborate script of the streets. Much of this may be viewed as symbolic display, but it works to maintain a certain ordering of affairs in the public arena.

In the presence of police officers, who clearly have the upper hand, black youths check themselves. They defer to the police or try to avoid them. And some black men, because of their profound distrust of the criminal justice system, say they would never allow a white policeman to arrest them. A young black male told me, "A white policeman would never go out of his way for a black man."

After about fifteen minutes the policemen finished their talk and said their good-byes. Meanwhile I was simply a nonperson, not their equal, and my time and business were clearly secondary in their minds. As we drove slowly up and down the streets, Officer Riley continued to nod, speak, and wave to people. Finally he gave up, saying he was "sorry, but maybe we'll have some luck tonight or tomorrow. I'll stay on it, and hopefully we'll get your car back." He then offered me a ride home, which I gladly accepted. On the way Officer Riley talked about his own misfortunes with theft, attempting to commiserate with me. I saw one of my white colleagues on a street corner near my house, reading a newspaper while waiting for a bus. As the patrol car pulled up to the light, he casually looked over at me, looked away, then looked again with astonishment. "Eli! Is that you? Are you okay? What's the trouble?" I quickly assured him that everything was all right, that I was with the policeman because my car had been stolen. But my colleague looked unconvinced. The light changed and Officer Riley drove toward my house. He again expressed his regret for my predicament but said he was hopeful. We parted company and I never saw him again. But the next morning at 9:00 I got a call that my car had been found and I could come and retrieve it.

There are some who charge—and as this account indicates, perhaps with good reason—that the police are primarily agents of the middle class who are working to make the area more hospitable to middle-class people at the expense of the lower classes. It is obvious that the police assume whites in the community are at least middle class and are trustworthy on the streets. Hence the police may be seen primarily as protecting "law-abiding" middle-class whites against anonymous "criminal" black males.

To be white is to be seen by the police—at least superficially—as an ally, eligible for consideration and for much more deferential treatment than that accorded blacks in general.

This attitude may be grounded in the backgrounds of the police themselves. Many have grown up in Eastern City's "ethnic" neighborhoods.[2] They may serve what they perceive as their own class and neighborhood interests, which often translates as keeping blacks "in their place"—away from neighborhoods that are socially defined as "white." In trying to do their job, the police appear to engage in an informal policy of monitoring young black men as a means of controlling crime, and often they seem to go beyond the bounds of duty. The following field note shows what pressures and racism young black men in the Village may endure at the hands of the police:

> At 8:30 on a Thursday evening in June I saw a police car stopped on a side street near the Village. Beside the car stood a policeman with a young black man. I pulled up behind the police car and waited to see what would happen. When the policeman released the young man, I got out of my car and asked the youth for an interview.
>
> "So what did he say to you when they stopped you? What was the problem?" I asked. "I was just coming around the corner, and he stopped me, asked me what was my name, and all that. And what I had in my bag. And where I was coming from. Where I lived, you know, all the basic stuff, I guess. Then he searched me down and, you know, asked me who were the supposedly tough guys around here? That's about it. I couldn't tell him who they are. How do I know? Other gang members could, but I'm not from a gang, you know. But he tried to put me in a gang bag, though." "How old are you?" I asked. "I'm seventeen, I'll be eighteen next month." "Did he give any reason for stopping you?" "No, he didn't. He just wanted my address, where I lived, where I was coming from, that kind of thing. I don't have no police record or nothin'. I guess he stopped me on principle, 'cause I'm black." "How does that make you feel?" I asked. "Well, it doesn't bother me too much, you know, as long as I know that I hadn't done nothin', but I guess it just happens around here. They just stop young black guys and ask 'em questions, you know. What can you do?"

On the streets late at night, the average young black man is suspicious of others he encounters, and he is particularly wary of the police. If he is dressed in the uniform of the "gangster," such as a black leather jacket, sneakers, and a "gangster cap," if he is carrying a radio or a suspicious bag (which may be confiscated), or if he is moving too fast or too slow, the police may stop him. As part of the routine, they search him and make him sit in the police car while they run a check to see whether there is a "detainer" on him. If there is nothing, he is allowed to go on his way. After this ordeal the youth is often left afraid, sometimes shaking, and uncertain about the area he had previously taken for granted. He is upset in part because he is painfully aware of how close he has come to being in "big trouble." He knows of other youths who have gotten into a "world of trouble" simply by being on the streets at the wrong time or when the police were pursuing a criminal. In these circumstances, particularly at night, it is relatively easy for one black man to be mistaken for another. Over the years, while walking through the neighborhood I have on occasion been stopped and questioned by police chasing a mugger, but after explaining myself I was released.

Many youths, however, have reason to fear such mistaken identity or harassment, since they might be jailed, if only for a short time, and would have to post bail money and pay legal fees to extricate themselves from the mess (Anderson 1986). When law-abiding blacks are ensnared by the criminal justice system, the scenario may proceed as follows. A young man is arbitrarily stopped by the police and questioned. If he cannot effectively negotiate with the officer(s), he may be accused of a crime and arrested. To resolve this situation he needs financial resources, which for him are in short supply. If he does not have money for an attorney, which often happens, he is left to a public defender who may be more interested in going along with the court system than in fighting for a poor black person. Without legal support, he may well wind up "doing time" even if he is innocent of the charges brought against him. The next time he is stopped for questioning he will have a record, which will make detention all the more likely.

Because the young black man is aware of many cases when an "innocent" black person was wrongly accused and detained, he develops an "attitude" toward the police. The street word for police is "the man," signifying a certain machismo, power, and authority. He becomes concerned when he notices "the man" in the community or when the police focus on him because he is outside his own neighborhood. The youth knows, or soon finds out, that he exists in a legally precarious state. Hence he is motivated to avoid the police, and his public life becomes severely circumscribed.

To obtain fair treatment when confronted by the police, the young man may wage a campaign for social regard so intense that at times it borders on obsequiousness. As one streetwise black youth said: "If you show a cop that you nice and not a smartass, they be nice to you. They talk to you like the man you are. You gonna get ignorant like a little kid, they gonna get ignorant with you." Young black males often are particularly deferential toward the police even when they are completely within their rights and have done nothing wrong. Most often this is not out of blind acceptance or respect for the "law," but because they know the police can cause them hardship. When confronted or arrested, they adopt a particular style of behavior to get on the policeman's good side. Some simply "go limp" or politely ask, "What seems to be the trouble, officer?" This pose requires a deference that is in sharp contrast with the youths' more usual image, but many seem to take it in stride or not even to realize it. Because they are concerned primarily with staying out of trouble, and because they perceive the police as arbitrary in their use of power, many defer in an equally arbitrary way. Because of these pressures, however, black youths tend to be especially mindful of the police and, when they are around, to watch their own behavior in public. Many have come to expect harassment and are inured to it; they simply tolerate it as part of living in the Village-Northton.

After a certain age, say twenty-three or twenty-four, a black man may no longer be stopped so often, but he continues to be the object of police scrutiny. As one twenty-seven-year-old black college graduate speculated:

> I think they see me with my little bag with papers in it. They see me with penny loafers on. I have a tie on, some days. They don't stop me so much now. See, it depends on the circumstances. If something goes down, and they hear that the guy had on a big black coat, I may be the one. But when I was younger, they could just stop me, carte blanche, any old time. Name taken, searched, and this went on endlessly. From the time I was about twelve until I was sixteen or

seventeen, Endlessly, endlessly. And I come from a lower-middle-class black neighborhood, OK, that borders a white neighborhood. One neighborhood is all black, and one is all white. OK, just because we were so close to that neighborhood, we were stopped endlessly. And it happened even more when we went up into a suburban community. When we would ride up and out to the suburbs, we were stopped every time we did it.

If it happened today, now that I'm older. I would really be upset. In the old days when I was younger, I didn't know any better. You just expected it, you knew it was gonna happen. Cops would come up. "What you doing, where you coming from?" Say things to you. They might even call you nigger.

Such scrutiny and harassment by local police makes black youths see them as a problem to get beyond, to deal with, and their attempts affect their overall behavior. To avoid encounters with the man, some streetwise young men camouflage themselves, giving up the urban uniform and emblems that identify them as "legitimate" objects of police attention. They may adopt a more conventional presentation of self, wearing chinos, sweat suits, and generally more conservative dress. Some youths have been known to "ditch" a favorite jacket if they see others wearing one like it, because wearing it increases their chances of being mistaken for someone else who may have committed a crime.

But such strategies do not always work over the long run and must be constantly modified. For instance, because so many young ghetto blacks have begun to wear Fila and Adidas sweat suits as status symbols, such dress has become incorporated into the public image generally associated with young black males. These athletic suits, particularly the more expensive and colorful ones, along with high-priced sneakers. have become the leisure dress of successful drug dealers, and other youths will often mimic their wardrobe to "go for bad" in the quest for local esteem. Hence what was once a "square" mark of distinction approximating the conventions the wider culture has been adopted by a neighborhood group devalued by that same culture.

...

"Downtown" Police and Local Police

In attempting to manage the police—and by implication to manage themselves—some black youths have developed a working conception of the police in certain public areas of the Village-Northton. Those who spend a good amount of their time on these corners, and thus observing the police, have come to distinguish between the "downtown" police and the "regular" local police.

The local police are the ones who spend time in the area; normally they drive around in patrol cars, often one officer to a car. These officers usually make a kind of working peace with the young men on the streets; for example, they know the names of some of them and may even befriend a young boy. Thus they offer an image of the police department different from that displayed by the "downtown" police. The downtown police are distant, impersonal, and often actively looking for "trouble." They are known to swoop down arbitrarily on gatherings of black youths standing on a street corner; they might punch them around, call them names, and administer other kinds of abuse, apparently for sport. A young Northton man gave the following narrative about his experiences with the police.

And I happen to live in a violent part. There's a real difference between the violence level in the Village and the violence level in Northton. In the night-time it's more dangerous over there.

It's so bad now, they got downtown cops over there now. They doin' a good job bringin' the highway patrol over there. Regular cops don't like that. You can tell that. They even try to emphasize to us the certain category. Highway patrol come up, he leave, they say somethin' about it. "We can do our job over here." We call [downtown police] Nazis. They about six feet eight, seven feet. We walkin', they jump out. "You run, and we'll blow your nigger brains out." I hate bein' called a nigger. I want to say somethin' but get myself in trouble.

When a cop do somethin', nothing happen to 'em. They come from downtown. From what I heard some of 'em don't even wear their real badge numbers. So you have to put up with that. Just keep your mouth shut when they stop you, that's all. Forget about questions, get against the wall, just obey 'em. "Put all that out right there"—might get rough with you now. They snatch you by the shirt, throw you against the wall, pat you hard, and grab you by the arms, and say, "Get outta here." They call you nigger this and little black this, and things like that. I take that. Some of the fellas get mad. It's a whole different world.

Yeah, they lookin' for trouble. They gotta look for trouble when you got five, eight police cars together and they laughin' and talkin', start teasin' people. One night we were at a bar, we read in the paper that the downtown cops comin' to straighten things out. Same night, three police cars, downtown cops with their boots on, they pull the sticks out, beatin' around the corner, chase into bars. My friend Todd, one of 'em grabbed him and knocked the shit out of him. He punched 'im, a little short white guy. They start a riot. Cops started that shit. Everybody start seein' how wrong the cops was—they start throwin' bricks and bottles, cussin' 'em out. They lock my boy up; they had to let him go. He was just standin' on the corner, they snatch him like that.

One time one of 'em took a gun and began hittin' people. My boy had a little hickie from that. He didn't know who the cop was, because there was no such thing as a badge number. They have phony badge numbers. You can tell they're tougher, the way they dress, plus they're bigger. They have boots, trooper pants, blond hair, blue eyes, even black [eyes]. And they seven feet tall, and six foot six inches and six foot eight inches. Big! They the rough cops. You don't get smart with them or they beat the shit out of you in front of everybody, they don't care.

We call 'em Nazis. Even the blacks among them. They ride along with 'em. They stand there and watch a white cop beat your brains out. What takes me out is the next day you don't see em. Never see 'em again, go down there, come back, and they ride right back downtown, come back, do their little dirty work, go back downtown, and put their real badges on. You see 'em with a forty-five or fifty-five number: "Ain't no such number here. I'm sorry, son." Plus, they got unmarked cars. No sense takin' 'em to court. But when that happened at that bar, another black cop from the sixteenth [local] district, ridin' a real car, came back and said, "Why don't y'all go on over to the sixteenth district and file a complaint? Them musclin' cops was wrong. Beatin' people." So about ten people went over there; sixteenth district knew nothin' about it. They come in unmarked cars, they must have been downtown cops. Some of 'em do it. Some of 'em are off duty, on their way home. District commander told us they do that. They have a patrol over there, but them cops from downtown have control of them cops. Have bigger ranks and bigger guns. They carry .357s and regular cops carry little .38s. Downtown cops are all around. They carry magnums.

Two cars the other night. We sittin' on the steps playing cards. Somebody called the cops. We turn around and see four regular police cars and two highway police cars. We drinkin' beer and playin' cards. Police get out and say you're gamblin. We say we got nothin' but cards here, we bet no money. They said all right, got back in their cars, and drove away. Downtown cops dressed up like troopers. That's intimidation. Damn!

You call a cop. they don't come. My boy got shot, we had to take him to the hospital ourselves. A cop said. "You know who did it?" We said no. He said. "Well, I hope he dies if y'all don't say nothing." What he say that for? My boy said, "I hope your mother die," he told the cop right to his face. And I was grabbin' another cop, and he made a complaint about that. There were a lot of witnesses. Even the nurse behind the counter said the cop had no business saying nothin' like that. He said it loud. "I hope he dies." Nothin' like that should be comin' from a cop.

Such behavior by formal agents of social control may reduce the crime rate, but it raises questions about social justice and civil rights. Many of the old-time liberal white residents of the Village view the police with some ambivalence. They want their streets and homes defended, but many are convinced that the police manhandle "kids" and mete out an arbitrary form of "justice." These feelings make many of them reluctant to call the police when they are needed, and they may even be less than completely cooperative after a crime has been committed. They know that far too often the police simply "go out and pick up some poor black kid." Yet they do cooperate, if ambivalently, with these agents of social control.

In an effort to gain some balance in the emerging picture of the police in the Village-Northton, I interviewed local officers. The following edited conversation with Officer George Dickens (white) helps place in context the fears and concerns of local residents, including black males:

I'm sympathetic with the people who live in this neighborhood [the Village-Northton), who I feel are victims of drugs. There are a tremendous number of decent, hardworking people who are just trying to live their life in peace and quiet, not cause any problems for their neighbors, not cause any problems for themselves. They just go about their own business and don't bother anyone. The drug situation as it exists in Northton today causes them untold problems. And some of the young kids are involved in one way or another with this drug culture. As a result, they're gonna come into conflict even with the police they respect and have some rapport with.

We just went out last week on Thursday and locked up ten young men on Cherry Street, because over a period of about a week, we had undercover police officers making drug buys from those young men. This was very well documented and detailed. They were videotaped selling the drugs. And as a result, right now, if you walk down Cherry Street, it's pretty much a ghost town; there's nobody out. [Before, Cherry Street was notorious for drug traffic.] Not only were people buying drugs there, but it was a very active street. There's been some shock value as a result of all those arrests at one time.

Now, there's two reactions to that. The [television] reporters went out and interviewed some people who said, "Aw, the police overreacted, they locked up innocent people. It was terrible, it was harassment." One of the neighbors from Cherry Street called me on Thursday, and she was outraged. Because she said, "Officer, it's not fair. We've been working with the district for well over a year trying to solve some of the problems on Cherry Street." But most of the neighbors were thrilled that the police came and locked all those kids up. So you're getting two conflicting reactions here. One from the people that live there that just wanta be left alone, alright? Who are really being harassed by the drug trade and everything that's involved in it. And then you have a reaction from the people that are in one way or another either indirectly connected or directed connected, where they say, "You know, if a young man is selling drugs, to him that's a job." And if he gets arrested, he's out of a job. The family's lost their income. So they're not gonna pretty much want anybody to come in there to make arrests. So you've got contradicting elements of the community there. My philosophy is that we're going to try to make Northton livable. If that means we have to arrest some of the residents of Northton, that's what we have to do.

You talk to Tyrone Pitts, you know the group that they formed was formed because of a reaction to complaints against one of the officers of how the teenagers were being harassed. And it turned out that basically what he [the officer] was doing was harassing drug dealers. When Northton against Drugs actually formed and seemed to jell, they developed a close working relationship with the police here. For that reason, they felt the officer was doing his job.

I've been here eighteen months. I've seen this neighborhood go from ... Let me say, this is the only place I've ever worked where I've seen a rapport between the police department and the general community like the one we have right now. I've never seen it anyplace else before coming here. And I'm not gonna claim credit because this happened while I happened to be here. I think a lot of different factors were involved. I think the community was ready to work with the police because of the terrible situation in reference to crack. My favorite expression when talking about crack is "crack changed everything." Crack changed the rules of how the police and the community have to interact with each other. Crack changed the rules about how the criminal justice system is gonna work, whether it works well or poorly. Crack is causing the prisons to be overcrowded. Crack is gonna cause the people that do drug rehabilitation to be overworked. It's gonna cause a wide variety of things.

And I think the reason the rapport between the police and the community in Northton developed at the time it did is very simply that drugs to a certain extent made many areas in this city unlivable.

In effect the officer is saying that the residents, regardless of former attitudes, are now inclined to be more sympathetic with the police and to work with them. And at the same time, the police are more inclined to work with the residents. Thus, not only are the police and the black residents of Northton working together, but different groups in the Village and Northton are working with each other against drugs. In effect, law-abiding citizens are coming together, regardless of race, ethnicity, and class. He continues:

Both of us (police and the community] are willing to say, "Look, let's try to help each other." The nice thing about what was started here is that it's spreading to the rest of the city. If we don't work together, this problem is gonna devour us. It's gonna eat us alive. It's a state of emergency, more or less.

In the past there was significant negative feeling among young black men about the "downtown" cops coming into the community and harassing them. In large part these feelings continue to run strong, though many young men appear to "know the score" and to be resigned to their situation, accommodating and attempting to live with it. But as the general community feels under attack, some residents are willing to forgo certain legal and civil rights and undergo personal inconvenience in hopes of obtaining a sense of law and order. The officer continues:

Today we don't have too many complaints about police harassment in the community. Historically there were these complaints, and in almost any minority neighborhood in Eastern City where I ever worked there was more or less a feeling of that [harassment]. It wasn't just Northton; it was a feeling that the police were the enemy. I can honestly say that for the first time in my career I don't feel that people look at me like I'm the enemy. And it feels nice; it feels real good not to be the enemy, ha-ha. I think we [the police] realize that a lot of the problems here [in the Village-Northton] are related to drugs. I think the neighborhood realizes that too. And it's a matter of "Who are we gonna be angry with? Are we gonna be angry with the police because we feel like they're this army of occupation, or are we gonna argue with these people who are selling drugs to our kids and shooting up our neighborhoods and generally causing havoc in the area? Who deserves the anger more?" And I think, to a large extent, people of the Village-Northton decided it was the drug dealers and not the police.

I would say there are probably isolated incidents where the police would stop a male in an area where there is a lot of drugs, and this guy may be perfectly innocent, not guilty of doing anything at all. And yet he's stopped by the police because he's specifically in that area, on that street corner where we know drugs are going hog wild. So there may be isolated incidents of that. At the same time, I'd say I know for a fact that our complaints against police in this division, the whole division, were down about 45 percent. If there are complaints, if there are instances of abuse by the police, I would expect that our complaints would be going up. But they're not; they're dropping.

Such is the dilemma many Villagers face when they must report a crime or deal in some direct way with the police. Stories about police prejudice against blacks are often traded at Village get-togethers. Cynicism about the effectiveness of the police mixed with community suspicion of their behavior toward blacks keeps middle-class Villagers from embracing the notion that they must rely heavily on the formal means of social control to maintain even the minimum freedom of movement they enjoy on the streets.

Many residents of the Village, especially those who see themselves as the "old guard" or "old-timers," who were around during the good old days when antiwar and antiracist protest was a major concern, sigh and turn their heads when they see the criminal justice system operating in the ways described here. They express hope that "things will work out," that tensions will ease, that crime will decrease and police behavior will improve. Yet as incivility and crime become increasing problems in the neighborhood, whites become less tolerant of anonymous blacks and more inclined to embrace the police as their heroes.

Such criminal and social justice issues, crystallized on the streets, strain relations between the newcomers and many of the old guard, but in the present context of drug-related crime and violence in the Village-Northton, many of the old-timers are adopting a "law and order" approach to crime and public safety, laying blame more directly on those they see as responsible for such crimes, though they retain some ambivalence. Newcomers can share such feelings with an increasing number of old-time "liberal" residents. As one middle-aged white woman who has lived in the Village for fifteen years said:

> When I call the police, they respond. I've got no complaints. They are fine for me. I know they sometimes mistreat black males. But let's face it, most of the crime is committed by them, and so they can simply tolerate more scrutiny. But that's them.

Gentrifiers and the local old-timers who join them, and some traditional residents continue to fear, care more for their own safety and well-being than for the rights of young blacks accused of wrongdoing. Yet reliance on the police, even by an increasing number of former liberals, may be traced to a general feeling of oppression at the hands of street criminals, whom many believe are most often black. As these feelings intensify and as more yuppies and students inhabit the area and press the local government for services, especially police protection, the police may be required to "ride herd" more stringently on the youthful black population. Thus young black males are often singled out as the "bad" element in an otherwise healthy diversity, and the tensions between the lower-class black ghetto and the middle and upper-class white community increase rather than diminish.

Endnotes

[1]See Rubinstein (1973); Fogelson (1977); Reiss (1971); Bittner (1967); Banton (1964).
[2]For an illuminating typology of police work that draws a distinction between "fraternal" and "professional" codes of behavior, see Wilson (1968).

References

Anderson, Elijah, 1986. "Of Old Heads and Young Boys: Notes on the Urban Black Experience." Unpublished paper commissioned by the National Research Council. Committee on the Status of Black Americans, 1986.
Banton, Michael. 1964. *The Policeman and the Community*. New York: Basic Books.
Bittner, Egon. 1967. "The Police on Skid Row." *American Sociological Review 32* (October): 699–715.
Fogelson, Robert. 1977. *Big City Police*. Cambridge: Harvard University Press.
Reiss, Albert J. 1971. *The Police and the Public*. New Haven: Yale University.
Rubinstein, Jonathan. 1973. *City Police*. (New York: Farrar, Straus, and Giroux, 1973).
Wilson, James Q., 1968. "The Police and the Delinquent in Two Cities." In *Controlling Delinquents*, ed., Stanton Wheeler. New York: John Wiley.

Section III:
Institutional Imbalance
and Spatial Arrangements

Typically, when urban scholars consider spatial arrangements in society, it usually pertains to concerns covered by ecological studies. Urban ecological researchers often draw from the early work of sociologists Robert Park, Ernest Burgess, and Homer Hoyt—each of whom envisioned different spatial models of how cities were laid out. While each model has its own unique features, critics tend to question the models for suggesting that cities merely consist of various uniform zones and that they thrive from natural competition, large population movements, and basic societal growth.[1] Other scholars recognize, however, that growth is an important dynamic in cities, as they consider the idea of an urban growth machine.[2] This so-called growth machine involves a coalescence of various social institutions and actors interested in profitable private sector growth. However, this machine is also not without its own criticisms. Accordingly, in the articles of the following section the authors move away from urban ecological notions of growth. Instead, they appear to embrace, implicitly, a broad critique of the urban growth machine. They focus on interactions between forces of growth that they believe engender manipulation and improper stewardship of urban space, while often having negative social consequences.

Sociologists John Logan and Harvey Molotch characterize collusion between public and private actors as urban growth coalitions.[3] Urban growth coalitions—typically made up of bankers, business people, corporate property owners, developers, politicians, and investors—seek to spark population growth, the market value of land, and the city's economy through investment and development. Influential actors who direct urban growth coalitions are preoccupied with the exchange (or market) value of urban space and seek urban expansion at almost any cost.[4] A major critique of the urban growth machine stems from this assertion. In other words, qualitative dimensions of public space for the use of parks, museums and libraries are often disregarded in favor of growth agendas, creating tension between community residents and growth coalition advocates. Unfortunately, for many urban areas, the growth agenda often prevails as public policy.[5]

Although urban growth agendas continue to be alive and well today, some criticize the perspective as harmful to urban areas. For example, geographer Jason Hackworth in his recent book, *The Neoliberal City*, analyzes the relationship between policy makers, private developers, banks, and bond-rating agencies. He points out that collusion between these actors—which facilitated misleading bond rating practices regarding public space—(1) helped distort the historical concept behind the need for affordable housing, (2) undermined public policy regarding public housing construction, and (3) inflated the costs of homes in the private housing market, which ultimately contributed to the 2008 housing-market collapse that economist Thomas Sowell discusses in *The Housing Boom and Bust*.[6]

The New York Times ran a story in January 2008 entitled "Private Cash Sets Agenda for Urban Infrastructure." The paper reports that despite budgetary disruptions of plans by the mayor of New Haven, CT, John DeStefano Jr., to restore urban neighborhoods, Yale University is moving forward with a massive rebuilding project in the city. The project, according to *The New York Times*, involves use of public space, as the university works with private developers to enhance the downtown area with shops and fancy restaurants. Regarding this seeming dominance of public space, Mayor DeStefano is quoted as saying, "For us, infrastructure spending has come to mean growing the university. Yale has the money, and what they get from us is the approval to grow."[7] Does this implicate a shame of governance? The answer, in this instance, largely rests on one's view of where public and private interests begin and end. The readings in this section provide a further opportunity (implicitly) to consider the notion of private vs. public interest.

First, Peter Dreier et al., from the book *Place Matters*, discuss how neglect of the federal government influenced economic segregation in cities and suburban sprawl. They review the merits of free market arguments and insist that actions of the federal government (along with coordinated private interests) promoted the growth of suburban communities, at the expense of cities. They briefly discuss, for example, the role that transportation and the defense industry played regarding city vs. suburban spatial inequities. In the second article, Jeanie Wylie discusses an agreement between General Motors and the City of Detroit to build a new Cadillac Plant in a section of the city inhabited largely by working class whites of Polish descent. GM and Detroit public officials argued that the new plant would create jobs, while the residents of Poletown faced the prospects of being evicted from their homes to accommodate the project, causing sympathizers to exclaim that, "This is not Russia."

In the third article, George Lipsitz provides an historical account of sports stadium development in St. Louis, Los Angeles, and Houston. He uses the Warner model of urban growth to evaluate the public benefit of new stadiums—relative to other urban problems in each city—and discusses whether committing public funds for these projects are worthwhile city investments. Next, in an original study, Henrik Lebuhn considers urban politics and the privatization of farm space in the city. Specifically, he discusses actions taken that undermine the existence of urban farmlands in Los Angeles, as public officials appear to cooperate with private land developers. He argues that the decision to cater to private interests for the land amounts to a betrayal of immigrant farmers in Los Angeles, as well as an open assault on public space. In the fifth section, Deirdre Pfeiffer studies Cabrini Green, a "redeveloping African-American public housing community near downtown Chicago." By employing a critical discourse approach, Pfeiffer shows that the unfortunate displacement of Cabrini Green residents was facilitated by agreements between Chicago policy makers and urban elites who utilized strategies such as neighborhood renaming, resident denigration, and neoliberal relocation narratives to help dislodge Cabrini Green residents from their homes.

In the final piece, Douglass Massey and Nancy Denton, from their book *American Apartheid*, discuss the future of urban ghettos. They argue that covenants between government entities and private citizens helped contribute to a social dilemma whereby problematic social divisions become virtually impossible to disentangle. They insist that disentangling race and class dynamics will require coordinated efforts by the federal government if we ever hope to seriously address poor conditions in the inner-cities of the U.S. This piece leads us into the consideration of race, class, and education matters discussed in Section IV of this volume.

Endnotes

[1]John J. Macionis and Vincent N. Parrillo. *Cities and Urban Life* 5th edition (Boston: Prentice Hall, 2007).

[2]Harvey Molotch. "The City as a Growth Machine." *American Journal of Sociology* 82, 309–333, 1976.

[3]John Logan and Harvey Molotch. *Urban Fortunes: The Political Economy of Space* (Berkeley: University of California Press, 2007).

[4]Mike Savage and Alan Warde. *Urban Sociology, Capitalism and Modernity* (New York: Continuum Publishing Company, 1993).

[5]Randy Stoeker writes in *Defending Community* about a struggle between community organizers and the growth coalition, as the coalition attempts to overtake Cedar Riverside, a section of Minneapolis, Minnesota (Philadelphia, PA: Temple University Press, 1994).

[6]Jason Hackworth. *The Neoliberal City: Governance, Ideology, and Development in American Urbanism* (Ithaca, NY: Cornell University Press, 2007); Thomas Sowell. *The Housing Boom and Bust* (New York: Basic Books, 2009).

[7]*New York Times* article: <http://www.nytimes.com/2008/01/06/business/06haven.html>

Promoting Segregation[*]

Peter Dreier, John Mollenkopf, and Todd Swanstrom

The Roads Not Taken

Martin Wuest, an electrical engineer, gets up at 3:15 every morning so he can get to work at Pericom, a semiconductor company in San Jose, California. He lives in Los Banos, an old farm town eighty-six miles from San Jose. If he leaves his house at 3:50 A.M., he can usually make the drive in ninety minutes. If he leaves later, it takes a lot longer. He gets to his office by 5:30 A.M. More than one-third of the residents of Los Banos join Wuest in rising before dawn to fight their way through heavy freeway traffic to commute to Silicon Valley, the high-tech region around San Jose. Many of these families moved to Los Banos because they could not afford to live any closer. The median house price in Silicon Valley rose from $397,533 in October 1999 to $530,000 a year later, and the average monthly rent of an apartment is over $1,000. To accommodate them, Los Banos has allowed developers to build large tracts of single-family homes and apartments that cost less than half the price of those in Silicon Valley. Although the people living in Los Banos pay lower housing costs, they face long commuting times, less family time together, and more family stress.[1]

Few would dispute our contention that place matters in people's lives, but some would disagree with how we interpret this claim. Some would say, "Sure, some places are better than others, but this only reflects individual preferences and ability to consume. It has always been this way. If you make money, you can afford to live in a good neighborhood. If you are poor, you can't. It is only natural that people of different economic classes sort themselves out into different neighborhoods. It is a matter of personal preferences, market forces, and cultural values." In the case of Martin Wuest, the high-technology boom caused housing prices to soar in Silicon Valley. Given his income level, Wuest chose to trade longer commuting times for lower housing costs. Some would say that this was simply a rational decision, not the result of any plot to constrain his choices.

In this chapter, we dispute the contention that sprawl and segregation simply result from rational decisions made in the marketplace. Geographic sprawl and spatial inequalities were not the inevitable result of high-tech growth in the San Jose metropolitan area. Instead, these outcomes were shaped by a whole series of government actions, ranging from freeway construction and tax policies to local zoning policies, as well as inactions,

---

*Peter Drier, John Mollenkopf, and Todd Swantrom, *Place Matters: Metropolitics for the Twenty-First Century* (Lawrence: University Press of Kansas, 2001). Reprinted with permission.

particularly the failure to build adequate supplies of moderately priced rental housing, public transit, and socially integrated communities. Although Martin Wuest undoubtedly made the best choice from among the options available to him, previous political decisions had a lot to say about what these options would be.

In fact, government politics play a crucial role in producing and aggravating metropolitan inequalities. A recent survey asked 149 leading urban scholars to identify the most important influences on the American metropolitan areas since 1950. They identified "the overwhelming impact of the federal government on American metropolis, especially through policies that intentionally or unintentionally promoted suburbanization and sprawl."[2] Federal policies have had two major consequences. First, they have consistently favored investment in suburbs and disinvestment from central cities. These policies provided incentives for businesses and middle-class Americans to move to suburbs while deterring poor Americans from doing so. Government policies have also favored concentrating the poor in central cities. Second, federal (and state) policies encouraged economic competition and political fragmentation within metropolitan areas, primarily by allowing "local autonomy" over taxation, land use, housing, and education, but also by failing to provide incentives for regional governance or cooperation. The power of each suburb to set its own rules and the competition among local governments for tax-generating development have powerfully promoted economic segregation and suburban sprawl. Both federal policies and the jurisdictional ground rules have created an uneven playing field that fosters the conditions we have already described.

The Free Market Perspective

The conservative conventional wisdom has it the other way around: government policies are biased in favor of cities, wasting huge amounts of money in a futile effort to stem urban decline driven by powerful market forces. This misperception is rooted in historical amnesia and fails to appreciate the influence of government and the power of place.

Although government policies have long been biased against central cities, these biases were especially pronounced from World War II through the 1960s. Once suburban sprawl and economic segregation had gained momentum, the federal government did enact a series of policies to stem urban decline, such as urban renewal and revenue sharing. But these policies were largely designed to protect central business districts, not reverse the dynamic of economic segregation and suburban sprawl. Only belatedly, and with few resources, did they even seek to address worsening conditions in central-city neighborhoods.

Many scholars have reinforced the conventional wisdom that suburbanization and economic segregation are the natural products of a free marketplace. They assume that people with similar incomes have similar preferences for government services, thus confirming the folk wisdom that "birds of a feather flock together." It is only natural that rich people choose to live in the same suburban areas with other rich people. This perspective represents the way many people think about metropolitan development. Only by challenging this conventional wisdom can we overcome the widespread cynicism that government can do little to counter economic and racial segregation and metropolitan sprawl.

Those who defend economic segregation generally view it as an expression of individual choices made in a free market. In a provocative article in the conservative journal *National Review*, Llewellyn Rockwell argued that "[t]he housing policy of a free society ought to be simple: people should be able to live where they want, using their own money and engaging in voluntary market exchanges." According to Rockwell, "markets mean choice, and with choice comes sorting. People tend to choose to work, socialize, and live with others in their own social, religious, cultural, and economic group. There's nothing wrong with that. In fact, it creates real diversity among neighborhoods." This has traditionally led to "neighborhoods centered on one group or another, whether WASP, Greek, Ukrainian, Italian, black, Chinese, or whatever."[3] Accordingly, society actually has less economic and racial segregation than is ideal, because government has interfered in this "natural system" by engaging in "social engineering" that imposes poor people and racial minorities on communities that would otherwise choose to be more homogeneous. Those who defend segregation from this perspective view the outcome not just as maximizing efficiency and free choice but as creating a superior moral climate. Rockwell, for example, calls segregation a "natural pattern, a product of rational choice," which "makes possible strong communities."[4] Fred Siegel adds that sprawl is "an expression of the upward mobility and growth in home-ownership generated by our past half-century of economic success." Larger incomes require bigger homes on more land, forcing our metro areas to stretch out. Sprawl is "part of the price we're paying for creating something new on the face of the earth: the first mass upper-middle class."[5]

These commentators believe that economic segregation is morally just. Howard Husock argues in a report for the conservative Heritage Foundation that "socioeconomic status is a universal sorting principle in American cities. People of like social rank tend to live together and apart from those of unlike rank." Moving to better neighborhoods is a mark of one's status, which, Husock argues, should be earned by hard work. Economic segregation reflects the rightful ability of those who have good values, whose hard work and saving are rewarded by the market, to move into good neighborhoods. Those who lack good middle-class values, who are lazy and live only in the present, do not deserve to live in such neighborhoods. If left to the free market, they would not be able to afford to. Programs like the Department of Housing and Urban Development's (HUD's) Moving to Opportunity, which provides vouchers to low-income families so that they can pay for private apartments in better-off suburbs, violate this moral order. Subsidized low-income housing developments in middle-class neighborhoods are equally bad because they "[rob] the poor of the will and even the means to climb the neighborhood ladder on their own." They are, Husock says, an "ill-gotten gain," a "reward not commensurate with accomplishment."[6]

In a *New Republic* article entitled "Suburban Myth: The Case for Sprawl," Gregg Easterbrook acknowledges that the desire of white people to "escape contact with blacks" promotes suburbanization, but he argues that their primary motivation is the preference for "[d]etached homes, verdant lawns [and] lower crime rates," which "represents a lifelong dream" to most Americans, regardless of race. People also move to suburbs to escape the "corruption and mismanagement" of urban governments, Easterbrook argues, especially "disastrous inner-city school systems." Acknowledging that suburban sprawl creates environmental problems, Easterbrook nevertheless believes that the benefits outweigh the costs. He associates cities with "high density tower housing" and "cramped quarters." In contrast, suburban housing tracts make widespread home ownership possible. Suburban shopping malls are a "furiously efficient means of retailing." Automobiles "promote economic efficiency and personal freedom" and, despite traffic congestion, typically get people to and from places more quickly than public transit would.[7] Freeways allow people to commute from homes in one suburb to jobs in another; subways and light railways, built along fixed corridors, do not offer nearly as much convenience and flexibility. Sprawl, he concludes, is "economically efficient."[8]

Some defenders of sprawl believe that central cities are becoming obsolete. *Washington Post* reporter Joel Garreau celebrated the emergence of "edge cities." The Gwinnett Place mall outside Atlanta, the Schaumburg area outside Chicago, the Bridgewater Mall area in central New Jersey, and Tysons Corner outside Washington. D.C., constitute the "hearths of civilization," according to Garreau. "Americans are individualists," he writes. "The automobile is the finest expression of transportation individualism ever devised."[9] Thanks to cheap land, highway access, and distance from central cities, farmland and open space on the urban periphery have become attractive for development. Edge cities are now practically self-sustaining. People can live, work, shop, visit their doctors, eat at nice restaurants, and attend plays and movies in the suburbs. They no longer need a big, central urban "hub." Moreover, Garreau says, none of this was planned by public officials or government bureaucrats. It came about because pioneering entrepreneurs recognized these exurban possibilities, invested in them, and attracted other entrepreneurs. What some view as ugly sprawl, sterile housing tracts, and congested highways, Garreau views as a symbol of entrepreneurial innovation.

In this view, government efforts to work against this logic of metropolitan growth and edge-city development are doomed to fail. Tamar Jacoby and Fred Siegel argue that government should instead seek to improve inner-city economic conditions by using tax breaks and loans to entice private businesses to locate in ghettos and by providing grants to community-based organizations to sponsor retail stores or provide social services. Regulating banks to lend in areas where they otherwise would not do so will inevitably backfire, they say, because government bureaucrats create too many rules and obstacles. They do not understand how the private market works or the flexibility that individual entrepreneurs require. Government programs just thwart the entrepreneurial spirit of inner-city businesspeople.[10] Instead, Harvard Business School professor Michael Porter tells us, government should get out of the way and allow the "competitive advantage of the inner city" to foster economic improvements in poor urban neighborhoods.[11]

Given the reality that most private choices—by individuals as well as businesses—about metropolitan location are shaped by local government taxes, infrastructure, services, and schools, scholars working from the free-market perspective have incorporated the local public sector into their analysis. This is called "public choice" theory. Its proponents view the multiplicity of local governments within metropolitan areas as creating an intergovernmental marketplace parallel to the private market. This promotes consumer choice. Just as shoppers can choose from among brands of towels, toothpastes, or television sets, households can choose where to live from an array of cities and suburbs.[12] Each jurisdiction represents a distinct bundle of amenities and services at a distinct price in taxation. Since people have different tastes in cities, just as they have different tastes in clothing, public choice scholars view this arrangement as the most efficient way to allocate public goods and services.

Charles Tiebout's 1956 classic essay "A Pure Theory of Local Expenditures" provided the first systematic statement of this view:

The consumer-voter may be viewed as picking that community which best satisfies his preference pattern for public goods.... The greater the number of communities and the greater the variance among them, the closer the consumer will come to fully realizing his preference position.[13]

For public choice theorists, choosing a detergent and choosing a local government have much in common: "Individual choices differ for public goods and services as well as for private. Some consumers want more freeways; others want a rapid transit system instead. Some prefer local parks; others, larger private backyards."[14] Tiebout and those who embrace his argument. including Elinor and Vincent Ostrom, Paul Peterson, and Mark Schneider, view the competition among local jurisdictions as creating an efficient and responsive market for public services (although interference by government bureaucrats and other special interests distort the marketplace).[15]

Public choice theory justifies economic segregation on the grounds that people with similar tastes for public goods and a similar ability to pay for them will naturally settle in local government jurisdictions that provide those goods. According to Robert Warren, public choice theory "assumes that a metropolitan area is composed of diverse communities of interests which are territorially distinct from one another and which have different preferences for goods and services in the public sector."[16] While acknowledging that regional governments may be more efficient in providing air pollution control, transportation, and hospital services, the public choice perspective argues that most services are best provided by local governments, because, according to Werner Hirsch, proximity leads to more "effective citizen-consumer feedback into the government sector," better management, less corruption, and greater efficiency.[17] In other words, competition forces each government to be more efficient and more responsive to its citizens' concerns. If it does not meet their needs, people will move to a more responsive jurisdiction. Fragmented, competitive metropolitan areas provide a cornucopia of choices that maximize household satisfaction.

These critics believe that government plays a role in guiding metropolitan development, but they argue that government should adapt to market trends (or, following public choice theory, imitate the market). To be sure, they recognize that unregulated markets can generate environmental problems, racial separation, and urban ghettos, but they think that any attempt to "cure" these ills will only make things worse by violating human nature and introducing inefficiencies into the market. A metropolitan-wide government, for example, would only eliminate or reduce consumer choice.

The Myth of the "Free" Market

The public choice perspective has two major flaws. The first is the assumption that markets are actually "free" of government influence. Although people do make real choices among alternatives in housing, business location, and other markets, government policies shape every aspect of how they make those choices and what they have to choose from. Indeed, government establishes the regulatory and legal framework that makes it possible to have functioning markets at all. Markets therefore cannot be isolated from government, public policy, and politics. The "free market" is an abstraction, not a reality. Garreau hardly acknowledges that edge cities have grown up around and depend entirely on publicly funded highways and other government facilities. Local governments do compete for residents and investors, but the rules of the game under which they do so are neither free nor fair. They do not give all people and places an equal chance to succeed. In fact, they are strongly biased away from central cities and toward suburban jurisdictions.

Moreover, paths taken or not taken in the past frame current choices. Easterbrook may be right that cars are more efficient than public transit today, but he ignores what might have been if, earlier in the twentieth century, investment in public transit had been expanded rather than withdrawn. Likewise, the view that suburban home ownership reflects people's preferences ignores the reality that government programs and private lenders for many years refused to provide mortgages to members of many different racial and ethnic groups who would have been happy to remain in urban neighborhoods and strongly favored single-family dwellings over rental housing, cooperative apartments, and the like. Far from bowing to market forces, government policies have actually shaped them from the beginning.

The second major flaw is that public choice theory seems to work better for middle-class home owners than for the inner-city poor. It ignores all the other features of society that constrain or empower people's ability to choose. Most obviously, people with fewer means (or the wrong skin color) have a highly constricted range of choice. The market not only fails people who live in poverty; it punishes them through the negative effects of concentrated poverty. Let us now look in some detail at how government has shaped the construction of the current state of metropolitan America.

Local Government Fragmentation and Land-Use Control

A fundamental force propelling economic segregation and suburban sprawl is the nature of local jurisdictional arrangements in the United States, specifically the fact that we grant wide latitude and autonomy to local governments. They regulate land use, provide crucial public services (such as education and infrastructure), and finance them with local taxes. As a result, local governments engage in a beggar-thy-neighbor competition with one another. In the competition for favored residents and investments, each jurisdiction has a strong incentive to adopt zoning and development policies that exclude potential residents with incomes below the median for their jurisdiction or who require more costly services. The better-off may view these people as "free riders" who do not pay enough taxes for the services they use. From the viewpoint of fiscal self-interest, this is a rational position. Widespread discriminatory practices in the rental, sales, and financing of housing reinforce this exclusion by price and income.[18] Similarly, each jurisdiction seeks new businesses that will pay more tax revenues than the costs of the services they will require. As the federal and state governments devolve responsibility for more programs to the local level, the fragmented nature of local government becomes even more important. This resulting dynamic strongly promotes economic segregation and suburban sprawl.

Out of this competition comes a pecking order of jurisdictions. Each tries to be more exclusive than the next. At the top end, exclusive and expensive suburbs provide their residents with excellent public services at a relatively small tax cost in relation to housing values and incomes. At the bottom, distressed suburbs and central cities provide housing of last resort for all those whom suburban jurisdictions can exclude by reason of low income, lack of mobility, or race. Over time. the loss of well-to-do residents can undermine the ability of a city to attract commercial investments. Suburbs are arrayed according to the incomes of their residents and their commercial tax bases. Inner-ring suburbs that house working-class families with school-age children and that have little commercial wealth are not in a good position to compete in this intergovernmental marketplace. Businesses have also sought out, and sometimes even created, suburban jurisdictions to provide them with tax havens and few regulations, thus siphoning off badly needed business investment from other municipalities.[19]

From the 1940s to the 1990s, this dynamic encouraged much of the mobile white middle class and, more recently, the black, Asian, and Hispanic middle class to move to suburbs. Those rendered immobile by discrimination and low incomes, especially the minority poor, were constrained to live in expanding urban, and sometimes suburban, ghettos. At some distance from them, yet still within city limits, are middle-income households that, depending on local circumstances, chose to remain in the city. These include gradually shrinking white ethnic neighborhoods (whose residents may have loyalties to the local church or the neighborhood ethnic stores and culture), emerging immigrant enclaves, zones where young people seek to start their careers, and defended enclaves (such as gated communities) of the urban elite. Despite the persistence of these groups in the city, the real median household income of city residents declined significantly compared with that in the surrounding suburbs.

These ground rules also encourage towns and regions to engage in "bidding wars" for manufacturing plants, "big-box" stores like Wal-Marts and Kmarts, shopping centers, industrial parks, luxury housing, and even sports franchises.

For example, three adjacent cities in southern California (Oxnard, Ventura, and Camarillo) kept outbidding one another (with tax breaks) to attract large stores to their respective shopping centers. After several years of such maneuvering, one council member concluded, "this is not about creating new business. This is about spending $30 million to move two stores three miles."[20] The competition for business investment results in a "race to the bottom" in which the tax burden is gradually shifted from businesses to residents. The resulting development does little to help poor areas pull themselves up. After Detroit offered generous incentives for private companies to locate within the city, surrounding suburbs responded by offering the same incentives.[21] Whichever locality "wins" the bidding war ends up with fewer tax revenues to provide public services.

Every other major democracy in Europe and Canada exercises greater national control over land use than does the United States.[22] Here, local municipalities retain great power over land use (as well as local schools). This control enables them to determine what kind of businesses and housing get built and who can afford them.[23] Of course, suburbanization could have happened in the absence of metropolitan political fragmentation. Cities could have expanded their boundaries to encompass the spreading of population and jobs. With some exceptions, this did not happen.

In the United States, states charter local governments, which are not even mentioned in the U.S. Constitution. In the nineteenth century, state laws generally made it easy for growing central cities to annex new territory as their populations expanded. Early in the twentieth century, however, states revised their laws to make this more difficult and to enable residents of outlying areas to incorporate new suburban municipalities.[24] Although some cities (mostly in the South and West) retained the ability to annex adjacent suburban areas, most cities are trapped within their political boundaries.[25] States gave local governments the authority to tax, regulate land uses, and establish their own public school systems. Instead of promoting metropolitan government and consolidation, these laws encourage balkanization.

Local governments use zoning laws, which divide localities into districts, or zones, to segregate land uses and to limit access of potential unwanted new residents and land uses. (Although free-market conservatives decry government intervention, only a few have said anything about the restrictive nature of suburban zoning laws.) Racial zoning, such as South Africa's apartheid system, was struck down by the Supreme Court in 1917, but the federal courts have upheld zoning based on economic distinctions.[26] Los Angeles passed the first zoning ordinance in 1909, creating residential, light industry, and heavy industry zones. Later laws added zones for open space and retail shops. But later zoning laws went further, seeking to favor some kinds of housing over others. Some early planners described apartment buildings as "polluting" or "tainting" single-family residential areas.[27] In 1926, the U.S. Supreme Court (in Euclid v. Ambler) allowed the Cleveland suburb of Euclid to ban apartment buildings from neighborhoods with single-family housing. Zoning increasingly became a way to protect property values and to exclude "noxious" land uses, including apartment buildings.

States have the ultimate authority to regulate land use, but, encouraged by the federal government, they began to delegate that responsibility to local governments in the 1920s. Early state statutes were modeled on the 1924 *Standard State Zoning Enabling Act* and the 1928 *Standard City Planning Enabling Act* published by the U.S. Department of Commerce. By the late 1920s, 564 cities had zoning ordinances. The 1954 Housing Act provided federal funds for local, regional, and state planning and encouraged local zoning ordinances. By 1968, 65 percent of the 7,609 local governments in the nation's metropolitan areas had planning agencies that created and policed zoning laws.[28] Many federal task forces and commissions have recommended that Washington take a firmer stand on national land-use planning to promote efficient location of businesses and housing, to reduce geographic segregation based on income and race, and to protect the environment, but few of these recommendations have been accepted. In these and other ways, the federal government and the states have encouraged or condoned the nation's fragmented land-use practices and their social consequences.

Local zoning laws also allow municipalities to regulate the location and minimum lot size for various kinds of housing. Affluent suburbs have used "snob zoning" to limit housing for the poor. Many suburbs set minimum lot sizes (such as one-half acre per home) that increase the cost of housing and rule out the construction of dense housing—not just apartment buildings. but also bungalow-style single-family homes.[29] Intentionally or unintentionally (there is evidence of both), these zoning laws have the effect of excluding low-income and even middle-income families. They also restrict racial minorities, who generally have lower incomes than whites. Some suburbs that desire to limit school-age children, in order to avoid education costs, prohibit housing types favored by families with children.

Proponents of public choice theory believe that inequalities among local jurisdictions should balance themselves out over time as the market achieves "equilibrium." For the intergovernmental marketplace, this means that land prices should rise in successful areas, reducing their attractiveness to residents and investors, who will then be attracted to poor areas, where prices have fallen. But as the previous discussion has shown, spatial inequalities have become worse rather than better. The competition among fragmented local governments has led to a vicious circle of rising spatial inequality.

Federal Stealth Urban Policies

Urban policies are normally understood as those that are targeted to cities or to poor people who mostly live in cities. Almost all federal policies have spatial impacts, however, that may harm or benefit cities. Acknowledging this, the Carter administration during the 1970s experimented with an "Urban Impact Analysis," which would enable policy makers to anticipate the negative impacts of various policies on cities and thereby lessen them.[30] Many federal policies with profound impacts on cities and metropolitan development are implicit or indirect urban policies. Because many are invisible to people's political radar, we call them "stealth urban policies."[31]

When the New Deal initiated a large public works program during the 1930s to lift the nation out of the depression, its primary goal was to create jobs. But a secondary effect was to lift up cities, where most of the unemployed were located. Similarly, when the Reagan administration adopted policies to reduce inflation in the early 1980s that brought on a deep national recession, it harmed inner cities far more than other areas.[32] Because cities have a disproportionate share of low-income people, federal efforts to help poor people, such as Medicaid, food stamps, welfare, and job training programs, generally benefit cities more than suburbs. And when these programs are cut, poor urban neighborhoods are hurt the most.[33]

Here we examine [two] stealth urban policies: transportation [and] military spending, ... [Neither] of these policies was intended primarily to shape urban development, but each had profound urban impacts. In reality, these federal policies subsidized America's postwar suburban exodus (and still do) by pushing people and businesses out of cities and pulling them into suburbs. The idea that this happened purely as a result of the free market is a myth.

Transportation Policy: An Arranged Marriage with the Automobile

America's marriage to the automobile began early in the twentieth century. But in many ways, it was an arranged marriage, not just a love affair. Each time the nation courted mass transportation, powerful interests intervened, objecting to the arrangement. The "highway lobby," composed of the automobile, trucking, oil, rubber, steel, and road-building industries, literally paved the way to suburbia by promoting public road building over public transit and by keeping gas taxes low (by European standards).[34] By the 1920s, cars and trucks began to outstrip trolleys and trains as the major form of personal and business transportation.[35] While government officials looked the other way, the major car, truck, and bus companies purchased and dismantled many of the electric trolley lines that urban Americans relied on.[36] State governments earmarked tolls and gas taxes for road construction instead of public transit and launched major road-building programs. In 1934, Congress required states receiving federal highway funds to dedicate state turnpike tolls to road building.[37] The highway lobby was gaining momentum.

The federal Interstate Highway and Defense Act of 1956 sounded the final death knell for alternatives to the car as a source of metropolitan mobility. Although the ostensible purpose was to promote mobility across the country and get Americans quickly out of crowded cities in time of war (this was the height of the cold war), it would also powerfully promote suburbanization by building radial and ring freeways around the major cities. It set up the Highway Trust Fund, which used federal gas tax revenues to pay 90 percent of the freeway construction costs. Trust fund expenditures grew from $79 million in 1946 to $429 million in 1950 to $2.9 billion in 1960. It "ensured that the freeways would be self-propagating, because more freeways encouraged more automobile travel, generating more gasoline revenue that could only be used to build more highways."[38] Ultimately. it built 41,000 miles of roads.[39] Urban scholars ranked this program as the most important influence in shaping America's urban areas in the past half century.[40]

By 1997. the United States was spending $20.5 billion a year through the Highway Trust Fund.[41] But gas taxes by then covered only 60 percent of the cost of maintaining the federal highway system, so federal and state governments made up the rest. (This cost does not include the negative health consequences of pollution or the loss of economic productivity from employees stuck in traffic.) Most other industrial nations fund highways out of general revenues (as they also fund national rail systems and often regional commuter railways), forcing roads to compete with other national priorities.

America's car culture is premised on the belief that automobiles provide a degree of personal freedom and flexibility that public transit cannot. We have shown that the car culture poses many costs for suburbanites, including environmental damage, long commutes, and personal injuries. Even if we discount these costs, the irony of millions of Americans simultaneously exercising their personal freedom by driving their cars only to end up in traffic jams has been parodied in such films as *Falling Down* (1993) with Michael Douglas and Jean Luc Goddard's French film *Weekend* (1967). Drivers are spending significantly more time stuck in traffic. Since 1982, traffic gridlock has increased 700 percent in Indianapolis, 533 percent in Kansas City, 525 percent in Rochester, 480 percent in Colorado Springs, and 440 percent in Salt Lake City. These were the worst increases, but even areas with the smallest increases (Phoenix with 19 percent, Houston with 32 percent, Philadelphia with 40 percent, Honolulu with 63 percent, and San Francisco with 69 percent) experienced significantly more traffic congestion.[42] Americans now spend 8 billion hours a year stuck in traffic.[43] According to Jane Holtz Kay, "On the coasts that hold two-thirds of all Americans, the long-suffering 'BosWash' and the newer 'Los Diegos' freeways greet their share of the day's 80 million car commuters, and, with a screech of brakes, the love song of freedom and mobility goes flat."[44]

Throughout the twentieth century, advocates for public transit argued and battled for a more balanced federal transportation strategy. They won a number of victories. In the 1970s, neighborhood groups protested federal and state plans to build a highway through Boston's working-class neighborhoods and persuaded the U.S. Department of Transportation to halt the highway and divert funds to build a subway line. In recent decades, Atlanta, Miami, Baltimore, Buffalo, Detroit, Los Angeles, Washington, D.C., and San Francisco have all built new subway lines using federal funds shared from gas tax revenues. But federal policy had already cast the die in favor of roads and cars. Between 1975 and 1995, the United States spent $1.15 trillion for roads and highways, compared with $187 billion for mass transit and only $13 billion for Amtrak, the nation's interurban train system.[45] Highway construction continues to expand, exacerbating sprawl and undermining the economies of older cities and suburbs.[46] As a result, mass transit ridership is much lower in American cities than in Europe, Japan, and Canada, accounting for only 3 percent of all travel, one fifth the Western European average.[47]

Our car-dominated transportation system was premised on individual choice, but it has reduced choice in many ways. Most Americans have no choice but to use the automobile. You need one to get to your job, buy groceries, or visit friends. In Canadian and European cities, households make great use of cars but can also live in pedestrian-friendly neighborhoods where they can rely on mass transit. Many live quite easily without using their cars often and can even do without them. The United States chose not to take this road.

Military Spending: More than Just Defense

Most Americans think that the search for cheaper land and lower taxes, along with the rise of truck transportation, inevitably shifted major manufacturing plants to suburban and outlying locations. Obviously, government transportation policies had an enormous impact on this trend, but so did the federal government's siting of military facilities and distribution of defense contracts. Throughout the post-World War II period, military spending has accounted for the largest part of the federal budget. Pentagon decisions about where to locate military facilities and where to grant defense contracts greatly influenced regional development patterns. They are America's de facto "industrial policy," a form of government planning that has dramatically shaped the location of businesses and jobs.

Before World War II, almost all manufacturing plants were located in the nation's central cities. When the war began, the federal government took control (though not ownership) of the nation's major manufacturing industries in order to mobilize resources for the war effort. Companies that built commercial airplanes were drafted to produce military aircraft; firms that produced clothing were conscripted to manufacture uniforms; firms that turned out automobiles and freighters began making tanks and battleships for military use. America's business leaders were wary of the potential implications of this government takeover, so President Roosevelt appointed corporate executives to run the War Production Board (WPB).

Rather than retool existing plants, many of which sat underutilized during the depression, the WPB executives decided to build new plants and to locate most of them (government funded but privately owned) in suburban areas. "In New York, Detroit, Baltimore, and Pittsburgh, for example, new investment was located outside the central cities twice or more as heavily as before the war. This pattern also held for such Sunbelt cities as Los Angeles, Dallas, Houston and San Diego." The leaders of the nation's largest industrial corporations used "government financing to reconstruct the private sector's capital base along new and more desirable lines." Suburban locations were desirable because they were "largely beyond the reach of the unions," which had a strong presence in the existing factories, and were not governed by big-city mayors, who were often sympathetic to unions.[48] These location decisions had a major impact on postwar America.

Mobilization for World War II also strongly affected the regional location of employment (with disproportionate shares of wartime investment being located outside the preexisting industrial base in the urban North) and population (prompting a northward flow of blacks and a westward and southward flow of whites). The Defense Department's support for the aerospace and electronics industries continued these shifts in the cold war era.[49] After World War II, key congressmen continued to utilize the "Pentagon pork barrel" to bring jobs to firms and workers in their districts, disproportionately in suburban areas. The ripple effects of Pentagon spending dramatically changed the population and employment map of the entire country.[50]

Even in the metropolitan areas that won the Pentagon sweepstakes, most Pentagon dollars went to the suburbs, not the central cities. One study compared the military contracts and salaries coming into each city with the amount of federal taxes drained out of each city to the Pentagon. In 1990 alone, eighteen of the twenty-five largest cities suffered a loss of $24 billion. New York City alone lost $8.4 billion a year; Los Angeles, $3.3 billion; Chicago, $3.1 billion; Houston, $1.7 billion; Dallas, $731 million; and Detroit, over $900 million. In Los Angeles, taxpayers sent $4.74 billion to the Pentagon and received $1.47 billion back, for a net loss of $3.27 billion, or $3,000 per family.[51] The employment impact of this drain-off of funds is equally dramatic.

Even those cities gaining dollars and jobs from the Pentagon have discovered that depending on military contracts makes them vulnerable to "downturns in the military spending cycle."[52] Both Seattle (dominated by Boeing, the nation's largest defense contractor) and St. Louis (where defense contractor McDonnell-Douglas is the largest employer) experienced severe economic hard times when the Pentagon reduced its funding for specific weapon systems or selected another contractor. Politics influence the rise and fall of regions and cities as a result of Pentagon spending.[53]

The free-market view of urban decline and suburban sprawl is wrong. Federal policies toward metropolitan areas did not waste billions of dollars on programs targeted at cities in a futile effort to reshape powerful market forces. To the contrary, from a free-market perspective, federal policies toward metropolitan areas were an outstanding "success"; they powerfully promoted economic segregation and suburban sprawl. (Of course, the social and economic costs of this "success" were extremely high.)

The political, economic, and social landscape that we take for granted is a product of federal and state policies that shaped individual and corporate decision making. Each major policy initiative began with serious debates about substantially different options. Powerful interest groups (such as the highway lobby and home-building industry) got exactly what they wanted—government support for suburbanization and metropolitan segregation. Had national policy makers been prompted to make different choices—for example, to support public transportation, to provide subsidies for mixed-income housing, to invest defense dollars and other public facilities in cities—our current metropolitan landscape would look substantially different.

Looking more narrowly at the policies and programs overtly targeted at central cities and poor neighborhoods, they partly failed. Despite billions of dollars spent on bolstering central-city business districts, central cities have lost population and jobs and become poorer relative to their suburbs. These targeted policies failed partly because far more governmental resources were devoted to promoting suburbanization. Spending on home owner subsidies was several magnitudes larger than spending on low-income housing programs; far more was spent on highways than on mass transit.

Even those urban programs most directly targeted to the urban poor were fundamentally flawed. They did not acknowledge that the problems facing poor people and poor neighborhoods are only one part of a larger dynamic of regional growth. Deeply propelled by decades of government support, this regional dynamic is hard to reshape. We have described the many ways in which it developed a self-reinforcing momentum. Compensatory programs, after the fact, are bound to have only marginal effects, especially when they do not recalibrate the institutional arrangements and incentive systems that promote economic segregation and suburban sprawl.

The federal government put its full weight behind suburbanization, refusing, for example, to insure loans in cities and integrated neighborhoods, thus encouraging red lining of cities. After governments and banks shunned economically and racially integrated neighborhoods, this decline became a self-fulfilling prophecy. Even if governments and banks no longer discriminate, spatial inequalities have a momentum of their own. The concentration of poverty leads to fewer jobs, higher crime, unhealthier environments, and fewer shopping opportunities. As a result, those who have the wherewithal flee to better neighborhoods, accentuating the economic and social decline of inner cities and distressed suburbs.

Endnotes

[1] Rebecca Trouson and John Johnson, "Housing Strain Unravels Community Ties," *Los Angeles Times*, January 7, 2001; *Raising the Roof: California Housing Development Projections and Constraints 1997–2000* (Sacramento: California Department of Housing and Community Development, 2000), exhibit 45, "Housing Cost Burden by Income and Tenure for Selected California Metropolitan Areas: 1988–1995; p. 164; Chris Brenner, *Growing Together or Drifting Apart? A Status Report on Social and Economic Well-Being in Silicon Valley* (San Jose, Calif.: Working Partnerships and Economic Policy Institute, January 1998).

[2] Robert Fishman, "The American Metropolis at Century's End: Past and Future Influences," *Housing Policy Debate* 11, no. 1 (2000): 199–213. The survey was conducted for the Fannie Mae Foundation among members of the Society for American City and Regional Planning History; the article can be found at www.fanniemaefoundation.org/research/facts/wi99s1.html.

[3] Llewellyn H. Rockwell, Jr., "The Ghost of Gautreaux," *National Review*, March 7, 1994, pp. 57–59.

[4] Ibid.

[5] Fred Siegel, "The Sunny Side of Sprawl," *New Democrat* (March-April 1999): 20–21. See also Fred Siegel, "Is Regional Government the Answer?" *Public Interest* (fall 1999): 85–98; Fred Barnes, "Suburban Beauty: Why Sprawl Works," *Weekly Standard*, May 22, 2000, pp. 27–30.

[6] Howard Husock, "Mocking the Middle Class: The Perverse Effects of Housing Subsidies," *Heritage Foundation Policy Review* (spring 1991); 96–101. Bovard agrees that federal government programs to help the poor escape the ghetto "amount to a project to dictate where welfare recipients live in every county, city and cranny across the nation." James Bovard, "Suburban Guerrilla," *American Spectator* (September 1994): 26–32.

[7] Nevertheless, 76 percent of transit riders had a total trip time of less than thirty minutes, 57 percent less than twenty minutes, and 25 percent less than ten minutes. David F. Schulz, "Urban Transportation System Characteristics, Condition and Performance" (paper prepared for the Conference on Transportation Issues in Large U.S. Cities, Transportation Research Board, Detroit, June 28–30, 1998).

[8] Gregg Easterbrook, "Suburban Myth: The Case for Sprawl," *New Republic*, March 15, 1999, pp. 18–21.

[9]Joel Garreau, *Edge City: Life on the New Frontier* (New York: Doubleday, 1991), p. 242. See also Philip Langdon, *A Better Place to Live: Reshaping the American Suburb* (New York: Harper, 1994).

[10]Tamar Jacoby and Fred Siegel, "Growing the Inner City?" *New Republic*, August 23, 1999.

[11]Michael E. Porter, "The Competitive Advantage of the Inner City," *Harvard Business Review* (May-June 1995): 55–71. Porter's article triggered a major debate on this topic. See Thomas Boston and Catherine Ross, eds., *The Inner City: Urban Poverty and Economic Development in the Next Century* (New Brunswick, N.J.: Transaction Books, 1997). Also see Bennett Harrison and Amy K. Glasmeier, "Why Business Alone Won't Redevelop the Inner City," *Economic Development Quarterly* 11, no. 1 (1997): 28–38; Timothy Bates, "Michael Porter's Conservative Agenda Will Not Revitalize America's Inner Cities," *Economic Development Quarterly* 11, no. 1 (February 1997): 39–44.

[12]The same argument is applied to business location decisions, but here we focus on residential choice (or the lack thereof).

[13]Charles M. Tiebout, "A Pure Theory of Local Expenditure," *Journal of Political Economy* 64, no. 5 (October 1956): 418.

[14]Robert Bish and Robert Warren, "Scale and Monopoly Problems in Urban Government Services," *Urban Affairs Quarterly 8* (September 1972): 99.

[15]Tiebout, "A Pure Theory of Public Expenditure," pp. 416–24; Vincent Ostrom, Charles Tiebout, and Roland Warren, "The Organization of Government in Metropolitan Areas," *American Political Science Review* 55 (1961): 835–42; Vincent Ostrom, Robert Bish, and Elinor Ostrom, *Local Government in the United States* (San Francisco: Institute for Contemporary Analysis, 1988); Paul Peterson, *City Limits* (Chicago: University of Chicago Press, 1981); Mark Schneider, *The Competitive City: The Political Economy of Suburbia* (Pittsburgh: University of Pittsburgh Press, 1989). For an excellent summary of the public choice perspective, see G. Ross Stephens and Nelson Wikstrom, *Metropolitan Government and Governance: Theoretical Perspectives, Empirical Analysis, and the Future* (New York: Oxford University Press, 2000).

[16]Robert Warren, "A Municipal Services Market Model of Metropolitan Organization," *Journal of the American Institute of Planners* 30 (August 1964): 198–99.

[17]Werner Z. Hirsch, "Local Versus Areawide Urban Government Services," *National Tax Journal* 17 (December 1964): 331–39.

[18]Douglas S. Massey and Nancy A. Denton, *American Apartheid: Segregation and the Making of the Underclass* (Cambridge, Mass.: Harvard University Press, 1993), pp. 96–114, 187–212. Margery Austin Turner and Ron Wienk, "The Persistence of Segregation in Urban Areas: Contributing Causes," in *Housing Markets and Residential Mobility*, ed. G. Thomas Kingsley and Margery Austin Turner (Washington, D.C.: Urban Institute Press, 1993), pp. 193–216.

[19]Gary J. Miller, *Cities by Contract: The Politics of Incorporation* (Cambridge, Mass.: MIT Press, 1981).

[20]William Fulton, *The Reluctant Metropolis: The Politics of Urban Growth in Los Angeles* (Point Arena, Calif.: Solano Press, 1997), p. 279.

[21]John E. Anderson and Robert W. Wassmer, *Bidding for Business: The Efficacy of Local Economic Development Incentives in a Metropolitan Area* (Kalamazoo, Mich.: W.

E. Upjohn Institute for Employment Research, 1999), available at http://www.csus.edu/indiv/w/wassmerr/upjohn.htm.

[22]See, for example, United Nations Center for Human Settlements (HABITAT), *An Urbanizing World: Global Report on Human Settlements: 1996* (London: Oxford University Press, 1996); Charles Abrams, "The Uses of Land in Cities," *Scientific American* (September 1965): 225–31.

[23]See Gerald E. Frug, "The City as a Legal Concept," *Harvard Law Review* 93, no. 6 (April 1980): 1057–1154; Gerald E. Frug, "Decentering Decentralization," *University of Chicago Law Review* 60, no. 2 (spring 1993): 253–73; Gerald E. Frug, "The Geography of Community," *Stanford Law Review* 48, no. 5 (May 1996): 1047–94; Gerald E. Frug, *City Making: Building Communities Without Building Walls* (Princeton, N.J.: Princeton University Press, 1999); Sidney Plotkin, *Keep Out: The Struggle for Land Use Control* (Berkeley: University of California Press, 1987); Harvey M. Jacobs, "Fighting over Land," *Journal of the American Planning Association* 65, no. 2 , (spring 1999): 141–49.

[24]Kenneth Jackson, *Crabgrass Frontier* (New York: Oxford University Press, 1985); David Rusk, *Cities Without Suburbs*, 2d ed. (Washington, D.C.: Woodrow Wilson Center Press, 1995).

[25]Rusk, *Cities Without Suburbs*.

[26]The Court struck down racial zoning in *Buchanan v. Warley*, 245 U.S. 60. (1917).

[27]Gwendolyn Wright, *Building the Dream* (Cambridge, Mass.: MIT Press, 1983), p. 213.

[28]Mary K. Nenno and Paul C. Brophey, *Housing and Local Government* (Washington, D.C.: National Association of Housing and Redevelopment Officers, n.d.), p. 7.

[29]Among many others on this topic, see Alan Mallach, *Inclusionary Housing Programs* (New Brunswick, N.J.: Rutgers University Center for Urban Policy Research, 1984).

[30]Ann R. Markusen, "The Urban Impact Analysis: A Critical Forecast," in *The Urban Impact of Federal Policies*, ed. Norman Glickman (Baltimore: Johns Hopkins University Press, 1979).

[31]We borrow this term from Bernard H. Rass and Myron A. Levine, *Urban Politics: Power in Metropolitan America*, 5th ed. (Itasca, Ill.: F. E. Peacock, 1996), p. 434.

[32]Harold Wolman, "The Reagan Urban Policy and Its Impacts," *Urban Affairs Quarterly* 21, no. 3 (March 1986): 311–35.

[33]Bruce Katz and Kate Carnevale, "The State of Welfare Caseloads in America's Cities" (Washington, D.C.: Brookings Institution Center of Urban and Metropolitan Policy, 1998).

[34]James Flink, *The Car Culture* (Cambridge, Mass.: MIT Press, 1975); Kenneth Jackson, *Crabgrass Frontier: The Suburbanization of the United States* (New York: Oxford University Press, 1985); Jane Holtz Kay, *Asphalt Nation: How the Automobile Took over America and How We Can Take It Back* (New York: Crown Publishers, 1997); Helen Leavitt, *Superhighway-Superhoax* (New York: Doubleday, 1970); Pietro S. Nivola, *Laws of the Landscape: How Policies Shape Cities in Europe and America* (Washington, D.C.: Brookings Institution Press, 1999).

[35]By the mid–1920s, 56 percent of American families owned an automobile, according to Nivola, *Laws of the Landscape*, p. 11.

[36]See Bradford C. Snell, "American Ground Transport: A Proposal for Restructuring the Automobile, Truck, Bus, and Rail Industries" (presented to the Subcommittee on Antitrust and Monopoly of the Committee on the Judiciary, U.S. Senate, February 26, 1974).

[37]Nivola, *Laws of the Landscape*, p. 13.

[38]Howard P. Chudacoff and Judith E. Smith, *The Evolution of American Urban Society*, 4th ed. (Englewood Cliffs, N.J.: Prentice-Hall, 1994), p. 260.

[39]Fishman, *American Metropolis*, p. 3.

[40]Ibid., p. 2.

[41]U.S. Bureau of the Census, *Statistical Abstract of the United States*: 2000, p. 625.

[42]Texas Transportation Institute, *Urban Mobility Study* (College Station: Texas A&M University, November 1999).

[43]Kay, *Asphalt Nation*, p. 14.

[44]Ibid.

[45]Nivola, *Laws of the Landscape*, p. 15.

[46]Timothy Egan, "The Freeway, Its Cost and 2 Cities' Destinies," *New York Times*, July 14, 1999.

[47]Nivola, *Laws of the Landscape*, p. 15.

[48]John H. Mollenkopf, *The Contested City* (Princeton, N.J.: Princeton University Press, 1983), p. 105.

[49]See ibid., pp. 102–9, on World War II; Ann Markusen, Peter Hall, Scott Campbell, and Sabrina District, *The Rise of the Gunbelt: The Military Remapping of Industrial America* (New York: Oxford University Press, 1991).

[50]Ann Markusen and Joel Yudken, *Dismantling the Cold War Economy* (New York: Basic Books, 1992); Markusen et al., *Rise of the Gunbelt* (New York: Oxford University Press, 1991). Military research and development and weapons production have spawned new industries and new fields, but in doing so, much of the nation's resources and scientific expertise have been diverted from civilian production and research. Likewise, military production and research and the siting of facilities help some areas but drain others.

[51]*Report to the Boston Redevelopment Authority* (Lansing, Mich.: Employment Research Associates, 1992), reported in Steven Greenhouse, "Study Says Big Cities Don't Get Fair Share of Military Spending," *New York Times*, May 12, 1992, p. A20, and in Marion Anderson and Peter Dreier, "How the Pentagon Redlines America's Cities," *Planners Network* (May 1993): 3–4.

[52]Markuson and Yudken, *Dismantling the Cold War Economy*, p. 173.

[53]For example, in September 1992, President Bush, far behind Governor Clinton in the Missouri polls, traveled to St. Louis to announce the sale to Saudi Arabia of F-15 jet fighters, which are manufactured by McDonnell-Douglas, the state's largest employer. The sale was highly questionable on defense and foreign policy grounds, but Bush made little pretense of discussion geopolitics. He emphasized the 7,000 local jobs generated by the weapon.

This is Detroit USA, Not Russia[*]

Jeanie Wylie

This is the story of the spirited, integrated, lower-middle-class urban community in Detroit that refused to die until the bulldozers of corporate socialism destroyed its physical being. The story has an epic quality that speaks to the future as well as the past. The sovereign power of the world's largest automobile manufacturer—General Motors—sighted the community's 465 acres—hundreds of homes, schools, churches, retail stores, small producers, and a hospital. Its imperious demands for city hall to exercise eminent domain over the area for an automated luxury-car factory were conveyed. A former socialist and civil rights advocate, Mayor Coleman Young moved to condemn the neighborhood under the state's new "quick take" law. Over $350 million of local, state, and federal subsidies were placed on the sovereign's table as an enticement for the plant's construction within Detroit's city limits instead of at a nearby location that would have saved Poletown with its 4,200 residents. The corporate sovereign told the political bureaucracy to move quickly to flatten, clear, and prepare the area or risk losing the factory to other jurisdictions. Negotiations and arrangements, even those in writing between city hall and General Motors, were concealed. All necessary city council approvals and permits were secured in record time. Epidemics of arson began breaking out in Poletown, adding fire to the combined power of the corporate state.

The people of Poletown were at first plainly stunned. These were avowedly patriotic Americans whose sons fought in World War I and World War II and later police actions in Asia. They were devout churchgoers, as the twelve churches testified. They were community people helping and consoling and enjoying each other up and down and across the streets. Poletown had a sense of history—the late-nineteenth-century settlement by Eastern European immigrants, their important role in the sit-down strikes leading to the creation of the United Auto Workers Union, the sober adjustment to an integrated neighborhood without disruption, and the neighborly rituals and communal projects going back decades—that gave spice and remembrance to everyday talk on porches, between windows of close-by homes, and in the neat gardens and sidewalks that spelled a comfortable familiarity with roots.

Then suddenly, as if issued from the guns of Fort Sumter, the news imploded on them. General Motors wanted their homeland and the news came not from the GM Building but from city hall. The first hearing brought disbelief, but the reality of the planned demolition was conveyed to them by the emissaries of condemnation who invaded the neighborhood in the early fall of 1980. It was urgent that Poletowners reach out for help, but there was no extended hand. Other citizen groups, muzzled by the grants machine that Washington provided city governments, looked the other way. The UAW chose its priority—the factory—and declined to credit the claims that both factory and community could co-exist with some acreage and local adjustments. The Catholic archdiocese saw an opportunity to sell its churches and consolidate its patronage, diminishing due to outward immigration of a younger generation to the suburbs. The lawyers were ridden with the conflict between their desire to retain more lucrative clients and their concern not to offend the establishment and thus curtail their careers, while Poletown's representative, George Crockett, and senators Donald Reigle and Carl Levin refused even to meet with them, much less represent their pleas for help in any way. Poletown was a community abandoned to its lonely fate of extinction. Even the courts became a mirror image of the power structure that wanted what Rome warranted for Carthage—*delenda est* Poletown. In perhaps the most extreme judicial sanction behind corporate power against individual property rights, a majority of the judges deciding the Poletown cases up to the Michigan Supreme Court ruled that a city government could take private property by eminent domain and transfer it to a profit-making corporation. Such is the extension of the "public purpose" rationale for eminent domain that General Motors' proposal was defined as a "public purpose."

The destruction of Poletown took place during an auto industry recession brought about by the now widely acknowledged inefficiency, waste, and mismanagement of its leadership that led foreign competitors with more fuel-efficient cars to expand their market share. The top executives did not resign, but many auto workers were laid off in the Detroit region. As the auto companies became temporarily weaker economically, they became stronger politically. Their demands on governments for abatements, lenient enforcement, and direct subsidies became commands meekly accepted. Michigan Supreme Court justices Fitzgerald and Ryan wrote in their dissent: "Eminent domain is an attribute of sovereignty. When individual citizens are forced to suffer great social dislocation to permit private corporations to construct plants where they deem it most profitable, one is left to wonder who the sovereign is." Assailing the majority's opinion that pronounced lawful the taking of Poletown by the City of Detroit for General Motors, the dissenters wrote that "there is virtually no limit to the use of condemnation to aid private businesses... No homeowner's, merchant's, or manufacturer's property, however productive or valuable to its owner, is immune from condemnation for the benefit of other private interests that will put it to a 'higher use.'"

Almost unmentioned in the discourses over the Poletown controversy was the fact that taxpayers inside and outside that enclave were also paying for the direct and indirect subsidies woven together by the mayor and handed to the giant automaker. Thus GM took, and made their victims pay, an added premium on top.

Writ large, Poletown becomes a metaphor for the politics of abandonment, where the rule of power in an economic recession rides roughshod over the rule of law with scarcely a murmur of protest from a clutch of countervailing constituencies that society was entitled to rely upon in a crunch. It becomes a metaphor for institutionalized deceit, prevarication, and betrayal as the ballooning costs of subsidizing GM continue to pile on the City of Detroit while an ineffective robotic factory limps along with a work force less than half that promised by the company as a key inducement to the city's demolition power and its corporate welfare package. In fact, one industry insider said that the Poletown plant was the "single worst implementation of computer-integrated manufacturing in the United States."

There will be more to the Poletown story as the insiders and participators begin to unencumber their consciences and speak about the machinations. Perhaps the media, which reported the personal tragedies of Poletown but ducked the hard investigative job of going behind the visuals to the backroom powerplays and exchanges, will take a retrospective and prospective look at the demolition decision now nearing its tenth anniversary. At least, they may pay factual tribute to the survivors of Poletown, whose warnings have borne truth, and to those martyrs, such as Father Joseph Karasiewicz, of their beloved community who lost their breath of life when the set fires, the bulldozers, the steel ball pulverized the place where they lived, worked, played, and prayed from their childhood to older age. Someday, too, a plaintiff will pursue Michigan's "quick-take" law to the Supreme Court of the United States as an unconstitutional taking of one's private property for another private property's profit and benefit.

The end of the physical Poletown, where now a parking lot and shrubbery surround a factory that occupies only one-sixth of the total seized acreage, does not end its lesson for future corporate-city hall aggressions. Before going down it showed that a defenseless but stalwart community can jolt a city and a corporate giant to their heels and demonstrated that much can be learned from its loss: the next communities who choose survival over servility will be more likely to prevail.

—Ralph Nader

There is a state of emergency within the city and bold, far-reaching and innovative initiatives, beginning with the city's Central Industrial Park Project, must be undertaken immediately to deal with the foundations of this crisis.

—Mayor Coleman Young. September 10, 1980, letter to the
Council on Environmental Quality

In late June of 1980, just four months before the presidential election, Mayor Coleman Young and General Motors chairman Thomas Murphy announced that a new $500 million Cadillac plant would be built in the center of Detroit—on a site including the northern third of Poletown. The Central Industrial Park Project would demonstrate GM's fidelity to southeastern Michigan and serve as a replacement for two older Detroit Cadillac plants that GM had announced would probably close by 1983. The two older Cadillac plants had employed 15,000 people as recently as 1979. The new one, which they said would produce 1983 Cadillac Sevilles and Eldorados, was projected to employ 6,000.

. . .

GM's announcement that it would build in Detroit was greeted with banner headlines and a spirit of festivity downtown. This factory, and the one under construction in suburban Pontiac, were, after all, the first auto plants to be built in Michigan since the 1950s. They appeared to be a promise on GM's part that it would not allow the area's industrial infrastructure to become obsolete. The Poletown plant was projected to provide 6,000 union jobs and tens of thousands of spin-off jobs for parts suppliers and service stores.

Detroit officials were delighted, even though they would have to evict 4,200 people from Poletown homes and businesses, to provide the "greenfield site" General Motors wanted. They had been trying to sell the city to corporate investors for some time. So when GM made its announcement, city officials speculated that the corporation's decision to locate a new multimillion-dollar facility in Detroit would lure other companies to do the same.

…

> *This is America, not Russia. We're not going to let you do this. We're going to fight like hell.*

> —Josephine Jakubowski, Poletown resident

The first Poletown residents to become aware of General Motors' plan for the neighborhood were Tom Olechowski and Richard Hodas. They stumbled on the information inadvertently through a June 23, 1980 *Free Press* story outlining the area's potential for renewal.

…

Word of GM's plans for the Poletown community spread from house to house like wildfire. During the first several weeks, residents clustered on the streets, reading and rereading the relocation information that had been hand delivered to them by the police. They received visits from appraisers. They were informed they could attend a public meeting on July 9.

The situation was utterly foreign to everyone in the neighborhood. Residents were unsure how to assess the scope and method of the project, much less how to organize to oppose it. Ken Fireman, a veteran city hall reporter for the *Detroit Free Press*, noted at the outset that GM and the city had designed their project with the intent of moving it along as quickly as possible in order to prevent strong opposition from developing. The formality of the documents presented and the speed with which things seemed to be being accomplished did serve to knock residents off balance.

Bernice and Harold Kaczynski were in North Carolina, visiting their daughter, son-in-law, and a new-born grandchild, when their sons called to tell them that they were soon to lose their home. They cut short their vacation and headed back.

"People couldn't believe it," Bernice Kaczynski explained.

> They thought it would be something that would pass by. They couldn't believe they were going to take this [Immaculate Conception] church. Everybody believed the project would take two, three, maybe five years. People said, "How can they take the property so quick? You know you have a chance to fight this and it will take years." And then we started to learn about the quick-take law at our own meetings at Immaculate Conception where people were looking into it. They came up and says, "Hey, Act 87—do you know what it's all about?" And that's where we learned about the quick-take law and about its

being valid, that Governor Milliken passed it through in April and in June they told us this is how they're going to operate here.

Ann Giannini, who prior to the news of the project had never met Bernice but soon became a very close friend, said the reaction was much the same on her block. People just failed to acknowledge that everything that was familiar to them could be destroyed by a city edict. "My husband didn't believe it from the beginning anyway," she explained. "He was always kidding about it until they started tearing the houses down, and then he saw it was really going to happen. Most of the old folks—they are in their seventies—they just didn't want to get involved in it because they didn't believe it was going to happen. You couldn't get them to understand it.

"I've been married almost fifty years and our anniversary is going to be next July," Giannini added. "So on our golden wedding anniversary we're going to get kicked out of our house. I got up this morning and I was going through the house singing and my husband is looking at me. He says what the hell am I doing singing? I'm getting kicked out of my house, it's raining outside…" She laughed. "I say I don't give up. We don't want to go because, although it's not much, it's all we have. I always said the only place I'd move to from here was Mount Olivet [Cemetery]."

Fr. Malcolm Maloney, pastor at St. John's Roman Catholic Church, did bury a Poletown resident soon after the project was announced. Maloney recalled that most of his parishioners were distressed. Some had never celebrated Christmas in any other church. But one incident in particular stood out in his mind. A woman in her forties, who carried scars from falls caused by epilepsy, came to his office with a blue HUD relocation booklet in her hands. Maloney was concerned about her because she seemed frightened and disoriented. He tried to reach her family and her doctor but finally sent her home with the phone number of a shelter where he suggested she stay for a while.

"She walked back to her building, leaving her little blue book on my desk," Maloney said. "Some guy tried to grab her purse when she got home. She went up the stairs and jumped out the window. She was killed." Maloney paused. "So how would you feel? You get a notice of displacement—none of it having anything to do with saving your house…." He shook his head. Another of his parishioners had a heart attack and was hospitalized when she saw the first woman plunge from her apartment window next door.

Confusion permeated the neighborhood. While many people refused to believe that the neighborhood was truly in jeopardy, others insisted that the neighborhood was doomed and that there was no point in resisting General Motors. The news media, of course, reinforced the latter perception. Newspaper and TV coverage generally rejoiced about the Cadillac plant project; the mourning of residents only served as a minor dissonant counterpoint to the story.

Rumors flew wildly—one in particular, which warned that if you didn't sell your house quickly, the city would run out of money and you'd lose your home and neighborhood for next to nothing.

But when the first public meetings were called at Parke elementary and Kettering high schools, 1,000 people showed up and most of them were angry. They listened to presentations by city council members, representatives from CEDD,* an appraiser, staff people from the state and national Historic Preservation councils, the Citizens District Council,

---

*Editors' Note: Community and Economic Development Department.

and GM officials. They were shown slides of the Oklahoma prototype plant, of the new plant site design, and of alternate housing available in Detroit. Then a brief question-and-answer period followed, during which those who got to speak were limited to three minutes. Residents repeatedly asked why the citizens weren't allowed to vote on whether they should be displaced by General Motors. They asked whether GM had made any binding commitments about the number of jobs it would provide at the plant and whether the city council was really going to give the corporation a tax abatement on top of everything else. They also questioned the amounts of money people would be offered for their homes, when they would receive it, and whether the elderly would be able to get mortgages.[1]

Donald Ludwig, a Poletown resident and former GM engineer, gave the city council a written statement raising his objections, among them the concern that the plant would be highly automated and that the relocation would traumatize residents. Ludwig, a price cost analyst for the Army, complimented Poletown residents for not allowing their homes to fall into tax delinquency and HUD-ownership, a process he called "being HUDized." And he regretted that the homes would be taken over by CEDD official Emmett Moten instead—a process he called being "Motenized." "It is a pathetic sight," he wrote, "to see aged couples hugging each other, sobbing on the sidewalks, looking at their homes perhaps for the last time before being Motenized. Such scenes are not pleasant and it is not imaginable that a great city like Detroit could be so cold-hearted and gluttonous for the almighty buck."

John Saber's complaints were equally passionate and brought down the house at the Parke School hearing. Saber, sixty-eight, railed at the city council members: "I been living in this neighborhood for over forty-six years, and I don't intend to move because you con artists are trying to pull a rip off. Nobody can tell me up to eighty percent of the value of that house, how much that house is worth. To me it is a million dollars. My house has a brand new bathtub and I don't intend to move to a clunker, God-damned, cockroach-infested house that you pick out. I want to live on Kanter and I love every rotten board in that house."[2]

To the surprise of Emmett Moten and other city officials who had expected their cooperation in selling the GM project to neighborhood residents, Olechowski and Hodas handed out leaflets urging people to fight the GM project. They invited residents to a Poletown Neighborhood Council meeting in the basement of the Immaculate Conception Church. According to Hodas, most of the people attending the public hearing were very hostile to the demolition of their neighborhood. But some were mollified when city officials invited people to sign up for jobs preparing the GM site. Plus, he said, people were told they could apply to be paid appointees on the Citizens District Council (CDC) that the mayor would soon create.

Nearly 400 people attended the first meeting of the Poletown Neighborhood Council. Some of the residents had already begun organizing on their own. Lists of the names and addresses of city council members, the mayor, and the chairman of General Motors were passed from hand to hand. People pooled envelopes and stamps. Second generation Poletown residents, some of whom had studied at area colleges, helped their families and neighbors put their objections into writing.

It was at these early Poletown meetings that the Kaczynskis, the Crosbys, the Dockerys, and Karen Apollonio first met the Gianninis and the Jakubowskis. Bonds began to form in a number of directions as people recognized in each other the same resolve to stop the project or, at least, to make it as publicly costly as possible for the city and GM.

The prevailing sentiment in the neighborhood seemed to be that the neighborhood and the plant could co-exist. Residents resented being portrayed in the media as people whose selfish concerns posed an obstacle to the possibility of a new plant and jobs. "It's not the plant we're against," explained Hodas, who was elected vice president of the PNC. "It's the uprooting of history and human beings. We've seen the plans and we know that the site of the Immaculate Conception [Church] is supposed to be a flat 50-car parking lot. We've tried to talk them into building vertical parking structures, which would be more efficient, but they won't even talk to us about it."[3]

Residents also resented the way city officials were implying that sacrificing the neighborhood was no great loss, since it was already blighted and deteriorating. "They say this is a slum area," complained Sally Harris, a Poletown resident who was laid off from GM's Chevrolet Gear and Axle plant. "They don't know how good it is. We probably get along better than people out in Grosse Pointe. We all have to scuffle to make it and everyone looks out for everybody else. You keep thinking you're making some moves in your life, and then something like this comes along and you have to start all over again… The only way I would really be satisfied about moving is if they built that plant and gave me a job. But it's not going to happen. They're going to put robots in there and nobody's going to have a job."[4]

Many residents also expressed a strong sense of betrayal by an America they had believed in and fought for in the past. Harold Kaczynski, who fought in World War II and sent several of his children into the Service, complained, "I fought for this country for four years, and what do I get? They're trying to run me out of my home. I don't think that's justice. I'm not selling and I'm not moving. I'm not moving until the bulldozers come and knock me down in it. I got nothing to lose."[5]

Walter Jakubowski, retired from Chrysler, felt much the same way. "I've lived here for 60 years," he told the *Michigan Catholic*.

> My parents lived in this house. Two of my children were born upstairs because we couldn't afford hospitals during the war. I went to that [Immaculate Conception] church as a boy. I was married there. My children were baptized there. And now they want to tear it all down. I'll fight that. It's just too hard to take. I want to live here. If I didn't I could have moved a long time ago…. We're not interested in how much they'll give us for our homes. A house can be replaced. But you can't replace memories. A neighborhood is your life and a church the hub of your social and religious life. If they destroy all that, what do you have left? The government talks about protecting human rights in Asia and Africa, but they're trampling human rights in their own backyard. There is no democracy. You have democracy as long as you don't tangle with the power structure.[6]

The PNC meetings themselves were bold stabs at challenging the project, but they were hampered somewhat by the de facto leadership of Tom Olechowski who became the group's president partly because he was involved in organizing the area prior to the announcement of the GM project but also because he claimed to have connections at city hall and in the state capitol. Many Poletown residents said in retrospect that Olechowski served a real purpose in pulling the organization together and in giving people confidence that they could dare to argue with the authorities. But his leadership was the cause of much doubt and dissension. People complained that he was from the southern part of Poletown, which would not be affected by the plant site demolition, and that he also had a tendency to play his cards too close to his chest. Olechowski insisted on meeting with political and corporate leaders himself and discouraged others from trying to make contact on their own.

Olechowski's first objective may well have been a wise one. He wanted to establish a clear name for the neighborhood, so that the media would refer to the area by a community name rather than as the "proposed Central Industrial Park" area. It proved effective to designate the area as "Poletown," a name popular at the turn of the century. Non-Polish residents complained that the name alienated them, but it did recall the area's history. Consequently, the neighborhood was perceived as having an essence prior to and distinct from the Cadillac plant project. Within a few weeks the media had adopted the name.

This so infuriated the mayor that he denounced Poletown as a myth and constantly referred to the area as "so-called Poletown." Young's constant attacks on the integrity of the neighborhood earned him the hostility of many Poletown residents. "When he first got into office he was doing good," explained Bernice Kaczynski. "But when he got re-elected he started going another way. I'm saying now 'a mayor is a mayor: The black politician isn't going to do any more for me than the White politician because he never listened to me anyway. And now, he's calling us a myth."

Early on, a Citizens District Council (CDC) was set up by the mayor. This body was supposed to represent the public interest and oversee the project in compliance with Public Act 198. Hodas was asked to provide the names of ten community leaders for appointment to the CDC. Hodas did this, only to discover that business owners who were in favor of the GM project had also assembled a list of ten names. Officials at CEDD selected five names from each list.

The chairperson of the newly formed CDC, James Paczkowski, attended most of the early PNC meetings. According to residents who hoped to stop the GM project, he came intending to disrupt the meetings and to discredit the PNC leadership. "We couldn't stop him from coming, they were open meetings," Bernice Kaczynski explained, "but when he came in he caused a lot of chaos. That's how we found out about the Act 87, which is the eminent domain law, the quick-take law. We checked into that because he came to discredit Tom because he felt Tom didn't tell us about it. So Tom, I guess, wasn't aware of it at that point and that cost, because when the people finally found out what the Act 87 was, they were down on Tom for not telling us about it."

It was hard for residents to figure out the validity of these kinds of complaints, because the technicalities of the law under which they were being evicted were completely new to them. Most residents complained that when they tried to call city relocation offices or CEDD, the lines were busy or their calls were not returned. Deciphering the truth of the situation was nearly impossible and the pressure of time shortened most people's patience.

In addition, many Poletown residents were not used to having to challenge the government. Except for those with a labor union past, they had never been in a position to try to manipulate the political process. Some people tended to believe that if the Congress and the president learned about the situation they would intervene personally and put a stop to it. They believed that elected officials would put the rights of American citizens before the interests of General Motors. At one meeting an elderly woman expressed surprise when she reported, "I wrote a letter to President Carter, and I wrote about what's going on here. And

I didn't get an answer from him, but somebody in his office answered me and told me that the president doesn't answer letters. He has a staff working for him, and he says they can't do anything but referred me to the HUD office downtown."

Clearly there was a need for someone to provide perspective. But Olechowski may have stepped beyond his limits when he promised at meetings to check out and pursue the multifarious suggestions that were raised. Eventually, residents became irritated with his lack of follow-through.

Fr. Malcolm Maloney, a newcomer to Poletown who was appointed pastor of St. John's church just a few weeks before the GM project was made public, complained later that "there was a lot of dissatisfaction over the way meetings were run. Practically everyone wanted to resist but it seemed like a couple of big egos got off on a head trip. They wanted everything to fall under their banner. Every week their goals changed. They had demands that they were going to make that were really good, but the next week they changed and they had added a whole new set." Maloney started to pursue independent plans to sue the city, which he finally abandoned, when Fr. Joseph Karasiewicz, of the Immaculate Conception Church, gave his financial support to Olechowski's endeavors.

However, most agree that while Olechowski assumed the most visible power position in the Poletown resistance, another second string of leadership was forming. In fact, Olechowski's mobilization of the PNC did buy time for others who wanted to become active in Poletown. Karen Apollonio, who lived with her parents on Mitchell Street, teamed up with Bob Giannini, whose parents lived on the other side of East Grand Boulevard. Working with some other second-generation Poletown residents, like Connie Patrick, Pat Barszenki, and David Tylenda, they started planning more confrontational demonstrations by late September.

In four short months Poletown residents had banded together in a way that demonstrated a clear neighborhood identity. Their spokesman was articulate and passionate, even if his leadership was questioned. And the layer of leadership which was in the making promised more aggressive mailings, phone-calling efforts, and protests. The people who hung in behind the younger and less visible leaders, like Apollonio and Giannini, were primarily women, many of them elderly. These women may have taken the biggest risks of any when they decided to challenge the institutions they had depended on for so many years.

Rather than subside in disillusionment and bitterness, many of Poletown's women learned to fight back, carrying the American flag and the crucifix with them to protests. They drafted letters to their elected representatives, who rarely bothered to respond. They petitioned GM for a meeting to consider whether an alternative plant configuration could accommodate the plant and the neighborhood. And finally, they overcame their hesitancy and were willing to march down city streets with signs and chants.

All of this took a toll. Many of the women had to leave husbands and families to attend endless meetings. They had to expose themselves to the hostility of people who didn't share their views. They had to learn to speak out against critics who were often better-educated and more influential than they were.

Of course the city and GM were not standing still in the interim. While Poletown residents were aligning themselves and learning to grapple with the laws and executives that threatened their homes, the city and GM pushed ahead relentlessly toward clearing the land by May 1, 1981.

By fall Poletown residents were preparing to file suit and readying themselves for their first demonstration. But by then the city had already officially designated Poletown the Central Industrial Park Project. It had gotten a waiver from the Council on Environmental Quality to expedite preparation of the Environmental Impact Statement and contracted researchers to complete it. The city had held two public hearings to satisfy state and federal requirements and amended its application for federal monies to include an advance of $60.5 million in block grant monies to free up Section 108 loans. It had completed all its relocation surveys and 85 percent of its parcel appraisals.[7] In addition, the city's Economic Development Corporation (EDC) had passed a resolution stating that construction of the plant would serve a public purpose—a measure required to enable the city to use the new quicktake law to condemn people's homes.

Moreover, the city and GM had secured the support of the Roman Catholic archdiocese and the United Auto Workers. The union issued a brief statement commending GM for being socially responsible enough to build in Detroit. The church described itself as taking a neutral posture; however, it encouraged its Poletown parish priests to help their congregations move out by relying on Catholic Social Services. It also made the two priests cochairs of a church committee intended to defuse criticism and dissatisfaction with the project.

Both Poletown Catholic priests were new to their parishes. Fr. Malcolm Maloney, a Capuchin priest, arrived at St. John's one week after he had learned it was to be demolished. Fr. Joseph Karasiewicz, pastor of Immaculate Conception, had been at that church for only one year. However, Karasiewicz had a long history in the neighborhood. He had been raised in southern Poletown and had been carried into the Immaculate Conception Church (ICC) when he was only two years old.[8]

...

In late September, twenty black and white Poletown residents picketed outside St. John's Church during a Sunday mass. They were angry that the priest was preparing his parishioners to leave rather than to fight. (Maloney felt the battle was to be fought in court, not in the streets by his parishioners.) The protestors resented the forums which Maloney held at his church for parishioners to learn about the relocation process from city officials. They saw his whole approach as a betrayal. Their signs read: "The church supports GM," "Fr. Maloney—Present Day Shogun Priest," and "GM Desecrates Churches for Profit."

Maloney responded to the demonstration in the *Detroit Free Press:* "These people outside, these neighbors, their approach is atrocious. That's why they get a 'no' from the start. They don't want to discuss. They back you into a corner... I hope this relocation doesn't happen, but if it does, it will happen soon and we've got to be ready... I'm afraid of how this is going to affect the little old lady in her kitchen, wondering what's happening as the wrecking boom hits her building. There are a lot of people who are going to die over this. We are trying to bring in the social workers to help."[9]

Maloney started receiving hate mail, some of it scrawled on toilet paper, from other Poletown residents. "I became the guy on the scene who was the bishop's boy," he said. "They needed a fall guy. I felt like the Old Testament prophets when Jerusalem was going to be destroyed. They got stoned and persecuted, because they were telling people to leave. But we started telling people, 'You'd better move out. We'll help you.'"

Olechowski denounced the picket at the next PNC meeting, but those involved were satisfied with the results and pleased by the press coverage it generated. "It worked," Bernice Kaczynski said later. "We started to be noticed. We, as residents of Poletown, were being heard for the first time and not in some basement of a church. It was a new venture for all of us. We mostly raised our kids. You stay home with the kids and you elect your politicians to work for you and here the politicians were taking over and we had no say-so. And so it was nice to see the reaction of everyone. My son, who came home from the Navy, helped make the billboards. It was nice. There was a little bit of everybody there. Everybody we could get on short notice."

Karasiewicz's early role in the Poletown struggle was much more low-profile. He had an innate sympathy with the residents that probably came from his background in the area. (His father had been a janitor at Ford Motor Company by day and a shoemaker by night. His mother had been a seamstress and had taken in boarders.) Like others in the area Karasiewicz doubted that the project would actually be put through.

"I think a number of people never thought it would be a reality," Karasiewicz said, "because the money wasn't available and nobody thought GM would go through with it. GM was threatening to go to the sun belt. I thought it wouldn't affect the church at all and I hoped it wouldn't affect the people either, at least the majority of them."

In time, Karasiewicz became extremely outspoken about the project, and his critics would suggest that this was a radical deviation from his early position. However, when asked by a reporter for the *Michigan Catholic* in October what he thought of the archdiocesan committee he cochaired, Karasiewicz said he was upset that it "does not have as its goal to forestall the plant from reaching into the residential areas. They want to recruit as much help as possible for this committee, which doesn't make that much sense to me. It's like saying, 'We won't help you live, but when you die, we'll dress you up real nice.'"[10]

City officials spent time in September lining up the support of the Advisory Council on Historic Preservation (ACHP). The ACHP, a national agency intended to help protect historic structures that are either on or eligible to be on the National Register, had the right to make suggestions about ways to minimize the destruction of historic structures during the completion of projects. The first representative sent from Washington, Patrick Steele, toured the area and concluded that "the ethnic background" of Poletown entitled it to protection. But his superior, Robert Garvey, arranged to take his own tour of Poletown with Emmett Moten. Steele says Moten described the neighborhood as a rundown residential area and pointed out that it stood in the way of a $700 million development project. Garvey reportedly told Moten: "I don't see anything historic about this. I don't see that it would be a problem." Steele complained that at a policy briefing session "I was told, at two different times, that 'this is no time for integrity.' Shortly after that we had a policy committee session. Nobody came out and said anything direct, but it was pretty clear that we were going to give the needed papers to Detroit."[11]

On October 14, the city held its third public hearing. Like the previous ones it was top-heavy with presentations by GM and city officials. The question-and-answer period followed several hours of pro-plant talk by the panelists. Residents were allowed a few minutes to speak and were frequently angry that their questions were deflected, not answered.

Fr. Francis Skalski, rector of St. Hyacinth's Church in southern Poletown, attended. "I remember the meeting at Kettering High School very vividly," he said. "It was a mass meeting. There was about a thousand people there. It was hard to believe the amount of people there—blacks and whites and everyone. At that meeting I don't think they had more than six people speaking for the project. All the people there, young and old and middle-aged people, were against the project. Especially vocal were the people presently working for General Motors—they said they'd be losing jobs.

"My position throughout the whole thing was that you can't barter with a giant," Skalski added.

> I was probably the only one who said we don't need the project in this part of the city. I felt you couldn't win concessions from the city or GM. I brought up the fact that it was a shame that people like General Motors were coming in and taking over an area from poor people. It reminds me of a medieval king—there's a massive area, a nice big fence in front of their property, beautiful landscaping, and behind they have their castle—their plant. But nobody outside the neighborhood would listen to us. They thought we were antilabor, antijobs, just antiprogress when we started to fight. No one was giving too much attention to the fact of eminent domain, that this was a precedent-making affair.

At that meeting, residents were given a pamphlet titled *Acquisition Notice—When the City Acquires your Property*. This provided simplistic explanations for why the state could take your property against your will. There was no mention of the recent revisions in state law which were facilitating the GM project. Worse, there was a blatantly misleading paragraph stating that "in most states" residents who sued the condemning agency would have to pay their own attorneys' and appraisers' fees. The pamphlet failed to mention that in Michigan this was not the case. The Michigan Condemnation Act provided that the condemning agency would always pay appraisers and would also pay attorney fees if successfully sued. Emmett Donnelly, a representative of the Christian Service Department, pointed out the error and asked the city to amend the pamphlet. This was done within two weeks, but any Poletown residents who received only the first issue would presume that the state had no responsibility to help residents make their claims defensible in court.

Olechowski asked the city and GM officials at the meeting if residents could have forty days to consult with architects and industrial engineers to develop alternative site configurations which could accommodate the plant and the neighborhood. The request was denied.

Sandra Kotz, a Poletown mother at the meeting, accosted the city council and won rounds of applause. "My child is attending the same school that her grandfather attended," Kotz said. "I'm upset that I will never be able to afford to buy one of the cars that this plant will produce. Why don't they move it out to Grosse Pointe or Birmingham where the rich people live? You're taking away our freedom. You're not asking us—you're telling us. We're being ruled just like the gestapo."[12]

The next day, the draft Environmental Impact Statement was released, indicating that the city had adequately considered other possible sites and recommending approval of the project. The city's Economic Development Corporation, which was staffed by the Economic Growth Corporation, authorized a "letter of commitment" to GM. And on October 20, the city council's planning commission approved the project despite its concern about "real risks to the city in terms of financing and human impact." The report also said "the direct economic benefits to the city in terms of additional revenue have been somewhat overstated in the draft EIS."

In October Poletown residents began to express fear about living alone. The arson rate in the neighborhood had doubled since the project was announced, and even police arson investigators said that fires plaguing the neighborhood were a direct result of the GM project. But in the meantime residents worried that their neighbors would sell and move, leaving them next door to abandoned houses. The neighborhood began to feel transitional.

On October 31, the city council approved the project, declaring it "hereby determined to be for the use and benefit of the public." The only councilperson to vote against the project was Ken Cockrel, a Marxist known city-wide for his independence. On that same day, HUD authorized the city to draw on its $60.5 million in Section 108 loan guarantees.

The Poletown Neighborhood Council's efforts to challenge the constitutionality of Michigan's Uniform Condemnation Act were hampered by the group's difficulty in finding an attorney. This was partly attributable to Olechowski's preference for big-name Polish attorneys. But Poletown residents claimed it was also because most Detroit attorneys were unwilling to tackle General Motors and city hall. The PNC would eventually issue a press release to this effect.

Finally, labor attorney Ronald Reosti agreed to take the case, despite the fact that the PNC could not back the litigation financially nor coordinate a legal team to help with the case. Reosti decided to challenge the constitutionality of taking private homes for corporate profit. An expedited hearing was scheduled before Judge George Martin, a retired judge contracted by the city for the duration of the Poletown project. Reosti's motion for a temporary injunction to halt the taking and demolition of property until the legal issues were resolved was refused.

"This project violates the basic constitutionally guaranteed rights of the residents of Poletown," Reosti explained to the press. "If the court allows this takeover, it will set a precedent which can be used to undermine and erode the rights of citizens and neighborhoods in any part of our city or in any city in the country."[13]

In November and December Poletown residents picketed city hall and the Economic Development Corporation. At the EDC demonstration, protestors were denied access to the entire building which housed the Detroit Economic Growth Corporation, the EDC, and the Chamber of Commerce. When Jim Delcamp, a Poletown resident, and Nick Kubiak, whose aunt lived in Poletown, tried to insist that it was a public building, they were arrested. The charges were eventually dropped. At city hall, a group gathered to leaflet. One of those present was Teofilo Lucero, an American Indian in his seventies, who came to the demonstration in full Indian headdress. At PNC meetings Lucero was always the one who insisted that the government would be unrelenting in its relocation of the residents. He urged immediate action and was disappointed by people's confidence in letter-writing:

> People here are facing the same thing that the American Indian faced. We've been relocated ever since the white man came here. Our treaties meant nothing to them. And that's just about what our city fathers, GM, the mayor, the lawyers, the judges, and the governor are doing to us now. I said we got to retaliate before they hire the planners, but the residents didn't believe things were going to go through.
>
> The old people will never start over again. They'll be put in nursing homes. People here don't want that. They want to live here and die here. But what does GM and the city care? All they care about is the Almighty Dollar. We don't want that. We want to be humanly treated. Now you know what it's like to be relocated. It's a trail of tears.

One of Poletown's early demonstrations was a march through the neighborhood, which organizers hoped would draw the media into the neighborhood and force them to look closely at its character. Residents carried signs that read: "GM says get back—We say fight back." Members of the Revolutionary Socialists League who lived in the area helped organize the march, making some of their political skills available to Poletown residents. No other Left groups were willing to involve themselves, either because of the mayor's former reputation as a radical or because they saw battles for property as "petty bourgeois."

When he took the Poletown case, Reosti said he broke ranks with Detroit's Left lawyers, many of whom openly said that challenging the mayor was tantamount to facilitating racism. "I kept looking over my shoulder," he said.

> But I don't think it's proper for a corporation to extort these conditions. The residents are as concerned about jobs as anyone else. But to hold this neighborhood hostage to the loss of jobs is to concede that the GM plan is the only way to save jobs, and that is simply not true.
>
> Instead of using its vast energies and know-how to develop a plan for this urban area, GM has arbitrarily insisted on enough acreage to accommodate a plant designed for a flat, open area because that is what they did in Oklahoma. To force this design on this neighborhood and this city establishes the "government/business partnership" as a one-way deal. ... GM could have its plant and at the same time save much of the Poletown neighborhood and millions in tax dollars with a more efficient design. There are several alternatives to allow for building the plant and saving both the neighborhood and taxpayer dollars. The neighborhood is still functioning; people still want to live in Poletown. Some have decided to leave, but the great majority will maintain this community.[14]

Reosti was given just under three weeks to present his case to Judge Martin. He presented several alternate design configurations which had been prepared by a local architect. Each one included the plant, its power plant, and rail lines but also accommodated the neighborhood. A primary change from the GM site design was the creation of a vertical parking structure and rooftop parking.

Reosti argued that the city's use of eminent domain was unconstitutional because it primarily benefitted General Motors and the exchange of private property for such a purpose was illegal. He argued that taking the entire 465-acre site was an abuse of discretion because the construction of parking structures would eliminate the need to take the whole neighborhood. The absence of any such changes in GM's original design indicated that GM had forced the city's hand. Reosti also argued that Poletown, because of its history and ethnicity, was an area resource warranting protection under the Michigan Environmental Protection Act (MEPA).

Mayor Young testified before the court that unemployment was at a crisis level of 18 percent as compared to a national rate of 8 percent. Unemployment for minorities was estimated at 30 percent. The mayor also said that Detroit's industrial facilities were largely obsolete, which resulted in decreasing employment and a decreasing population in the City of Detroit. Young testified to the relentless efforts of the city to lure new industries into Detroit.

Judge Martin stated at the outset that his purview was relatively narrow, because he was bound by the quick-take statute to presume that an agency's finding of necessity to take the property was legitimate, unless there was evidence of "fraud, error of law, or abuse of discretion." The broader questions—such as whether it would be wise to take hundreds of parcels of property to build a Cadillac plant—were outside his jurisdiction.

Martin ruled that Poletown's presentation fell "far short" of proving the city abused its discretion because the city examined the residences and the people affected by the proposed plant, offered relocation help, and provided financial assistance for relocation. "General Motors held no gun to the head of the City of Detroit," Martin wrote, adding, "General Motors could go elsewhere." No doubt, the judge's intent was to show GM had not insisted on this particular site for the Cadillac plant, but he unintentionally acknowledged the argument of Poletown residents, which was that by threatening to leave Detroit GM *was* putting a gun to the head of the city.

Martin also ruled that the city's refusal to insist on the construction of parking structures was not an abuse of discretion but simply "having regard for all the features involved, including how workers rush to parking spaces on entering and exiting." The judge dismissed the MEPA argument, saying that the protection of cultural resources was outside the scope of the act.

Most importantly, Martin wrote that construction of the plant would serve primarily a public purpose, because "unemployment deeply affects the lives of citizens and of the city and state in which they are resident. Governor Milliken has approved this project, and it comes most definitely within the goal of federal programs. In large part how a city and state can avoid more decline depends upon the employment of its citizens. *The emphasis on this project is not upon GM but upon the employment and attendant revitalization of the city.* The use of the power of eminent domain for the Central Industrial Park Project serves a public purpose because the use of such power is indispensable in order for the city and EOC to take action to 'alleviate and prevent conditions of unemployment.'" (Emphasis added.)[15]

The Poletown Neighborhood Council immediately appealed the decision to the state court of appeals, as well as applying to the State supreme court for an appeals court bypass.[16] But by the third week of December, the city began demolishing Dodge Main and some of the very first residents began to leave. Many people held their breath through the Christmas season. Their faith was lodged in court appeals for the duration, but they were painfully aware of neighbors who were already searching for new homes.

"The court decision was a rotten deal," Mary Mitchell, a Poletown resident, complained. "When Judge Martin ruled in favor of GM, it was telling me you might as well give in. It was like saying, 'I work for the city, I get my paycheck from the city and I'm not supposed to go against them.' They say judges are supposed to be impartial. They're working hand in hand—the city, Reagan, big business. I wish the poor people and private citizens had control over the city, as much power as GM has. I feel anger and helplessness because of the whole situation. Why me? Why this area? I don't know what to do, who to turn to. I felt I didn't have the power to overcome big business."[17]

During this same time, residents began to receive notices giving them 20 days to "object to the necessity" of the city's condemnation. The city began to remove water meters from some homes. And the arson in the area began to escalate. Residents complained that they were being subjected to psychological warfare. While all the wheels were being greased with public agencies in Washington and with the UAW and the archdiocese in Detroit, the comfort and the safety of their neighborhood were being disrupted in an effort to deliberately undermine their ability to resist.

"1 think the city is behind it to scare people out," Carol Dockery, a mother of five, explained. "I blame General Motors and the city and these damn businesses that wouldn't stand behind us. If all the people would stand together, it would make a difference. It's something I've never seen before. I've got an education out of all this, I'll tell you."

Early on, most Poletown business owners were put in touch with condemnation attorneys who assured them that selling their properties to the city could be immensely profitable. They would be able to sue the city for monies above and beyond the assessed value, partly because the law required that the condemning agency help prevent the relocated business from going bankrupt. So few of them did more than make a token financial contribution to the community's resistance. In fact, the attorneys did eventually succeed in forcing the city to spend at least $100 million more than it had originally estimated for property acquisition and relocation.

One business owner who attempted to fight the project was Eddie Niedbala, owner of the Chene Trombly Market. Niedbala bought his market, renowned both for its homemade kielbasa and for its record sales of state lottery tickets, for $50,000 in 1947. Niedbala was popular in many circles and claimed the mayor as a "personal friend." An autographed picture of Coleman Young hung on a wall in the store.

When Niedbala first heard about the project, he telephoned Young. He was told, "'Don't fight it, you're going to lose.' And I says, 'You're full of it. I am going to fight it.'"

> I called [Senator Carl] Levin. I called [Senator Don] Riegle. I went right down the chain of command. I found out there's nobody to stop this. Nobody wanted to stop it. They wanted the plant. Young wants this plant bad and I can't blame him. Detroit needs that plant. But they could have made it smaller. GM is getting it for nothing so they take what they can get.

> I think the whole shot was illegal. The quick-take law, Public Act 87, that is wrong. I told that to the mayor. I told that to anybody that would listen. They just confiscated my property. It's just as bad as Russia. It's confiscation. I'm not being funny. They gave me half of what I paid for this place in 1947. I remodelled my whole upstairs living quarters. They're taking my home and my business for $34,000."[18]

Twenty-six months after the project was announced, after the Chene Trombly Market was destroyed, Niedbala died of a heart attack.

It was never precisely determined how many of Poletown's residents were willing to leave the area. The Citizens District Council claimed 70 percent of the people it interviewed wanted to leave, but researchers from the Social Research Application of Montana called the CDC study unscientific and published their own results which showed that two-thirds of the residents wanted to remain in the neighborhood.

Recent residents and renters were the group most likely to take the city's offer of money and go. Each renter was offered $4,000 to relocate. It doubtless did not escape the city's attention that most renters were young black families living below the poverty line.

These people could have been formidable adversaries to the mayor if they had chosen to fight the project, particularly since the mayor often charged that people resisting the GM project were racists. Young claimed that no one had protested the destruction of Black Bottom for freeway construction, because the neighborhood was black. He insisted Poletown generated interest only because it was white. This argument could fly only if the majority of Poletown's black residents, who constituted half the community's population, did not fight the project.

But for the many who wanted to stay in Poletown, the primary question was not how much money they would be offered for their homes. Again and again residents explained that they were fighting for principle.

"If we allow this to happen, our ethnic backgrounds, our religious backgrounds, our America has no way to stand because we're laughing at the laws men gave their lives for," Fisher complained from his Famous Bar-B-Q Restaurant. "Some of these people are affected mentally. They walk around like they're drunk, some of them saying 'What am I going to do?' Invariably we get a phone call or two every day. 'Did you hear anything, Carl? Do you know anything?' Who's to stop the same thing that happened in Germany? It may sound ridiculous to a lot of people, but then a lot of things sounded ridiculous to me until I seen with my own eyes what went on in Germany.

"I spent a whole year with the third armored division and I seen it all," Fisher said. "We spearheaded all the first army's moves. We were the first ones to overrun and release a German concentration camp. What we seen is deeply embedded in my mind. And I say it can happen any place. This is what we're allowing to happen here."

...

Not a single institution in the city of Detroit rallied on behalf of the Poletown residents. Residents attempted to contact the chief executives at General Motors, the mayor and his staff at CEDD, the cardinal and his adjuncts at the archdiocese, the local and high court judges, news editors and station managers, officials at the United Auto Workers, Detroit area clergy, community groups, and members of the Left.[19] None took the time to respond in a genuine manner. None even advocated a meeting of all parties to discuss possible compromises. For a variety of reasons, all of which could be reduced to a collusion of class, the power brokers in Detroit embraced GM's Cadillac project.

At every possible juncture these institutions—some of which Poletown residents had been prepared to fight and die for—rejected the community's appeals. Some people confided to Poletown residents that they did believe something needed to be done, but they would add that publicly they would endorse the plant since GM might move out of state. Detroit, they said, should do everything possible to accommodate the automaker.

Endnotes

[1]City of Detroit, Community and Economic Development Department, transcript, public hearing at Kettering High School, 14 Oct. 1980.

[2]*Poletown Lives!* transcript, p. 9. This Poletown documentary was produced by Information Factory and can be previewed by writing to 3512 Courville, Detroit, Mich. 48224.

[3]Harry Cook, "Members Rail at Poletown Church's Sale," *Detroit Free Press*, 24 Feb. 1981, A–3.

[4]"You Have to Start All Over Again," Workers' League in Detroit, *Bulletin*, 17 Feb. 1981.

[5]*Poletown Lives!* transcript, p. 1.

[6]Thomas Ewald, "Poletown!" *Michigan Catholic*, 15 Aug. 1980, p. 1; *Poletown Lives!* transcript, p. 12.

[7]Sandy Livingston, *Poletown Chronology*, Center for the Study of Responsive Law, 1982.

[8]James Ricci, "The Iron Priest of Poletown," *Detroit Free Press*, 15 May 1981, D–1.

[9]Stephen Franklin, "GM Protestors Picket Church," *Detroit Free Press*, 29 Sept. 1980, A–3.

[10]Thomas Ewald, "Poletown Church Group Hopes to Ease Resettlement Fight," *Michigan Catholic*, 3 Oct. 1980, p. 1.

[11]Patrick Steele, Advisory Council on Historic Preservation, telephone interview with Gene Stilp, winter, 1981.

[12]Bill Vann, "Protest GM Demolition Plan," *Bulletin*, 17 Oct. 1980, p. 12.

[13]Ronald Reosti, statement to the Poletown Neighborhood Council, 3 March 1981.

[14]Ibid.

[15]George T. Martin, *Findings of Fact and Law, Poletown Neighborhood Council v. City of Detroit and the Detroit Economic Development Corp.*, 8 Dec. 1980, Third Judicial Circuit Court of Michigan.

[16]During this time, Bob Giannini and Pat Barszenski organized a raffle to help provide money for court costs. Residents raised $1,000 by raffling three baskets of liquor.

[17]"We're Like a Testing Ground," *Bulletin*, 24 March 1981, p. 13.

[18]Patricia Chargot, Luther Jackson, "Big Court Battle Looms over GM Site," *Detroit Free Press*, 9 Nov. 1980, A–3; David Moberg, "GM Retools Detroit," In *These Times*, 4 Feb. 1981, p. 1; and Eddie Niedbala, with CSRL representative, Detroit, 10 June, 1981.

[19]Eventually, the Poletown Neighborhood Council decided to use certified mail so they could at least prove that their letters had been received.

Sports Stadiums: Good or Bad?*

George Lipsitz

When civic leaders in St. Louis, Los Angeles, and Houston decided to support construction of new sports stadia in their cities in the 1960s, their concerns went far beyond the desire to improve facilities for baseball and football games. The mass popularity of sports and the close relationship between civic identity and local teams made construction of sports facilities an important tool for promoting public and private spending aimed at solving problems of civic development. In each city the manner of financing and the method of locating the stadium responded to the local legacy of urban history. Consequently, public debates about stadium building involved larger questions about the nature of each metropolis and the amenities its form of development offered to its citizens.

Each city built the stadium appropriate to its stage of development. St. Louis planned Busch Stadium as the focal point of downtown urban renewal designed to transform that old industrial city into a modern center of commerce and finance. Los Angeles used the advantages of a growing population, available land, and a sophisticated freeway network to attract private capital for Dodger Stadium which called attention to that City's transition from a regional manufacturing and trading center into a national metropolis. And Houston used the speculative capital and promotional skill of some of its entrepreneurs to build the Astrodome as the anchor of a convention and hotel complex capable of advertising the rapid growth and technological resources of that emerging international city.

Supporters of each stadium presented themselves as proponents of the welfare of the entire population while downplaying the specific local interests helped and hurt by their plans. They boasted about the amount of private investment stimulated by the stadia without detailing the direct and indirect public subsidies required to make those investments viable. Voters in each city approved revenue bonds for land clearance and construction in anticipation of widely distributed benefits that never materialized. Yet the campaigns by stadium boosters did not take place in a vacuum; they responded to very real long-term trends that left civic leaders with few options. Two of those trends, the "Warner Model" of urban growth and the entry of the state into large scale capital accumulation for the private sector, set definitive parameters for decisions about stadium building in U.S. cities in the 1960s.

As outlined by urban historian Sam Bass Warner, U.S. cities have consistently attempted to solve their problems by extending the physical boundaries of the metropolis and by pooling low-risk wealthy populations in protected zones (Warner, 1962, 1972). As

*George Lipsitz, "Sports Stadia and Urban Development: A Tale of Three Cities." *Journal of Sport and Social Issues* 8 2: 1–18, 1984. Reprinted with permission.

early as the mid-nineteenth century, elites in cities like St. Louis moved to "private places" and residential suburbs to escape the overcrowding, disease, and pollution of the core city. Rather than supporting the collective cost of cleaning up the by-products of industrialization, they acted as individuals to build new residential neighborhoods on inexpensive land. This brought safety and pleasant surroundings to those who could afford them, but only at the expense of exacerbating conditions in older areas. Correctly viewing themselves as trapped in dirty and dangerous neighborhoods with inadequate access to vital public services, poor people followed the elite out of the central city. Willing to pay more than market value to escape the squalor of the slums, these residents often had little capital left over to make needed repairs or improvements, or even to make rental and mortgage payments. As a result, neighborhoods between slums and suburbs rapidly deteriorated into satellite slums, which in turn, pushed the elite even farther from the central city.

That process left downtown areas ringed with concentric circles of slums. It prematurely exhausted housing stock, and increased the costs of transportation, water, and electrical service by dispersing the population over an area that lost the economies of scale made possible by dense settlement. Yet the waste of resources and immiseration of the poor provided benefits for the rich. Those able to escape the costs of urbanization enjoyed comfortable homes in pleasant surroundings, gaining full benefit of services they purchased individually but passing along the increased costs of city services mandated by dispersed population to the public at large. Distance acted as an informal policeman for the rich, separating them from the resentments and envy of the poor. Class segregation made life cheaper for the upper and middle classes who pooled low-cost and low-risk populations in residential neighborhoods and suburbs, leaving high-risk populations without the resources to pay for the police and fire protection, insurance, medical, and educational costs, and street and sidewalk repair needed in their environment.

The Warner Model shaped development in older industrial cities, but it also characterized relations between cities and regions. Elite populations and industries abandoned whole cities as they had once abandoned older neighborhoods in pursuit of expansion to inexpensive land and low cost labor in the south and west. Between 1940 and 1970, the west and south increased their share of the nation's income from 33% to 43%, and their share of the population went from 42% in 1940 to 48% in 1970 (Abbott, 1981: 15). "Sunbelt" cities escaped the costs of years of decay and could offer lower taxes and more pleasant surroundings to industries interested in relocating. But they could do so precisely because the desire to escape the consequences of urban growth had so damaged older industrial cities in the first place.

The second historical trend influencing the nature of stadium construction in these cities had a briefer, but no less powerful legacy. Defense spending for World War II ended the Great Depression, and government spending in the postwar era fueled economic growth and prosperity (Eakins, 1969). Federal home loan policies, defense spending, highway construction, and urban renewal all played major roles in enabling the federal government to channel tax dollars into the private sector. To urban America, the role of the government in capital accumulation manifested itself in federal aid, but as well in local pro-growth coalitions seeking to use public funds as a stimulus for economic expansion.

The residual effects of the Warner Model emphasized the need for a progrowth coalition in St. Louis in the 1950s, one aimed at reversing the declining quality of life within the city and its disadvantages in competing for capital with sunbelt cities like Los Angeles and Houston. Yet those cities had coalitions too, and they worked to the positive trends in capital flight toward their regions that accompanied sustained and rapid growth. In St. Louis, Los Angeles, and Houston, leaders of the public and private sectors cooperated to build stadia as part of a larger strategy for urban growth consistent with the realities imposed by the Warner Model and by the increasing role of the state in capital accumulation.

St. Louis

In St. Louis stadium construction played a pivotal role in attempts at building a post-industrial city within the shell of a nineteenth century industrial metropolis. Established in the eighteenth century as a center for commerce, St. Louis became an industrial city in the 1800s, and then sank into slow and steady economic decline in this century (Primm, 1981). In the years immediately after World War II it suffered from federal policies that impacted on many cities of its type—home loan policies that favored single family suburban housing over renovation of inner city units (Jackson, 1980), defense spending which encouraged location of new plants outside the city limits (Ashton, 1978: 73), and federal highways that subsidized the costs of commuting and a more dispersed pattern of settlement (de Leon and Ems, 1973, Williams 1973). The movement of factories and people to the suburbs began in the nineteenth century, but by 1950 it had produced a real crisis threatening the future of St. Louis.

As they surveyed the dilapidated housing and crumbling economic infrastructure of their city, corporate leaders in St. Louis confronted an imposing array of problems. Slum housing encircled the downtown area inhibiting mercantile or corporate office expansion. The exodus of population and industry left behind large concentrations of high cost and high risk populations without the tax base required to attend to their many needs. Even though the city had the lowest per capita debt of any major city, budget deficits still exceeded $4 million per year, and voters rejected six municipal bond initiatives between 1945 and 1951 (Adde, 1960: 200). Worse yet, urban economists predicted a continued decline in the manufacturing sector of the U.S. economy, and they warned cities that only office activities and commercial shopping could expect to prosper in older industrial cities (Vernon, 1967, Mollenkopf, 1975: 127).

In order to address those problems, corporate leaders in St. Louis formed Civic Progress. Organized with the approval of Mayor Joseph Darst in 1953 who called it "the conscience of the community" the organization consisted exclusively of the chief executive officers of major corporations (Judd, 1979: 361–2). Inspired by Pittsburgh's Allegheny Conference on Development, Civic Progress attempted to reshape downtown St. Louis and turn it into an attractive center for shopping and corporate headquarters (Mollenkopf, 1975: 134, Sheak, 1971).

Members of Civic Progress also sought to direct slum clearance, urban redevelopment, and government spending along lines conducive to their own interests. Slum clearance and urban renewal could improve property values and make room for corporate expansion for firms with fixed investments in older areas. Tourist attractions and recreational events could bring money into the city and make it easier to attract top executive talent in competition with businesses in other regions (Sheak, 1971).

One leader of Civic Progress had a particular interest in that kind of urban redevelopment. August A. Busch, Jr., the pampered son of the most successful family in the brewing industry, used his corporation's money to purchase the St. Louis Cardinals baseball team in 1953 for $3 million. Hailed as a civic benefactor whose purchase kept the team in the city, Busch immediately attempted to use the team to make money for the brewery. He changed the name of their stadium from Sportsman's Park to Budweiser Park in order to advertise Anheuser-Busch's best-selling product. League officials objected to this crass commercialism and forced Busch to relent and name the stadium after his family—Busch Stadium, but then he had the brewery introduce a new product, Busch Beer, to capitalize on the free publicity provided by the stadium (*Fortune*, 1954, 1956, 1973, 1979).

In 1953 Busch led a Civic Progress delegation to Pittsburgh to observe the Allegheny Conference on Community Development. "The great thing we saw up there" he reported back to Civic Progress, "are the city, state, and federal government funds being spent for the good of Pittsburgh" (Raymond Tucker Papers, 1953). Busch had a notion about the "good of St. Louis" that coincided with his view of the good of Anheuser-Busch, and he urged St. Louis to follow Pittsburgh's example.

With Busch's participation, Civic Progess supported urban renewal that demolished slum neighborhoods in the Mill Creed Valley just west of the downtown central business district. That demolition left almost 30,000 poor people homeless and the city never developed adequate plans to relocate them. Urban renewal created a cleared out abandoned zone between central city office buildings in which Civic Progress firms had fixed investments and the poor people residing on the other sides of the urban renewal district.

Civic Progress secured $32 million in federal money to anchor the eastern part of downtown redevelopment with the Gateway Arch, $264 million to build a highway network around downtown, and additional millions in federal funds to build a convention center north of downtown and a shopping mall to the west. But the key item in downtown redevelopment proved to be the stadium.

Unlike other urban renewal projects, the stadium cleared no slum housing and made no contribution to the creation of more dwellings. Nevertheless, Civic Progress succeeded in getting the area for the proposed stadium declared "blighted" and consequently availed itself of opportunities to form a redevelopment corporation that could acquire land for a stadium through powers of condemnation and eminent domain established for urban renewal and slum clearance purposes.

For Anheuser-Busch, a new stadium enhanced the value of the Cardinal franchise, offered the prospect of more attendance and better revenues, and transferred costs of stadium construction, parking garages, street construction and lighting to other parties. In addition, it stabilized urban redevelopment in the section of downtown closest to the Anheuser-Busch brewery. The company put up $5 million to buy stock in the Civic Center Redevelopment Corporation that built and operated the stadium, but in return, Anheuser-Busch received access to a $20 million stadium without having to incur land acquisition costs, construction costs, or taxes (*Leif J. Sverdrup Papers*, 1960). But even more important benefits for the brewery and for other Civic Progress corporations came from the stadium's utility as a device for tax breaks for downtown corporate enterprises.

Missouri's "353" Redevelopment Law allowed businesses engaged in redevelopment of "blighted" areas to avoid all taxes on their property for ten years and to pay only half taxes for fifteen years after that. By including the stadium as a project qualified for such subsidy, the city and state opened the door for other profit-oriented business to tax advantages for locating in areas designated blighted whether those areas included slums or not, or whether or not such development served public purposes. In the case of the stadium, land cleared for redevelopment by the demolition of slums in the Mill Creek Valley (the "buffer zone" west of downtown) stood vacant while even more demolition took place downtown to make room for the stadium. Only by placing the stadium downtown could it serve as a wedge to secure tax breaks for adjacent businesses.

Small business owners displaced by the stadium project tried to warn the public about the dangers of such subsidy. In an advertisement in the November 21, 1961 *St. Louis Globe-Democrat*, they argued against the proposed stadium because it used public money to subsidize the transfer of choice real estate to profit-oriented business and because tax concessions granted to downtown business would then have to be made up by the rest of the city. They asked taxpayers

> Is it right that this kind of profit and private ownership be allowed to create many major problems for the City—and major problems for YOU, too—such as higher taxes on top of the already heavy tax load you bear?

But proponents of the stadium answered that it took that kind of sure profit-making to attract the capital necessary to build the stadium and that only a downtown site presented that opportunity, (*St. Louis Globe-Democrat* editorial, December 5, 1961, *Sverdrup Papers*, 1961).

On March 6, 1962 St. Louis voters approved a $6 million bond issue for sidewalk, street, and lighting improvements in the stadium area. Civic Progress corporations raised $20 million to establish equity for a $31 million loan from the Equitable Assurance Company, a firm with $900 million already invested in the city and a company soon to locate its new corporate headquarters within the tax sheltered redevelopment area (*St. Louis Commerce*, July 1961). Boosters promised that the stadium would bring people downtown to shop and that even with the generous tax provisions of the "353" law, the area which paid only $108,000 in taxes before construction of the stadium would supply to the city $540,000 in payments in lieu of taxes within ten years (Land Clearance and Redevelopment Agency, 1961).

Those estimates proved incorrect. Despite $135 million worth of development in office buildings, hotels, parking garages, and other ventures, the Civic Center Redevelopment Area paid only $259,324 to the city in lieu of taxes in 1976, and downtown retail establishments perceived no increase in business because of the stadium. The facility itself lost from $300,000 to $900,000 per year for the Civic Center Redevelopment Corporation (*Nation's Business*, 1977:110). Yet the baseball club, or to be specific the brewery that owned it, escaped the expense of those losses and along with investors in the office buildings, hotels, and parking garages around the stadium, it enjoyed a bonanza of tax subsidized profits.

To August A. Busch and the other members of Civic Progress the stadium exemplified the bright future of St. Louis. The old Sportsman's Park stood in an industrial neighborhood on the city's North Side—a remnant of a time when skilled labor and dense population made St. Louis a major city. The stadium anchored a gleaming downtown with a sparse population but many offices and cultural attractions. A subsidiary agency of Civic Progress, Downtown St. Louis, Incorporated, celebrated this in a 1968 report that claimed that "all great cities have in common two characteristics, an exciting downtown filled with a great variety of shops, theatres, museums, and other attractions" coupled with "a large middle class population residing near downtown possessing the purchasing power and tastes to help sustain its activities" (Sheak, 1971: 4).

After nearly two decades of this kind of development, corporations represented in Civic Progress netted profits of $892 million *per year*. Nearly twice the total assets of the city, this sum amounted to eight times the city budget, and seventy times its expenditure on health, housing, and welfare. And therein lay the problem. Even when development like the stadium fulfilled their promise for investors, they created problems for the rest of the city. While nearly $200 million of new construction projects in the 1960s and 1970s paid no taxes under the "353" redevelopment provisions, homeowners found themselves charged higher taxes for fewer services. Urban renewal's destruction of slums reduced the city's housing stock by 24,500 units between 1960 and 1970, and almost one fourth of the remaining housing had serious deficiencies. That housing disaster drove poor people into once stable residential areas creating new slums in the city's north side and west end. The combination of spreading slums, high taxes, and declining services accelerated the flight of the city's middle class tax base to the suburbs. Between 1966 and 1977 assessed valuation of real property in St. Louis fell from $1.59 billion to $1.37 billion. Property taxes as a share of city government and total tax revenue fell from 30% to 20% with consequent increases in even more regressive forms of taxation like the general sales tax which increased 110% between 1972 and 1978 (Schmandt et al. 1979: 9–12).

Downtown redevelopment also encouraged unwise investments that imposed further burdens on taxpayers. Even though marketing studies as early as 1954 showed that land costs and inadequate services made the downtown riverfront undesirable for residential development, St. Louis granted "353" tax abatement to the developers of the Mansion House Center (Adde, 1969: 200). Out of town investors like the General Electric Pension Fund, Mellon National Bank, and the John Hancock Corporation combined for more than $50 million worth of capital in the project. By 1972, Hancock and Mellon fell $375,000 behind in FHA insured mortgage payments causing the federal government to take over the mortgages. Individual inverstors in the center profited from the default and subsequent bankruptcy of Mansion House due to federal tax laws, but the waste of capital and resources in St. Louis made Mansion House a disaster for local taxpayers (*Business Week*, 1972: 78, *Community Development Agency Report*, 1977).

In 1981, Anheuser-Busch demanded ownership of Busch Stadium and control over revenue from parking, concessions, and adjacent offices and hotels as an inducement to keep the team in St. Louis. The brewery offered $30.2 million as a purchase price, a figure ridiculed as outrageously low, even by Civic Progress officials serving on the board of the Civic Center Redevelopment Corporation (*Wall Street Journal*, June 8, 1981: 29). When the Apex Oil Company submitted a bid of $59.9 million for the same property, Anheuser-Busch broke off negotiations with Civic Center Redevelopment Corporation and used its influence over the May Department Stores Charitable Trust, the Laclede Gas Company, and Mercantile Trust to privately secure a controlling interest in the redevelopment corporation thereby becoming the owner of the stadium and adjacent properties (*Wall Street Journal*, July 29, 1981:15). The brewery paid $3 million for the Cardinal team in 1953, and invested an additional $5 million in its purchase of stock in the Civic Center Redevelopment Corporation in 1960, plus an undisclosed amount to win voting control of that organization in 1981 For that investment, it received free publicity for thirty years, profit from baseball operations, access to a modern and centrally-located stadium and eventually ownership of it along with a large part of downtown St. Louis. At the same time, the brewery could afford to spend $38 million to recreate the African veldt in Tampa, Florida in its theme park, Busch Gardens. It even built a Swiss chalet in the middle of the recreation of the veldt as a tribute to Busch's Swiss wife. Yet due to the "353" law, taxpayers who witnessed the closing of the only full service hospital in the Black community, the curtailment of music, art, and sports in some public schools, and a disastrous cut in city services, wound up subsidizing the brewery and the other business like Equitable Assurance, General American Life, Pet Milk, and Union Electric with offices in the redevelopment area (*Fortune*, January 1979).

That brought St. Louis full circle with the Warner Model. Urban renewal attempted to reclaim downtown areas threatened by slums in order to reconstitute the city. Yet in the creation of a new low-cost low-risk zone downtown, the St. Louis elite shifted the burdens of urban growth onto others as they had always done. And by building corporate office buildings and a stadium rather than factories or housing, they accelerated the national tendencies of the Warner Model—the flight of capital and employment to other parts of the nation and the rest of the world.

The diminishing importance of industry to the U.S. domestic economy, the dilapidation of housing stock and industrial infrastructure in St. Louis, and the high costs of land clearance motivated business and government to devise structures to accumulate capital for the private sector. Broad popular support for the stadium brought narrow benefits for a few but did not reverse the effect of the Warner Model. To a sunbelt city like Los Angeles, the decline of St. Louis and other older industrial cities brought important benefits. Free of some of the local costs of traditional urban industrial development, it nonetheless also responded to the government's role in capital accumulation and land clearance, and in its own way dealt with the legacy of the Warner Model in industrial cities.

Los Angeles

Settled as a trading center in the eighteenth century, Los Angeles became an important railroad terminal after the Civil War, and a dominant city in its region by 1940. No city enjoyed as much sustained or rapid growth after 1850, and by 1930 almost 38% of California's population—and 18% of the population of the eleven westernmost states—resided in Los Angeles. Between 1936 and 1939 more than 200,000 new residents moved to the metropolis, but it took defense spending for World War II and afterwards to turn Los Angeles into America's second largest center for population and its third largest center for manufacturing (*Southern California Research Council*, 1958).

During World War II the federal government spent $30 billion on direct defense spending in the west including $2 billion for new plant and equipment (Abbott, 1981:16). Government spending on shipyards, aircraft plants, and related research and development activities made Los Angeles the only diversified manufacturing center outside the northeast (Warner, 1972). The role of the state in capital accumulation during and after World War II made its presence felt more in Los Angeles than in any other city through enormous defense spending on aerospace and related industries, elaborate highway construction programs, and extensive subsidies for low density single family dwelling by federal home loan agencies. These formed the basis for a spectacular growth in population and allowed for new uses of urban space that transcended some of the costs and some of the constraints of the Warner Model in older industrial cities.

Five hundred new residents per day moved to Los Angeles between 1945 and 1955 for a ten year total of 1,725,000 migrants: more than the combined total populations of Baltimore and Pittsburgh (*Southern California Research Council*, 1958). They moved into a city with widely scattered housing, industry, and commerce with no dominant downtown core. As early as the 1920s, the Los Angeles County Planning Commission favored dispersed settlement and encouraged that kind of development (Abbott, 1981:16) The local elite invested heavily in selling suburban land to newcomers and as a result had little fear of peripheral development eclipsing the downtown core (Halberstam, 1979:164). And the rapid growth of freeways instead of mass transit allowed for multicentered development that did not have to radiate outward from the central city (Warner, 1972: 138).

Yet Los Angeles did have slums and its growth resembled that of cities more closely in tune with the Warner Model in important respects. The discriminatory policies of realtors and the federal home loan agencies excluded minorities from much of the city's new suburban housing (*NAACP Papers*, 1945, *HOLC Papers*, 1939). The city refused to spend $10 million in federal appropriations for slum clearance between 1937 and 1940 because its officials refused to acknowledge the existence of slums even though the Home Owners Loan Corporation files showed extensive blight and substandard housing in Black and Mexican-American neighborhoods (*California Eagle*, May 1, 1949, *National Urban League Papers*, 1949, *HOLC Papers*, 1939). The Regional Plan Commission used zoning powers to encourage concentration of minorities in older and less desirable districts—by 1950 almost 95% of the Los Angeles Black community lived in the central district (*NAACP Papers*, 1945).

As in cities conventionally ruled by the Warner Model, Los Angeles produced better living conditions for those on the periphery by enabling them to escape the overcrowding and social costs of the center city. Poor people in Los Angeles remained trapped in clearly marked areas and the political fragmentation of the region engendered by urban sprawl meant that they received fewer concessions in the form of public services and amenities from government than did the poor in older industrial cities.

Los Angeles voters provided a graphic example of their unwillingness to distribute the costs of urban growth evenly in an election in 1952 when they rejected federally sponsored public housing on the basis of a campaign which portrayed such spending as "creeping socialism" (Hines, 1982, Henderson, 1980). That election curtailed development of a public housing project in the Chavez Ravine area near downtown, leaving the land to be used for another as yet undesignated public purpose. Yet eviction had already started and the city continued to move residents out, even though it had no viable plan for the land. That land attracted Walter O'Malley and his Brooklyn Dodgers baseball team to Los Angeles, and that land eventually provided the site for Dodger Stadium.

Walter O'Malley cultivated an interest in baseball in the 1940s when he began taking his clients to games in Brooklyn's Ebbets Field. A lawyer specializing in bankruptcies, he became involved in the Dodger organization while restructuring its debt to one of his clients—the Brooklyn Trust Company. He became part owner of the ballclub in 1945 and assumed full control in 1950 for a purchase price of $2 million. O'Malley and the Dodgers made money in the early 1950s but by the middle of the decade, the Warner Model of development caught up with Brooklyn and the neighborhood around the Dodger ballpark (Kahn, 1973: 377–378).

Brooklyn suffered from all the forces that helped develop Los Angeles. Defense spending shifted tax dollars from the east to the west coast, FHA loans providing mortgage insurance for single family home owners subsidized a new and growing suburban city like Los Angeles at the expense of older multi-family dwelling dominated cities like Brooklyn, and the federal highway program encouraged movement of industry away from older industrial centers like New York. Within Brooklyn, the exodus of population to the suburbs of Long Island and New Jersey left behind deteriorated formerly middle class neighborhoods. Once the hub of a thriving community, Ebbetts Field appeared increasingly inaccessible and undesirable to the mobile segments of the population.[1]

Unhappy with a small old ballpark served by only one subway line, O'Malley got the state of New York to authorize construction of a new stadium at the intersection of Atlantic and Flatbush avenues. The Dodger owner sold Ebbetts Field and two minor league ballparks for $5 million and prepared to invest that sum in the new stadium. But land acquisition proved difficult in the face of rising prices and neighborhood opposition, and New York City authorities eventually quashed the project because of the terrible traffic problems it would create. Aware of the benefits reaped by the Boston Braves from their 1953 franchise shift to Milwaukee, O'Malley began to look for a city that could offer what Brooklyn could not, and Los Angeles proved to be irresistible (Kahn, 1973: 389, *New York Times*, January 3, 1958: 21).

The city government of Los Angeles had purchased more than three hundred acres of land at Chavez Ravine from the Housing Authority for $800,000 after the 1952 referendum.[2] Mayor Norris Poulson offered the land to O'Malley as an inducement for him to move the team to Los Angeles and build a stadium on that site. O'Malley called the land "two hundred and ten taxable acres of hill ground that would be of interest only to goats"— a disingenuous description of a neighborhood that housed 1800 families and which occupied a choice location near downtown and at the intersection of three major freeways. After complex negotiations, the city agreed to give to O'Malley 315 acres of land worth anywhere from $2 million to $6, mineral rights under that land, a ninety-nine year lease, all revenues from parking, concessions, and tickets, $4.7 million in land preparation costs, and $5,000 of free surveying donated by Howard Hughes. In return, O'Malley promised to provide the capital for a $20 million stadium (Poulson, 1966: 333, Coll, 1983: 61; Henderson, 1980, *New York Times*, June 4, 1958: 1).

Opponents of the agreement led by City Council members John C. Holland and James C. Corman doubted the wisdom and legality of the plan. Private citizens filed lawsuits arguing that land acquired for slum clearance and other "public purposes" should not be handed over to a private profit-making business. City Council hearings probed the necessity of supplying three hundred acres of land in a choice location for a stadium and parking lot that required only 100 acres, and a committee of the state legislature looked into the part of the agreement that turned over land owned by the state to the Dodgers (*New York Times*, January 23, 1958: 31, March 26, 1958: 49, March 27, 1958: 44, April 23, 1958: 43, June 4, 1958: 1).

Taxpayers forced a referendum on the Chavez Ravine Stadium held June 3, 1958. The city and the Dodgers promised to build a stadium with private funds at the very time that San Francisco and other cities assumed that the only viable sports complexes had to be municipally owned and leased to the teams. They also threatened that the Dodgers would move out of Los Angeles as they had moved out of Brooklyn if they did not have a suitable stadium. With the aid of a last minute telethon starring Debbie Reynolds and Ronald Reagan, voters approved the team's lease by a vote of 345,435 in favor and 321,142 against (Poulson, 1966: 206, Henderson, 1980, *New York Times*, June 6, 1958:17).

The Los Angeles electorate that voted against public housing in 1952 as "creeping socialism," six years later turned over a huge chunk of downtown real estate, $4.7 million in services, and mineral rights to allow a millionaire to make even more money. The city government that rejected aid for slum clearance in the 1930s replaced the homes of Chavez Ravine residents with a stadium that housed no one. But a population swelled by the decline of older industrial cities all over the country, found that its very size and prospects for growth attracted a private capital investment that would not have been made in Brooklyn.

Walter O'Malley put up $20 million of his own money to build Dodger Stadium. Unlike Horace Stoneham in San Francisco he did not ask the city to build its own stadium, and unlike August A. Busch in St. Louis he received no help from other private investors interested in tax abatement; in fact Dodger stadium paid taxes to the city amounting to $800,000 per year by 1965. Yet the growth of Los Angeles and the ideal location of Dodger Stadium made O'Malley the dominant economic force in baseball and gave him a substantial private fortune at a relatively low cost. Tax revenue from Dodger Stadium every year exceeded the purchase price of Chavez Ravine for the city, but had that land put to other uses it would certainly have generated more tax income (Poulson, 1966: 333. Henderson, 1980).

The push factor out of Brooklyn and the pull factor into Los Angeles followed the Warner Model and enabled Los Angeles to spend less on its stadium than St. Louis and receive more income from it. The role of the state in large scale capital accumulation for the private sector provided the model for the city of Los Angeles' generous lease with the Dodgers which gave them land for a stadium that other cities could not give, land taken from slum dwellers with the promise of relocating them in new housing in that neighborhood. No less than in St. Louis, the sports stadium in Los Angeles won subsidies for the rich at the expense of the more needy elements of the population, and like St. Louis it also offered some benefits to the public at large: in St. Louis, downtown redevelopment; in Los Angeles, property that paid taxes. By contrast. Houston enjoyed the benefits of the up side of the Warner Model, yet constructed a stadium that cost taxpayers more money than the ones in St. Louis or Los Angeles, yet provided far fewer public benefits.

Houston

Founded as a speculative venture by two New York businessmen in the 1830s, Houston enjoyed steady growth in the 19th and 20th centuries. Construction of the Houston Ship Channel made the city the nation's second largest port, and the oil booms of the early twentieth century made it a regional center for commerce and trade. In the depression decade of the 1930s when St. Louis lost population and Los Angeles grew by 25%, Houston's population increased by 51% (Primm, 1981: 442, HOLC Files, 1942). Yet Houston lacked the qualities necessary to be a major city in the industrial era. Unlike St. Louis with its river location and access to key railroad routes, Houston could not easily tap large markets in nearby population centers, nor could it readily obtain industrial raw materials. Unlike Los Angeles which served as the terminus of continental trade and the pre-eminent port on the

Pacific, Houston enjoyed no clear cut and obvious advantages over other cities as a site for manufacturing.

Economic growth in Houston hinged on enterprises with small numbers of workers and lots of capital. Deprived of the private capital accumulation that built industry in St. Louis in the 19th century, or the kinds of public spending that made Los Angeles a manufacturing center during World War II, Houston remained a regional trade center until the 1960s. Its working class experienced a fragmentation that left it spread throughout the region physically, and unorganized at the point of production. In St. Louis, ward bosses forced the elite to share some measure of power and public services with the working class, but in Houston the Chamber of Commerce pretty much ran the city as it pleased for its own benefit. Their philosophy, consistent with their role in the economy, called for low taxation and minimal government services.

In the 1940s Houston spent less than $1 per capita on public health per year—the American Public Health Association standards called for $1.75 to $2.25 per capita. The city delayed work on a full care public hospital in the 1950s to protest federal "red tape" consisting of reasonable regulations ensuring its fair and efficient operation. School board members opposed the federal school lunch program as "socialism" until 1967. Completely hostile to public city planning or zoning (although rife with restrictive covenants and deed restrictions on the private level), Houston could not qualify for federal urban renewal or model cities anti-poverty funds for years because it could not meet congressional guidelines mandating local commitment to orderly and equitable development (*National Urban League Papers*, 1945, McComb, 1981: 227, 443, *National Commission on Urban Problems*, 1967).

Without comprehensive planning and with only limited public expenditures, Houston invented new variations on the Warner Model. Downtown businessmen enjoyed the advantages of concentrated development in their business transactions, but weak political government and dispersed settlement enabled them to run away from the problems of the poor. Lack of public transportation confined poor and minority populations to undesirable areas, dispersed population made the costs of public services prohibitively expensive, and low taxation meant that the wealthy could keep more of the city's wealth for themselves. Sprawling over scattered subdivisions characterized by cul-de-sacs and few through streets, development undermined the public character of urban life and divided the city into privatized zones. The absence of zoning, street maintenance, and lighting in the rest of the city made private subdivisions all that much more attractive to those who could afford to live in them. Without the shared public space and transportation of St. Louis, or the careful planning of freeways that characterized Los Angeles, Houston's version evolved into the greatest possible private reward for the smallest possible public expenditure.

As had been the case with Los Angeles, federal spending propelled Houston to the first rank of U.S. cities in the postwar era. Federal flood control measures, the highway program, and home loan policies facilitated growth, and the location of the National Aeronautics and Space Administration Center in Houston provided a boost to local research and development operations. Air conditioning made the city's debilitating climate less oppressive to newcomers, and the prosperity of the oil industry engendered favorable conditions for ancillary business activities. Almost overnight, Houston changed from a regional center of commerce into an international metropolis. It skipped the industrial stage and became the first great American post-industrial city.

Oil money built the skyscrapers dominating the downtown skyline in Houston. Oil money secured the influence and provided the land that served as the site for NASA. And oil money led the way in bringing major league baseball to Houston. Securing an expansion franchise became an important goal for local boosters eager to publicize the spectacular growth of their city. Attracting new capital and encouraging relocation of corporate headquarters could be made easier if the rest of the country acknowledged the "big league" status of Houston. So they launched plans to build a stadium capable of securing a team and of symbolizing the city's identity.

Roy Hofheinz, a local entrepreneur and sometimes Mayor and County Judge, led the efforts to acquire a team and build the stadium. He formed an alliance with H.E. Bob Smith, a local oil magnate with extensive holdings near Bray's Bayou, seven miles southwest of downtown and near the burgeoning medical center. Together they created the Houston Sports Association which proposed a domed stadium—a necessity for baseball in Houston given the local heat, rain, and mosquitoes, but also an appropriate symbol of the new technologies and new possibilities innate to Houston's growth (Cartwright, 1968: 10).

Unlike Busch Stadium or Dodger Stadium, the Astrodome did not usurp land intended for other purposes or aggravate the displacement of poor people from their homes. But it did reflect a kind of decision making and a set of priorities consistent with the Houston ideal of metropolitan life.

Hofheinz and Smith proposed to raise $6 million and asked the city and county government to come up with the remaining $31 million for the Astrodome. They selected land owned by Smith near Bray's Bayou as the stadium site—land previously without value because of its tendency to flood. Building the Astrodome made it economically feasible to control the flooding and consequently added value to surrounding properties owned by Smith. Judge Hofheinz and his associate proposed four luxury hotels and an amusement park as part of their project as well as a small convention hall to supplement use of the Astrodome for that purpose. Once local authorities committed themselves to bond issues to finance the Astrodome, Smith and Hofheinz sold luxury boxes to corporations (who could deduct their purchases from their taxes) to raise their $6 million (McComb, 1981: 443, Cartwright, 1968: 11).

Houston voters approved the revenue bonds needed for the Astrodome in a bitterly contested election in 1961. Smith and Hofheinz contributed only $6 million out of the eventual $45 million required to build the stadium with the county ($31.6 million), city ($3.7 million) and other sources making up the difference. H.E. Bob Smith "donated" $4 million in land for right of way and access roads, the Texas Highway Department accelerated by five years its plans to construct a highway adjacent to the stadium, and even the federal government helped out Judge Hofheinz by granting $750,000 to him in return for designating the Astrodome an "emergency fallout shelter" in case of nuclear war (Cartwright. 1968: 11). In return, the Houston Sports Association took out a forty year lease on the building from the county at a maximum rent of $750,000 per year.

Houston trusted the skill of its entrepreneurs and made a public investment greater than had been done in St. Louis or Los Angeles. The city that refused to subsidize school lunches voted to risk $37 million of direct public spending on a private profit making venture. It demanded almost nothing in return—merely $750,000 a year in rent to be used toward retiring the revenue bonds and for meeting operating expenses. But that proved to be a mistake. In 1965 Hofheinz and Smith had a disagreement and Hofheinz had to borrow

$7 million to buy out his partner. The financial structure of his enterprise never recovered, and despite some profitable years (like 1966 when the Houston Sports Association made a profit of $3 million), Hofheinz fell deeply in debt ($38 million by 1975) and had to surrender control of the Astrodome and related properties to the Ford Motor Credit Company and the General Electric Credit Company (Cartwright, 1968: 11, McComb, 1981: 443, *New York Times*, June 25, 1975: 36, May 13, 1979: A10).

The Astrodome lost $569,000 in 1971 (Burck 1973: 106) and has continued to lose money ever since. The taxpayers financed Judge Hofheinz's high living and grandiose schemes (he had a palatial suite and a private bowling alley built for himself in the stadium) and they continue to pay debt servicing and maintenance on the facility (air conditioning must be run around the clock all year round). In 1983 voters recognized the Astrodome and Astrohall's inadequacies as a convention site when they approved funds to build a downtown convention center over the strong objections of the Houston Sports Association which warned that the new center would only compound the economic difficulties facing the Astrodome (*Houston Post*, November 9, 1983: 1).

Houston voters made a major commitment to the Astrodome for very little public return. At least in St. Louis tax abatement did revitalize part of downtown, and in Los Angeles modest grants of land and capital created a tax generating property. Houston created a spectacular opportunity for private investors with few public controls or responsibilities. That reckless process brought major league baseball to Houston and created an impressive and expensive structure. But the glitter proved short lived and the long range consequences costly. If Houston had more margin for error because of its advantageous position on the up side of the Warner Model, its refusal to plan rationally for growth or to share the benefits of public expenditures connected to the Astrodome portends an ominous future. For the short-sightedness behind the construction of the Astrodome reflects an urban philosophy present in other areas of life in Houston as well.

As with the Astrodome, Houston has attempted to address problems like land subsidence or traffic safety with the minimum public expenditure. Rapid growth in population without expenditures for new supplies of surface water has caused the land in the city to sink at an alarming rate. Houston is now four feet lower than it was in 1900, but if current trends continue, the affluent western section of the city will sink four more feet in the next twenty years. Downtown could sink 14 feet in the next 40 years. Last summer the Brownwood subdivision in Baytown endured another of the many floods which have plagued its existence and the entire property had to be condemned and abandoned. Flooding and subsidence threaten an investment of more than $100 billion in the heart of the city, but Houston has no master plan to deal with this threat (*New York Times*, September 26, 1982: 28, *Houston Chronicle*, September 29, 1983: section 2, page 3).

Similarly, low public expenditures and poor planning for road construction and highway safety have created a nightmare for Houston drivers. Local residents lost $1.9 billion in 1981 ($800 per person) because of traffic congestion. Delays in traffic cost $750 million in work time, $340 million in extra vehicle insurance costs, and $790 million in wasted fuel. In 1983, 317 motorists died in traffic accidents in Houston, more than in Dallas and San Antonio combined. The National Safety Council statistics from 1977 to 1982 identified Houston as the most dangerous city to drive in among cities with a population of more than one million, and insurance claims to Houston residents as a result of automobile accidents amounted to $253 million in 1982. Yet the city continued its inadequate lighting, poor road maintenance, and designed streets and freeways because collectively it has such a limited commitment to public expenditures as a means of solving public problems (*Houston Post*, April 7, 1984: 1B, *Houston Post Magazine*, April 22, 1984:6). Just as reckless and poorly planned private investments for the Astrodome created a public burden for the taxpayers, reckless and poorly planned development in Houston has produced immediate profits for a few at the risk of catastrophic social problems (and expenditures) in the years ahead.

Conclusion

...

Concentrated economic and political power may ultimately rely on ideological legitimacy inculcated through covert cultural mechanisms, but in the short run they often act openly and crudely to advance their own interests. The construction of Busch Stadium, Dodger Stadium, and the Astrodome demonstrate how the symbolic purposes of sport and civic imagery merge with private economic goals and public urban development.

In each of these cities, private entrepreneurs received lavish subsidies to build a stadium. Each city had business and political leaders eager to boast about the limits of public liability while evading full disclosure about the extensive private opportunities that the stadia created. All three team owners presented their plans as exemplary in comparison with those in other cities. And all three succeeded, at least to a degree. St. Louis revived its downtown office sector; Los Angeles and Houston secured major league franchises and added prestige and pride. But any expenditure on that scale would have some success; a more appropriate index of the success or failure of stadium building would evaluate it in relation to the long range trends of the Warner Model and of capital accumulation by the public sector for the benefit of private investors.

Unlike public investment in health, education, or productive industry, the rewards of stadium building tend to accrue to a small group of wealthy individuals. The rewards reaped from these projects by August A. Busch, Walter O'Malley, and Roy Hofheinz tended to stay with them and their business associates while urban problems accelerated. But given what we know of the Warner Model, that should not surprise. Creation of pleasant and profitable zones for the rich do not solve urban problems. In fact, by accelerating the distance between rich and poor and by draining off resources from pressing social needs, they eventually cause problems for everyone including the rich. And the role of the state in capital accumulation means that the schemes do not even have to be rational. If a Mansion House in St. Louis or Astrodome in Houston fails, taxpayers will be there to pay the debts and absolve investors from any responsibility.

Critics of stadium projects note that voters opposed to bond issues for schools, hospitals, or highways seem eager to subsidize private sports teams. But as scientist Arthur Johnson observes in his work on professional sports and public policy, expenditures for a stadium can be easily hidden in future budgets and their overall cost is low enough to have no disruptive effect on the tax structure (Johnson, 1982: 23–24). Money for building a stadium is simply not there for building low-cost housing under our system. It is not that the voters make an incorrect choice; it is that the nature of our system gives them no meaningful choice in the first place. And so the schemes of stadium builders that promise great rewards for no risk seem like reasonable propositions and expenditures on genuine public needs seem excessive and unproductive.

Construction of new sports facilities do not significantly enrich cities, but they can not by themselves be faulted for urban blight.[3] Rather they typify the kinds of wasteful expenditures our society makes. St. Louis has its Busch Stadium and downtown office buildings, but it steadily loses industry, population, federal funds, and hope. Los Angeles cheers the success of the Dodgers and welcomes the tax revenues paid by the O'Malley family, but the accumulated costs of urban growth now portend severe disparities between available jobs and the skills of the labor force, between housing demand and housing supply, and between the comforts of the rich and the desperate needs of the poor. Houston emerges from a decade of extraordinary growth still able to pay the bills and the maintenance on Judge Hofheinz's Astrodome, but it can look ahead to enormously costly expenses as it tries to adjust its water quality, transportation, and education to the underserved population that inhabits it. And if these cities follow the practices of the Warner Model and the dump the costs of urban growth on the poor, they will confront the same decay and blight which began in the 19th century, but which today threatens to leave the nation with limited purchasing power, low production, and a disintegrating public life.

When civic leaders decided to support stadium construction in the 1960s in these cities, they operated in harmony with the legacy of urban decision making in this country over the past one hundred years. They hoped that benefits channeled to the few would trickle down to the many, but in no case has that happened. Their grandiose promises about civic improvement could only be fulfilled by a form of public spending that refused to plunder the poor for the benefit of the rich, that did not make one citizen's elevation contingent upon the degradation of another, and which created genuine collective resources like decent housing, good health, advanced education, and widely dispersed consumer purchasing power. Such measures would be enormously costly. But perhaps not as costly as continuing to transfer public land and public funds and public resources to those who need it least. People like Busch, O'Malley, and Hofheinz can find other sources of capital for their teams, stadia, recreations of the African veldt and Swiss chalets, but where else but from public resources can the rest of us get the means of preserving the shared public life that has made cities bearable in the past and which might enable them to survive in the future?

Endnotes

[1] See Barry Jacobs, "Sentimental Journey: Brooklyn After the Dodgers," *New York Affairs*. 1983, 7 (4) 139–148.

[2] Thomas Hines, "Housing, Baseball and Creeping Socialism," *Journal of Urban History*. February, 1982, p. 140, gives the figure as $1,279,000. The transaction was complicated and Hines and Poulson may not be describing exactly the same land. In either case there is reason to believe Hines' observation that the federal government lost $4 million by having to return land cleared for public housing to the city.

[3] Stadium backers often claim that their projects will bring revenues into the city, but such claims usually amount to no more than public relations ploys to attract tax dollars. Cities may collect entertainment taxes from tickets and small amounts of private spending and small numbers of jobs may be generated by such investment, but the added costs of city services and the lost opportunity costs of the other uses for land and capital in favor of stadia more than offset any gain. In St. Louis $200 million of new construction in the heart of downtown pays only a few hundred thousand dollars in taxes, in Los Angeles Dodger

Stadium certainly generates less revenue than equivalent private enterprise on the same site, and in Houston the Astrodome loses money for the taxpayers.

References

Abbott, C. 1981 *The New Urban America—Growth and Politics in Sunbelt Cities*. (Chapel Hill: University of North Carolina).

Adde, L. 1969 *Nine Cities: The Anatomy of Urban Renewal*. (Washington, D.C.: Urban Land Institute).

Ashton, P. 1978 "The Political Economy of Suburban Development" in *Marxism and the Metropolis*, ed. Tabb. W. and Sawers, L. (New York: Oxford University Press).

Burck, C. 1973 "The Superstadium Game," *Fortune*. March. 104–107.

Business Week. 1972. February 19, 78.

California Eagle. 1949 May 1, 1; 1954 April 22, 4.

Cartwright, G. 1968 "A Barnum Named Hofheinz, A Big Top Called Astrodome," *New York Times Magazine*. July 21. 10–11.

Coli, S. 1983 "Dynasty," *California Magazine*. July. 59–135.

Community Development Agency 1977 *Annual Report*. (St. Louis: Community Development Agency).

de leon, P. and Ems, J. 1973 "The Impact of Highways Upon Metropolitan Dispersion: St. Louis." (San Diego: Rand Corporation).

Eakins, D. 1969 "Business Planners and America's Postwar Expansion" in *Corporations and the Cold War*, ed, Horowitz, D. (New York: Monthly Review Press).

Fortune. 1954. "Businessmen in the News." March. 39; 1956 "Spirited Businessmen of St. Louis." July. 119; 1973 "Superstadium Game." March. 104–107; 1979 "August Busch Brews Up a New Spirit in St. Louis." January. 92–96 .

Halberstam, D. 1979 *The Powers That Be*. (New York: Dell).

Henderson, C. 1980 "Los Angeles and the Dodger War, 1957–1962," *Southern California Quarterly*. Fall. 261–289.

Hines, T. 1982 "Housing, Baseball and Creeping Socialism," *Journal of Urban History*. February, 1982. 123–144.

Home Owners Loan Corporation Files. 1939 City Survey Files. St. louis, Los Angeles. Houston. National Archives, Washington, D.C. 1942 City Survey Files. St. Louis. Los Angeles. Houston. National Archives, Washington, D.C.

Houston Chronicle. 1983. "We're Sinking and Flooding and Nobody's Doing Much About It." September 29. Section 2, 3.

Houston Post. 1983 November 9, 1. 1984 "Tab for Repairing Roads a Bargain," April 7, Section B1. "Mean Streets." April 22. *The Magazine*, 6.

Jackson, K. 1980 "Race, Ethnicity, and Real Estate Appraisal," *Journal of Urban History*. August. 419–452.

Johnson, A. 1982 "The Uneasy Partnership," North American Society for the Sociology of Sport Conference. (Toronto) November 3–8.

Judd, D. 1979 *The Politics of American Cities*. (New York: Dell).

Kahn, R. 1973 *The Boys of Summer*. (New York: New American Library).

Kasson, J. 1978 *Amusing The Million*. (New York: Hill and Wang).

Land Clearance and Redevelopment Agency 1961 *Facts About Urban Renewal*. (St. Louis: Land Clearance and Redevelopment Agency).

McComb, D. 1981 *Houston, A History*. (Austin, Texas: University of Texas Press).

Mollenkopf, J. 1978 "The Postwar Politics of Urban Development," in *Marxism and the Metropolis*, ed. Tabb, W. and Sawers, L. (New York: Oxford University Press).

National Association for the Advancement of Colored People Papers 1945 Chapter Files. Los Angeles. St. Louis. Houston. Library of Congress, Washington, D.C.

National Commission on Urban Problems 1967 Hearings. St. Louis. Houston. (Washington, D.C.: U.S. Government Printing Office).

National Urban League Papers 1949 Chapter Files. Library of Congress, Washington. D.C.

Nation's Business 1978 "Here Comes The King of the Beer Business." November. 66–73.

New York Times 1958. January 3, 21; January 23, 31; March 26, 49; March 27, 44; June 4, 1; June 6, 17; 1975 June 25, 36; 1979 May 13, A10; 1982 September 26, 28.

Poulson, N. 1966 *Oral History Interview.* Powell Library, University of California, Los Angeles.

Primm, J.N. 1981 *Lion of the Valley.* (Boulder, Colorado: Pruett).

St. Louis Globe-Democrat 1961. November 21. December 5.

Schmandt, H. et al. 1979 "Case Studies of the Impact of Federal Aid on Major Cities," Brookings Institution. October.

Sheak, A. 1971 "Rape of St. Louis." (St. Louis: Radical Action for People). 1972 "Interlocking Directorates: Centers of Power in St. Louis," (St. Louis: Radical Action for People).

Southern California Research Council 1958 Cost of Metropolitan Growth. (Los Angeles: Southern California Research Council).

Sverdrup, I. 1960 Collected Papers, Washington University Libraries, St. Louis, Missouri. 1961 Collected Papers, Washington University Libraries, St. Louis, Missouri.

Tucker, R. 1953 Collected Papers, Washington University Libraries, St. Louis, Missouri.

Tygiel, J. 1983 *Baseball's Great Experiment.* (New York: Oxford University Press).

Vernon, R. 1967 "The Changing Economic Function of the Central City" in James Q. Wilson, ed. *Urban Renewal: The Record and the Controversy* (Cambridge: Harvard University Press).

Wall Street Journal 1981 "Anheuser-Busch Cos. Rebuffed in Second Bid for Stadium Properties." June 8, 29. "Anheuser-Busch Says It Has Won Bidding for St. Louis Stadium." July 29, 15. "Anheuser-Busch Claim of Control Over Firm Contested by Apex Oil." August 5. 34.

Warner, S. 1962 *Streetcar Suburbs.* (Cambridge: Harvard University Pres); 1972 *The Urban Wilderness.* (New York: Harper and Row).

Williams, B. 1973 "St. Louis, A City and Its Suburbs." (San Diego: Rand Corporation).

Entrepreneurial Urban Politics and the Privatization of Public Space: Lessons from South Central L.A.*

Henrik Lebuhn

Introduction

On June 13, 2006, the Los Angeles County Sheriff's Dept. evicted the nation's largest community garden in South Central, L.A. Small social justice magazines and internet forums like Indymedia as well as major daily newspapers like the *Los Angeles Times* and *Berliner Zeitung* reported on this local conflict.[1] After several years of struggle, investor Ralph Horowitz evicted 300 families, many of them Latino immigrants, from the urban land they had been farming on since 1992. Hundreds of neighbors and dozens of grassroots groups as well as celebrities like Daryl Hannah and Joan Baez had joined the South Central Farmers in their attempt to defend the public land and prevent City Hall from sealing the deal with a private investor. From 2005 to 2006, farmers and activists occupied the gardens 24/7 to protest the imminent eviction. Eventually investor Ralph Horowitz was able to enforce his property rights. In 2003, he had purchased the land from the city of L.A. in order to develop a large warehouse complex, promising employment opportunities to South Central and tax revenues to the city. Three years later, in June 2006, the farmers had to leave and the gardens were demolished.

Similar conflicts regarding the valorization of urban space, public infrastructure, and goods and services are taking place in several cities and metropolitan regions in western democracies. For a short historic moment, the Keynesian welfare state had protected important spheres of society from market forces. Today, neo-liberal globalization has seized almost all areas of life and subjected them to the logic of capital.

Cities play an important role in the current process of global reorganization of political and economic power. They are not only the geographical sites where social inequalities, processes of political exclusion and new societal contradictions unfold. They are also the political and economic centers, where globalization 'takes place' (see Sassen 1991). Cities

---

*Henrik Lehbun, "Entrepreneurial Urban Politics and the Privatization of Public Space: Lessons from South Central L.A." Unpublished 2010. Printed with permission of the author.

are important agents that create the specific political and economic forms, within which these processes are being articulated, and they are the places, where the social struggles that shape neo-liberal globalization take place on a daily basis (Brenner and Theodore 2002). This understanding of the urban arena crucially builds on the work of David Harvey. In 1989, he described how cities enter a moment of transformation under the conditions of the crisis of the welfare state, increasing mobility of capital and global competition. More and more, Harvey stated, cities will act like private corporations—they become "entrepreneurial cites"—competing for investment, employment opportunities and tax revenues (Harvey 1989).

In this discussion, I want to use Harvey's concept of "entrepreneurial urban politics" as a framework to analyze the conflict over the South Central Farm in L.A. I will argue that in L.A., entrepreneurial urban politics have created a political environment that renders groups like the South Central Farmers marginal and gives private investors like Ralph Horowitz a decisive advantage in the political arena.

Entrepreneurial Urban Politics

Since the early 1980s, cities have been undergoing a radical restructuring process. Throughout western industrialized societies, urban politics have been increasingly defined by questions of economic development, industrial growth and inter-urban competition. David Harvey's concept of "entrepreneurial urban politics" tries to grasp these historic tendencies (Harvey 1989) and has become very influential since then (see for example Brenner 2003; Clarke and Gaile 1998; Jessop 1997; Mayer 1994). It refers to an urban agenda in which "traditional local boosterism is integrated with the use of local governmental powers to try and attract external sources of funding, new direct investment, or new employment sources" (Harvey 1989: 7). Under the conditions of neo-liberal globalization—deregulation of financial markets and increasing mobility of goods and capital, deindustrialization and outsourcing of manual production from the US and Western Europe to Latin America and Asia, dualization of labor markets and structural unemployment in many "first world" economies, federal budget cutbacks for urban programs and social services, etc.—cities subject themselves evermore to the logic of private management and sound micro economics. Margit Mayer identifies three major tendencies that define this trend (Mayer 1994; Mayer 1999):

1. With respect to activating economic policies, the local and regional considerations gain significant influence in all developed industrial nations. Examples for this trend include local boosterism for mega projects such as the Olympic Games in Los Angeles (1984) or Potsdamer Platz in Berlin (1990s), local "tax presents" for private corporations and the privatization of public goods and services on the municipal level. Local image campaigns are supposed to brand each city with specific (yet in fact interchangeable) features: innovation, creativity, success, etc.

2. At the same time, social policies are subordinated to economic and employment policies. Public spending for affordable housing, culture, education, social services and health care decline in many cities while prestigious commercial projects like convention centers, sport stadiums and high end research facilities (e.g. life sciences) receive generous funding.

3. Within this process, the local political arena opens up for civil society actors like non-profit organizations, consulting firms and even grassroots groups. They are integrated into the urban regime through new forms of public-private partnership. Governance structures and networks emerge and bring public, semi-public and private actors together. However, the new opportunities to participate in urban politics—ranging from planning procedures to publicly sponsored services—go hand in hand with increasing pressure on the so-called "third sector" to follow the rules of "Realpolitik."

In sum, entrepreneurial urban politics can be described as a strategy to deal with the local consequences of structural transformations on a national and global scale. But far from solving these challenges, entrepreneurial urban politics play an important role in producing and re-producing the vicious circle they are struggling with. As scholars like Saskia Sassen has pointed out, successful global cities produce particular local conflicts (Sassen 1999). Many entrepreneurial cities struggle with severe financial crisis due to giant business subsidies and lack of tax revenues; they have to deal with severe social polarization, segregation and inequality; and they face dramatic social and social-spatial conflicts. Even if cities successfully master the pressure of regional and global competition, it doesn't necessarily mean that this 'pays off', at least not if we look at the city from a perspective of how livable it actually is for the majority of its inhabitants.

The Struggle over the South Central Farm in L.A.

Rather than focusing on individual politicians, coalitions and alliances, I will argue that entrepreneurial urban politics have shaped the political landscape in L.A. in specific ways that gave the investor and his interest in the commercial use of the land a structural advantage over the grassroots coalition that tried to keep the land available to the public as a large inner-city community garden.

At 14 acres, South Central Farm was probably the largest community garden in the United States, located right on the border between the district of South Central, L.A., and the city of Vernon (for more details about the history of the garden see Kuipers 2006).[2]

Around 1986, the city of Los Angeles was planning a large trash incinerator project, known as LANCER. The first incinerator was to be built in South Central. Searching for a site, the city took a 14-acre property on Alameda Street and 41st Street by eminent domain, and paid the owner Ralph Horowitz $4.7 million. But the incinerator was never built. Strong environmental protests forced then mayor Tom Bradley to pull the plug on LANCER. Instead, the property in South Central was abandoned.

The story continues in 1992. After the uprisings in Los Angeles, the city government was desperately looking into possibilities for social programs in marginalized neighborhoods, especially in South Central. When they approached the Regional Foodbank, located right across the street from the original LANCER site, the Foodbank suggested making the wasteland available for low-income families to farm. City Hall agreed and within a few months, families from South Central and other neighborhoods cleaned the trash up, divided the property into plots, and started to grow fruits and vegetables. The Foodbank officially administered the land, but in fact, turning the 14-acres of industrial wasteland into a community garden was a grassroots effort.

So starting in 1992/1993, about 300 low-income families, mostly migrants from Mexico and other Latin American countries, many of them undocumented, were farming the land. The farmers could easily cover about one third of their food demand through the gardens. On weekends, neighbors and friends stopped by to trade, sell and give away fruits, vegetables and herbs. In places like Vernon or South Central, where the average family income is about $1,500 per month,[3] this form of solidarity economy makes a huge difference for everyone.

Besides being an important factor of support for low-income households, the garden also became a fascinating microcosm of Latin American biodiversity, and for many Latino farmers it provided a place of cultural identity, a home, and a source of collective memory in the heart of L.A. After surveying the Farm's flora and conducting interviews with several farmers, anthropologist Devon G. Peña wrote:

> Imagine a space where families gather everyday to work on the community farm. Imagine they have made this special place into a sustainable source of local food. They have created an edible landscape, a green mosaic conjoined from a wide variety of native food crops, medicinal plants, fruit trees, creepers, crawlers, and cacti. Imagine that the people plant family heirloom seeds that have been carefully selected over the generations. Imagine the seeds are at least five thousand years old and are drawn from the ancestral crops of the Americas. Imagine a space where indigenous women cultivate heirloom crops and weave visions and memories of their cultural identity and heritage into the landscape. They are making place; they are making home. Imagine the passing of their knowledge to the next generation in memories of plant stories and the social and ecological skills of the farmer. Imagine youth eagerly assisting with the cultivation of heirloom maíz, frijol, calabaza, guayaba, chipilin, and chilacayote. Imagine youth who know hundreds of wild and cultivated plants, their nutritional and medicinal properties, and what it takes to grow them naturally. Now imagine this space is located not in rural Mexico, say Oaxaca or Michoacan. Instead, imagine it is located in the heart of the urban core of one of the world's largest and most important global cities, Los Angeles, California. (Peña 2005)

The garden was sandwiched between the low-income residential areas of South Central and the industrial landscape of Vernon, on the so-called Alameda Corridor, an area that is mostly commercial. For many years, the corridor has been an important transportation link to the ports of Los Angeles and Long Beach. In 1997, the city began construction on a $2.4 billion rail expressway, that runs about 20-miles from the ports through eight cities to downtown Los Angeles, where it connects to transcontinental rail lines (Erie 2004). This obviously gives *any* property along the Alameda Corridor a strategic value for trade related investment. No surprise that the original owner of the property started to pressure the city to sell him the land back. In 1995, when planning and preparations for the Alameda Corridor were in full speed, Ralph Horowitz approached City Hall for the first time. It was not until 2003, however, that he cut a deal with the local government and bought the land back for $5 million. Negotiations took place behind closed doors, and generous donations were made to City Hall members—something very typical for the neo-liberal privatization of public space and public goods.

In 2003 conflict broke out over the farmland: The farmers refused to leave the gardens. Instead they filed a lawsuit against the city to win time for a campaign. Although they lost the lawsuit, they managed to build an impressive coalition to defend the gardens. The strategic step was to name themselves the 'South Central FARMERS'. This allowed them to frame the conflict as a struggle for a cross-ethnic project (as opposed to a Latino-project), as a fight for food security, as an environmental issue, and to point out its positive effects on neighborhood security. In this way they were able to mobilize more than 50 local and regional environmental organizations, students' initiatives, migrant networks, and grassroots groups, and to get a lot of support from local and eventually even national and international media. Not to forget: The gardens themselves served as a physical space of organization, mobilization and community building through face-to-face communication.

In spring 2006, at the peak of the conflict, Mayor Antonio Villaraigosa tried to negotiate between Horowitz and the farmers. However, facing a budget deficit of $271 million in 2006 and a long-term debt of almost $10 billion,[4] the mayor was not going to offer to buy the land back. Instead, the most promising option to solve the conflict was an offer by the *Trust for Public Land* to raise $16 million to buy the property from Horowitz and turn the Farm into an environmental community project. However, Horowitz insisted on evicting the farmers. He told the magazine *Clamor*:

> "My plans are market-driven. When we get the property back, we're gonna determine what the viable use is depending on the market conditions and we'll do that. If someone was in need of a manufacturing plant or a warehouse, we'd do that for them.... We'd market the property for lease, and real-estate brokers would bring people who wanted to do something, and then the negotiations would start."[5]

After the eviction of June 2006, the South Central Farmers split up, but part of the group still continues to work under the same name. A neighborhood center across the street from the original site of the Farm functions as an anchor in the community. And recently, some of the farmers were offered land in Bakersfield, CA. They are not farming in South Central anymore, but maintain roots in the community and give their project a new dimension trying to survive as a Community Supported Agriculture (CSA) and market farm.[6]

The Making of a Global City

In order to fully understand the conflict over the South Central Farm, we will now take a closer look at a number of historic and contemporary aspects of L.A. politics and economic policies. Like many U.S. cities, Los Angeles was strongly affected by the global economic crisis of 1973 and the process of political and economic restructuring that would follow. First of all, the crisis of the 1970s led to massive job cuts in L.A.'s industrial sector, especially in the automobile industry. Between 1978 and 1982, the closure of several plants resulted in the loss of 75,000 jobs, each of them leading to additional loss of employment opportunities in local businesses and small-scale manufacturers surrounding larger industries. With the end of the "Cold War," the crisis expanded to the aerospace defense industry, one of L.A.'s strongest economic sectors, with the U.S. government being the principal client. Between 1988 and 1991, about 60,000 jobs were lost in this sector (Scott 2002: 175–176). But in comparison to other major U.S. cities, the "crisis of Fordism"[7] went hand-in-hand with a successful transformation of the city to an international center for finance-, service- and trade- related industries. Parallel to the industrial crisis, the latter sectors, as well as insurance and real estate businesses, experienced modest or even rapid growth. In the late 1980s, eminent L.A. scholar Ed Soja stated that the tertiarization of the regional economy was proceeding rapidly (Soja 1989: 200).

Ultimately, the economic development of the 1980s was characterized by a shift from production to service and the retail sector, but also by a dramatic bifurcation of these labor markets into (1) a segment of relatively well-paid and secure jobs that require higher quali-fications and (2) a precarious segment of low-skilled labor. Another sector that remained strong in LA., but experienced similar tendencies of employment bifurcation was manufac-turing. "As late as the early 1980s, two-thirds of L.A. manufacturing jobs were in higher-paid, often unionized industries such as autos, tires, electronics, and aerospace.... By the year 2000, nearly half of the regional manufacturing employment was in lower-wage sec-tors, exemplified by garment, furniture, toy manufacturing, and food processing" (Gottlieb, Vallianatos, Freer, and Dreier 2005: 85–86).

The restructuring of L.A.'s economic and political landscape starting in the 1970s is closely linked to a particular name: Tom Bradley, who was mayor of Los Angeles from 1973 to 1993. Like no other individual protagonist, he stands for entrepreneurial policies that aimed at turning Los Angeles into an attractive locality for capital investment while trying to pacify the tensions of racial polarization and social fragmentation in the city. For the era of the 1970s and 1980s, Roger Keil states that "Southern California was on the threshold of becoming a world city region. Two characteristics of the emerging Bradley regime accounted for these changing circumstances: the (incomplete) integration of racial and ethnic minorities as well as the working class into the regime; and the programmatic commitment to the erection of the of the world city citadel." (Keil 1998b: 74).

By the end of the 1980s, the urban landscape of L.A. was branded with all major land-marks of a successful global city: international convention centers, concert halls and sport stadiums, commercial tourist attractions, shopping malls, but above all futuristic skyscrap-ers of

> international banks, expensive hotels and corporate headquarters. "In the zone stretching from downtown to the ocean and branching south to the airport (LAX) are over sixty major corporate headquarters, a dozen banks and sav-ings and loan companies with assets over one billion dollars, five of the eight largest international accounting firms, two-thirds of the 200 million square feet of high-rise office space in the region, a battalion of corporate law offices unri-valled off the east coast, and the national nucleus of the American military-industrial complex" (Soja 1989: 210).

However, L.A.'s impressive economic restructuring rests on the fundamentals of a growing social polarization. Los Angeles' global city status was achieved by a specific eco-nomic mixture that combines high-tech production, global financial business and regional trade with the blatant exploitation of precarious labor, especially in the cleaning service industry, in gastronomy and low-tech manufacturing (e.g. sweat shops). Weak unions and a virtually unlimited supply of cheap and easily exploitable labor, mostly provided by poor immigrants from Latin America and other world regions, constitute the "dark side" of L.A.'s outstanding economic performance. The enormous social inequalities resulting from this economic structure combined with everyday racism and social exclusion became crucial factors for the 1992 riots, during which L.A.'s marginalized inner-city neighborhoods literally exploded.

In 1993, after the end of the Bradley era, Republican Richard Riordan took over the mayor's office and the political forces shifted even further towards capital. The entrepreneurial urban politics of the 1970s and 1980s continued, but in comparison to his predecessor, Riordan didn't even make an attempt to include the working class into his urban growth politics. Roger Keil states that it may be the goal of many city governments to convert their administrations into organizations that look like private corporations, however, Richard Riordan literally personalized this goal (see Keil 1998a: 90). This "personal style" in L.A. politics would not change substantially until the election of Antonio Villaraigosa in May 2005.

Finally, a crucial factor for L.A.'s prominent economic position is the city's role as a major site of inter-regional trade between the US and the Pacific Rim.[8] In a way, it seems almost ironic that one of the most obvious effects of the globalization is an enormous increase in import and export of very "classical" goods. In Los Angeles, globalization can literally be measured by looking at the growing number of containers passing through the region. Hence, L.A.'s international air- and seaports and their continental infrastructure connections are among the busiest in the world. In 2001, the value of goods and materials passing through L.A. amounted to $270 billion (Erie 2004: 10). Large amounts of these goods are needed for manufacturing processes in the Greater L.A. Region or are being sold to local consumers. In 2001, the gross domestic product (GDP) of the five regional counties (taken together)—Los Angeles, Orange, Ventura, San Bernardino and Riverside—amounted to $651 billion exceeding even the GDP of countries like Mexico, Spain and India. L.A.'s leading role as a trade hub that connects the interior of the US and the Pacific Rim brings us to a specific aspect of entrepreneurial urban politics in L.A. that had an immediate impact on the conflict over the South Central Farm.

Trade, Investment and the Alameda Corridor

Much of the cargo being transported through the Greater L.A. Region has to pass the Alameda Corridor. The Alameda Corridor is a transportation route that runs from the ports of Long Beach and Los Angeles 20-miles north to downtown Los Angeles, primarily along and adjacent to Alameda Street. It's a 20-mile "bottleneck" that connects the most important ports of the region to the transcontinental rail network near downtown. Starting in 1997 the Alameda Corridor was extended and developed by public agencies and private companies from the Greater L.A. Region. The project was successfully finished in 2002 and is an expression and a result of L.A.'s increasing role as a strategic nodal point for international trade. More importantly in this context, it also played a crucial role for the privatization and the demolition of the South Central Farm.

Historically, L.A.'s transcontinental railway lines established in the 19th and 20th century connected the interior of the country to the settlements and centers of economic activity located near today's downtown. Transcontinental railway lines do not reach the ports of L.A. Instead, the different railway lines end near downtown L.A. For that reason, much of the cargo reaching or leaving the ports of L.A. has to pass through the Alameda Corridor. As one can easily imagine, this constitutes immense logistic challenges for inter-regional trade and transportation. Neither the function of the Alameda Corridor as an important transportation link, nor the commercial use of properties along the Corridor is really new. However, starting in the 1970s and with Los Angeles' ascent toward a global city status, international trade became crucial for the economic development of the entire region—and so did the Alameda Corridor.

In L.A., the neo-liberal deregulation of global markets and the sharpening inter-urban competition for capital manifested themselves through an immense increase in trade and transportation. Within a short period of time, Los Angeles lost its character as "Fordist production site" catering to the domestic market and the gateway to the Pacific Rim.

It is not surprising then that the origins of the Alameda Corridor development, carried out in the late 1990s, can be traced back to the beginning of the neo-liberal era under Ronald Reagan. In the early 1980s, the city commissioned two studies to look at the rapid increase of trade and the problems associated with it along Alameda Corridor. In the mid–1990s, the NAFTA-agreement and the liberalization of trade between Mexico, Canada and the US further sharpened the situation as they led to dynamic economic growth in Southern California. In 2001, the ports of San Pedro Bay and Los Angeles ranked third among the world's busiest harbors following Hong Kong and Singapore.[9] For the years 2000 to 2020, experts predict an increase in cargo turn-over of 175 percent (Erie 2004:145).

In order to respond to this situation, a $2.4 billion rail expressway was built to drastically expand the capacity of the Alameda Corridor. Between 1997 and 2002, four railroad branch lines were consolidated, more than 200 grade crossings eliminated and a 10-mile open trench for cargo trains was built. The project also improved conditions for street level transportation by improving streets, eliminating traffic lights and building bridges for pedestrians. Overall, the goal was to shift more cargo traffic to rail and improve the efficiency of freight movements as well as of automobiles on nearby roads.

Crucial for the success of the Alameda Corridor project was the foundation of a regional planning agency. In 1989, the *Alameda Corridor Transportation Authority* (ACTA) was established and still manages all tasks related to the mega project.[10] ACTA not only brings representatives of the port authority, the *Metropolitan Transportation Authority* (MTA) and the city of Los Angeles together, but also includes politicians from all other cities the Alameda Corridor cuts through: Vernon, Huntington Park, South Gate, Lynwood, Compton and Carson. ACTA is a prime example for the creation of regional governance structures in order to deal with the specific task of combining economic policies as well as transportation and environmental issues.

But how does the development of the Alameda Corridor relate to the privatization and demolition of the South Central Farm? The answer is quite simple: The strategic public (and private) investment into the Alameda Corridor secured Los Angeles' role as the gateway for US trade with the Pacific Rim. The city's investment in local and regional infrastructure upgrades the locality, creates a favorable business environment and generates employment and tax revenues. In fact, with dozens of daily trains using the Corridor, the project has already generated revenues of $6.5 million via transportation fees.[11] But more importantly for our case, the new Alameda Corridor gives any property along it a strategic value for trade related investment. Under these conditions, it is not surprising that investor Horowitz pressured City Hall to sell the land back to him. Once construction on the Corridor had started in 1997, it was clear that the South Central Farm—bordering on its East side to the Alameda Corridor—would soon become prime real estate. We can therefore argue that the development of the Alameda Corridor had an indirect, but very important impact on the question of *how*, *by whom* and *for what purpose* the 14-acres of land, on which the South Central Farm was located, should be used: it clearly privileged commercial over non-commercial use.

Conclusion

In this chapter, I used the example of the South Central Farm in Los Angeles to analyze and illustrate the effects of entrepreneurial urban politics for conflicts over public and private urban space. The analysis did not focus much on the alliances and conflicts between local politicians, grassroots groups, business interest groups, and other entities and individuals involved in the conflict, but on the impact that larger political and economic changes had. This is not to say that the dynamics between local stakeholders do not play an important role for the conflicts over public space and public assets.

However, the aim of this chapter was to understand the structural component of this type of conflict. Local stakeholders do not act independently from their economic, political and institutional environment. Their goals, tactics and strategies—their "logic of action"—heavily depend on how the urban political arena is shaped. My argument is then that entrepreneurial urban politics pre-structure the political field, on which the conflicts over public space take place, in a way that privileges commercial interests over non-commercial interests, and that give investors and developers a decisive advantage over grassroots groups and politicians that try to "defend" the public realm against its privatization and valorization. David Harvey emphasizes the structural component even more: He argues that in the entrepreneurial city, "even the most resolute and avant-garde municipal socialists will find themselves, in the end, playing the capitalist game and performing as agents of discipline for the very processes they are trying to resist." (Harvey 1989: 5)

This finally leads me to two important conclusions: First, urban scholars and activists who defend "the public sphere" against the current tendency of privatization need to develop strategies to democratize local institutions, governance structures, and decision making procedures. How can we strengthen grassroots groups like the South Central Farmers? How can we include and safeguard their voice within the local political arena? How can we create local political institutions with strong participatory and inclusive elements? Secondly, the political dynamics that have led to the emergence of urban entrepreneurial governance structures are rooted in larger societal transformations on different scales. Entrepreneurial urban politics are closely tied to the larger project of neo-liberal globalization. Cites are crucial political sites, where the "actually existing neo-liberalism" is being shaped (Brenner and Theodore 2002; Brenner and Theodore 2005). This diagnosis implies, however, that we are looking at local changes as much as we are dealing with the consequence of political and economic shifts on the national and even global level. Grassroots groups and local politicians who want to build alliances against entrepreneurial urban politics will, therefore, have to address fundamental questions on various scales beyond the urban arena, such as federal funding for urban programs, welfare and labor market politics, and regional agreements over (free-)trade and private investment. In order to do this, urban actors will have to look for allies outside their cities and maybe even countries. This is an incredibly difficult political project – but a necessary one, if we want to address the contradictions between entrepreneurial urban politics and urban social justice in a livable city.

Endnotes

[1] See for example: Hector Becerra, Megan Garvey and Steve Hymon, "L.A. Garden Shut Down; 40 Arrested," *Los Angeles Times*, June 14, 2006.

[2] In the following overview, I will not be able to touch on all details of the conflict. For a comprehensive analysis see Lebuhn (2008). See also the Oscar-nominated documentary "The Garden" (see: http://www.thegardenmovie.com/ accessed on November 21, 2009) as well as Franceschini and Tucker's forthcoming book on urban farming in the US.

[3] City of Los Angeles Demographics, 2000 Census. Complete data-set online at http://cityplanning.lacity.org (accessed on November 28, 2006).

[4] See: City of Los Angeles. 2005. "Economic and Demographic Information," Appendix A, Los Angeles, May 2005.

[5] Quoted from: *Clamor*. 2006. "14 Acres. Conversations Across Chasms in South Central Los Angeles." *Clamor* Nr. 36, Spring 2006, online at: http://www.clamormagazine.org/issues/36/people.php (accessed on November 17, 2009).

[6] For more information about the South Central Farmers see: http://www.southcentralfarmers.com/ (accessed on November 17, 2009).

[7] The crisis of Fordism is associated with a period in U.S. history whereby modes of production are being challenged by stunted economic growth and profits.

[8] For trade related data and information about the Alameda Corridor project, I will refer to the excellent and well researched book on trade, infrastructure and regional development by Erie (2004). More recent data can be found online, for example at http://www.laedc.org/ (accessed on November 20, 2009) and http://www.portoflosangeles.org/ (accessed on November 20, 2009), however, the data cited here refers to the period of the conflict over the South Central Farm in the early 2000s.

[9] Both ports together had an annual turn-over of almost 10 million 'twenty-foot equivalent units' (TEU), with each TEU equaling about one container. See: "Special Report: World's Top 50 Container Ports." 2002, July 8–14. Pp. 22–27 in *Journal of Commerce Week*.

[10] See http://www.acta.org (accessed on November 21, 2009).

[11] Source: http://www.acta.org (accessed on December 15, 2009).

Bibliography

Brenner, Neil. 2003. "'Glocalization' as a State Spatial Strategy: Urban Entrepreneurialism and the New Politics of Uneven Development in Western Europe." Pp. 197–215 in *Remaking the Global Economy*, edited by J. Peck and H. W. C. Yeung. London, Thousand Oaks, New Delhi: Sage.

Brenner, Neil and Nik Theodore. 2002. "Cities and the Geographies of 'Actually Existing Neoliberalism'." *Antipode* 34: 349–379.

—. 2005. "Neoliberalism and the Urban Condition." *City* 9:101–107.

Caraley, Demetrios. 1992. "Washington Abandons the Cities." *Political Science Quarterly* 107:1–30.

Clarke, Susan E. and Gary L. Gaile. 1998. *The Work of Cities*. Minneapolis: University of Minnesota Press.

Erie, Steven P. 2004. *Globalizing L.A.: Trade, Infrastructure and Regional Development*. Stanford: Stanford University Press.

Franceschini, Amy and Daniel Tucker. forthcoming 2010. *Farm Together Now*. San Francisco: Chronicle Books.

Gottlieb, Robert, Mark Vallianatos, Regina M. Freer, and Peter Dreier. 2005. *The Next Los Angeles. The Struggle for a Livable City*. Berkeley, Los Angeles, London: University of California Press.

Harvey, David. 1989. "From Managerialism to Entrepreneurialism: The Tranformation in Urban Governance in Late Capitalism." *Geografiska Annaler* 71 B: 3–18.

Jessop, Bob. 1997. "The Entrepreneurial City: Re-Imaging Localities, Redesigning Economic Governance, or Restructuring Capital?" Pp. 28–41 in *Transforming Cities: Contested Governance and New Spatial Divisions*, edited by N. Jewson and S. MacGregor. London: Routledge.

Keil, Roger. 1998a. "Globalization Makes States: Perspectives of Local Governance in the Age of the World City." *Review of International Political Economy* 5: 616–646.

—. 1998b. *Los Angeles: Globalization, Urbanization and Social Struggle*. Chichester: Wiley.

Kuipers, Dean. 2006. "Trouble in the Garden." *Los Angeles CityBeat*.

LAEDC. 2004. *The South Los Angeles Area Economic Overview 2004*. Los Angeles: Los Angeles County Economic Development Corporation (LAEDC).

Lebuhn, Henrik. 2008. *Stadt in Bewegung. Mikrokonflikte um den öffentlichen Raum in Berlin und Los Angeles*. Münster: Westfälisches Dampfboot.

Mayer, Margit. 1994. "Post-Fordist City Politics." Pp. 316–337 in *Post-Fordism: A Reader*, edited by A. Amin. Oxford: Basil Blackwell.

—. 1999. "Urban Movements and Urban Theory in the Late–20th-Century City." Pp. 209–238 in *The Urban Moment. Cosmopolitan Essays on the Late 20th-Century City*, edited by R. A. Beauregard and S. Body-Gendrot. London, New Delhi: Sage.

—. 2009. "Social Cohesion and Anti-Poverty Policies in US Cities." Pp. 311–334 in *Social Cohesion in Europe and the Americas/Cohesión Social en Europa y las Américas*, edited by H. Koff. Brussels: Peter Lang Publishing.

Peña, Devon G. 2005. *Farmers Feeding Families: Agroecology in South Central Los Angeles*,. Lecture presented to the Environmental Science, Policy, and Management Colloquium; University of California, Berkeley (October 10, 2005).

Sassen, Saskia. 1991. *The Global City: New York, London, Tokyo*. Princeton: Princeton University Press.

—. 1999. "Whose City Is It? Globalization and the Formation of New Claims." Pp. 99–118 in *The Urban Moment. Cosmopolitan Essays on the Late 20th-Century City*, edited by R. A. Beauregard and S. Body-Gendrot. London, New Delhi: Sage.

SCAG. 2005. *The State of the Region 2005. Measuring Regional Progress*. Los Angeles: Southern California Association of Governments (SCAG).

Scott, Allen J. 2002. "Industrial Urbanism in Late-Twentieth-Century Southern California." Pp. 163–179 in *From Chicago to L.A. Making Sense of Urban Theory*, edited by M. J. Dear. Thousand Oaks, London, New Dehli: Sage Publications.

Soja, Edward. 1989. *Postmodern Geographies. The Reassertion of Space in Critical Social Theory*. London, New York: Verso.

Spencer, James H. and Paul Ong. 2004. "An Analysis of the Los Angeles Revitalization Zone: Are Place-Based Investment Strategies Effective Under Moderate Economic Conditions?" *Economic Development Quarterly 2004* 18: 368–383.

Moving Out of Cabrini Green, Chicago[*]

Dierdre Pfeiffer

Introduction

Cabrini Green is a redeveloping African-American public housing community near downtown Chicago. In 2000, the Chicago Housing Authority (CHA) initiated a plan to demolish existing buildings and replace them with mixed-income complexes. New upscale condominiums and town homes are appearing on the sites of old resident homes and landmarks, brandishing names such as "Old Town Square" and "North Town Village." Since the policy requires almost all residents to relocate from their neighborhood away from informal support networks and jobs, most have opposed the plan since its inception. In April 2004, the CHA dispensed more than 300 eviction notices to area tenants. Shortly after, residents began to inscribe the name "Cabrini" around the community, over new trashcans and advertising signs, and most prominently over a storefront on a busy arterial road.

In Cabrini Green, the use of language and naming is central to implementing and contesting the process of redevelopment. In what follows, I narrate the residential history of the neighborhood designated "Cabrini Green" in the 1960s. I then employ a critical discourse approach to examine how Chicago urban elites use neighborhood renaming, resident denigration, and neoliberal relocation narratives to displace public housing tenants and carry out redevelopment. Finally, I show that residents recognize the discursive constructions that enable the implementation of redevelopment and contest it in rhetorical ways. To displacement from their community, tenant activists reframe public housing redevelopment as a "human rights crisis." As evidenced by these tactics, redeveloping Cabrini Green is inherently a discursive site, a space marked by "cultural production and political struggle" (Conquergood 1992: 97).

A Critical Discourse Approach

With its roots in critical linguistics, critical discourse analysis (CDA) is a perspective that seeks to understand how and why language affects social change. It stems from the conception that language constructions serve to reproduce power, dominance and hegemony by

[*] Deirdre Pfeiffer, "Displacement Through Discourse: Implementing and Contesting Public Housing Development in Cabrini Green." *Urban Anthropology & Studies of Cultural Systems and World Economic Development* 35 1: 39–74, 2006. Reprinted with permission of The Institute.

naturalizing social disparities. Critical discourse analysts aim to demystify the causal rela-tionships between the production of language and broader social and political-economic processes to examine how these practices "arise out of and are ideologically shaped by relations of power and struggles over power; and to explore how the opacity of these rela-tionships between discourse and society is itself a factor securing power and hegemony" (Fairclough 1993:135; Fowler et al. 1979; van Dijk 1993).

The following analysis is grounded in the theory that inequality is enacted, legitimized and sustained by discourse manipulation and control over the spaces of ideological produc-tion. Chicago housing policymakers and developers were able to disseminate discrimina-tory texts and displace low-income minorities from their homes because of their unequal media access. Instead of using their position to promote debate and purvey equitable solutions to the affordable housing shortage, they naturalized dominant underclass public housing discourses, which in turn stripped vulnerable race and class groups of power and resources (van Dijk 1993; Fairclough 2000; Erjavec 2001).

Although many studies have focused on top-down discourses of dominance, few have examined bottom-up discourses of resistance (van Dijk 1993). In this paper, I show the interaction between urban elites' dominant constructions and public residents' subversive manipulations. To document and assess the discursive factors that simultaneously enable and frustrate public housing redevelopment, I integrate textual analysis with ethnographic methodologies. I analyzed hundreds of documents, such as newspaper articles, advertise-ments, and policy statements, and interviewed 20 upper-income residents and 70 public housing tenants to examine how these language constructs erupted in their daily speech. In addition, during the summers of 2003 and 2004, I was in the community almost every day. I participated in a neighborhood book club and attended all community policing and redevelopment meetings, park events, and many mixed-income social gatherings. Every week, I documented CHA board and committee meetings, as well as Cabrini Green court proceedings and resident activism.

The Social Production of Cabrini Green

In his 1929 study *The Gold Coast and the Slum*, Chicago school sociologist Harvey Zor-baugh describes the Lower North Side of Chicago as a place "in the process of evolution" (Zorbaugh 1929: viii). Indeed, for more than 150 years, residents have identified the land bounded by Halsted Street, Chicago Avenue, Orleans Street, and North Avenue by many names. Although a variety of ethnic and racial groups have established residence in the area, it has remained a low-income community.

Shortly after the city's incorporation in 1837, German immigrants settled in the area. After the Chicago fire devastated the district in 1871, however, they moved further north and were succeeded by newly arrived Swedish immigrants. By 1890, there were more than 10,000 people of Swedish descent, the largest concentration outside Sweden and Finland, and the neighborhood consequently became known as "Swede Town." Concurrently, a small contingent of Irish immigrants settled at the juncture of the river and its north branch in an area called "Kilgubbin" or "the Patch." Comprised of wooden homes adjacent to tanneries, lumber mills, coal yards, and a gas plant, outsiders labeled the district "Smokey Hollow" and "Little Hell." At the turn of the century, Sicilian immigration outpaced that of other ethnic groups. Many Swedes migrated further north to Lakeview and Andersonville, and Chicagoans renamed the area "Little Sicily" (Pacyga and Skenett 1986; Grossman et al. 2004).

During the first wave of black migration to the north in the 1920s, African-Americans settled in the Lower North Side. To accommodate the new arrivals, the CHA razed many of the area's dilapidated tenement buildings and constructed a 586-unit row home complex in their place. The Francis Cabrini Homes opened for occupancy in 1942.[1] By 1949, African-Americans constituted 40% of the development and the majority of the surrounding neighborhood. Some current public housing residents described community life during this period as "the United Nations," since Puerto Ricans, Italian-Americans, and Chinese-Americans also occupied apartments. As blacks continued to migrate from the south throughout the 1950s, however, their need for adequate housing grew. The CHA completed the 1,896-unit Cabrini Extension in 1958 and the 1,096-unit William Green Homes in 1962.[2] The area took on yet another name, "Cabrini Green."

After the CHA changed leadership in the mid–1950s, they discouraged integration in tenant and site selection. By 1959 blacks occupied 75% of Cabrini Green apartments.[3] Conditions deteriorated because of federal and local cuts to maintenance and security and policy changes over rent payment. The 1968 Brooke Amendment to the U.S. Housing Act, for instance, required all residents to contribute 25% of their income to rent. Although policymakers wrote the amendment as a strategy to increase available funds for public housing construction and maintenance, housing authorities lost money and had to cut services when wealthier residents moved out (Hirsch 1983; Marciniak 1986; von Hoffman 1998).

When Martin Luther King was assassinated that same year, riots erupted in Cabrini Green. Residents who burned and looted stores along Oak Street were beaten by local police and the National Guard. Shortly after this event, the CHA stopped screening tenants, thus increasing the presence of ex-convicts, gang members, and drug users, which further reduced maintenance. Many Cabrini Green tenants attribute the CHA and the city's subsequent neglect of their neighborhood to this event. Wanda Hopkins recalls:

> I think they gave up on us. I still believe the city… said those people are not civilized, that's the only way that they would allow us to live in trash. It was some days that trash was so high in those buildings that I wouldn't stay in my house, 'cause I lived right at the garbage chute and it was just horrible. I think the maintenance people were told that they just didn't have to do it anymore. That's what I think (Hopkins cited in Whitaker 2000: 121).

In 1975, President Nixon placed a moratorium on public housing construction, expanding waitlists at existing, deteriorating developments. Ten years later, President Reagan reduced federal funding for public housing maintenance, rehabilitation, and construction from $35 to $7 billion annually. These decisions rendered the crumbling exteriors of Cabrini Green a permanent feature of the urban landscape (Bauman 2000; Biles 2000).

During the 1970s, the quality of public housing continued to decline as the need for low-income shelter grew. Between 1977 and 1981, the Chicago Standard Metropolitan Statistical Area experienced a 14% decrease in jobs. After the big steel industries such as Wisconsin Steel and U.S. Steelworks closed in the 1980s, more than 10,000 people became unemployed. Chicago permanently lost 150,000 manufacturing jobs by the end of the decade. Not only were public housing residents unable to achieve social mobility through adequately paid employment, but also working-class Chicagoans struggled to make mortgage and rent payments with slashed wages (Squires et al. 1987; Ranney 2003).

Rather than provide shelter for those left unemployed and inadequately housed by deindustrialization and social welfare cutbacks, many municipalities, such as Chicago, institutionalized gentrification and proactively rid their center cities of low-income minorities to increase property tax revenues. In 1968, the Chicago Department of Urban Renewal instituted "Project Chicago-Orleans," which classified the area as "a slum" and "blighted" and led to the development of an upscale 2,600-unit complex on its northeastern boundary. Sure enough, between 1980 and 1990, the median sale price of a single-family home in the area tripled from $138,000 to $700,000. The black population declined by 7,000, while the white population grew by 4,000 (Bennett and Reed 1999). Having provoked upper-and middle-class investment, city officials rendered the Cabrini Green neighborhood vulnerable to redevelopment (Marciniak 1986).

Considering the extent of public housing deterioration, politicians' reluctance to fund social welfare programs and cities' ambitions for inner-city redevelopment, federal policymakers forged a new public housing policy. In the fall of 1992, the Department of Housing and Urban Development (HUD) laid out three main strategies to "revitalize" public housing: 1) deconcentration through site construction, 2) income mixing in new developments, and 3) self-sufficiency programs. They claimed that mixed-income development would make neighborhoods more stable and residents upwardly mobile, thus decreasing governmental financial responsibility (Epp 1998). Later that year, the Department of Veteran's Affairs and HUD created "Housing Opportunities for People Everywhere" (HOPE VI), a funding program local housing authorities could use to redevelop public housing tracts into mixed-income communities. Overwhelmingly, the purpose of HOPE VI was to mitigate the stigma of public housing through "integration." Policymakers, ignoring that governmental funding cutbacks literally caused the deterioration and poverty they so deplored, enacted the reduction of the number of low-income residents in public housing, arguing that residents' behaviors and attitudes jeopardized neighborhoods' ability to attract private investment, the keystone of "healthy" communities.

In 1993, CHA board chairman Vincent Lane successfully applied for a $50 million HOPE VI grant to realize pro-growth goals through the demolition of Cabrini Green. Three years later, Mayor Richard M. Daley implemented the Near North Redevelopment Initiative (NNRI), a neighborhood "revitalization" plan that would use HOPE VI funds to demolish Cabrini Green and redevelop it as a mixed-income area. Media reports painted a harrowing portrait of the community. Journalists modified "Cabrini-Green" with the adjective "notorious" and included pictures of burnt buildings and descriptions of gang activity and violence. Such underclass formations stripped the neighborhood of its human qualities and garnered public support for demolition (Bennett and Reed 1999).

Bottles popped in CHA headquarters after HUD approved their "Plan for Transformation" in February 2000. The Plan is a $1.6 billion policy to demolish 15,000 public housing units by 2009 and "transform" "isolated" public housing neighborhoods into mixed-income communities. Inclusive in name, mixed-income development in Chicago is exclusive in practice. Due to rigid tenancy requirements, policy analysts estimate that only 11% of tenants will be eligible to return to their redeveloped communities (Wilen 2003). Instead, most leaseholders must use vouchers to find their own housing elsewhere, a daunting task considering racism and classism in the private market. Since African-American women head 84% of public housing families, and 64% of Cabrini Green women are under

21 years of age, the lives of young black women are disproportionately disrupted by this Plan (Fleming 2003).

Cabrini Green as Family

Although 18,000 people officially lived in Cabrini Green in 1968, currently fewer than 5,000 reside there. Most leaseholders are African-American women with children. A large proportion of residents are non-leaseholders who live with family and friends or squat in vacant apartments. Deidre, a tenant activist who moved out in 1998 and is waiting for her replacement unit, contends that 60% of the people who live in the community have formal jobs and are hardworking and considerate neighbors.[4]

Residents live in the high-rise William Green Homes on the north side of Division Street, or on the south side of Division Street in the Cabrini Extension red mid-rises, or the Francis Cabrini row homes. They call these places the "whites," "reds," and "row homes." Division Street divides the community not only physically, but also socially. Residents in the whites attend different schools and parks than those in the reds or row homes, and some avoid spaces out of fear of gang retaliation.[5] Despite these divides, many tenants strongly identified with Cabrini Green. They emphasized that it was more than a place where they had an apartment, that the entire area was their home. It was where they grew up, where their roots were. Carol, a resident activist, explained: "There's a sense of security, an extension of family in Cabrini Green."[6] Even when residents move out of the community, they still identify it as their home and return on weekends to visit families and attend barbecues and weekly community gatherings, called "Old School parties."[7]

Tenants contest public housing redevelopment primarily because they desire to preserve their community which, despite constant denigration, continues to provide them with vital informal support networks.[8] A few years ago, resident activists and the Local Advisory Council (LAC), initiated the "One Community, One Cabrini Green" campaign to form solidarity against the CHAs demolition plans.[9] After CHA officials served eight red and white buildings eviction notices in April 2004, they were sued by residents, who contended that the CHA violated a contract that enabled them to participate in the redevelopment planning process.[10] Tenant leaders and their lawyers argued that the notices were "forced evictions," and thus violated residents' "human right" to housing. They cited the negative effects of resident relocation, which include removal from social services and informal support networks, vulnerability to gang harassment, and homelessness, and maintained that a phased redevelopment process was more humane (*Cabrini-Green Local Advisory Council v. Chicago Housing Authority 2004*).

In early August 2004, the judge ruled in the plaintiffs' favor by requiring CHA to preserve two buildings slated for demolition to house residents who desired to stay in the community during redevelopment. Despite this opportunity, people continued to move out of their apartments and cite bad living conditions as their primary reason for relocation. Cabrini Green tenants insist CHA officials purposefully mismanaged their buildings as a strategy to force them to leave their community. Indeed, many families live with rat infestation, broken elevators, sewage overflow, and flooding in their apartments.[11] Linking mismanagement with relocation, tenants joke: "If there's a moving truck outside of the building, the elevators are working. If there's no truck, they're not working." To defy the crumbling exteriors of their buildings, residents keep clean, comfortable apartments. Others expose CHA's mismanagement to the press.[12] But to many, it is a vicious cycle. Once enough people leave because of bad maintenance, CHA officials can justify even lower levels of maintenance, which then can lead to total vacancy.

If the physical space of Cabrini Green is renamed, redeveloped, and occupied overwhelmingly by more affluent white households, what will become of the lives and social networks of the people who call the community their home, their family? Once Wardell Yotaghan, a deceased resident activist, pointed to a drawing of the Cabrini Green buildings and declared: "When they're gone, we're gone." Can a community exist outside of a physical space, an anchor point? Yolanda, a nurse's aide and mother of three, does not want to wait to find out. "I've been here my whole life," she explained before a residents' meeting. "I don't want to leave, especially now, just as it's cleaning up."

Renaming Cabrini Green as "Old Town"

Although bad management is displacing Cabrini Green residents physically, they are being displaced discursively by the renaming of their community. A few years ago, cardboard placards announced the coming of new developments such as "Old Town Square" and "Old Town Village." Now developers assert the permanence of these designations by installing lightpost banners and stone markers etched with these names. The new heavy markers stand in contrast to the dilapidated identifiers of Cabrini Green.[13] In an illustrated brochure of the new mixed-income developments, the CHA endorses this conversion. The new community names emerge boldly in front of the architectural renderings, while the old public housing neighborhood names disappear into the background.

The concrete markers, banners, and advertisements renaming the community as "Old Town" penetrate the perceptions of new owners and designate a community exclusively based on race and class. Standing on Larrabee Street between the Cabrini Green white rises and the Old Town Square town homes, when I asked white people what the community was called they said "Old Town" whereas African-American pedestrians identified the area as "Cabrini Green." In interviews, upper-income residents identified Old Town as "quaint," "close to downtown," "exciting," and "connected to everything," yet some characterized Cabrini Green as "ugly," "depressing," and "isolated." A few of the newer people are aware of private developers' attempts to profit by redefining the community. Jane, a white married woman in her 30s who moved into Old Town Square three years ago, explains: "Old Towns started appearing everywhere around here to raise rents. The whole process is propagated by the city, and usually the community is not strong enough or cohesive enough to fight it." As another homeowner exclaimed: "Old Town names are real estate names... now real estate groups decide what to call a community!"

Real estate marketers selectively preserve components of the built environment and erase others, articulating a "landscape of consumption" (Zukin 1993). In brochures, private developers promote the area as a community composed of private stores and name-brand businesses: Crunch Gym, Crate and Barrel, and Whole Foods. While real estate map makers identify these places as landmarks, they omit Cabrini Green buildings, community centers, and stores or replace them with architectural renderings of low-rise town homes. Private development leaves few public places for people of different race and class backgrounds to exist together, let alone talk to one another. Because of their lower-class status, public housing residents feel unwelcome in many of the commercial spaces that have defined their community's redevelopment. Of all the new construction in the area, only the Near North Public Library, Seward Park, and the police station are open to residents regardless of their consumption ability.

A "culture of fear" surrounds low-income minority communities like Cabrini Green (Glassner 2000). When I asked new and incoming residents where they walked in the area, most admitted to feeling comfortable only in commercial areas. Documenting the walking patterns of white owners, I realized that most men and women turned onto another street before reaching Cabrini Green or the Marshall Field Garden and Apartment Homes, a low-income African-American development on the northeast side of Division Street. Alex, a white 35-year-old married financial consultant who lives in a condominium near Marshall Field, told me that his wife prefers to drive their SUV to the grocery store four blocks away rather than walk by the African-American men on the street. At times, upper-income white residents would ask me if the rumors of violence they heard about Cabrini Green were true. Eddie, a single white investor who lives in Old Town Village West, once asked if I heard about the white guy who was killed recently just walking down Division Street. "Sometimes I get the urge to walk around the area and meet some of the people who live here," he confessed, "but then I remember where I am and decide against it."

Old Town signifies investment security through controlled "diversity." Even though city officials and some private developers market redeveloping Cabrini Green as a "mixed-income" community, in many ways this designation is a misnomer. With 30% public housing units, the North Town Village complex represents the highest income mix. Most of the other so-called mixed-income developments have fewer than 10% public housing residents. In buildings with fewer than 50 units, this often translates into one or two low-income tenants. Although some upper-income owners describe themselves as "progressive" for moving into a community characterized by its "diversity," when probed, most desired an area composed of racial, rather than economic, heterogeneity. One afternoon, Alex confided in me:

> I like the idea that it's diverse and the whole culture that goes with it. I don't mind the music or the way people outfit their cars, I think it's fascinating. And I'd love to get to know them, experience a different culture than my own... But then again, there are things here that we don't like, like the trash. You see young mothers, not married, walking around the street. And I don't approve of the way they raise their kids, hitting them on the streets... Honestly, I would like to see the rest of Cabrini Green go. First we welcomed it, but now... I don't want to see minorities go. I want to see it get more diverse, but instead have professionals or even working-class.

As evident from these examples, developers and city officials alter neighborhood names to foster a private landscape that excludes low-income minorities and constructs a space comprised of racial, rather than class, diversity. This process renders the area "safe" for investment by remaking a black space white. Thus renaming not only accelerates the displacement of Cabrini Green residents, but also it gradually removes them from the neighborhood history.[14]

The "Notorious" Cabrini Green

Just as private developers and CHA officials erase the identities and histories of threatening and unprofitable Cabrini Green buildings and residents by renaming the community "Old Town," so do they generate public support for redevelopment by describing Cabrini Green and its inhabitants with tropes of disease and decay (Conquergood 1992; Bennett and Reed 1999). In these portrayals, CHA officials, journalists, and neoliberal academics reduce recent public housing history to crimes, drugs, gangs, and isolation. Harping on the deterioration of the physical environment is a particularly potent way of justifying its demolition. By reifying the social actors responsible for these processes, writers, policymakers and politicians link the environment's condition to residents' character. This in turn, constructs them as "undeserving" poor, people incapable and unworthy of planning for their futures (Katz 1989, Bennett and Reed 1999, Goode and Maskoysky 2001; Fleming 2003).

Academics and policymakers have long denigrated low-income neighborhoods as dysfunctional, disorganized, and devoid of community.[15] Poor black public housing residents have been doubly blamed for their socioeconomic position. In the 1980s, for instance, President Reagan dubbed black female welfare recipients as "welfare queens," a label that stems from racist conceptions of African-Americans as lazy, immoral and oversexed. In addition, the term "the projects" continues to carry a bad connotation for many Americans, conjuring up images of crime, filth, and rampant drug use. Lawrence Vale notes that "[n]o place in the contemporary United States, with the possible exceptions of prisons and certain hospitals, stigmatizes people in as many debilitating ways as a distressed inner-city public housing project" (Vale 2002:13). Many outsiders can identify a distinct public housing culture defined by joblessness, substance addiction, and teenage pregnancy. These stereotypes are so deeply woven into the public's perception of subsidized housing that President Carter professed during his presidential campaign that "public… and subsidized housing are not dirty words…" (Carter cited in Bauman 2000: 248).

Journalists and media organizations have consistently reproduced these conceptions, crippling the public's perception of Cabrini Green. After July 1970, when a sniper shot and killed two Chicago police officers outside a Cabrini Green high-rise, coverage incited people's fear of the development. White media elites at the *Chicago Tribune* and *Chicago Sun-Times* ran stories that exacerbated and legitimized existing stereotypes to appeal to their suburban readership. Typical headlines during this period read: "Cabrini-Green Area Thieves Prey on Women Drivers in Daylight" (Keegan 1979) and "Suburban Man Found Dead at Cabrini" (*Chicago Sun-Times*, 1986). Ed Marciniak, a former aide to Chicago Mayor Richard J. Daley, explains: "In an unprecedented way, the mass media has shaped the image of the Cabrini-Green neighborhood as much as the residents themselves" (Marciniak 1986: 39).[16]

Alex, who travels frequently because of his consulting job, told me that "everyone has heard of that place. When I travel, people always know what Cabrini Green is. People are shocked that I live there." Another owner, who was a social worker and wanted public housing residents to live in their redeveloped communities, was frustrated by the reaction she gets when she tells people that CHA officials are demolishing Cabrini Green: "good riddance." Other upper-income residents joked that it was easy to give people directions to the area since all seasoned Chicagoans knew to avoid it. When Eddie first started seeing his current girlfriend, he worried that she would never come visit him since he lived adjacent to Cabrini Green. "She thought she would get raped or killed if she drove through here at night," he explained. Nine months into the relationship, his girlfriend slept over regularly. Except for finding a syringe on the lawn one morning, he recounted his experience living in the community like any other.

Although violent incidents still occur in Cabrini Green, crime has dropped consistently since January 1999. Between the summers 2003 and 2004, the area experienced more than an 8% reduction in total crimes, including a 33% reduction in homicides, a 17% reduction in aggravated assault, and a 20% reduction in motor vehicle theft. While the 1991 murder rate was 18 per 100,000 persons and 7% of city murders happened in the district, in 2004 it had decreased to 7 and less than 2% of city murders occurred in the area. For more than 15 years, the area has ranked in the quartile encompassing the Chicago districts with the lowest homicide rates (Chicago Police Department 2004; Alderden and Lavery 2004: 25).[17]

Also contrary to disseminated stereotypes, a large portion of Cabrini Green residents and the majority of Cabrini Green women with children are in the labor force. According to 2000 census while 52% of residents worked during 1999, 75% of those who worked were women. Of this group, 36% worked full time. In addition, 66% of women with children at home worked in the labor force ("Census 2000 Summary File 3-Sample Data").[18]

Eager to get a sense of the public discourse entrenching these stereotypes and propelling redevelopment, I reviewed adjectival descriptors used to describe Chicago public housing and its inhabitants from more than 100 local and national newspaper articles written between 1999 and 2004. Here is a random sample of building characterizations:

> Isolated, vacant, deteriorating, demolished, dangerous, shadows, oppressive, notorious, crippled, overwhelmed, corrosive, grim monoliths, hell hole, chaotic, raggedy, prison-like, reeking, a symbol of failure, overwhelmed by crime, trouble spot, sticking point, outdated, sprawling, dismantled, coming down, half-empty, dilapidated, vast, devastating, enclaves of poverty, last resorts, shabby, unsafe, substandard, torn-down, decrepit, distressed, dead-end destination, bleak and battered, falling one by one, mismanaged, disrespected, vertical ghettos.

Viewed as a whole, these terms construct Cabrini Green as a "geography of abnormality," a black hole of degeneration (Cresswell 1997). When journalists condemn the built environment, they often implicate the residents, "othering" them. Indeed, they have described public housing tenants as:

> Excluded, unemployed, single mothers, casualties, anxious, desperate, vulnerable, victims, agitated, wary, industrious, stigmatized, poor, driven, ready for change, dependent, problems, don't fit, socially isolated, patient, trapped, frustrated, displaced, pushed out, angry, suspicious, scared, in poor shape, opposed, stung, stereotyped, scrutinized.

In using these terms, journalists insinuate that public housing and its inhabitants are a threat to social order. They suggest that either the environment fosters maladjusted behavior in its residents and should be destroyed, or that people do not take care of their buildings and should be denied the "privilege" of public housing. In this way, these words and phrases serve as a rallying call for action and pave the way for ideological debates about the value of public housing and policy changes to its present maintenance, construction, and rehabilitation. Tim Cresswell emphasizes that diction has "consequences 'on the ground' for thousands of people whose lives are deemed 'out of place'" (Cresswell 1997: 339). He warns that negative depictions of people propagated publicly can lead to discriminatory treatment: in the eyes of the white suburban public, low-income minorities are the way media officials describe them. Cresswell concludes: "The metaphorical understandings are as much actions as the physical actions themselves. Once an inner-city resident is understood to be a weed, he or she can be treated like one" (Cresswell 1997: 343).

Such underclass formations reinforce public housing dismantlement by disempowering residents and stripping them of respect. This frustrates not only their participation in the planning process, but also their ability to return to their redeveloped communities. After I told Ernestine, a 60-year-old African-American woman who lives in Old Town Square, that Cabrini Green LAC members sued the CHA for serving them eviction notices, she exclaimed:

> They think they have the right to have over 50% of the new places built, they want to have all this input in what's going on in the area. But they live in CHA! They're not making their keep… They're not paying taxes, many of the people over there don't read the paper, don't work jobs. They should be on their feet! One of my pet peeves is that I don't think they should have stayed here all these years not getting a job. And then they don't want to make space for others; they think it's their legacy!

Just as these stereotypes do not reflect neighborhood conditions such as declining crime and resident employment, so are they counter empirical to the day-to-day life experiences of people in the community. Like many ethnic enclaves, Cabrini Green residents have barbecues in the park, chat in the playground, and play basketball on the courts. Teenagers work summer jobs for the LAC or the local grocery store. For these reasons, tenants express their fury that people who do not know them stereotype them and reduce them to agentless subjects defined by their race and income, characterized by their "immoral" behavior.[19] Outraged by the titillating descriptions of Cabrini Green residents living in filth and disorder, Carol circulated a poster around Chicago depicting the insides of residents' apartments, floral couches, candles and all. Like Carol, Anita also was infuriated that some people think all public housing residents are lazy freeloaders. Before a court hearing one day, she explained to me that a few Cabrini Green residents even paid close to market-rate rents. "People have such a bad perception of Cabrini, the 'notorious' Cabrini Green, but it's not all like that."

Unmasking CHA's Relocation Narratives

During the late fall 2004 and early winter 2005, CHA officials and Leo Burnett staff, the CHA's publicity firm, erected advertisements that portrayed public housing redevelopment as empowering to residents, primarily because it enabled them to move from "chaotic" public spaces to seemingly private homes of their own.[20] This discourse appeared on posters as resident testimonies in Chicago bus stations, el trains and newspaper advertisements. I first encountered one of these posters in early January 2005 while riding the red line train from Evanston to Cabrini Green. At the top of the poster was a picture of a smiling African-American woman; at the bottom the letters CHA were superimposed over the word "CHANGE." The text read:

> Dalphine Allen Jasper will never forget growing up in Henry Horner. She lived with her mom and two sisters in a tiny two-bedroom apartment surrounded by gangs and drugs. "It was a nightmare."

> But Dalphine didn't give up. She vowed to make a better life for her family and enrolled in Malcolm X College. Shortly after, her hard work paid off. Dalphine moved into a new, three-bedroom Chicago Housing Authority home, the kind she always longed for.

> Today Dalphine is about to buy her own home. And, following in her footsteps, her oldest son attends Malcolm X College, while her two younger kids plan to do the same.

In this advertisement, CHA officials celebrate Dalphine's denigration of her public housing living environment and decision to move into a subsidized unit in a privately managed mixed-income community. This narrative is convenient for CHA because it stipulates that social mobility occurs fthrough altering one's behavior, and that poverty is a consequence of antisocial choices. By ignoring the broader political-economic processes that further impoverish people, such as social program cutbacks, corporate deregulation and trade liberalization, CHA officials place responsibility on poor people, rather than the government, to alleviate their own precarious economic situations, letting themselves off the hook.

They also obscure the process of public housing redevelopment from tenant displacement. Rather than empowering residents, public housing redevelopment accentuates their poverty by denying them safe, decent, and affordable housing. Even though CRA officials contend that all lease-holding tenants are "legally entitled to return to a new or rehabbed unit, so long as they remain lease compliant," they deny lease compliance on small infractions, such as paying bills a day late. In addition, few households can meet the standards required even to establish eligibility to apply for one of these units, such as full time employment and good credit. Finally, since policymakers imposed income floors on public housing residency in mixed-income developments, often the very poor are denied units.

Cabrini Green residents frequently express their frustration with the bureaucracy of assigning units in mixed-income developments. For months, Melody, a relocated executive assistant, has tried to reserve a new unit for her elderly godmother, who lives without working elevators in a Cabrini Green red rise. She complains that:

> [t]here are staff inconsistencies, so much bureaucracy to work through in these developments. I've tried to find my godmother a place in a new mixed-income development. She got a place, but they've been doing paperwork since December [2003] on it! Then they came back to us and said no unit was available because she had supposedly turned down four units in the past.

CHA also has a reputation among Cabrini Green residents of "losing" people who temporarily relocate out of the community. Rumor holds that when the North Town Village mixed-income development was finished, CHA officials had to scrounge up residents to live there. For these reasons, Deidre encourages people to try and stay in their communities during redevelopment, because "if you don't go anywhere, they can't lose you!"

Other people fear a lowered quality of life in the mixed-income complexes. Many feel that management will police them heavily and blame them for problems when they occur. Indeed, the sense of equality evoked by the term "mixed-income" is misleading: public housing residents are subjected to harsher rules than other occupants. After they are selected to move in, potential inhabitants must pass a drug screening test and take classes on appropriate home maintenance and community behavior. In this way, they are quarantined from upper-income white owners until they are sanitized of their past "pathological" behavioral habits. As one subsidized North Town Village tenant confessed, "They treat us like five year-olds."

Once inside the development, public housing residents are reprimanded by management and security guards for engaging in activities that fall outside of middle-class cultural norms, such as congregating on stairwells or holding large outdoor barbecues. Through these policies, management officials validate one set of social practices over another. On one hand, they seek to quell "lower-class" behaviors that some upper-income owners perceive as disorderly and threatening. On the other hand, they assume that if they compel public housing residents to acquire "middle-class" values, such as cleanliness and regular employment, they will experience social mobility.

Although a few public housing residents are able to obtain units in mixed-income developments and relocate within their community, 89% of leaseholders are given housing choice vouchers to find their own housing elsewhere (Wilen 2003). Recent studies have shown that between 82 and 97% of voucher holders relocate into primarily segregated low-income neighborhoods on the far south and west sides of the city (Venkatesh 2002; Venkatesh et al. 2004; Lewis and Ward 2003; Fisher 2003). Thus rather than integrating public housing residents into the broader urban fabric, public housing redevelopment exacerbates existing segregation patterns. In fact, this process further isolates residents from the informal local support networks that enable them to raise children while working low-income jobs, which hinders their attainment of self-sufficiency. Not only do the new neighborhoods lack these connections, but also they can produce potentially life threatening relationships, especially when the area is occupied by an opposing gang. As Gail, a Cabrini Green tenant patrol leader, expressed:

> My sister used to live down the hall from me and take care of my kids, but she just decided to take one of the vouchers and now she is moving out west. Unfortunately, the area she's moving to has a lot of gangs and drugs. There aren't many stores and the schools aren't too good. But she thinks she found a nice house. I worry about her and told her to go look at the place at night to see who's hanging out and all, especially since she has a 14-year-old son who is also a father.

Compounding these threats, many people who move into market-rate housing are unable to afford their utility bills. Beauty Turner, a reporter for the *Residents' Journal*, described the situation of a recently displaced family before a resident activist meeting:[21]

This woman saw her yearly bills go up from $1,000 to $8,000; they caught up with her in the private market. When I visited her, she was living with just candles lighting the house. She had Christmas with her family by candlelight … and this was with young children running around too! I went to the CHA to tell them about the situation, and they said, "We'll take care of it, but please, Beauty, don't write a story about it!"[22]

For these reasons, some residents see relocation as leading to imminent homelessness. Indeed, recent studies show that three of every 10 residents who relocate from public housing are unable to use their vouchers (Bennett and Reed 1999; Venkatesh 2002; Lewis and Ward 2003). In addition, the number of homeless shelters has more than tripled since the implementation of the Plan for Transformation (Wilen 2004). Residents recognize these trends and choose to contest relocation rather than accept a life "on the streets." During a Cabrini Green town hall meeting, a 21-year-old college student, visibly agitated, stood up and exclaimed: "We're sitting on prime land; people don't realize it and take these vouchers. Cabrini was built to be torn down! People think we're coming up and out when we leave, but we're walking into hell. We're going to be on the streets!"

As evident from these testimonies, a policy of vouchering-out is thus not empowering but disabling to most public housing residents. It takes away the social safety net of reliable housing and places them in the hands of private market landlords who, in a rapidly gentrifying city, have little incentive to ensure that they are adequately sheltered. The CHA's "free market empowerment" discourse also undermines residents' political agency. By disseminating these texts. they stipulate that residents only are empowered by refusing public services and denigrate tenants who decide to stay in public housing. These tactics effectively enervate contestation campaigns and garner support for demolition, conditions that enable them to proceed unobstructed with the privatization of public land. Residents recognize that local housing policymakers are valuing profit making over public welfare and in turn have started to reframe redevelopment as a "human rights crisis."[23]

Public Housing Redevelopment as a "Human Rights Crisis"

On March 4, 2005, I stood on the steps of the Organization of American States (OAS) in Washington D.C. with Cabrini Green residents and other public housing tenants, squatters, and homeless men and women from across the eastern United States. Although we came from different backgrounds and lived hundreds of miles apart, we were joined by our signs and chants that proclaimed "housing is a human right." Later that day, Carol testified in front of the OAS Inter-American Commission on Human Rights and asserted that public housing redevelopment violated tenants' human rights. Back in Chicago, WBEZ, the public radio station, ran a segment on Cabrini Green residents' campaign to stop the human rights violations inflicted by the Plan for Transformation. How was a group of public housing activists able to insert the language of "human rights" into a dominant redevelopment discourse that perpetually represented them as undeserving poor?

The Coalition to Protect Public Housing (CPPH) meets weekly in a pink and purple linoleum tiled room in the Cabrini Row Houses Tenant Management offices near a wall taped with a poem titled "Don't Quit." In the fall of 1996, Carol formed the Coalition with Wardell Yotaghan, a Rockwell Gardens public housing resident, to protest the CHA's plans to demolish public housing. With the help of local non-profits and community-based organizations, they led marches on City Hall, secured a Relocation Rights Contract for displaced tenants, and undertook a Chicago rental market analysis. Despite their efforts, the Plan for Transformation passed in early 2000. Afterwards, it became apparent that they needed a new framework to refocus public attention on resident displacement.

For years, Carol has carried Article 25, Section 1 of the 1948 Universal Declaration of Human Rights in her purse, which gives everyone:

> [t]he right to a standard of living adequate for the health and well-being of himself and of his family, including food, clothing, housing and medical care and necessary social services, and the right to security in the event of unemployment, sickness, disability, widowhood, old age or other lack of livelihood circumstances beyond his control (General Assembly of the United Nations 1948).

However, it was not until CPPH members received positive feedback on a housing and human rights workshop at the 2004 Chicago Social Forum that they formally incorporated the human rights framework into their agenda at their annual retreat later that year.[24] Ten months later, the Mertz Gilmore Foundation awarded the group $100,000 to implement a "housing is a human right" campaign in Chicago. Ever since, many residents and local activists have referred to demolition inflicted by the Plan for Transformation as a "human rights crisis."

The United States has ratified four international treaties and conventions that support residents' right to housing. The International Convention on the Elimination of All Forms of Racial Discrimination prevents housing-based racial discrimination, while the American Convention on Human Rights requires states to provide adequate housing to people of different income groups. Both the International Covenant on Civil and Political Rights and the UN Commission on Human Rights Resolution 19993/77 protect residents from forceful entry and eviction. Since the millennium, lawyers have increasingly referenced international human rights agreements in their legal arguments. The Supreme Court has become not only more receptive to hearing cases that employ this framework, but also it frequently cities European and international legal standards in its decisions (Leavitt 2003).[25]

In addition to inserting human rights language into their suit against the CHA and testimony before the OAS, in April 2004 Cabrini Green residents also focused worldwide attention on Chicago public housing demolition by taking Miloon Kothari, the Special Rapporteur on Adequate Housing to the UN Commission on Human Rights, on a tour of the community. On December 10th, 2004, also known as International Human Rights Day, Kothari issued a solidarity statement to the Cabrini Green residents. It states:

> What we are witnessing in Chicago today is occurring all across the United States, and in fact across the world. Governments are dismantling social housing, housing subsidies and affirmative actions for low-income people in the name of liberalization and are placing primacy in the market and privatization as a panacea to solve the global crisis of millions living in inadequate and insecure housing... Such policies are a clear violation of the commitment of States across the world to International human rights instruments (Kothari 2004).

Just as residents are displaced through physical and discursive measures, so do they contest redevelopment in tangible and rhetorical ways. By applying human rights discourse to the public housing debate, tenants perform a "symbolic inversion" and expose the global political-economic forces driving the privatization of their community (Babcock 1978; Stallybrass and White 1986: 17). Residents also build their discursive power by asserting that they are not only citizens, but also political citizens capable of altering the current course of redevelopment in the city. In using the language of human rights, they become equated with the discerning public, rather than separated by class. Since such discourse questions government morality and promotes human interest, it carries valuable political capital. Indeed, residents use its language strategically to plug their name and agenda into local and national publications: "Build First. One Move. Resident Control" and "Redevelop, don't displace." During an interview with the *Los Angeles Times* in January 2004, for example, Deidre responded to every question with variants of "housing is a human right" and "public housing demolition is a human rights crisis," so much that in another article, the CHA articulated that they were not violating tenants' human rights (Pride 2005).

Changing the diction people use to talk about public housing is not only crucial to improving the public's perception of its tenants, but also to countering the dominant privatist consensus that garners public support for demolition (Maskovsky 2001). The human rights framework has the potential to restore faith in public value, and thus salvage the Cabrini Green community, a stubborn remnant of the American semi-welfare state. At a town hall meeting in August 2004, Carol motivated a roomful of Cabrini Green residents by declaring: "We give up too fast. If we take a stand, we'll be better people for it. The only reason Cabrini Green is standing is because people have come up to the plate to fight. We don't need to be welcomed back; we need to be the welcomers! If we leave, it's no longer ours. If we stay, it's ours."

Conclusion: Towards a More Equitable Public Housing Policy

In this paper, I have argued that discursive strategies, such as neighborhood renaming, resident denigration and neoliberal relocation narratives, have contributed to public housing redevelopment and tenant displacement. In turn, residents successfully subvert dominant discourses to stall demolition and stay in their communities. However, to ensure that public housing redevelopment results in a more equitable outcome, three conditions must be met.

First, CHA officials should pursue a phased redevelopment process that incorporates the history of low-income residents. Instead of demolishing all Cabrini Green buildings at once, they should preserve enough buildings so that all tenants who desire to live in their redeveloped neighborhood stay in the area during construction. This will not only preserve vital informal support networks, but also protect tenants from territorial violence and homelessness. In addition, new community names should acknowledge, rather than erase, the histories of past tenants. Designations such as 'The Greens" or "Cabrini Place" are more inclusive and preserve the historical black identity of the space.

Second, journalists and other media officials should omit terms such as "the projects" from public housing reporting and resist temptations to simplify, sensationalize, and criminalize complex low-income communities. To more accurately represent the public housing experience, news organizations and schools should recruit, train and hire individuals from low-income minority backgrounds. Last, since empowerment narratives obstruct the real processes of displacement and segregation from public housing redevelopment, progressive planners, city officials, and other local leaders should partner with public housing residents to hold citywide forums and debates to address injustices. Only through such actions will we create a new language to arrive at more equitable solutions to the low-income housing crisis.

Acknowledgments

I want to thank Rebecca Severson, Ivan Watkins and Alaka Wali at the Field Museum's Center for Cultural Understanding and Change for first giving me the opportunity to research public housing redevelopment in Cabrini Green. I also am indebted to Henry Binford for introducing me to Chicago public housing history and Micaela di Leonardo for guiding me as an activist ethnographer. Without the generous support of the National Science Foundation, the Friends of Anthropology, and the Office of Fellowships Undergraduate Summer Research Grant at Northwestern University, this study would not have been possible. I dedicate this paper to the residents of Cabrini Green. I can only hope that these findings will improve their lives in a meaningful way.

Endnotes

[1]Francis Cabrini was the first canonized American saint. The CHA initially reserved 80% of Cabrini units for displaced Italians and 20% for blacks. After World War II broke out, however, the CRA shifted priority to housing war workers and returning veterans. While southern blacks who migrated to work in industries were still eligible for occupancy, many of the 380 Italians displaced by the project were unable to return. In retribution, some community members restricted black use of local parks. In April 1943, shots were fired into a black-occupied Cabrini apartment, inciting a riot. See Hirsch 1983: 45–46 for more information on this event.

[2]William Green was a past president of the American Federation of Labor.

[3]Other Chicago public developments were similarly segregated. Of the 33 projects approved by the CHA in the 1950s and 1960s, 25 were located in census tracts at least 75% black. At the projects' completion, however, only one was located in an area less than 84% black. With the exception of seven projects, the rest were constructed in neighborhoods in excess of 95% black. In the 1966 Gautreaux case, Judge Richard B. Austin found that CHA housing was 99% black occupied, and that 99.5% of projects were in black or racially changing neighborhoods. He stipulated that future housing be built in white areas. Chicago Mayor Richard J. Daley responded by bringing public housing construction to a near standstill. While 1,000 units were constructed annually between 1950 and 1966, development fell to 114 units annually between 1969 and 1980. See Hirsch 1983, Jackson 1985 and Marciniak 1986.

[4]Although the tenant activists requested that I use their real names, I have changed the names of other public housing and upper-income residents.

[5]In an extreme case, Trina, a lifelong resident of the red rises, has never visited Stanton Park in the white rises. Since opposing gangs occupied the area, she avoided it out of fear. Resident-initiated truces and increased police presence has limited gang activity in recent years.

[6]Whenever I walked around with Deidre, we rarely reached our destination without someone running out to hug her or yell, "Hey girl! How you doin'?"

[7]On Friday and Sunday, the Division Street bus is packed with people coming back and forth. Once I witnessed a mother and daughter get on the westbound bus and read "Cabrini Green in Words and Pictures," a history of the community through resident interviews.

[8]Neighbors rely on each other for day care, household supplies, and small loans.

[9]The LAC is a body of locally elected residents that represents their development at the Central Advisory Council, which negotiates with the CHA on matters affecting public housing residents. The group also holds neighborhood-wide functions such as talent shows and Back to School nights, and members wear yellow t-shirts emblazoned with the slogan, "One Community, One Cabrini Green."

[10] In a 1996 suit over the Near North Redevelopment Initiative, residents won the right to negotiate redevelopment plans with the CHA. The ruling enabled the CHA to demolish three buildings, but also it required them to build 700 public housing units in their place. The LAC was made a joint partner in the process. Although the CHA demolished three buildings in 2000, 1158 N. Cleveland, 1150–1160 N. Sedgwick, and 500–502 Oak, most of the replacement units have yet to be built. Presently more than 200 of the units are not even funded. See *Cabrini-Green Local Advisory Council vs. Chicago Housing Authority*. 2000. Consent Decree. U.S. District Court for the Northern District of Illinois Eastern Division, 96C6949, signed October."

[11]One elderly resident lamented that rainwater inundates her walls during thunderstorms. Initially she contacted CHA repeatedly, pleading with them to fix the problem. After 15 years of inadequate response, however, she "learned to live with it." Resident activists report that some tenants become informal "painters and plumbers" after years of mismanagement.

[12]Deidre recalls: "Last winter some of the pipes burst in these buildings, and there was a lot of flooding, ice started forming on the floors. Since CHA wanted people to leave, they didn't do anything about it. They even started blackmailing people, threatening "vagrants" who lived in the building. But I wanted to expose this kind of mismanagement to the press. One day I lined up residents outside the building for a press conference. At the press conference, one of the press people fell down on the ice, and it was only after that incident that CRA started to fix the problems that people were having."

[13]For instance, the large, tombstone-like "Old Town Village West" rock on the corner of Division Street and Crosby Avenue overwhelms the faded iron "Cabrini Green" gate further down the road.

[14]One summer afternoon in 2003, Janice, a relocated Cabrini Green church secretary, took me on a tour of the neighborhood as it "used to be." "See those town homes over there?" she said, pointing to a series of single family homes. "That's where Cooley School was (as in the 1975 film "Cooley High"). And on the other side of Larrabee, where those new homes are?" She gestured to the Old Town Village West development. "There used to be buildings there. And see over there, those brick buildings?" she said, indicating the red rises served most recently with demolition notices. "That's where I grew up. I heard they're tearing those down to build new town homes."

[15]See Zorbaugh 1929, Lewis 1966, and Wilson 1987.

[16]So prevalent was the "Cabrini Green" stigma, that by the 1980s, public housing tenants and area churches began to refer to their community as the "Near North Side," see Marciniak 1986, pg. 112.

[17]Of the crimes occurring in the district, some residents insist that the vast majority of perpetrators live outside the area.

[18]To disaggregate Census statistics for Cabrini Green, I selected data for African-Americans in tracts encompassing the development.

[19]After I read Carol the list of people's perceptions about Cabrini Green, she retorted: "If you go into some of the houses in Cabrini Green, you would think you were in one of those lakefront houses. We don't just sit around and watch 'All My Children.' I go to the office everyday." She smiled and added, "We tape 'All My Children' so we can watch it when we get home."

[20]In the summer 2004, the CHA initiated a $650,000 media campaign to promote positive perceptions of public housing relocation.

[21]The *Residents' Journal* is a bi-monthly publication written by and for public housing residents.

[22]She later shook her head and smiled, adding, "You can't tell a fighter not to fight; you can't tell a writer not to write."

[23]Public housing redevelopment is a highly profit-making venture. In 1998, public housing units comprised 5% of the total US real estate market, an estimated value of 90 billion dollars. See Epp (1998: 122). Realizing its market-rate value, one Cabrini Green tenant actually put her unit up for rent in a local paper.

[24]The Chicago Social Forum is a component of the World Social Forum, which initiates dialogue between human rights organizations from around the world.

[25]See *Daryl Renard Atkins v. Virginia.* 2002. No. 00–8452, *Barbara Grutter v. Lee Bollinger et al.* 2003. No. 02–241; and *John Geddes Lawrence and Tyron Garner v. Texas* 2003. No. 02–102.

References

Alderden, Megan, and Timothy Lavery (2004). *2004 Murder Analysis*. Chicago: Chicago Police Department.

Babcock, Barbara (ed.) (1978). *The Reversible World: Symbolic Inversion in Art and Society*. Ithaca, NY: Cornell University Press.

Barbara Grutter v. Lee Bollinger et al. 2003 No. 02–241.

Bauman, John F. (2000). "Jimmy Carter, Patricia Roberts Hanis, and Housing Policy in the Age of Limits." In *From Tenements To The Taylor Homes*, John F. Bauman, Roger Biles, and Kristin M. Szyivian (eds.). University Park: The Pennsylvania State University Press, pp. 246–264.

Bennett, Larry, and Adolph Reed, Jr. (1999). "The New Face of Urban Renewal: The Near North Redevelopment Initiative and the Cabrini-Green Neighborhood." In *Without Justice For All: The New Liberalism and Our Retreat from Racial Inequality*, Adolph Reed Jr. (ed.). Boulder: Westview Press, pp. 175–211.

Biles, Roger (2000). "Public Housing and the Postwar Urban Renaissance, 1949–1973." In *From Tenements To The Taylor Homes*, John F. Bauman, Roger Biles, and Kristin M. Szylvian (eds.). University Park: The Pennsylvania State University Press, pp. 143–162.

Cabrini-Green Local Advisory Council vs. Chicago Housing Authority 2000. Consent Decree. U.S. District Court for the Northern District of Illinois Eastern Division, 96C6949, signed October.

Cabrini-Green Local Advisory Council, et al. v. Chicago Housing Authority, et al. 2004. No. 04 C 3792.

Chicago Police Department (2004). Index Crime Summary: January-September 2004, compiled by the Research and Analysis Section of Research and Development. Year to Date Index Crime Statistics: December 2004. Chicago: Chicago Police Department.

Chicago Sun-Times (1986). "Suburban Man Found Dead at Cabrini." *Chicago Sun-Times*, February 19: 28.

Conquergood, Dwight (1992). "Life in Big Red: Struggles and Accommodations in a Chicago Polyethnic Tenement." In *Structuring Diversity*, Louise Lamphere (ed.). Chicago: University of Chicago Press, pp. 95–145.

Cresswell, Tim (1997). "Weeds, Plagues, and Bodily Secretions: A Geographical Interpretation of Metaphors of Displacement." *Annals of the Association of American Geographers* 87(2): 330–345.

Daryl Renard Atkins v. Virginia. 2002. No. 00–8452.

Epp, Gayle (1998). "Emerging Strategies for Revitalizing Public Housing." In *New Directions in Urban Public Housing*, David P. Varady, Wolfgang F. E. Preiser, and Francis P. Russell (eds.). New Brunswick: Rutgers, pp. 121–141.

Erjavec, Kannen (2001). "Media Representation of the Discrimination Against the Roma in Eastern Europe: the Case of Slovenia." *Discourse and Society* 12(6): 699–727.

Fairclough, Norman (1993). "Critical Discourse Analysis and the Marketization of Public Discourse: The Universities." *Discourse and Society* 4(2): 133–168.

Fairclough, Norman (2000). "Language and Neo-liberalism." *Discourse and Society.* 11(2): 147–148.

Fisher, Paul (2003). *Where Are the Public Housing Families Going? An Update.* Chicago: National Center on Poverty Law.

Fleming, David (2003). "Subjects of the Inner City: Writing the People of Cabrini-Green." In *Towards a Rhetoric of Everyday Life*, Martin Nystrand and John Duffy (eds.) Madison: The University of Wisconsin Press, pp. 207–244.

Fowler, Roger, Robert Hodge, Ginthere Kress, and Tony Trew (eds.) (1979). *Language and Control.* London: Routledge and Kegan Paul.

General Assembly of the United Nations. (1948). Adopted and proclaimed by resolution 217 A (III), December 10. Available on the internet at: http://www.un.org/Overview/rights.html. Accessed on April 17, 2006.

Glassner, Barry (2000). *The Culture of Fear: Why Americans Are Afraid of the Wrong Things.* New York: Basic Books.

Goode, Judith, and Jeff Maskovsky (eds.). (2001). *The New Poverty Studies: The Ethnography of Power, Politics, and Impoverished People in the United States.* New York: New York University Press.

Grossman, James R., Ann Durkin Keating, and Janice L. Reiff (eds). (2004). *The Encyclopedia of Chicago.* Chicago: The University of Chicago Press.

Hirsch, Arnold R. (1983). *The Making of the Second Ghetto: Race and Housing in Chicago 1940–1960.* Cambridge: Cambridge University Press.

Jackson, Kenneth T. (1985). *Crabgrass Frontier: The Suburbanization of the United States.* Oxford: Oxford University Press.

John Geddes Lawrence and Tyron Gamer v. Texas 2003. No. 02–102.

Katz, Michael (1989). *The Undeserving Poor: From the War on Poverty to the War on Welfare*. New York: Pantheon Books.

Keegan, Anne (1979). "Cabrini-Green Area Thieves Prey on Women Drivers in Daylight." *Chicago Tribune*, February 9: 1.

Kothari, Miloon (2004). *Bring Human Rights Home*. Statement for International Human Rights Day, December 10, 2004. Available on the internet at: http://www.unhchr.ch/huricane/huricane.nsf/view01/ 0131163454A52BFOC1256F6500577634?opendocument.

Leavitt, Noah (2003). "Legal Globalization: Why U.S. Courts Should Be Able to Consider the Decisions of Foreign Courts and International Bodies." Find Law's Legal Commentary. Available on the internet at: http://writ.findlaw.com/leavitt/20031016.html

Lewis, Dan, and Cheryl Ward (2003). "The Plan for Transformation and the Residential Movements of Public Housing Residents." Research Paper, Institute for Policy Research at Northwestern University.

Lewis, Oscar (1966). "The Culture of Poverty." *Scientific American* 215(4): 19–25.

Marciniak, Ed (1986). *Reclaiming the Inner City: Chicago's Near North Revitalization Confronts Cabrini-Green*. Washington: National Center for Urban Ethnic Affairs.

Maskovsky, Jeff (2001). "Afterward: Beyond Privatist Consensus." In *The New Poverty Studies: The Ethnography of Power, Politics, and Impoverished People in the United States*, Judith Goode and Jeff Maskovsky (eds.). New York: New York University Press, pp. 470–482.

Pacyga, Dominic A., and Ellen Skerrett (1986). *Chicago: City of Neighborhoods*. Chicago: Loyola University Press.

Pride, Karen E. (2005). "Doll Draws Attention to Public Housing Demolition Debate." *Chicago Defender* February 8: 3.

Ranney, David (2003). *Global Decisions, Local Collisions: Urban Life in the New World Order*. Philadelphia: Temple University Press.

Squires, Gregory D., Larry Bennett, Kathleen McCourt, and Philip Nyden (1987). *Chicago: Race, Class, and the Response to Urban Decline*. Philadelphia: Temple University Press.

Stallybrass, Peter, and Allon White (1986). *The Politics and Poetics of Transgression*. Ithaca: Cornell University Press.

United States Census Office (2000). 2000 Summary File 3-Sample Data. Presence of Own Children Under 18 Years by Age of Own Children by Employment Status for Females 16 and Over. Universe: Black or African American Alone Females 16 Years and Over. Available on the internet at www.census.gov.

Vale, Lawrence J. (2002). *Reclaiming Public Housing: A Half Century of Struggle in Three Public Neighborhoods*. Cambridge: Harvard University Press.

van Dijk, Teun (1993). "Principles of Critical Discourse Analysis." *Discourse and Society*, 4(2): 249–283.

Venkatesh, Sudhir (2002). *The Robert Taylor Homes Relocation Study*. Columbia University in the City of New York: A Research Report from the Center for Urban Research and Policy.

Venkatesh, Sudir Alladi, Isil Celimli, Douglas Miller, Alexandra Murphy, and Beauty Turner (2004). *Chicago Public Housing Transformation: A Research Report*. New York City: Columbia University, Center for Urban Research and Policy.

Von Hoffman, Alexander (1998). "High Ambitions: The Past and Future of American Low-Income Housing Policy." In *New Directions in Urban Public Housing*, David P. Varady, Wolfgang F. E. Preiser, and Francis P. Russell (eds.). New Brunswick: Rutgers, pp. 3–22.

Whitaker, David T. (2000). *Cabrini Green in Words and Pictures*. Chicago: LPC Group.

Wilen, William P. (2003). Testimony of P. Wilen, Attorney. National Center on Poverty Law, prepared for the hearing on HOPE VI and the Low-Income Housing Crisis. Chicago, IL. November 10, 2003.

Wilen, William P. (2004). Remarks of William P. Wilen, Director of Housing Sargent Shriver National Center on Poverty Law. Chicago, IL: Coalition to Protect Public Housing, April Briefing, April 28.

Wilson, William Julius (1987). *The Truly Disadvantaged: The Inner City, the Underclass and Public Policy*. Chicago: University of Chicago Press.

Zorbaugh, Harvey Warren (1929). *The Gold Coast and the Slum: A Sociological Study of Chicago's Near North Side*. Chicago: The University of Chicago Press.

Zukin, Sharon (1993). *Landscapes of Power: From Detroit to Disney World*. Berkeley: University of California Press.

Solving Ghetto America[*]

Doug Massey and Nancy Denton

The isolation of Negro from white communities is increasing rather than decreasing... Negro poverty is not white poverty. Many of its causes... are the same. But there are differences—deep, corrosive, obstinate differences—radiating painful roots into the community, the family, and the nature of the individual.

—President Lyndon Johnson, address to Howard University, June 4, 1965

After persisting for more than fifty years, the black ghetto will not be dismantled by passing a few amendments to existing laws or by implementing a smattering of bureaucratic reforms.[1] The ghetto is part and parcel of modern American society; it was manufactured by whites earlier in the century to isolate and control growing urban black populations, and it is maintained today by a set of institutions, attitudes, and practices that are deeply embedded in the structure of American life. Indeed, as conditions in the ghetto have worsened and as poor blacks have adapted socially and culturally to this deteriorating environment, the ghetto has assumed even greater importance as an institutional tool for isolating the by-products of racial oppression: crime, drugs, violence, illiteracy, poverty, despair, and their growing social and economic costs.

For the walls of the ghetto to be breached at this point will require an unprecedented commitment by the public and a fundamental change in leadership at the highest levels. Residential segregation will only be eliminated from American society when federal authorities, backed by the American people, become directly involved in guaranteeing open housing markets and eliminating discrimination from public life. Rather than relying on private individuals to identify and prosecute those who break the law, the U.S. Department of Housing and Urban Development and the Office of the Attorney General must throw their full institutional weight into locating instances of housing discrimination and bringing those who violate the Fair Housing Act to justice; they must vigorously prosecute white racists who harass and intimidate blacks seeking to exercise their rights of residen-

*Douglas Massey and Nancy Denton, *American Apartheid: Segregation and the Making of the Underclass* (Cambridge, MA: Harvard University Press, 1993). Copyright © 1993 by the President and Fellows of Harvard College. Reprinted by permission of the publisher.

tial freedom; and they must establish new bureaucratic mechanisms to counterbalance the forces that continue to sustain the residential color line.

Given the fact that black poverty is exacerbated, reinforced, and perpetuated by racial segregation, that black-white segregation has not moderated despite the federal policies tried so far, and that the social costs of segregation inevitably cannot be contained in the ghetto, we argue that the nation has no choice but to launch a bold new initiative to eradicate the ghetto and eliminate segregation from American life. To do otherwise is to condemn the United States and the American people to a future of economic stagnation, social fragmentation, and political paralysis.

Race, Class, and Public Policy

In the United States today, public policy discussions regarding the urban underclass frequently devolve into debates on the importance of race versus class. However one defines the underclass, it is clear that African-Americans are overrepresented within in it. People who trace their ancestry to Africa are at greater risk than others of falling into poverty, remaining there for a long time, and residing in very poor neighborhoods. On almost any measure of social and economic well-being, blacks and Puerto Ricans come out near the bottom.

The complex of social and economic problems that beset people of African origin has led many observers to emphasize race over class in developing remedies for the urban underclass.[2] According to these theories, institutional racism is pervasive, denying blacks equal access to the resources and benefits of American society, notably in education and employment. Given this assessment, these observers urge the adoption of racial remedies to assist urban minorities; proposals include everything from special preference in education to affirmative action in employment.

Other observers emphasize class over race. The liberal variant of the class argument holds that blacks have been caught in a web of institutional and industrial change.[3] Like other migrants, they arrived in cities to take low-skilled jobs in manufacturing, but they had the bad fortune to become established in this sector just as rising energy costs, changing technologies, and increased foreign competition brought a wave of plant closings and layoffs. The service economy that arose to replace manufacturing industries generated high-paying jobs for those with education, but poorly paid jobs for those without it.

Just as this transformation was undermining the economic foundations of the black working class, the class theorists argue, the civil rights revolution opened up new opportunities for educated minorities. After the passage of the 1964 Civil Rights Act, well-educated blacks were recruited into positions of responsibility in government, academia, and business, and thus provided the basis for a new black middle class.[4] But civil rights laws could not provide high-paying jobs to poorly educated minorities when there were no jobs to give out. As a result, the class structure of the black community bifurcated into an affluent class whose fortunes were improving and a poverty class whose position was deteriorating.[5]

The conservative variant of the class argument focuses on the deleterious consequences of government policies intended to improve the economic position of the poor.[6] According to conservative reasoning, federal antipoverty programs implemented during the 1960s—notably the increases in Aid to Families with Dependent Children—altered the incentives governing the behavior of poor men and women. The accessibility and generosity of federal welfare programs reduced the attractiveness of marriage to poor women, increased the benefits of out-of-wedlock childbearing, and reduced the appeal of low-wage labor for poor men. As a result, female-headed families proliferated, rates of unwed childbearing rose, and male labor force participation rates fell. These trends drove poverty rates upward and created a population of persistently poor, welfare-dependent families.

Race- and class-based explanations for the underclass are frequently discussed as if they were mutually exclusive. Although liberal and conservative class theorists may differ with respect to the specific explanations they propose, both agree that white racism plays a minor role as a continuing cause of urban poverty; except for acknowledging the historical legacy of racism, their accounts are essentially race-neutral. Race theorists, in contrast, insist on the primacy of race in American society and emphasize its continuing role in perpetuating urban poverty; they view class-based explanations suspiciously, seeing them as self-serving ideologies that blame the victim.[7]

By presenting the case for segregation's present role as a central cause of urban poverty, we seek to end the specious opposition of race and class. The issue is not whether race or class perpetuates the urban underclass, but how race *and* class *interact* to undermine the social and economic well-being of black Americans. We argue that race operates powerfully through urban housing markets and that racial segregation interacts with black structure to produce a uniquely disadvantaged neighborhood environment for African-Americans.

If the decline of manufacturing, the suburbanization of employment, and the proliferation of unskilled service jobs brought rising rates of poverty and income inequality to blacks, the negative consequences of these trends were exacerbated and magnified by segregation. Segregation concentrated the deprivation created during the 1970s and 1980s to yield intense levels of social and economic isolation. As poverty was concentrated, moreover, so were all social traits associated with it, producing a structural niche within which welfare dependency and joblessness could flourish and become normative. The expectations of the urban poor were changed not so much by generous AFDC payments as by the spatial concentration of welfare recipients, a condition that was structurally built into the black experience by segregation.

If our viewpoint is correct, then public policies must address both race and class issues if they are to be successful. Race-conscious steps need to be taken to dismantle the institutional apparatus of segregation, and class-specific policies must be implemented to improve the socioeconomic status of minorities. By themselves, programs targeted to low-income minorities will fail because they will be swamped by powerful environmental influences arising from the disastrous neighborhood conditions that blacks experience because of segregation. Likewise, efforts to reduce segregation will falter unless blacks acquire the socioeconomic resources that enable them to take full advantage of urban housing markets and the benefits they distribute.

Although we focus in this chapter on how to end racial segregation in American cities, the policies we advocate cannot be pursued to the exclusion of broader efforts to raise the class standing of urban minorities. Programs to dismantle the ghetto must be accompanied by vigorous efforts to end discrimination in other spheres of American life and by class-specific policies designed to raise educational levels, improve the quality of public schools, create employment, reduce crime, and strengthen the family. Only a simultaneous attack along all fronts has any hope of breaking the cycle of poverty that has become deeply rooted within the ghetto. Before discussing policies to end residential segregation, however, we take a quick look at preliminary data from the 1990 Census to see if there is any hint of progress toward integration under current policies.

. . .

Past Integration Efforts: A Scorecard

During the 1970s and 1980s, the fight to end racial segregation was spearheaded by individuals and by private fair housing organizations. The National Committee Against Discrimination in Housing was founded in 1950 with a small coterie of local open housing groups, but after 1968 additional chapters were set up around the country to take advantage of new enforcement mechanisms created by the Fair Housing Act; presently the NCDH has seventy-five local affiliates.[8] These local chapters assist individuals in filing and pursuing fair housing suits: they supply low-cost legal advice to victims of discrimination; they organize testing efforts; they assist litigants in compiling evidence of discrimination; and they provide legal counsel to plaintiffs in trial proceedings.

Though hamstrung by weak enforcement provisions in the Fair Housing Act itself and hampered by limited financial resources, personnel shortages, and a lack of community support, these private organizations have established a variety of legal precedents to enable the more effective prosecution of housing discriminators. Over the years they have gradually expanded the list of parties with legal standing to file fair housing suits; they have firmly established the housing audit as an acceptable method for proving discrimination in court; and they have succeeded in declaring a variety of real estate practices illegal under the Fair Housing Act.[9]

Despite these successes, however, discrimination and segregation persist in urban America. The heroic efforts of individual victims, idealistic activists, and dedicated organizations are not enough to dismantle the institutional apparatus of segregation. Whereas the processes that perpetuate segregation are pervasive and institutionalized, fair housing enforcement has been individual, sporadic, and confined to a small number of isolated cases (since 1968, only about four hundred fair housing cases have been decided).[10] Rather than eliminating the systemic foundations of segregation, private efforts have only chipped away at its facade.

Although the 1988 amendments provide tougher penalties against those who violate the Fair Housing Act and make it easier to prosecute discriminators, the basic organization of enforcement still relies heavily on individuals. As long as the Fair Housing Act is enforced by these "private attorneys general" rather than by federal authorities, it is unlikely to be effective.

Proof of the inefficacy of individual enforcement comes from Chicago, which has led the nation in fair housing litigation. Since 1966, the Leadership Council for Metropolitan Open Communities has mounted an aggressive campaign against residential segregation in the Chicago metropolitan area.[11] It has established affirmative real estate marketing programs; it has filed numerous fair housing complaints against realtors and developers; it has repeatedly defeated discriminators in court; it has pioneered the use of testers to uncover those guilty of a "pattern and practice" of discrimination; and it has taken the lead in prosecuting HUD and the Chicago Housing Authority for promoting racial segregation in public housing.[12]

As a result of these efforts, litigation initiated in Chicago has produced some of the most important fair housing rulings of the past two decades, including such landmark cases as *Hills v. Gautreaux*, which confirmed HUD's complicity in promoting public housing segregation;[13] *Metropolitan Housing Development Corporation v. Village of Arlington Heights*, which paved the way for an effects criterion in proving Title VIII violations;[14] *Gladstone Realtors v. Village of Bellwood*, which significantly expanded standing to file suit under the Fair Housing Act;[15] *Phillips v. Hunter*, which set a precedent for large punitive awards;[16] and *Williamson v. Hampton*, which helped to establish the legitimacy of testing as a method of proving discrimination in court.[17]

Probably no fair housing group in the country has been more energetic or successful in promoting equal housing opportunities than the Leadership Council for Metropolitan Open Communities and its allies; but despite its efforts, the Chicago metropolitan area remains one of the most segregated areas in the United States. In the twenty years since the passage of the Fair Housing Act, the level of black-white segregation has hardly changed; as of 1990 the index of black-white residential dissimilarity stood at 86, within 2 points of where it stood a decade earlier and within 5 points of its 1970 value. At the rate of change observed between 1980 and 1990, the level of racial segregation would not even reach 70 (still a very high level of segregation) until the year 2042.

Although Chicago's fair housing groups have pushed private fair housing enforcement to the legal limit, they have produced *essentially no change* in the degree of racial segregation within that urban area. If Chicago's vigorous fair housing efforts have been unable to bring about any significant movement toward residential desegregation, then private efforts in other metropolitan areas with large black populations are unlikely to succeed either.

Private enforcement of the Fair Housing Act is not the only weapon in the battle against housing segregation, however; integration maintenance programs have also been used.[18] These programs employ a variety of race-conscious techniques to maintain racially balanced populations within specific housing developments, apartment complexes, neighborhoods, or even entire communities. They are typically used in residential settings that lie near or adjacent to existing black areas and are likely to attract substantial black housing demand. White demand in such settings tends to be weak and sensitive to small changes in the relative number of blacks. In the absence of any intervention, white housing demand drops precipitously as black demand and the black percentage increase, leading to racial turnover and residential resegregation.

Integration maintenance programs intervene within targeted residential settings to forestall this process. The techniques of intervention vary depending on the setting, but all essentially work to maintain blacks as a minority. In apartment complexes and specific housing developments, such as New York's Starrett City or Chicago's Atrium Village, integration maintenance programs may involve the simple imposition of a racial quota.[19] The number of minority-and white-inhabited units is fixed, and separate waiting lists are created for each race. Given the disparity in white and black demand for integrated housing, the black list quickly grows to be several times longer than the white list. Most whites who seek housing in the complex are admitted rather quickly; blacks are forced to endure a long wait until a "black" unit is vacated.

When the targeted setting is an entire neighborhood or community, simple quotas cannot be employed and other methods must be used to maintain blacks as a minority. In order to prevent panic selling by whites, "For Sale" signs may be banned and special insurance schemes implemented to guarantee the value of white homes. Meanwhile, white housing demand is fostered by taking steps to improve the quality of schools and increase public security. At the same time, realtors are specially trained to engage in "reverse steering," whereby they deliberately encourage white homeseekers to consider units in integrated neighborhoods. Integration maintenance programs also engage in extensive public relations, including the preparation of attractive brochures, the placement of ads in magazines, recruiting white homeseekers at local universities, and working with employers and corporate relocation services to attract white residents.[20]

In contrast, little is done to make blacks aware of housing opportunities within the targeted area. Black racial concentrations within the community are carefully monitored, and special efforts are taken to avoid the development of black clusters. Landlords are often required to furnish monthly reports on the race of new tenants, and homeowners are asked to maintain logs of the race of potential buyers brought in by realtors. In contrast to whites, black homeseekers are steered away from black "clusters" toward homes in areas that are all white or that contain few black residents.[21]

Although integration maintenance programs are consistent with the spirit of residential desegregation, ultimately they operate by restricting black residential choice and violating the letter of the Fair Housing Act. They limit black housing options either directly, by applying quotas, or indirectly through a series of tactics designed to control the rate of black entry. As the geographers Robert Lake and Jessica Winslow point out, "ensconced in fair housing rhetoric, integration management relies on a highly restrictive interpretation of the goals and procedures of national fair housing policy. The maintenance of black minorities, rather than the guarantee of equal housing access, is the underlying objective of integration management programs."[22]

These violations leave fair housing advocates vulnerable to attack from interests opposed to the expansion of black civil rights…. [F]or example, during the early 1980s the Reagan Administration filed lawsuits attacking integration maintenance schemes implemented at New York's Starrett City development and elsewhere.[23] Civil rights groups were forced into the awkward position of devoting scarce time and resources to defending housing practices of questionable legality.

The most serious flaw of integration maintenance schemes, however, is that they do nothing to change the larger system of housing discrimination in the United States: they deal with the symptoms rather than the causes of residential segregation. Integrated settings are at risk of turnover in the first place because a racially biased housing market discourages black entry in most other neighborhoods, thereby funneling black demand to a few isolated areas close to existing black communities. Rather than seeking to change this discriminatory system of housing allocation, integration management programs accept it and seek to preserve a few islands of integration within a larger sea of racial exclusivity. Inevitably, many deserving black families with high aspirations for residential mobility are kept out so that a few privileged whites and blacks can enjoy the benefits of an economically stable, integrated neighborhood.

Public housing programs provide a third avenue for the promotion of residential integration. But as… case studies and statistical analyses have shown, local housing authorities, with the tacit support of the federal government, used public housing as an institutional means of reinforcing racial segregation during the period of rapid black integration from 1945 to 1970.[24] When it became clear after 1970 that local authorities would eventually have to conform to the affirmative mandate of the Fair Housing Act and locate new projects outside the ghetto, they decided to forgo federal housing funds and stopped constructing projects.[25]

During the early 1970s, the Nixon and Ford administrations shifted federal housing priorities away from the construction of large, authority-owned projects to the funding of small, scattered-site units erected by private developers.[26] Yet even these low-density subsidized housing programs encountered spirited resistance by neighborhoods and communities, especially in suburban areas where racial barriers were buttressed by restrictive zoning ordinances designed to maintain class integrity.[27] Fair housing groups were constantly forced into court to compel local authorities to conform to federal housing laws.

The most notorious case of resistance to public housing desegregation occurred in Yonkers, New York.[28] In 1980, the NAACP filed suit on behalf of black residents to end the city's forty-year practice of systematic segregation in subsidized housing. After a long period of discovery and an exhaustive ninety-day trial, Federal Judge Leonard B. Sand found Yonkers officials guilty of intentional discrimination in the location of federally subsidized housing. In his 1986 decision, *NAACP v. Yonkers Board of Education et al.*, the judge cited specific illegal activities that local officials had used to promote racial segregation: they had employed different procedural rules to select housing sites in white and black neighborhoods; they had readily acquiesced to racially motivated opposition to public housing construction; they had systematically located subsidized housing in black areas; they had refused to seek all of the Section 8 housing certificates for which they qualified although there was a pressing need for low-income housing; and they had limited the use of Section 8 certificates they did acquire to the black quadrant of the city.[29]

The judge ordered the city of Yonkers to designate a set of sites outside of the ghetto for the construction of two hundred new subsidized housing units and to develop a long-term plan for the desegregation of subsidized housing. City officials refused to comply, however, and obstructed all remedial efforts.[30]

Although Judge Sand's settlement was confirmed by a federal appeals court in December 1987, the city still refused to obey the court order, and during the summer of 1988 Yonkers made headlines by incurring $800,000 in fines as a result of a contempt-of-court citation for failure to comply. As the fines mounted daily, city officials undertook a vitriolic and racially based media campaign against the judge, the federal courts, black residents of Yonkers, and the NAACP. It was not until September 1988—eight years after the original lawsuit was filed and two years after the initial court order—that the City Council, under financial duress, finally accepted a plan to build the two hundred units on eight sites scattered among white neighborhoods of Yonkers, an action that was unlikely to alter the racial composition of any neighborhood or significantly change the structure of segregation.[31]

Although other attempts to desegregate public housing have not achieved the notoriety of the Yonkers case, they have met with similar hostility and organized political resistance. Events surrounding the Black Jack case, involving a nonprofit developer who sought to build subsidized housing in an unincorporated area outside of St. Louis, lasted seven years from start to finish; and by the time of the settlement, financing for construction had fallen through and the contested apartments were never built.[32] The *Gautreaux* case...dragged on for fifteen years until the U.S. Supreme Court finally settled it.[33] A proposal in the early 1980s to build 105 units of subsidized housing in a white neighborhood of Houston met with heated protests and marches until the plan was finally shelved, and a proposal for an eighty-unit development later met with a similar fate.[34]

Partly because of the staunch legal and political resistance that public housing desegregation efforts inspire, they have not been successful in promoting the broader integration of urban America. Even if scattered-site programs could be smoothly desegregated, moreover, the potential effect on overall segregation levels is limited by the small number of units involved. Scattered-site units constitute only about one-third of all public housing units in the United States, which, in turn, represent only 2 percent of the nation's total housing stock;[35] and even if the desegregation of scattered-site units could be achieved, it would leave intact the intense segregation of large, authority-owned housing projects. [36]

Dismantling the Ghetto

Public policies to end racial segregation must attack racial discrimination in private housing markets, where 98% of all dwellings are allocated. In particular, they must interrupt the institutionalized process of neighborhood racial turnover, which is the ultimate mechanism by which the ghetto is reproduced and maintained. Racial turnover is built into the structure of urban housing markets through a combination of white prejudice and racial discrimination, which restrict black access to most white neighborhoods and systematically channel black housing demand to a few black or racially mixed areas.

The elimination of racial barriers in urban housing markets requires the direct institutional involvement of the federal government. To an unprecedented degree the U.S. Department of Housing and Urban Development, in particular, must fully commit itself to fair housing enforcement.

First, HUD must increase its financial assistance to local fair housing organizations to increase their ability to investigate and prosecute individual complaints of housing discrimination. Grants made to local agencies dedicated to fair housing enforcement will enable them to expand their efforts by hiring more legal staff, implementing more extensive testing programs, and making their services more widely available. In the early history of fair housing, many testers and legal assistants were funded by federal programs such as the Comprehensive Education and Training Act and the Office of Economic Opportunity.[37] The elimination of these programs by the Reagan Administration undercut the ability of local organizations to enforce fair housing law, and these cuts must be restored if racial discrimination is to be overcome.

But spirited individual prosecution, even when federally assisted, is not enough. As a second step, HUD must establish a permanent testing program capable of identifying realtors who engage in a pattern of discrimination. A special unit dedicated to the regular administration of large-scale housing audits should be created in HUD under the Assistant Secretary for Fair Housing and Equal Opportunity. Audits of randomly selected realtors should be conducted annually within metropolitan areas that have large black communities, and when evidence of systematic discrimination is uncovered, the department should compile additional evidence and turn it over to the Attorney General for vigorous prosecution.

Neither of these two proposals requires significant changes in fair housing law. Indeed, the 1988 Fair Housing Amendments, in making it easier to pursue discriminations and increasing the costs for those who are caught, make the 1990s a particularly opportune time to redouble enforcement efforts. The new law authorized a Fair Housing Initiatives Program at HUD to fund state and local governments and nonprofit corporations seeking to carry out programs to prevent or eliminate discriminatory housing practices.[38] The amendments empowered HUD to initiate investigations on its own, without a prior complaint of discrimination, clearing the way for a bureaucratically based testing program.[39]

Racial discrimination is a problem not only in real estate transactions, however, but also in the home loan industry, where blacks are rejected at rates considerably above those of whites.[40] Congress therefore has required financial institutions to compile detailed racial data on their lending practices. The 1974 Equal Credit Opportunity Act requires them to tabulate the race of clients they accept and reject for home loans;[41] the 1975 Home Mortgage Disclosure Act requires them to report which neighborhoods receive mortgage funds;[42] and the 1977 Community Reinvestment Act requires them to demonstrate that they have provided credit to areas that have been unable to secure capital in the past.[43]

But despite these requirements, little has been done with these data to monitor lender compliance with fair housing statutes. As a third policy initiative, a staff should be created under the Assistant Secretary for Fair Housing and Equal Opportunity to scrutinize lending data for unusually high rates of rejection among minority applicants and black neighborhoods. When the rejection rates cannot be explained statistically by social, demographic, economic, or other background factors, a systematic case study of the bank's lending practices should be initiated. If clear evidence of discrimination is uncovered, the case should be referred to the Attorney General for prosecution, and if not, an equal opportunity lending plan should be conciliated, implemented, and monitored.

Because HUD continues to play a large role in overseeing federally subsidized housing, a fourth policy initiative must be a more vigorous promotion of desegregation under the affirmative mandate of the Fair Housing Act. Given the reality of intense opposition to the construction of projects outside the ghetto, significant desegregation is unlikely to occur by building new projects. More promise has been shown through the use of subsidized rental vouchers that enable poor blacks to obtain units through the private market. In one evaluation of the remedy arising from the *Gautreaux* decision, blacks who moved into integrated settings through the use of rental vouchers experienced greater success in education and employment than did a comparable group who remained behind in the ghetto; and, significantly, participants did not encounter the kind of white hostility commonly experienced by project inhabitants.[44] Funding for housing certificate programs authorized under Section 8 of the 1974 Housing and Community Development Act should therefore be expanded, and programs modeled on the Gautreaux Demonstration Project should be more widely implemented.

Finally, effective enforcement of the Fair Housing Act requires prompt judicial action and timely relief. Since 1968, fair housing enforcement has been a long, drawn-out, expensive, and emotionally draining process for plaintiffs, even if they ultimately prevail. Congress recognized this problem in 1988 when it passed amendments to create an administrative process for adjudicating fair housing cases; but acting on a motion by Senator Orrin Hatch of Utah, Congress also granted defendants the right to request a trial in federal court.[45]

Most accused discriminators elect to have their cases heard in federal court, which slows down the judicial process considerably and defeats the new administrative hearing process. Because defendants are usually realtors or developers with significant financial resources, a long trial provides them with a decided advantage over plaintiffs, whose resources are generally more modest. In order to expedite fair housing judgments and grant more timely relief to victims of discrimination, Congress should amend the Fair Housing Act to require that initial trials be held before an administrative law judge and to provide access to federal courts only upon appeal.

Even if these five policy initiatives are successful in lowering racial barriers in urban housing markets, however, they are not likely to end racial segregation unless black demand is simultaneously allowed to spread more evenly around metropolitan housing markets. To a great extent, blacks are reluctant to enter white neighborhoods because they fear becoming victims of racial hate crimes.[46] These fears can only be allayed by vigorous and swift punishment of those who commit crimes against minority families seeking to integrate white neighborhoods.

Given the overriding importance of residential mobility to individual well-being, and in view of the great social and economic harm done to the nation by segregation, hate crimes directed against black in-migrants must be considered more severe than ordinary acts of vandalism or assault. Rather than being left to local authorities, they should be prosecuted at the federal level as violations of the victim's civil rights. Stiff financial penalties and jail terms should be imposed, not in recognition of the severity of the vandalism or violence itself, but in acknowledgment of the serious damage that segregation does to the nation's well-being.

Black housing demand is also geographically skewed by racial segregation within the real estate industry itself. Most real estate brokers depend on the cooperation of other agents for sales and referrals, a fact that is formalized through multiple listing services (MLS). These services provide extensive listings of properties for sale or rent throughout a metropolitan area, and when MLS transactions are completed, the commission is divided between the participating agents. But these listings typically cover only white suburbs and select city neighborhoods, and are available only to agents serving those areas; brokers serving black communities generally do not have access to these services. Moreover, access is typically controlled by local real estate boards, and in some instances suburban brokers who sell to blacks have been denied membership on the board and hence prevented from using multiple listing services.[47]

Under prevailing marketing practices in the real estate industry, therefore, homeseekers living in segregated black neighborhoods do not have full access to information about wider housing opportunities, and black housing searches are consequently much less efficient than those of whites. Frequently blacks are forced to rely on drives through neighborhoods in search of "For Sale" signs.[48] If black demand is ever to be expressed naturally and widely, realtors serving black clients must be given complete access to multiple listing services. Congress should adopt legislation removing monopoly control of multiple listing services from local realty boards; access to the service should be open to all agents willing to pay a standard membership fee, irrespective of their race or that of their clients.

HUD should also establish new programs, and expand existing programs, to train realtors in fair housing marketing procedures. Agents catering primarily to white clients should be instructed about advertising and marketing methods to ensure that blacks in segregated communities gain access to information about housing opportunities outside the ghetto; agents serving the black share of the market should be trained to market homes throughout the metropolitan area and should be instructed especially in how to use multiple listing services. HUD officials and local fair housing groups should carefully monitor whether realtors serving blacks are given access to the MLS.

Such programs should be implemented in concert with a strengthening of the Voluntary Affirmative Marketing Agreement.[49] In strengthening the terms of the agreement, the list of realtors that signed it should once again be made public, the use of testers should be encouraged, and the responsibilities of realtors to enforce the Fair Housing Act should be spelled out explicitly.

Although it is important for HUD to work with the National Association of Realtors and local real estate boards, efforts should also be made to monitor realtor compliance with Title VIII. Ultimately the Assistant Secretary for Fair Housing and Equal Opportunity at HUD must take a more active role in overseeing real estate advertising and marketing practices, two areas that have received insufficient federal attention in the past. Realtors in selected metropolitan areas should be sampled and their advertising and marketing practices regularly examined for conformity with federal fair housing regulations. HUD should play a larger role in ensuring that black homeseekers are not being systematically and deliberately overlooked by prevailing marketing practices.

The Case for National Action

For the most part, the policies we have recommended do not require major changes in legislation. What they require is political will. Given the will to end segregation, the necessary funds and legislative measures will follow. But political will is precisely what has been lacking over the past several decades, and resistance to desegregation continues to be strong. For each proposal that is advanced to move the fair housing agenda forward, there are other efforts to set it back.

At the time the 1988 Fair Housing Amendments were being debated, for example, Senator Orrin Hatch of Utah introduced a bill endorsed by the National Association of Realtors to limit the filing of fair housing suits to parties actually intending to rent or buy real estate (as opposed to testers, fair housing staff members, or others banned by discriminatory practices), thereby attempting to undo twenty years of court decisions that had broadened the question of standing and made fair housing enforcement easier.[50] The Hatch bill also would have banned the hearing of fair housing cases before administrative law judges and relied instead on secret conciliation as the principal means of fair housing enforcement.[51]

After the Hatch bill was discarded in favor of legislation sponsored by Senators Kennedy and Specter, the Reagan Administration offered regulations implementing the amendments that could have banned a variety of affirmative marketing strategies used by fair housing organizaitions.[52] In addition, the National Association of Realtors attempted to limit funding for the Fair Housing Initiatives Program, which was intended to support local antidiscrimination efforts;[53] and in 1991, a House banking subcommittee quietly added a provision to pending legislation that would have exempted more than 85% of U.S. banks from the 1977 Community Reinvestment Act, which required financial institutions to meet the credit needs of low-income minority areas.[54] Later that year the Bush Administration proposed abolishing the U.S. Commission on Civil Rights,[55] which for years had kept pressure on HUD to improve fair housing enforcement.[56]

Although race has become embroiled in partisan politics during the 1980s and 1990s, residential desegregation is not intrinsically a cause of either the right or the left; it is neither liberal nor conservative, democrat, nor republican. Rather it is a bipartisan agenda in the national interest. The ghetto must be dismantled because only by ending segregation will we eliminate the manifold social and economic problems that follow from its persistence.

For conservatives, the cause of desegregation turns on the issue of market access. We have marshaled extensive evidence to show that one particular group—black Americans—is systematically denied full access to a crucial market. Housing markets are central to individual social and economic well-being because they distribute much more than shelter; they also distribute a variety of resources that shape and largely determine one's life chances. Along with housing, residential markets also allocate schooling, peer groups, safety, jobs, insurance costs, public services, home equity, and, ultimately, wealth. By tolerating the persistent and systematic disenfranchisement of blacks from housing markets, we send a clear signal to one group that hard work, individual enterprise, sacrifice, and aspirations don't matter; what determines one's life chances is the color of one's skin.

For liberals, the issue is one of unfinished business, for residential segregation is the most important item remaining on the nation's civil rights agenda. In many areas of civil life, desegregation has occurred; in the south, Jim Crow is dead, and throughout the country blacks are accepted in unions, sports, entertainment, journalism, politics, government, administration, and academia. Many barriers have fallen, but still the residential color line remains and from residential segregation follows a host of deadly social ills that continue to undercut and overwhelm the progress achieved in other areas.

Residential desegregation should be considered an effort of national unity; any other course of action is politically indefensible. For conservatives, turning away from the task means denying the importance of markets and individual enterprise; for liberals it means sweeping the last piece of unfinished civil rights business under the rug. Ultimately, however, residential desegregation requires a moral commitment and a bipartisan leadership that have been lacking among politicians for the past two decades. Without a willingness to lead and take risks on the part of elected officials, and without a will to change on the part of the American people, none of the legal changes and policy solutions we propose will succeed.

For America, the failure to end segregation will perpetuate a bitter dilemma that has long divided the nation. If segregation is permitted to continue, poverty will inevitably deepen and become more persistent within a large share of the black community, crime and drugs will become more firmly rooted, and social institutions will fragment further under the weight of deteriorating conditions. As racial inequality sharpens, white fears will grow, racial prejudices will be reinforced, and hostility toward blacks will increase, making the problems of racial justice and equal opportunity even more insoluble. Until we face up to the difficult task of dismantling the ghetto, the disastrous consequences of residential segregation will radiate outward to poison American society. Until we decide to end the long reign of American apartheid, we cannot hope to move forward as a people and a nation.

Endnotes

[1]Epigraph from "Remarks of the President at Howard University," in Lee Rainwater and William L. Yancey, *The Moynihan Report and the Politics of Controversy* (Cambridge: MIT Press, 1967), pp. 127–28.

[2]See Douglas G. Glasgow, T*he Black Underclass: Poverty, Unemployment, and Entrapment of Ghetto Youth* (San Francisco: Jossey-Bass, 1980); Alphonso Pinkney, *The*

Myth of Black Progress (Cambridge: Cambridge University Press, 1984); Charles V. Willie, "The Inclining Significance of Race," *Society* 15 (1978): 10, 12–15.

[3]See Theodore Hershberg, Alan N. Burstein, Eugene P. Ericksen, Stephanie W. Greenberg, and William L. Yancey, "A Tale of Three Cities: Blacks, Immigrants, and Opportunity in Philadelphia, 1850–1880, 1930, 1970," in Theodore Hershberg, ed., *Philadelphia: Work, Space, Family and Group Experience in the 19th Century* (New York: Oxford University Press, 1981), pp. 461–91; John D. Kasarda, "Caught in the Web of Change," *Society* 21 (1983): 41–47; John D. Kasarda, "Urban Change and Minority Opportunities," in Paul E. Peterson, ed., *The New Urban Reality* (Washington, D.C.: Brookings Institution, 1985), pp. 33–68; John D. Kasarda, "Jobs, Migration, and Emerging Urban Mismatches," in Michael G. H. McGeary and Lawrence E. Lynn, Jr. , eds., *Urban Change and Poverty* (Washington, D.C.: National Academy Press, 1988), pp. 148–98; John F. Kain, "Housing Segregation, Negro Employment, and Metropolitan Decentralization," *Quarterly Journal of Economics* 82 (1968): 175–97; William Julius Wilson, *The Declining Significance of Race: Blacks and Changing American Institutions* (Chicago, University of Chicago Press, 1978); William Julius Wilson, *The Truly Disadvantaged: The Inner City, the Underclass, and Urban Policy* (Chicago: University of Chicago, 1987).

[4]Bart Landry, *The New Black Middle Class* (Berkeley: University of California Press, 1987).

[5]Douglas S. Massey and Mitchell L. Eggers, "The Ecology of Inequality: Minorities and the Concentration of Poverty, 1970–1980," *American Journal of Sociology* 95 (1990): 1153–88.

[6]See Lawrence M. Mead, *Beyond Entitlement: The Social Obligations of Citizenship* (New York: Free Press, 1986); Charles Murray, *Losing Ground: American Social Policy, 1950–1980* (New York: Basic Books, 1984).

[7]William Ryan, *Blaming the Victim* (New York: Random House, 1971); Willie, "The Inclining Significance of Race."

[8]George R. Metcalf, *Fair Housing Comes of Age* (New York: Greenwood Press, 1986), pp. 198–221.

[9]Ibid., pp. 1–16, 86–137.

[10]Ibid., p. 3

[11]Brian J. L. Berry, *The Open Housing Question: Race and Housing in Chicago, 1966–1976* (Cambridge, MA: Ballinger, 1979); Robert McClory, "Segregation City," *Chicago Reader* 20 (1991): 1–29.

[12]McClory, "Segregation City."

[13]Harold Baron, *What is Gautreaux?* (Chicago: Business and Professional People for the Public Interest, 1990); McClory, "Segregation City"; Michael J. Verarelli, "Where Should HUD Locate Assisted Housing? The Evolution of Fair Housing Policy," in John M. Goering, ed., *Housing Desegregation and Federal Policy* (Chapel Hill: University of North Carolina Press, 1986), pp. 214–34; Irving Welfeld, "The Courts and Desegregated Housing: The Meaning (If Any) of the Gautreaux Case," *Public Interest* 45 (1976): 123–35.

[14]Metcalf, *Fair Housing Comes of Age*, pp. 65–72.

[15]Ibid., pp. 96–101.

[16]McClory, "Segregation City."

[17]Ibid.

[18]See Carole Goodwin, T*he Oak Park Strategy: Community Control of Racial Change* (Chicago: University of Chicago Press, 1979); Juliet Saltman, *A Fragile Movement: The*

Struggle for Neighborhood Stabilization (New York: Greenwood Press, 1990); Juliet Saltman, "Maintaining Racially Diverse Neighborhoods," *Urban Affairs Quarterly* 26 (1991): 416–41; Juliet Saltman, "Neighborhood Stabililzation: A Fragile Movement," *Sociological Quarterly* 31 (1990): 531–49.

[19]Metcalf, Fair Housing Comes of Age, pp. 205–221.

[20]Carole Goodwin, *The Oak Park Strategy*; Robert W. Lake and Jessica Winslow, "Integration Management: Municipal Constrains on Residential Mobility," *Urban Geography* 2 (1981): 311–26; Saltman, *A Fragile Movement*.

[21]Ibid.

[22]Lake and Winslow, "Integration Management," p. 323.

[23]Metcalf, *Fair Housing Comes of Age*, pp. 208–209.

[24]John F. Bauman, *Public Housing, Race, and Renewal: Urban Planning in Philadelphia, 1920–1974* (Philadelphia: Temple University Press, 1987); Adam Bickford and Douglas S. Massey, "Segregation in the Second Ghetto: Racial and Ethnic Segregation in U.S. Public Housing, 1977," *Social Forces* 69 (1991): 1011–36; Ira Goldstein and William L. Yancey, "Public Housing Projects, Blacks, and Public Policy: The Historical Ecology of Public Housing in Philadelphia," in John M. Goering, ed., *Housing Desegregation and Federal Policy* (Chapel Hill: University of North Carolina Press, 1986), pp. 262–89; Arnold R. Hirsch, *Making the Second Ghetto: Race and Housing in Chicago, 1940–1960* (Cambridge: Cambridge University Press, 1983).

[25]Bauman, *Making the Second Ghetto*, p. 257.

[26]R. Allen Hays, *The Federal Government and Urban Housing: Ideology and Change in Public Policy* (Albany: State University of New York Press, 1985), pp. 137–72.

[27]Michael N. Danielson, *The Politics of Exclusion* (New York: Columbia University Press, 1976), pp. 50–106; Metcalf, *Fair Housing Comes of Age*, pp. 149–62.

[28]Joan Magagna and Brian Hefferman, "City of Yonkers: A Bitterly Fought Civil Rights Case," *Trends in Housing* 27 (1988): 1, 9.

[29]Ibid.

[30]Ibid.

[31]George C. Calster and Heather Keeney, "Subsidized Housing and Racial Change in Yonkers, NY: Are the Fears Justified?" Working Paper, Urban Studies Program, College of Wooster, Wooster, Ohio, 1989.

[32]Metcalf, *Fair Housing Comes of Age*, p. 116–24.

[33]McClory, "Segregation City."

[34]Franklin James, Betty McCummings, and Eileen Tynan, *Minorities in the Sunbelt* (New Brunswick, NJ: Rutgers Center for Urban Policy Research, 1984), pp. 125–55.

[35]John S. Adams, *Housing America in the 1980s* (New York: Russell Sage, 1987).

[36]Bickford and Massey, "Segregation in the Second Ghetto."

[37]See Metcalf, *Fair Housing Comes of Age*, pp. 93–94; Berry, *The Open Housing Question*, p. 72.

[38]U.S. Department of Housing and Urban Development, Office of the Assistant Secretary for Fair Housing and Equal Opportunity, "Fair Housing Initiatives Program: Final Rule," *Federal Register*, vol. 54, no. 27 (1989): 6492–6502, February 10.

[39]U.S. Department of Housing and Urban Development, *The State of Fair Housing* (Washington, D.C.: U.S. Government Printing Office, 1989), pp. 1–3.

[40]Bill Dedman, "Blacks Denied S&L Loans Twice as Often as Whites," *Atlanta Journal–Constitution*, 1988, January 22, p. 1.

[41]Beth J. Lief and Susan Goering, "The Implementeation of the Federal Mandate for Fair Housing," in Gary A. Tobin, ed., *Divided Neighborhoods: Changing Patterns of Racial Segregation* (Newbury Park, CA: Sage Publications, 1987), pp. 227–67.

[42]Metcalf, *Fair Housing Comes of Age*, pp. 103–104.

[43]Lief and Goering, "The Implementation of the Federal Mandate for Fair Housing."

[44]James E. Rosenbaum, Marilynn J. Kulieke, and Leonard S. Rubinowitz, "White Suburban Schools' Responses to Low-Income Black Children: Sources of Success and Problems," *Urban Review* 20 (1988): 28–41; James E. Rosenbaum and Susan J. Popkin, "Employment and Earnings of Low-Income Blacks Who Move to Middle Class Suburbs," in Christopher Jencks and Paul E. Peterson, eds., *The Urban Underclass* (Washington, D.C.: Brookings Institution, 1991), pp. 342–56; James E. Rosenbaum and Susan J. Popkin, "Economic and Social Impacts of Housing Integration," Center for Urban Affiars and Policy Research, Northwestern University, 1990.

[45]Robert G. Schwemm, *Housing Discrimination: Law and Litigation* (New York: Clark Boardman, 1990), pp. 5.6–5.11.

[46]Reynolds Farley, Suzanne Bianchi, and Diane Colasanto, "Barriers to the Racial Integration of Neighborhoods: The Detroit Case," *Annals of the American Academy of Political and Social Science* 441 (1979): 97–113.

[47]John Yinger, "The Racial Dimension of Urban Housing Markets in the 1980s," in Gary A. Tobin, ed., *Divided Neighborhoods: Changing Patterns of Racial Segregation* (Newbury Park, CA: Sage Publications, 1987), pp. 43–67.

[48]Robert W. Lake, "The Fair Housing Act in a Discriminatory Market: The Persisting Dilemma," *Journal of the American Planning Association* 47 (1981): 48–58.

[49]Metcalf, *Fair Housing Comes of Age*, pp. 15–26.

[50]Testimony of Mr. Robert Butters, Association Counsel, National Association of Realtors, Hearings Before the Subcommittee on the Constitution of the Committee on the Judiciary, United States Senate, One Hundredth Congress, First Session, on S. 558. (Washington, D.C.: U.S. Government Printing Office, 1988), pp. 108–131.

[51]Ibid.

[52]George C. Galster, "HUD Could Forbid Affirmative Marketing Strategies," *Trends in Housing* 27 (1988): 3.

[53]U.S. Department of Housing and Urban Development, "Fair Housing Initiatives Program."

[54]The ploy was foiled by Senator Alan Dixon of Illinois, the Chair of the Senate banking subcommittee, who vowed to block any attempt to weaken the law's fair housing provisions; see "Dixon Hits Move to Ease Community Lending Rule," *Chicago Tribune*, May 31, 1991, Sec. 3, p. 1.

[55]"Headliners: Agency in Decline," *New York Times*, Sunday, October 13, 1991, Sec. 3, p. 9.

[56]See U.S. Commission on Civil Rights, *A Report of the Racial and Ethnic Impact of the Section 235 Program* (Washington, D.C.: U.S. Government Printing Office, 1971); U.S. Commission on Civil Rights, *Equal Opportunity in Housing* (Washington, D.C.: U.S. Government Printing Office, 1974); U. S. Commission on Civil Rights, *The Federal Fair Housing Enforcement Effort* (Washington D.C.: U.S. Government Printing Office, 1979).

Section IV:
Institutional Implications:
Race, Class, Education

In the following section we take a look at studies that implicate institutions, government involvement, and their links to conditions relative to race, class, poverty, and education—conditions that indicate systems of stratification in most Western societies. Sociologists—relying on the insights of Weber—define social stratification as the hierarchical ranking of social class groups according to wealth, power, and prestige.[1] Thus, social stratification produces arrangements in society that help shape who gets what and why.[2] This is an important point to consider, as it has significant implications for shaping the life chances of individuals and families—chances that often involve access to resources, or lack thereof. In this section we include studies that examine conditions often associated with class, race, poverty and socio-economic status in cities, which we argue raise questions about access to resources, as well as the resolve of public institutions to provide equal access to those resources. First, we briefly review how other scholars have broadly discussed matters that influence social class stratification.

Today, it is not uncommon for researchers to challenge traditional ideas of class stratification, ideas that are customarily related to worker vs. management in labor relations; while others argue that a new paradigm of class is needed that is able to take into account the stability of socio-economic life. Sociologist Erik Olin Wright defends a traditional Marxian notion of stratification on the basis of class, arguing that those in the capitalist classes continue to thrive through their on-going ability to exploit the masses of working class families and individuals.[3] Conversely, Paul Kingston challenges the notion of the existence of distinctive classes of groups—groups believed to have formed from individuals in similar socio-economic situations. He argues in *The Classless Society* that while people may be similarly situated economically, their diverse life-styles and experiences undermine arguments about group solidarity by class. Instead, Kingston focuses on social hierarchies like income, occupational prestige, and cultural valuation, which produce what he calls "multi-rung ladders of continuous gradation." This argument appears to challenge the notion of coordinated efforts by the capitalist classes designed to exploit workers.[4] Still, other researchers suggest that the debate about class and social stratification should be modified to take into account more seriously *who has access to what, in the form of capital*, and the stability of their access to elements of financial, social, cultural, and credentialed capital.[5]

If we consider credentialed capital alone, which pertains to access to an education from elite colleges and universities, we are invariably led to think about who has access and to what and why, relative to class and race. Jonothan Kozol, in *Savage Inequalities,* links access to education to both racial disparities and impoverishment in American cities.[6] He employs a government culpability narrative regarding the reproduction of class and racial disparity in the U.S. by explaining how the implementation of policies favor more affluent residents, while further exacerbating—in cities—what some have referred to as the nihilism of black America.[7] Moreover, he challenges broad notions of meritocracy in the American educational system. Quoting educational scholar John Coons, Kozol writes "there is no graver threat to the capitalist system than the present cyclical replacement of the fittest of one generation by their artificially advantaged offspring".[8]

The articles included in this section trace the connections between social stratification and access to social resources such as education. They also remind us about the challenge of disentangling problems relative to race and class, as such efforts are often complicated by the actions of social institutions and confounded by a sometimes inexplicable role of governance. In the first article of the section, Mary Patillo, from her recent book *Black on the Block*, examines the dynamics of race, class, and education in North Kenwood-Oakland (NKO), a gentrified community in Chicago. In earlier chapters in her book, Patillo characterizes the status of middle-class blacks in the neighborhood as being in the position of a "middleman"—in other words, acting like a broker whose residential concerns fall between those of less well-off residents in the community and the power structures in Chicago. In the chapter from her book that we include in this volume, Patillo discusses how private dimensions of educational reform in NKO seem to benefit incoming middle-class blacks (in their middleman roles), but also undermine open access to adequate public schooling for the less well-off *original* residents of NKO.

In the second article of the section, Meghan Ashlin Rich also takes a look at the dynamics of race and class. Her study examines a neighborhood in Baltimore that has special-tax district status within the city, allowing it to finance various municipal services through an augmentation of existing funding mechanisms. However, Rich argues that while the community benefits from the arrangement, it also helps to support a neoliberal assault on the role of government, while undermining ideas regarding the role of governance to provide sufficient services for all city residents. Also, Rich discusses how the special-tax district complicates efforts to improve race and class integration of the community.

In the third piece, Jay Arena discusses the neoliberalizaton of Post-Katrina New Orleans. He argues that collusion between private and public actors erodes the idea of a people's "right to the city." This, Arena argues, disproportionately impacts African-Americans and the poor as they attempt to reclaim their original residency in New Orleans following the Hurricane Katrina evacuations in August of 2005. Next is a discussion by William Julius Wilson from his recent book, *More than Race*. Wilson overviews cultural arguments related to the causes of poverty, and consistent with the work of Elijah Anderson in *Code of the Streets*, he argues that structural factors continue to play a role in what is often believed to be outgrowths of culture in urban areas.[9] Overall, while helping to advance a government culpability narrative, Wilson discusses programs and institutions that help clarify the cultural-structural implications and causes of urban poverty.

The final piece in the section deals with spatial arrangements in New York City, as business elites work to re-assert upper class power in light of the city's fiscal crises that emanate from the mid-1970s. Hence, Kim Moody, in *From Welfare State to Real Estate*, argues that in response to fiscal crises of the mid-1970s and 1980s, business elites and government actors pushed for a new upper class-dominated agenda for New York City. The new agenda involved dismantling, undermining, and ignoring public dimensions of urban life to boost private real estate markets in the city—an agenda which, arguably, continues to influence the city today.

Endnotes

[1]John J. Macionis and Vincent N. Parrillo. *Cities and Urban Life* (Boston: Prentice Hall, 2007), 267.

[2]Harold R. Kerbo. *Social Stratification and Inequality* (New York: McGraw-Hill, 1996), 11.

[3]Erik Olin Wright. *Class Counts* (student ed.) (Cambridge: Cambridge University Press, 1977).

[4]Paul W. Kingston. *The Classless Society* (Stanford, CA: Stanford University Press, 2000).

[5]Robert Perrucci and Earl Wysong. *The New Class Society* (Lanham, MD: Rowman and Littlefield, 2003).

[6]Jonathan Kozol. *Savage Inequalities: Children in America's Schools* (New York: Harper Collins, 1991), p. 206.

[7]Cornell West. *Race Matters* (Boston: Beacon Press, 1993).

[8]Jonathan Kozol, p. 206.

[9]Elijah Anderson. *Code of the Streets: Decency, Violence, and the Moral Life of the Inner City* (New York: W.W. Norton, 2000).

The Middleman in the City*

Mary Patillo

When the North Kenwood-Oakland Conservation Plan was approved in 1992, there were three operating public elementary schools and one public high school in the neighborhood, all with abysmal records. When Mayor Richard M. Daley took control of the schools in 1995, the four-year graduation rate at the high school was only 58 percent. Twenty-three percent of the students there were chronically truant. In 1995, at Price Elementary School in North Kenwood fewer than 10 percent of the students were performing at or above national norms in reading and math. The students at Robinson, the elementary school in Oakland, performed only marginally better. The third elementary school was closed for low enrollment. It is no secret that high on the list of the things that people think about when choosing a neighborhood is schools. The schools in North Kenwood-Oakland in the early days of its revitalization were hardly attractive choices. What could be done?

The public discourse of school reform always emphasizes improving educational options for all families, including low-income residents. The available reform tools, however—schools with selective enrollment criteria, charter schools, small schools—make school reform more exclusive than its rhetoric suggests. Though none of these strategies "privatizes" public education, as critics often assert, each of the options available to North Kenwood-Oakland activists puts limits on the ability of neighborhood families to take advantage of the new schools. This is the power structure under which black brokers must operate. These were the "master's tools" with which the newcomer brokers tried to dismantle years of educational violence against North Kenwood-Oakland's children.[1]

The framework I employ here extends the middleman concept and adds to it a discussion of the contemporary emphasis in urban governance on "choice" and the personal initiative of residents who must choose from the array of resources available from the state. The model has changed from one in which cities "deliver" public services like education, health care, and protection from crime, to one in which residents "shop for" these goods in a service landscape that includes more nongovernmental, private subcontractors. An informant in Eric Klinenberg's analysis of the 1995 heat wave in Chicago, in which over seven hundred people died, said that the tragedy was an example of "murder by public policy." The public policies that this informant indicted, like those indicted in the aftermath of

---

*Mary Patillo, *Black on the Block: The Politics of Race and Class in the City* (Chicago: University of Chicago Press, 2007). Reprinted with permission.

Hurricane Katrina ten years later, were characteristic of an era of "reinvented government, administered with techniques and system values honed in the private sector and recently adapted to public institutions." Klinenberg refers to this new approach to urban service provision as the "entrepreneurial state," but in its general (and more global) guise it is referred to as "neoliberalism," or the promotion of unfettered free markets. "The embrace of public-private partnerships, deregulation, fiscal austerity, cross-subsidies, and market solutions have been characterized as a form of urban neoliberalism," writes geographer Nicholas Blomley. Political scientists Neil Brenner and Nik Theodore make the case that neoliberal ideologies can only be understood by investigating their local manifestations, where reliance on the market interacts with particular national, state, or municipal policy regimes, personalities, and histories.

Going back to the local, to what Brenner and Theodore call "actually existing neo-liberalism," is what Klinenberg did to explain the extreme death toll of the heat wave in Chicago, and what other scholars have done in analyzing urban labor markets, governance structures, gentrification, and school reform. For example, in line with the thrust of this chapter, Arlene Dávila's study of the gentrification of Spanish Harlem tracks the debates over the opening of a charter school that would be managed by a private, for-profit corpora-tion, Edison Schools, Inc. The proposal, despite its failure, was illustrative of the neoliberal belief that the private sector can offer a product that is superior to what is available in the public sector because it is less encumbered by legislative regulations, union contracts, and requirements for local participation.[2]

The critique of this new direction in urban governance and service provision focuses on the inequalities that often accompany such an approach. While regulations may constrain the flexibility that actors desire in order to experiment with best practices, they also exist to forestall dangerous experimentation or to make sure that the least powerful constituents are not left behind. Labor agreements may keep some workers on the job whose performance is less than stellar, but they also ensure decent pay and benefits, reasonable work hours and environments, and protection for workers from capricious hiring and firing decisions. And lay stakeholders may be unruly or simply a pain, but they represent an indispensable knowledge base in any effort aimed at improving their lives.

The particular inequality-producing properties of neoliberalism on which I focus in this chapter are those based on various levels of exclusion, often of people who are most in need of inclusion. As Klinenberg writes, the neoliberal managerial strategy "disproportion-ately empowers residents who are already endowed with the forms of social and cultural capital necessary to navigate through bureaucratic systems while in effect... punishing people who are least likely to have the social skills and resources necessary to obtain goods and services that they are most likely to need." In North Kenwood-Oakland, it is the middle and upper-income newcomers who are best positioned to take advantage of new schools envisioned under the rubric of the entrepreneurial state. This explains why they utilize their brokerage positions to foster such innovations in the neighborhood, energized by the overly optimistic expectation that their less-advantaged neighbors will be similarly equipped to get with the new program. The intentions are benign, and in many respects the routes taken by middle-class school brokers in North Kenwood-Oakland are the only ones possible as the city, state, and federal governments imagine a public school system in which involving private-sector partners improves the choices that parents have. Still, the limitations of such an approach exacerbate and reproduce already existing class inequalities in access to quality educations.

Education professor Pauline Lipman, who studies the reform of Chicago's schools, similarly acknowledges the laudable goals of all those involved, despite gravely unequal results:

> Current CPS policies represent a convergence of interests of financial elites and the city's political regime. But they are supported and accomplished by well-meaning educators at all levels of the school system, as well as many Chicagoans, operating out of a shared common sense that the policies will improve schools. This common sense is constructed out of real hopes and frustrations. It is bolstered by CPS's rhetoric of equity and resoluteness and the pragmatic logic of a quick fix through the blunt force of sanctions and punishment. Unequal educational experiences are rendered less visible by establishing standards and tests that promise equal treatment and rigor. Although new advanced academic programs involve a very small percentage of students, their well-advertised initiation serves to legitimate the current policy regime even as it helps to develop the city as a concentrated expression of new global inequalities.[3]

There is no question that something had to be done to remedy the disgraceful state of the schools in North Kenwood-Oakland. There is also no question that the activists who put in the hard work to make a difference wanted to improve the educational options available to parents. But the philosophies of reform rested on the logic of options rather than uniform excellence, on choice rather than universal provision, and on parents' ability to shop rather than the public sector's responsibility to deliver.

New Schools for All...Who Can Get In

The efforts in North Kenwood-Oakland were but one part of widespread changes in public school administration in the city of Chicago overall, sparked by the 1995 mayoral "takeover" of the public schools. With bipartisan support in the state legislature, Mayor Richard M. Daley won the right to independently manage the Chicago Public Schools (CPS), to decrease the size of the Chicago Board of Education, and to name both its members and the Chief Executive Officer of Schools. The change in the top school administrator's title, from superintendent to CEO, is a powerful symbolic indication of the new market model in which educational performance and accountability are grounded.

The educational initiatives in NKO happened in tandem with, and in many ways were reflections of, reforms at the city and state level, and were not completely restricted to the arena of schools. The consolidation of power under Mayor Daley meant that the same city leadership that was transforming public housing and enabling the resurgence of home buying and building in NKO was also addressing the poorly performing schools. All three endeavors were in the service of making Chicago an attractive place to live and work, and especially attractive to the middle class. In the cases of public housing and school reform the strategies were basically the same: clear the high-rises of their residents and the poorly performing schools of their students and then start from scratch. The infusion of middle-income families and children into the replacement buildings and schools would then encourage, pull up, support, or "overshadow" those poor neighbors and classmates who were able to return.

Like the mayor's administration, the alderman and the Conservation Community Council [CCC] in North Kenwood-Oakland knew that good schools were crucial for attracting higher-income home buyers. As a result, efforts coalesced around the transformation of two existing schools: the closing of Shakespeare Elementary School, to be reopened as two separate schools—Ariel Community Academy and the North Kenwood/Oakland Charter School—and the closure of Martin Luther King Jr. High School, to be reopened as Martin Luther King Jr. College Prep High School. The three resulting schools are essentially brand new, with completely new student bodies and rehabilitated buildings. Two other elementary schools in the neighborhood—Price and Robinson—have been the target of small-scale improvement efforts but remain neighborhood schools with general admissions, and high school students who cannot gain admission to King College Prep are sent to a nearby (low-performing) high school that has general admissions. After giving the histories of each of these efforts, I discuss the importance of black middle-class brokers to their implementation and examine how each reform strategy featured some level of exclusion. The stories illustrate the policy constraints within which brokers and their allies must operate, and how those constraints can create a gulf between intent and result, in this case in the form of limits on the scope of beneficiaries.

Ariel Community Academy is named after the first black-owned money-management firm in the country, Ariel Capital Management. Ariel's headquarters are in Chicago, and its founder and board chairman, John Rogers Jr., comes from a prestigious black Chicago family. In 1991, the Ariel Foundation established the I Have a Dream Program, which adopted the sixth-grade class at Shakespeare Elementary School in North Kenwood and committed to seeing its students through college, promising college scholarships as an incentive.[4] Two years after the program's inception, in the students' eighth-grade year, the Chicago Public Schools closed Shakespeare because of low enrollment. I Have a Dream staffers scrambled to find school placements for the nearly forty eighth graders that would further support their college-bound aspirations. Given the poor quality of the city's public schools, they ended up placing nearly all of their students in Catholic schools. "We were just looking for anything above what I considered educational malpractice," remembered Sarah Duncan, the program's director. "Most of the Catholic schools represented at least one step above that." While they got good "bulk" deals on tuition at the Catholic schools, it was a frustrating expenditure of resources and a sobering recognition that there were no free, public schools of high quality available to the students in their program.

The experience stirred the idea among Ariel Foundation employees of opening a school of their own. The Dreamers, as the students were called, would not directly benefit from a new school, but the Ariel staff was just as concerned about the next generation of neighborhood youth. When the group got a generous gift from an anonymous donor, staff from the Ariel Foundation and other volunteers began hammering out concrete plans for opening a new school. Things moved quickly, and reforms at the city level created opportunities for outside organizations to run public schools under a program called the small schools initiative. By 1995 they were submitting an application to CPS for a small school in North

Kenwood, and they were open for business by the 1996–1997 school year. At that time, the "small schools" movement was just beginning and the definition of the concept was still evolving. In the early years, there were no caps on class size or total enrollment. Also, small schools were not defined by local attendance boundaries and were required to accept students citywide, but now schools like Ariel can use "neighborhood preferences" in admissions.[5]

...

The I Have a Dream program also tapped the expertise and commitment of several black professionals who worked for the Ariel Foundation or served as mentors for the program's students. The Duncan siblings* were the ironic "local" faces (although neither lived in NKO), but there was also a group of dedicated black professional women who were equally instrumental in putting together the proposal for the new school. All of these players represent crisscrossing associations formed at the University of Chicago Lab School and Princeton and Harvard Universities, on basketball courts, in childhood neighborhoods, and through marriages and family relations, producing an interracial cadre of energetic, twenty-something do-gooders with the financial backing to make something happen. "As young, naive people we thought: this is ridiculous, anybody can do better than this," summed up Sarah Duncan, capturing their acute disappointment with the public school system and their bold and optimistic plan to make a difference. In the creation of Ariel Community Academy, there was not one middleman. Instead, the unofficial collaboration of black John Rogers Jr.'s philanthropy and white Sue Duncan's community involvement provided an umbrella under which the school could be born. Black professionals affiliated with the Ariel Foundation were key participants in the germination and implementation of ideas for changing the educational landscape of NKO. "It was very impressive people that were around the table," remarked Ruanda Garth, the Ariel School community liaison, about the lively planning process. This seat at the table is part of the job description of the middleman, and it explains how such people could broker new resources for the neighborhood from a public school system that was then in the midst of a takeover by the mayor's office.

The second educational initiative in NKO was the University of Chicago's North Kenwood/Oakland Charter School. The university had long been involved in after-school tutoring in and around Hyde Park through the Neighborhood Schools Program. In 1988, it got more actively involved in teaching and curricular issues through the Center for School Improvement. The center focused on teacher-training programs and on developing educational models that could reform whole schools. Yet even given the university's world-class reputation, few local schools were willing to turn over the administrative reigns to the center for its educational experiments. Like the Ariel school concept, the university charter school notion was born of frustration with what could be accomplished within the existing public school mold. And again like Ariel, changes afoot at the city and state levels offered new public education possibilities. In 1996, the state of Illinois passed the Charter Schools Law to "create a legitimate avenue for parents, teachers, and community members to take responsible risks and create new, innovative, and more flexible ways of educating children within the public school system." Later legislation authorized sixty charters across the state (in the early years an organization could open more than one school under a single char-

---

Editors' note: Sarah and Arne Duncan are Chicago-based school reform activists. Arne Duncan was named Barack Obama's Secretary of Education in 2009.

ter), with no more than thirty to be granted in Chicago. Charter schools are public schools, "open to any pupil who resides within the geographic boundaries of the area served by the local school board." They cannot charge tuition or set admissions criteria. But they are governed independently by the board of directors of the entity that runs them, as opposed to being managed and overseen by the local school board.[6]

The university turned to this legislation as an avenue to open a new school in which it could set the curriculum, hire the teachers, and put together the various reform pieces that were then scattered across the seven separate schools with which its staff worked. The university was already affiliated with a private school, the University of Chicago Lab School, but in this undertaking was explicitly interested in developing high-quality *public* education that would benefit students in the nearby low-performing schools in an inclusive manner.[7]

...

When the North Kenwood/Oakland Charter School first opened, roughly 60 percent of the student body came from outside the neighborhood. The school's directors tried hard to keep it as local as possible. They got permission not to provide bus service, so as to discourage outsiders, and they only recruited in the immediate area. Still, an "amazing underground" of information about educational options got the word out beyond the neighborhood's borders, prompting the school to have to be even more "aggressive" in marketing to local parents.[8]

Since new housing and new schools were indelibly intertwined, the new schools got some help in their marketing campaign from the builders of new homes. As if the construction sites and the smell of new lumber were not enough to signal the rebuilding of NKO, the private developers of nearly a hundred new homes and condominiums across the street from Shakespeare School, recognizing the synergy of homes and schools, posted a banner on the abandoned school building that read "Future Home of North Kenwood/Oakland Charter School." "I'll tell you what the developers did around here," reported one of the charter school's early staff members. "They put a big sign up on this building before we even moved in here. They did that. We didn't do it. They did it because that was the appeal." School revitalization and housing construction were mutually reinforcing signs of neighborhood change. One seemed impossible without the other. At the same time, people who could afford the expensive homes that were being built would never send their children to the unreformed local public schools, but they would love not to have to pay private school tuition. Banker Shannon Howard looked cautiously into the future of her child's education. "We'll see what happens once my kid gets to be school age. At this point, I kind of think he's going to private school, but it would be nice to not have to foot that bill. But it just depends. You can't really take a chance on education today." Residents like Mrs. Howard would have to be convinced of the excellence of the local public schools before they sent their children there, and the University of Chicago believed it could bring about that change of heart.

The final NKO school intervention was the conversion of King High School to King College Prep, a magnet high school for high-achieving students, officially known as a "selective enrollment school." King actually underwent two reforms. First, in 1997, King High School was "reconstituted," which in Chicago school reform parlance was the most drastic intervention possible. For King, it meant that half of its teachers were replaced and a completely new administration installed. The impetus for these actions was King's chronic poor performance. For the 1996–1997 school year, daily school attendance was at

70 percent, total student enrollment was less than half of the building's capacity, fewer than 60 percent of the students graduated in four years, and only 7 percent of students met state testing standards in reading. Post-reconstitution indicators showed very slow improvement in test scores and a steady decline in enrollment. This prompted a second intervention. In his announcement of the plans to turn King into a magnet high school, Chicago school board president Gery Chico remarked, "We're frustrated with King's failures. This is our way of getting some value out of the school."[9]

The name change and accompanying shift from a general education curriculum to a college preparatory curriculum might entice one to see this conversion as an unambiguously positive step. But King's conversion was even more drastic. Beginning in the fall of 1999, the school stopped accepting freshmen. As the 1971 modernist building gradually emptied, construction crews moved in for a complete multimillion-dollar renovation. King reopened in the fall of 2002 with two hundred freshmen, selected from a pool of more than a thousand applicants, all with above-average standardized tests scores. Unlike the two new elementary schools, the new King College Prep was unabashedly "selective."

Could local students meet King College Prep's new, higher admissions standards? When the school reopened in 2002, the first hurdle for admission was scoring at or above the national average on the Iowa Test of Basic Skills in both reading and math—a minimum of 229 in reading and 231 in math. At price Elementary School, which shared a campus with King, the average standardized test score for seventh graders was 225 in both areas: fewer than half of the Price students could even apply for King. Mean test scores at two other nearby elementary schools were similarly below the application threshold.[10] Qualifying to apply is only the first step in an admissions process that also requires a separate entrance exam, seventh-grade report cards, and attendance records. King College Prep—where each classroom was wired with a bank of new computers, and the recreational facilities included gymnastics equipment and a newly refurbished swimming pool—was essentially closed to more than half of North Kenwood-Oakland's local students. And then only one out of seven students who were qualified to apply got in. In its first freshman class, 13 percent of the students were from elementary schools in Hyde Park and Kenwood (including three students from the North Kenwood/Oakland Charter School), and 24 percent were from the Bronzeville area, the black communities to the west of North Kenwood-Oakland.[11]

The conversion of King High School was not a top-down affair. North Kenwood-Oakland had a well-placed ally in the CPS bureaucracy. Arne Duncan, who was already fully involved in education in the neighborhood through the I Have a Dream program and the Ariel Community Academy, became the project manager for magnet schools in 1998 and deputy chief of staff at Chicago Public Schools in 1999. As Alderman Preckwinkle and members of the CCC "were beginning to have real issues and concerns with regard to attracting home buyers to the area who had teenage young people, and where they would go to school" they began discussions with Duncan "with regard to creating a desirable high school for the area."[12] NKO's rebirth was synchronous with Mayor Daley's educational overhaul, which included a new magnet school for each of the city's six educational regions. Given Daley's plans, a magnet school was the most feasible means by which to achieve the end of improving King High School.

Whereas brokers in North Kenwood-Oakland saw themselves as forward-looking in considering the high school needs of newcomers, area real estate agents reported that most of their business came from young singles, childless couples, and younger families. Thus few newcomers had kids in King, and most were unaffected when it stopped being a local school. This explained the eerie silence as King died and was reborn. With no stake in its present and unanimous disapproval of its past, newcomers could more easily support a plan that would clean it out, commencing a new history for the high school as a school of choice. Alderman Preckwinkle remarked at the school's rededication ceremony that King had been "an embarrassment to me because in performance it was always near the bottom in the state and high school rankings. If we do not have quality public schools, we'll lose the working and middle-class families who are the backbone of the city."[13] While the alderman hid nothing in her explanation of why King needed so badly to be transformed, the problem facing Preckwinkle and officials citywide was not so much *losing* working- and middle-class families as *attracting* and *accommodating* them.

Overall, the changes at King High School, as well as the creation of Ariel Community Academy and the North Kenwood/Oakland Charter School, show a community wrestling with the realities that, while the existing schools were not justly serving the children in the neighborhood, the tools available for reforming them were also limited in their ability to deliver decent education in an equitable manner. Both the University of Chicago and the Ariel Foundation expressed a fervent desire to serve the low-income students who lived in North KenwoodOakland. The leadership of both schools has commented in hindsight that they did not anticipate how rapidly the neighborhood would change, and how much they would be unintentionally complicit in urging it on. When North Kenwood/Oakland Charter School came close to having half of its students not eligible for free and reduced lunches (that is, not low-income), the administration got worried. "A lot of schools would welcome what we're trying to avoid," remarked the charter school's director about its becoming attractive to middle-income parents.[14] But the designers of the university's charter school were not so excited, since their goal was to show success at a public school that looked like any other in Chicago, where 85 percent of the students are low-income. Hence, in this brief overview of the three new schools in the neighborhood, the contradictions between goals and results are already evident. In some cases, reformers were cognizant of the fact that the masters' tools—charter schools, small schools, and magnet schools—were exclusionary on some levels. Yet the imperatives of gentrification demanded some good schools *now*, even if only for a few, rather than good schools later for all.

. . .

New Schools Deliver

The enthusiasm with which each of these three schools has been greeted affirms the reality that they provide quality options where none had previously existed. Both of the elementary schools have waiting lists, and King College Prep receives at least seven applications for each student opening. At Ariel, for example, the principal explained that the admissions process, though ostensibly open regardless of students' abilities or where they live, has become competitive. It starts with a preference for siblings and family members of current students. "Most of the families, when they have younger children, they come here. If they have a cousin, a brother, a sister that moves in the neighborhood and has children, they come here." By the time family members are taken care of, there isn't much room left for unrelated community children, and even less for children from outside the neighborhood.

Because they must stick to enrollment limits, part of their definition as a "small school," they routinely turn interested students away.

Such demand is not an indication of protest and withdrawal, but rather of approval and participation. This story is not unlike black middlemen's stimulation of mortgage capital: North Kenwood-Oakland gained resources that it did not have before, this time in the form of new schools. As public schools, they do not discriminate by income and they are, in principle, open to any family that is interested. The new schools were the result of the social and political clout that newcomers represented in North Kenwood-Oakland, just as the mixed-income model predicts. Even when new residents were not visibly organized, their presence, and the desire to maintain the flow of new gentrifiers, motivated elected officials and members of the Conservation Community Council to push for what the neighborhood would surely need—good schools. With history as proof, the working-class and poor residents of NKO could not have done this on their own. It took the confluence of available policies, political greasing, and connected—and here is the critique of the mixed-income paradigm—respected people to get what every neighborhood and all citizens should receive, access to quality schools. The results are in the data.

Figure 1 shows data from the 2004–2005 academic year for the two new elementary schools (Ariel Community Academy and North Kenwood/Oakland Charter School), the two previously existing elementary schools in the neighborhood (Price and Robinson), and Fuller Elementary School, which is not in NKO proper but is the local school for students at the northern end of the neighborhood. All of the schools are over 90 percent African American. On the issue of socioeconomic composition, the two new schools are predominantly low-income: 81 percent of the students at Ariel come from low-income families, as

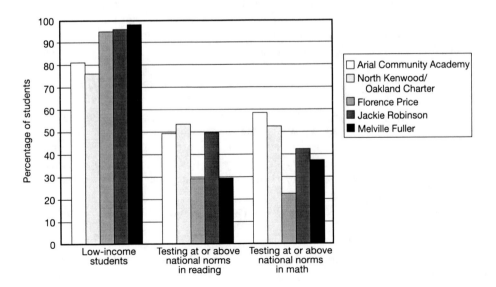

Figure 1.   Performance of North Kenwood-Oakland area elementary schools, 2004–2005. Chicago Public Schools, "School Test Score and Demographic Reports," http://research.cps.k12.il.us/ (accessed December 1, 2005); Illinois State Board of Education, " eReport Card Public Site," http://webprod1.isbe.net/ereportcard/publicsite/getSearchCrieteria.aspx (accessed December 1, 2005).

do 76 percent of the students at North Kenwood/Oakland Charter School.[15] Given these figures, these schools have been able to follow their original missions of educating disadvantaged students. However, these proportions are lower than the proportions of low-income students in the regular public schools in the neighborhood, which range from 95 percent to 98 percent, and lower than the citywide figure: overall, 85 percent of Chicago students come from low-income families. That is, Ariel and the NKO Charter School are more utilized by the neighborhood's (or the city's) nonpoor parents than are the regular schools, evidence of some measure of selection into these schools. As the principal at Ariel described it, "Initially, we started and they were about 96 percent [low-income] and it's dropping as the community gentrifies."

The lower proportion of low-income children at the new schools is also evidence of the capital necessary to secure a space for one's child in these schools. Middle-income families with more education and white-collar jobs are embedded in networks that discuss and access information about innovative and decent public schools, and they have the wherewithal to maneuver the sometimes complex procedures for applying and enrolling in them. You can contact Ariel to get an application and have it submitted by January, but you're unlikely to make it in before the siblings and other family members of current students. The charter school's application can be downloaded from its Web site or retrieved at the school, and must be submitted by March. The three-page form includes general family information, plus questions about the student's needs and talents. The application must be completed, signed, dated, and accompanied by the child's birth certificate to be considered for admission. But, the Web site notes, there are almost no slots available for grade schoolers. "Since siblings have priority for enrollment, we do not expect any openings in the other grades," the site explains.[16] The process for admission to King College Prep is considerably more arduous. It begins in November or December with an application that can only be obtained from a school counselor and which requires a letter from the counselor, test scores, attendance records, and additional student information. Students who qualify must then sit for a separate test. It is more like applying to college or graduate school than to high school.

Do the new schools, after all this, produce better student performance? Both new elementary schools have a greater proportion of their students testing at or above national norms in reading and math than their neighborhood school peers, although Robinson's scores in reading are comparable. Ariel and the charter school also beat out Chicago elementary schools overall in standardized test scores. The differences are not enormous, but they are notable, reaching as high as a 36 percentage point difference between Ariel and Price in math. Moreover, Price Elementary School, the school with the lowest performance outcomes, also has the highest enrollment.

Figure 2 presents data for King College Prep and three other public high schools. Dyett Academy High School is the local high school designated for most of North Kenwood-Oakland's teenagers now that King is a selective enrollment school, while Phillips Academy High School serves students in the northern third of the neighborhood. The figure also includes data for Kenwood Academy, which is located in the South Kenwood neighborhood and serves Hyde Park-South Kenwood students; it has a magnet component into which high-achieving students from across the city can be accepted. It has traditionally been one of the city's better public high schools, although not as good as the separate selective enrollment schools. At over fifteen hundred students it is at capacity and thus not an option for

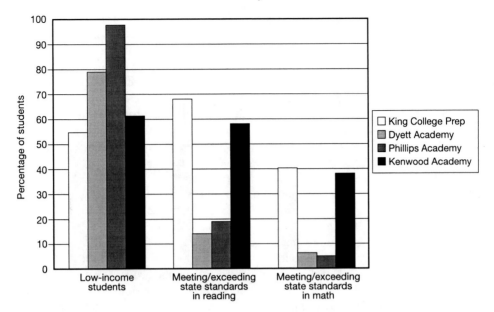

Figure 2. Performance of North Kenwood-Oakland area high schools, 2004–2005. Chicago Public Schools, "School Test Score and Demographic Reports," http://research.cps.k12.il.us/ (accessed December 1, 2005); Illinois State Board of Education, " eReport Card Public Site," http://webprod1.isbe.net/ereportcard/publicsite/getSearchCrieteria.aspx (accessed December 1, 2005).

high schoolers from North Kenwood-Oakland who cannot test into King. I include it here because it illustrates the stark division between North and South Kenwood. A school named Kenwood is not open to North Kenwood students, even though it is closer to many residents and clearly a better educational option than either Dyett or Phillips. The mobility rates at Dyett and Phillips (data not shown) suggest that these schools do not provide a curriculum that attracts and keeps students; 32 percent of the students at Dyett and 37 percent of those at Phillips enter or leave those schools *during the school year*, indicating a high degree of instability in the student populations. The mobility rate at King is only 4 percent.

The performance differences at the high school level are even more stark than among the elementary schools. King College Prep is doing exactly what city officials hoped it would do, attracting students from middle-income families. (Unlike some of the city's other magnet schools, King mostly attracts middle-income African-American families.) Barely over 50 percent of King's students are low-income, compared to 79 percent of the students at Dyett and 97 percent of the students at Phillips. And while King still has plenty room for improvement in performance, especially in math, its students do dramatically better on standardized tests than students at the nearby general admissions high schools, where fewer than 20 percent meet or exceed state standards in reading, and fewer than 10 percent do so in math. It is no surprise that King so roundly outperforms its competitors since it picked its students based on test scores. The point of this exercise, however, is to illustrate the severe *lack of choice* for North Kenwood-Oakland students who cannot enroll in King.

...

Each intervention signaled profound pessimism about the hope for the existing schools' restoration, and instead skirted or dismantled them. The school reforms executed the visions of the state politicians, who enacted the charter school legislation, and the mayor, who took control of the public schools and offered selective enrollment schools and small schools as solutions to low performance. Not only were these the only tools available, they were also the explicit tools utilized. In the Ariel and charter school cases, each group of school leaders opted out of the regular local public school mold because of their experience of working within an entrenched system of failure. They desired the flexibility and autonomy that new school management opportunities offered, but in buying into these new strategies they also participated in some of the more exclusionary features, of the new school types, such as forgoing local attendance boundaries and limiting enrollment. Along with the creation of King College Prep, the tools of the new entrepreneurial state created a tiered educational universe that put the onus on parents and students to choose their way into the best school options. While Chicago Public Schools officials claim that the regular (unreformed, neighborhood, general admission) public schools will eventually receive similar attention and resources, it is not always apparent how investments will trickle down to them when the more prestigious schools, like the magnet schools, have at times received nearly half of CPS's construction and renovation funds.[17]

In addition, a main tenet of this market approach to public goods is that competition will eventually lead to the total failure of some schools, just as some commercial ventures are run out of business by competition from better firms. In the end, this competitive weeding process will lead to improvement in the overall selection of schools. Paul Grogan and Tony Proscio take the philosophy to its Darwinian extreme, writing: "And finally, of course, it offers extinction to anyone unwilling to compete."[18] The political and ethical question is if we are prepared to slate some children—most likely the poor and minority ones—and the schools that educate them for extinction. Moreover, is it *just* to pit citizens with different abilities and unequal access to information against each other in competition for public goods?

Before the advent of school reform in North Kenwood-Oakland, parents who lived near Price, Robinson, and the old King, could do nothing, and on the first day of school in September they would still be sure that their child would have a desk in a classroom. The education they received once seated was subpar, to be sure; open access alone does not satisfy the state's duty to provide decent educations to its citizenry. In the neoliberal model, the attitude is that some of that burden should be passed on and shouldered by citizens themselves. Applications with due dates, waiting lists that must be checked, online distribution of forms and information, mandatory orientation sessions, test score reporting, additional testing—all these things require an informed and efficacious parent with considerable time to spend on researching school options and admissions procedures, not to mention Internet access.[19] As Klinenberg states, there is an expectation that residents "will be active consumers of public goods, expert 'customers' of city services made available in the market rather than 'citizens' entitled to social protection. This market model of governance creates a systemic *service mismatch*, whereby people having the weakest capabilities and greatest needs are the least likely to get them."[20]

The story of school reform falls squarely in this new model of service delivery, in which parents have to "shop for" schools. The relative underrepresentation of poor students at the three new schools is one indication that those with the greatest need for good schools—that is, those for whom good schools could contribute to intergenerational mobility—are less likely to be in them. Public goods are no longer broadly and equitably available, but instead constituents must be well-informed, industrious, and "entrepreneurial" enough to demand and search out the best public services. All others are consigned to languishing in bad public schools (and dilapidated housing and infirm public health facilities). As players in this new regime, black middlemen in North Kenwood-Oakland deliver a valuable commodity but on terms that overlook the preferences, talents, and limitations of indigenous working-class and poor families. Black professionals have the information and the networks to navigate a stratified public service infrastructure, and hence charter schools, small schools, and selective enrollment schools seem like unproblematic great ideas to them. But the error in this perspective (one that is now being recognized in calls for unfettered local access), and in the choice-based model that underlies many similar urban reforms, is that they expect the same of their less-advantaged neighbors.

Endnotes

[1] I ended chapter 3 with a discussion of my own position as a middleman. I have also been involved in a school reform effort in Chicago as a board member of the Urban Prep Charter Academy for Young Men, located in another poor African-American neighborhood in Chicago. Thus my observations of the transformation of schools in NKO and the utilization of various reform tools is also informed by my own philosophical and political quandaries as I participated in the creation of a charter school in another Chicago neighborhood.

[2] Klinenberg 2002, 139; Blomley 2004, 30; Brenner and Theodore 2002; Dávila 2004. For a popular endorsement of a neoliberal approach to transforming cities, see Grogan and Proscio 2000.

[3] Lipman 2002, 409–10.

[4] Ariel Mutual Funds, "Education Initiative," http://www.arielmutualfundsI.com/aei/aei_O_index.htm (accessed July 1, 2005).

[5] For a current definition of "small schools" in Chicago Public School parlance, see Chicago Public Schools, "Small Schools Get Results," http://www.smallschools.cps.k12.il.us/whataress.html (accessed July 1, 2005).

[6] "Charter Schools," 105 Illinois Compiled Statutes 5/Art.27A (1996).

[7] University of Chicago Center for Urban School Improvement, "About USI," http://usi.uchicago.edu/aboutnew.html (accessed July 1, 2005).

[8] Caitlin Devitt, "Charter School Strives to Achieve Its Mission," *Hyde Park Herald*, December 9, 1998, p. 19. Maurice Lee, "NK-O Charter School Aims to Attract More Local Kids," *Lakefront Outlook*, February 5, 2003, p. 7.

[9] For data on Chicago Public Schools, see http://www.cps.k12.il.us/. See also Deborah Bayliss, "King Will Be Magnet School, Says Board," *Hyde Park Herald*, June 30, 1999, p. 3.

[10] See http://www.cps.k12.il.us/ and http://research.cps.k12.il.us/.

[11] Lenore T. Adkins, "King off to Strong Start as Area Magnet School," *Hyde Park Herald*, September 25, 2002, p. 3.; Lenore T. Atkins, "School Officials Pin Hopes on $25M King," *Lakefront Outlook*, December 11, 2002, p. 2. North Kenwood-Oakland residents were not the only critics of the magnet school approach. Parents across the city questioned the politics behind the plan for and placement of magnet schools. See Janita Poe and Abdon M. Pallasch, "Chicago Schools Reach for Best as School Officials Try to Retain the City's Top Students with New Magnet Schools," *Chicago Tribune*, August 25, 1998, p. 1. For a

general history and analysis of Chicago school reform, with a focus on equity and justice, see also Lipman 2002.

[12]Personal communications with CCC chairman Shirley Newsome, December 8, 2004.

[13]Adkins, *Lakefront Outlook*, December 11, 2002, p. 1.

[14]Deborah Bayliss, "Charter Schools Asks Waiver for Neighborhood Kids," *Lakefront Outlook*, February 2, 2000, p. 5. The University of Chicago opened a second elementary school in Oakland in 2005. It is a charter school with *local* attendance boundaries, accepting all students who live within its catchment area. This was made possible by a change in the state law, which resulted from lobbying by the university, Alderman Preckwinkle, and state lawmakers from the area. The university's second elementary school serves an entirely new mixed-income HOPE VI community that is replacing the Ida B. Wells public housing project and other nearby projects. In an ironic twist, and despite the progressive intent of the change in the law, the new localism also has its problem. It guards the benefits of a well-supported, reformed elementary school for a community for which the designs stipulate that two-thirds of the new residents will be moderate-, middle-, and upper-income families, and one-third will be public housing families. The text of the amended law reads: "Enrollment in a charter school shall be open to any pupil who resides within the geographic boundaries of the area served by the local school board, provided that the board of education in a city having a population exceeding 500,000 may designate attendance boundaries for no more than one-third of the charter schools permitted in the city if the board of education determines that attendance boundaries are needed to relieve overcrowding or to better serve low-income and at-risk students" ("An Act in Relation to Education," Illinois Public Act 093–086, http://www.ilga.gov/legislation/publicacts/fulltext.asp?name=093–0861&GA=093; accessed July 1, 2005).

[15]Low-income students are defined as those qualifying for free or reduced-price school meals. Eligibility for this program is determined at the federal level and is based on the national poverty income guidelines. Families who earn up to 130 percent of the federal poverty line are eligible for free lunches; those who earn up to 185 percent of the poverty line pay a reduced price. Families in both of these categories are classified as low-income. The upper limit for annual income for a family of three for the 2004–2005 school year was $28,990, and for a family of four was $34,873. U.S. Department of Agriculture Food and Nutrition Service, http://www.fns.usda.gov/cnd/governance/notices/iegs/IEGs04–05.pdf.

[16]North Kenwood/Oakland Charter School, "The Application Process," http://nko.usi-schools.org/how_to_apply/index.shtml (accessed December 1, 2005).

[17]Schaeffer 2000. For a description of the Chicago Public Schools reform plan, see Chicago Public Schools, "Renaissance 2010," http://www.ren2010.cps.k12.il.us.

[18]Grogan and Proscio 2000, 215.

[19]As a mentor to a Chicago Public Schools eighth grader, I experienced firsthand the immense work that must go into securing a suitable high school placement. Most local public schools are still failing in Chicago, and thus I spent many hours mining the CPS Web site for public school alternatives. Each charter school has its own admissions process, and applications for the selective enrollment schools are due in December of the student's eighth grade year. It was a harrowing process.

[20]Klinenberg 2002, 142–43.

References

Blomley, Nicholas, 2004. *Unsettling the City: Urban Land and the Politics of Property.* New York: Routledge.

Brenner, Neil and Nik Theodore, 2002. *Spaces of Neoliberalism.* Malden, MA: Blackwell.

Dávila, Arlene M. 2004. *Barrio Dreams: Puerto Ricans, Latinos, and the Neoliberal City.* Berkeley, University of California Press.

Grogan, Paul S. and Tony Proscio. 2000. *Comeback Cities: A Blueprint for Urban Neighborhood Revival.* Boulder, CO: Westview Press.

Klinenberg, Eric. 2002. *Heatwave: A Social Autopsy of Disaster in Chicago.* Chicago: University of Chicago Press.

Lipman, Pauline. 2002. "Making the Global City, Making Inequality: The Political Economy and Cultural Politics of Chicago School Policy." *American Educational Reserach Journal* 39: 379–419.

Schaeffer, Brett. 2000. "Some See Elite Schools as Drain on System." *Catalyst* 12 (4): 12–13. http://www.catalyst-chicago.org/news/index.php?item=256&cat=23 (accessed December 1, 2005).

Special Taxes in Baltimore:
Good or Bad?*

Meghan Ashlin Rich

Introduction

Large social institutions can serve as anchors of stability in urban neighborhoods. Institutions such as hospitals, universities, public schools, libraries, businesses, and community organizations not only serve residents' specific everyday needs, but can also provide jobs, spur local economic growth, and attract newcomers to the area (Taub, Taylor, and Dunham 1984; Nyden, Lukehart, Maly, and Peterman 1998). This is particularly important for neighborhoods undergoing changes to population demographics. Taub, Taylor and Dunham's study (1984) of neighborhood change in the Chicago neighborhoods of Hyde Park-Kenwood and Lincoln Park shows how institutions (such as large universities) collaborated with their surrounding neighborhoods to help stem the tide of racial succession and white flight in the 1950s and 1960s. By working to stabilize a neighborhood, institutions can create and maintain racial integration in communities. Thus, a neighborhood undergoing racial transition may not fully resegregate in the future. However, racial and ethnic integration can be threatened by neighborhood revitalization efforts that lack specific intent to maintain population diversity, regardless of the presence of strong social institutions (Hodge 1980; Stoecker 1994).

This article will consider how homeowners in Village Heights,[1] a racially integrated neighborhood in Baltimore, Maryland, perceive barriers to and support systems for continued diversity in their neighborhood. A university, a special tax district program, and local public schools are three types of institutions that were seen as influencing the neighborhood; although these institutions do not maintain diversity by design, all affect racial and economic diversity in the neighborhood. For the purposes of this discussion, two types of neighborhood social institutions will be focused on: the Village Heights Benefits District Management Authority (VHBD), a quasi-governmental institution created in 1994 to oversee the "grime and crime" problems in the neighborhood; and the public schools in the neighborhood (an elementary school and a combined elementary/middle school). Both of

---

* Meghan Ashlin Rich, "Institutional Barriers and Racial Economic Integration." Unpublished 2010. Printed with permission of the author.

these institutions highlight the complicated relationship between grassroots neighborhood organizations, local government, and the privatization of public institutions in the urban realm (Hackworth 2007). I critically examine how middle class homeowners perceive these neighborhood institutions and consider how these institutions affect the race and class composition of the neighborhood. I argue that the failure of city government institutions (in this case, law enforcement, sanitation, and public schools) pushes residents to make one or more of the following decisions: 1) create their own quasi-governmental organizations to replace or amend government institutions; 2) avoid government institutions by "shopping" for private replacements, as in the case of private schools; or 3) exit the neighborhood for other neighborhoods that are perceived by residents as having effective government institutions. It is hoped that by understanding how residents in a racially integrated neighborhood perceive their community's social institutions we can better understand how these institutions become barriers to retaining a racially and economically diverse residential population in other urban neighborhoods.

Studies of Integrated Neighborhoods

Not every neighborhood that went through racial transition in the 1960s and 1970s has gone through the invasion-succession neighborhood transition process as described by Molotch in his classic study of a Chicago neighborhood (1972). Carole Goodwin (1979) described similar racial transitioning in Chicago's Oak Park neighborhood and found that racial change was controlled through organizational interventions. Today, Oak Park has a robust real estate market and is still known for being racially integrated. Goodwin not only studied the role of organizational culture and community institutions in maintaining a stable racially integrated neighborhood, but also investigated white residents' perceptions of racial change and community. She found that whites' perceptions of racial change and of local institutions have a substantial effect on their behavior, whether that behavior is demanding that social institutions do something about racial change or individual moving decisions. When there is perceived racial transition in a community, white residents reconstruct what their community means to them and make predictions about change (Goodwin 1979; see also Abrahamson 1959).

More recent studies of stable racially integrated neighborhoods have focused on variables that characterize the people living in racially integrated neighborhoods (young and childless) and similarities that exist among integrated neighborhoods (past racial stability, distance from minority concentration, high rates of rental housing, a thriving housing market, and stable institutions within the community) (Ellen 2000; Smith 1993). Nyden, Lukehart, Maly, and Peterman's 1998 study of current racially integrated neighborhoods noted the importance of residents' awareness of the neighborhood's stable diversity, as well as the presence of *social seams* ("points in the community where interaction between different ethnic and racial groups is sewn together in some way," such as a main street area 1998: 262). They found two distinct types of diverse neighborhoods: *diversity by direction* and *diversity by circumstance*. *Diversity by direction* communities, such as Sherman Park in Milwaukee, Wisconsin, tend to be "the most stable of the diverse communities because they have developed the institutional structures, social arrangements, and political-social environment needed to sustain their diversity" (Nyden, Lukehart, Maly, and Peterman 1998: 9). The social institutions within the neighborhood are set up to specifically promote racial diversity, and that diversity tends to be of a biracial (black and white) character. In contrast, *diversity by circumstance* neighborhoods, such as Rogers Park in Chicago, Illinois, tends to be multiracial and multiethnic, where no one group dominates all social institutions within the community. The median income tends to be much lower than that of more established *diverse by direction* neighborhoods, as large numbers of recent immigrants reside there. Religious organizations tend to be very important within these communities, as they create social seams between various ethnic groups (Nyden, Lukehart, Maly, and Peterman 1998).

As part of the Nyden et al. study, Ferman, Singleton, and DeMarco (1998) completed an in-depth study of the West Mount Airy neighborhood of Philadelphia, Pennsylvania. West Mount Airy is a racially and economically diverse neighborhood (in 1990 it was 52.6 percent white and 44.8 percent African-American) that did not succumb to the panic selling and white flight that struck other Philadelphia neighborhoods in the 1950s and 1960s. A number of institutions (such as West Mount Airy Neighbors) were organized to promote the neighborhood to possible in-movers as a stable, racially diverse neighborhood. This effort was to help quell white residents' fears that the neighborhood was deteriorating by focusing on quality of life issues, such as deterring crime and unscrupulous real estate practices. West Mount Airy Neighbors worked with the city government to integrate the public schools within the community. Cultural institutions, such as Allen's Lane Art Center, the Mount Airy Learning Tree, and Weaver's Way Food Co-Op, served as places for community activism, cultural learning, and cross-racial interaction (Ferman, Singleton, and DeMarco 1998).

Nevertheless, social interaction in West Mount Airy is not perfectly integrated. "Certain behavior patterns—in particular, organizational membership, where people shop, and where they send their children to school—reveal less integration than housing data would indicate" (Ferman, Singleton, and DeMarco 1998: 46). Ferman et al. (1998) point to the "race-class quagmire" in which residential choice and social interaction are affected by social class, but social class often cannot be disentangled from race. An analysis of the census tracts that make up West Mount Airy shows that the tracts that are majority African-American have an overall lower median household income than those in majority white tracts (Ferman, Singleton, and DeMarco 1998; also see Anderson 1990).

Description of Study

Neighborhood Setting

This research originates from a case study of Village Heights, an urban neighborhood in Baltimore that has been racially integrated for at least twenty years. Baltimore is a large Mid-Atlantic city with a majority of black residents (64.3 percent of the city's residents are black and 31.6 percent are white, U.S. Census Bureau, 2000). While Baltimore is highly racially segregated (Massey and Denton 1993), Village Heights is a neighborhood that Baltimoreans historically define by its residential diversity, including people of different races, ages, classes, sexual orientations, professions, and lifestyles. Using Ellen's (2000) definition that a neighborhood is integrated if its population is 10–50 percent black, Village Heights is considered statistically integrated (see Ellen, 2000 for a discussion of the various definitions of racial integration) because it is 50.7 percent white, 34.2 percent black, 10.6 percent Asian, 3 percent Hispanic (can be of any race), and 3 percent two or more races

In the 1950s and 1960s, when Baltimore experienced considerable decline in manufac-turing work and population loss, Village Heights promoted itself as an affordable, lively neighborhood with a bounty of Victorian rowhouses awaiting renovation. An initial wave of gentrification is part of the shared lore of neighborhood residents, and it informs the current residents' perceptions of community diversity. Today the neighborhood remains an attractive place to live and continues to experience gentrification. Prices of homes climbed in recent years, with the median home price in Village Heights rising from $128,000 in 2002 to $320,000 in 2007 (Live Baltimore Home Center Home Sales Statistics 2008). Most dwellings in the neighborhood are rental units; only 20.76 percent of residential units are owner occupied (U.S. Census Bureau 2000). Today, many of these multi-unit rentals are being converted back to single-family homes.

The neighborhood contains three designated business districts, a hospital, the main campus of a major university (Garrett University), and the City Museum of Art. Median family income for white residents ran between $51,563 and $75,326 in 1999 (across the three main census tracts within the neighborhood's boundaries), while it is substantially lower for black residents, running between $27,902 and $33,462. Whites in Village Heights have a higher median family income in comparison to the white median family income for Baltimore overall, which is $49,391 (U.S. Census Bureau 2000). (See Appendix, Table 1 for selected demographic information on Village Heights.)

Village Heights is one of the few neighborhoods in the United States that has created a quasi-governmental institution, the Village Heights Benefits District Management Author-ity (VHBD; also called the Benefits District for short), to oversee the "grime and crime" problems in the neighborhood. The catalyst for creating the VHBD was the murder of an engineer who worked in the neighborhood in 1993. Neighborhood activists and community organizations worked with the city and state government to create the first special benefits tax district in the United States that is a mixture of residential and commercial areas. In addition to the regular city tax assessment on property, all property owners within the Ben-efits District pay a surtax of 30 cents per 100 dollars of the assessed value of their property.[2] In effect, the approval of the VHBD by the residents of Village Heights (it was voted in by a majority of at least 58 percent) meant that residents in this community were willing to *tax themselves* if doing so improved the community. The organization is funded by the property owners' surtax, as well as various foundations, city grants, and contributions from local institutions (such as the university and hospital). In addition, the VHBD created an umbrella organization, which serves to connect four distinct neighborhoods (Village Heights, Ebett, South Village Heights, and Grantley), represented on the VHBD Board of Directors.[3] A foundation was set up to raise money for neighborhood security, sanitation, and community development. The foundation pays for a VHBD office staff, including an Executive Officer, a security team (with a few automobiles to help patrol the neighbor-hood), a street sanitation team, and other expenses related to community programs and outreach.

This study uses the Benefits District's boundaries as the boundaries for the neighbor-hood of Village Heights. I limited my interviews to homeowners/property owners who pay the Village Heights Benefits District (VHBD) tax. I included all four sections of VHBD because they include different aspects of the neighborhood (with Village Heights more stu-dent-oriented and white; Ebett, racially mixed and mostly homeowners; Grantley, majority black and working class; and South Village Heights, racially mixed with a large business district). Each subsection of the neighborhood has its own neighborhood associations, meeting about once a month.

The Benefits District: Defensive Tactic or Gating Program?

In Village Heights, there are many community groups working to ensure that the neighborhood is stable by addressing various quality of life issues. The VHBD, financially supported by a residential surtax and matching grants from Garrett University and private foundations, attempted to serve as a larger umbrella connecting the many community groups in the neighborhood and serving as an economic and political resource.

During the course of this study, the VHBD was up for reauthorization by the city council. This reinvigorated the controversy surrounding the program, with many neighborhood activists arguing strenuously for or against reauthorization. Not surprisingly, conflicts over the program were more complex than a fight over tax money and often stemmed from the deeply held beliefs of Villagers. Although everyone seemed to want the same thing for the neighborhood—a safe, clean, diverse, and lively community—what constitutes that kind of neighborhood and how that could be accomplished differed from person to person. Various community associations were urged to support the reauthorization through letters and emails to local politicians. All of the community associations under the VHBD officially supported reauthorization (many of whom worked closely with the VHBD and shared board members), except for the Ebett Improvement Association (which could not come to a consensus with their members on the matter) and the Edward Hill Homeowners' Association (which was formed in opposition to the VHBD). In a letter widely distributed at community meetings and on various websites, the president of the VHBD board of directors wrote to "Village Heights stakeholders":

> This spring the City Council must again decide whether the Village Heights Benefits District (VHBD) should be reauthorized and continue to operate for another four years. Without reauthorization, the VHBD will close its doors this year. No more street and alley sweeping or pickups of illegally dumped trash. No more safety team patrols. No more security cameras on Marshall Boulevard. No more Beverly Main Street program. No more housing code enforcement and marketing initiatives. No more support for community-led festivals, greening projects, safety initiatives. You get the picture … (VHBD Board of Directors letter to the community, 2006).

A longtime resident who had a hand in the design and implementation of the Benefits District described the original idea of the program to me:

> The Benefits District was helpful. (pause) Here's how it was envisioned. There was a core group of us who had little kids, and full time jobs, and we're doing all this neighborhood organizing. And we were *exhausted*. And there was a murder, a shooting on 11th Street, near where we lived. And we fliered one block, the 1100 block of Victoria and Ebett and 70 people came to a meeting. And it was the same old hand wringing, like "What are we going to do, what are we going to do?" We finally said, you know, we need *systematic solutions*

to some of the problems. Crime and grime type problems. And that's when we worked to create the Benefits District. Because the idea was that with this Benefits District we have professional staff that would leverage *us* who were willing to contribute some of our personal time. And so I think it's done that... (50-year-old white female, longtimer in Village Heights).

As shown in the quote above, the VHBD was originally envisioned as a public/private partnership to amend existing government services; mostly sanitation and public safety. This *neoliberal[4] project* originated at the grassroots level though neighborhood activists who were alarmed at the failure of local government to address what they perceived to be neighborhood problems[5]—problems that would be a major barrier to maintaining economic and residential stability in the neighborhood if they were not addressed. By *neoliberal project*, I am referring to an organized effort to privatize services and programs previously provided by government (Harvey 2005).

While many residents were dissatisfied with the VHBD program because it did not always deliver on its promises, there was a general level of fear of not having the program in place. Many Villagers thought that without the VHBD, the neighborhood might slip back into a state of decline. This is exemplified by one homeowner's response to the city council reauthorization of the program in the summer of 2006:

Well, it passed again, so we're happy with that. I'm happy with that, I won't speak globally. You know, when I first moved into the neighborhood that I moved into, I didn't know that there were some issues causing those 25 houses to be available. It's hard to, it's hard to, when you grow up in the Washington, D.C. suburbs, the whole concept is buying this house. And I wanted to *buy a house* in a neighborhood that I felt was safe, that looked safe, had all the trappings of a viable, living neighborhood but (pause) from what I didn't know was that there was some issues, and there were some scared and frightened people (pause) and one of the answers I think to that tension was the neighborhood banded together said, "We're going to give this a shot" (43-year-old African-American male, longtimer in Ebett).

Many homeowners, especially those who were newcomers and did not know a lot about the VHBD or what it did for the neighborhood, did not feel strongly for or against the existence of the program. However, they were not willing to completely dismantle the VHBD, fearing that the positive aspects of the neighborhood might disappear without an organized monitoring body. Even some longtimers who lived in the neighborhood at the inception of the program took a neutral stance on the issue. As long as the neighborhood was not in decline, many were willing to pay the special surtax:

Well, my opinion is I'm not really sure [if the Benefits District should exist], I kind of take the opposite approach which is, I don't really know what they give us, but the absence of them may not be a good thing either ... I understand that people criticize them and say we're not getting our money's worth ... But, I almost question that ... even though we're not getting what we think we deserve, without that it's just *chaos*. And how is anybody, how is it—like, the one thing it seems like they do is like at least keep their eye on what's going on, that's going to help, what's coming into Village Heights (34-year-old Asian female, longtimer in Village Heights).

One newcomer moved to the neighborhood specifically because she learned about the Benefits District, equating the VHBD with a stable future: "No, it was attractive to me ... It showed a cohesiveness to me. That, you know, a group of citizens had really established it a while back. It showed that there was organization in the community." She was not sure of the exact benefits she received through the VHBD, but was impressed that the neighborhood had institutionalized an activity that is normally done through volunteer associations. Many homeowners who felt ambivalent about the Benefits District were aware of a neighborhood contingent that was strongly opposed to the program. Some homeowners were appalled by people protesting the surtax, equating the protests with political conservatism. Even after moving out of the neighborhood, this 36-year-old white male homeowner marveled at the contention in his old neighborhood regarding the VHBD: "It seemed to make sense to me, that it was okay to pay some extra money to get some extra services. Um, but really the kicker for me was that the people who were opposed (chuckles) to the Benefits District lived directly across the street from us ... *You know how some people have like the issue of like abortion? ...* They are like ... *that way* about the Benefits District." A longtimer agreed:

> Ironically, I think that a neighbor that is most vehemently opposed to it and I share a very similar view in that if you are going to have something in a community, you're going to have to chuck money into the pot. And it has to be decided upon by somebody to use that money, but everybody has to pitch in. I mean, that's just life. You have to pay for other people. And sometimes the people who are better off have to pay for the people who are less well-off. And that's just sorta where we ideologically fall (34-year-old white male, longtimer in Village Heights).

The above quote further exemplifies the neoliberal argument for the Benefits District, in that middle class residents should pay for the services that they *choose* to have in their neighborhood, rather than face neglect by the city government. Pattillo's work (2007) on a gentrifying historically black neighborhood in Chicago points to this trend in urban governance: "The model has changed from one in which cities 'deliver' public services like education, health care, and protection from crime, to one in which residents 'shop for' these goods in a service landscape that includes more nongovernmental, private subcontractors" (Pattillo 2007: 150). This model can be seen in the proliferation of "Empowerment Zones" (EZs) and private charter schools in many urban neighborhoods, across the United States (Pattillo 2007; Dávila 2004).

Many residents who were critical of the Benefits District were quite clear in their comprehension of the privatization of public services in the neighborhood. There were a number of different arguments *against* the Benefits District, most having to do with the inability of the organization to deliver on its promises. For some interviewees, the contention was not simply over an extra tax.

> I think the Benefits District is just a *band aid* for people who are willing to pay *more*, and that's a shame. And basically what it does, it says, "Every other

neighborhood, we don't care about you. And you don't care about yourselves because you're not spending an extra tax to make it happen." So to me the *need*, quote unquote, for a Benefits District, is a symptom of a sick city. And Baltimore is a sick city (36-year-old white female, longtimer in Village Heights).

A common criticism of the VHBD was that it was started because of the failure of local government. The government is "off the hook" in its responsibility to keep the city's neighborhoods clean and safe because of organizations like VHBD. Another criticism was that the VHBD was an elitist program, run by middle-class whites (many hired from outside of the neighborhood) *for* middle-class whites in Village Heights, who allowed other neighborhoods in Baltimore to fend for themselves. The Benefits District program was also suspected of working with other neighborhood institutions, such as the Village Heights Community Association and Garrett University, to gentrify the neighborhood and push out lower income residents and renters. Furthermore, it was thought that the program created economic inequality between Baltimore neighborhoods, as other neighborhoods did not have the resources to create their own Benefits District (I term this idea the "the gating effect"). At a Grantley Community Association Meeting, an African-American congressional state representative from the Park Heights community (a neighborhood in Northwest Baltimore where the majority of residents are lower-income African-Americans), told the group that she was rebuffed by the City Council in her efforts to create a Benefits District in her community. In her story, the City Council took the position that a Benefits District would not work in a neighborhood that was already in economic dire straits. However, if Benefits Districts are reserved for neighborhoods that are somewhat economically stable, what alternatives exist for neighborhoods that have tipped into decline? This led some Villagers to wonder what happens outside of the protective umbrella of the VHBD.

I don't really know that much about the Benefits District and what it offers, because like I said, I didn't live here prior to it. I mean, I got the flyers and whatever. You know, I'm perfectly happy to pay extra for some sort of perceived value, although I do get troubled by the fact that, because there are motivated people in this neighborhood that can form a Benefits District, we do get something that other people who can't organize don't get. Or that we should be getting just because we pay taxes. Pen-Lucy (neighborhood in North Baltimore) doesn't have a Benefits District, and they have terrible problems with garbage (40-year-old white female, newcomer in Village Heights).

In addition to the gating effect of the VHBD, the extra surtax was viewed by some homeowners as a hardship on those who were not middle or upper income, as well as a sign of class inequality in the neighborhood (see Berrey, 2005 and Goode, 2001 for studies on middle class community groups' discourse in multiracial neighborhoods):

my question is, is to any reasonable person, so we need to employ an Executive Director (of the VHBD), making $80,000 plus with benefits, when we have people in our neighborhood who are making, or who are living on poverty levels. There are people in Grantley, who are going to bed at night without food. And the 50 to 100 dollars that they have to spend on the Benefits District will mean that they can't have heating, they won't have food, or that the children will not have any clothes (65-year-old white male, newcomer in Village Heights).

One homeowner pointed out that accountability was lost because the Benefits District institutionalized what was normally done through volunteer efforts. The institutionalization of grassroots community organizing was perceived as creating another level of unaccountable government bureaucracy. It is important to note that homeowners who had strong negative opinions about the VHBD were middle class, white, and of the minority opinion. However, across all homeowners, there was distrust of governmental institutions in response to policies that focused on Inner Harbor development and tourism at the expense of struggling residential neighborhoods.

At the time of this writing, the Benefits District is being reorganized around a new Executive Director and staff. It is likely that VHBD will be heavily debated by neighborhood residents until it goes up for reauthorization in 2010. Perhaps if the city council allowed residents within the district's boundaries to vote on the program, as they did at its inception, the community would be more accepting and knowledgeable about the possible benefits of retaining the VHBD. However, the Benefits District surtax rises with home values, making the combination of high property taxes and high VHBD surtaxes a burden on both longtimers and newcomers to Village Heights. While many homeowners fear what will happen to their neighborhood if the VHBD is not in place, the personal financial burden of funding the program may become too much to bear for the individual homeowner.

Perceptions of Neighborhood Public Schools

If the privatization of governmental services attempts to attract and retain the middle class in an integrated neighborhood, which aspects of neighborhood institutions drive them away? Research on integrated neighborhoods shows that successful integration often depends on desegregated neighborhood schools (Ferman, Singleton, and DeMarco 1998; Goodwin 1979; Saltman 1990). Saltman(1990) argues that one of the major external strategies for maintaining integration is a system-wide program to desegregate schools in a given city. "The presence of a systemwide school desegregation program removes from the target integrated neighborhood the onus of having a racially identifiable black school or schools. Since that integrated neighborhood is then no different from any other in the school system, affirmative marketing can proceed with maximum potential for success" (Saltman 1990: 396). If all the schools in a city were desegregated, there would be no push for whites to move out of an integrated neighborhood in search of an integrated school district.

In Baltimore, almost all public schools are segregated and have a majority of black students (only 9.4 percent of students enrolled in Baltimore City public schools were white in 2006). The two public schools in Village Heights, Francis Lowe Elementary School and Lewis Elementary/Middle School (also called The Lewis School), illustrate this trend. In the 2005–2006 school year, 10 white students attended Francis Lowe Elementary (compared to 197 black students), and 90 percent of the students were eligible for the free school lunch program. The characteristics of the student body at The Lewis School were similar: In the 2005–2006 school year, seven white students attended the school (in comparison to

477 black students), and 80.3 percent of the students were eligible for the free school lunch program (Baltimore City Public Schools, 2007).

While public schools/education was not the intended focus of this study, it was one of the top neighborhood concerns of homeowners interviewed. Out of 23 interviews with parents, only two sets of parents sent their children to local public schools, although a total of nine interviews were conducted with parents whose children had attended a Baltimore City public school at some point. According to longtimers, there was once some fluidity in Baltimore City about which school district one's child could attend. For parents who were well-informed (which often meant being in middle class social networks), parents could arrange for children in the Village Heights area to attend racially integrated elementary and middle schools in the Forest Dale district. It was thought by some parents in this study that once a child was in the Baltimore public school system, it was easier to transition that child to one of the public magnet high schools later on. At some point (it is unclear when this unofficial school enrollment policy ended), the district lines were strictly enforced by the city, causing some middle class parents to leave the neighborhood for the Forest Dale district. Because property in Forest Dale is much more expensive than in Village Heights (the median home price in Forest Dale in 2006 was $520,000 (Live Baltimore Home Center 2007), parents who wanted to (or needed to for financial reasons) send their children to public school either left the city altogether for suburban public schools or found a less expensive neighborhood that was still within Forest Dale school district (see DeSena, 2006 and Montgomery, 2006 for research on how middle class parents navigate urban public school systems).

The fact that middle class residents in Village Heights see their local public schools as unacceptable for their own children is a major barrier to full racial integration in the neighborhood. Because countless families have moved out of the neighborhood in search of other school districts, there is significant turnover in the neighborhood. Ebett residents joke about the "height rule": that when neighborhood children get to a certain height (the height of a 5-year-old, approximately), they suddenly disappear.

Not all families choose to exit because of public schools. Some stay, putting the money that would have been spent on a more expensive suburban home into private or parochial education. It is unknown how many parents in Village Heights choose to send their children to a local school, private or parochial school, or move from the neighborhood. However, my interviews broaden understanding of the circumstances underlying these choices and what it would take for local schools to be seen as viable by middle class homeowners. It should be noted that only three out of 29 newcomers were raising children in the neighborhood, which biases the sample (in comparison to 16 out of 26 longtimers who were raising/had raised children in the neighborhood). Even so, newcomers who did not have children at the time of their interview had strong opinions on sending their future children to local public schools.

Village Heights Parents' Schooling Strategies

The question "Should we stay or should we go?" is a common one among middle class parents in Village Heights. It dominates conversations at private social gatherings and public parks in the neighborhood. I asked the homeowner quoted below what she planned to do about schooling for her little girl, who had just turned five-years-old a few months before our interview. She explained:

Well, I'm not worried anymore, she's going to (Catholic school). Um, but yeah, it was an *enormous* issue, this time last year, and even earlier than that. That's when people, that's when people start worrying about, pretty much as soon as their kids can *walk*, you know, the first issue is, "Are you going to move, or are you going to stay? If you move, where are you going to move? If you stay, what are you going to do? Are you going to home school? Are you going scrape up, you know, eighteen thousand dollars a year for Shriver (School)? You know, what are you going to do?" In fact, there's sort of a joking rule among all the parents in the neighborhood, that it's considered rude to ask questions about the schools within the first five minutes of any conversation (laughs) (36 year-old white female, longtimer in Ebett).

Very few of the longtimers interviewed were willing to put their children in local schools. One of the white longtimer couples interviewed raised five children in the Village Heights. Their children attended a combination of local schools and public parochial schools outside of the neighborhood, depending on the needs of each child. Their children attended The Lewis School in the 1960s and early 1970s, a period in which the neighborhood schools were in the process of desegregation from majority white. By the late 1970s, when many whites had abandoned Baltimore public schools, a citizens' action group was formed called the Lewis-Lowe Education Corporation. Because both neighborhood schools were quickly resegregating to have a majority of black students, it was hoped that if middle-class parents became involved and dedicated resources to the schools then other middle-class Villagers would be more willing to send their children there. Three of the people I interviewed had been active in this group, and were dismayed that their activism was not taken up by subsequent generations of parents:

We were consciously... trying to make the public schools work for us and were insistent that we were going to do that. So for all the time that my kids were at Lewis in the seventies, and for all the time that they were there, they... there were a number of middle class parents, black and white, who were glad to be there, who were fighting to make it a good school (and) fought some rather vigorous battles to do that. But towards the end, after my kids had moved on to high school, because we turned Lewis into a K–8 school while we were there. But after that he moved on to high school and I was still volunteering over here (at Lewis), we couldn't replace ourselves. The next generation of parents, for whatever reason, were—it doesn't mean that they necessarily moved out of the neighborhood, but they were on all the waiting lists to get into private schools, or the parochial schools, or doing home schooling, or doing something besides going in, so now I think both Lewis and Lowe are about 99 percent black. So we lost that, that battle as far as, we won it for our own generation but we just couldn't keep it going (63-year-old white female, longtimer in Ebett).

I asked her why she thought that middle class parents gave up on working with the neighborhood public schools. She replied:

There's a perception, based in some reality, that urban public schools in places like Baltimore just do not provide a good education. Our experience contradicts that perception. But at the same time, people *really* shouldn't have to struggle the way we did, and fight the way we did to get the good education that we got. And to preserve it, and then to support the people who are providing it, which in this case at Lewis, is the principal… so I have kind of mixed feelings when I think about the parents who came after us. Because on the one hand, I'm *annoyed* that they didn't step up and continue to fight the good fight, and see how far they can take it. And on the other hand, I can see why they didn't (laughs) because it really was an enervating, very high maintenance kind of life to be living with two kids in public school, to make it work for us.

This homeowner's feelings were echoed by a longtimer couple who raised five children in the neighborhood when they said, "*There's people that move away instead of staying to do something about it.*" However, most respondents with children did not feel the need to move out of the neighborhood because they found alternate schools. Another white longtimer couple in Village Heights considered the local schools, but balked at sending their white children to a school with a black majority that was perceived as academically deficient (F=Female Respondent; M=Male Respondent):

F: I think there are problems in the local schools. I mean, we looked at them. We were thinking of Lewis, maybe, for a little while. But I think there needs to be more… to keep families in an area like this, there needs to be more emphasis in the schools. I mean, our kids went to a private school. I would have preferred to send them to public school I think, but we sent them in the city, but still, not in the neighborhood.

M: Just so I'm clear, our names aren't being used as far as these responses? I think the schools are as good as like Lewis, for example, was sort of this star or you know, was supposed to be a good school. As our kids were coming in, it sort of had lost a lot of the luster from where it had used to be. And to be quite honest, our kids would have probably been the only white kids in the school, which is very problematic for a kid as they're going through grade school. And you know, if the schools had been even to the point where they ultimately went, which is probably majority African-American, it still is a sense that there's not as much of an opportunity for kids to do what kids do all the time, which is pick on whoever is the odd man out. And you know, so I think in terms of the quality of the education, it wasn't up to what you could get, they went to (private Catholic school), it wasn't really up to that.

White parents' negative perceptions of the public schools were based on two ideas. First, that the schools had an overwhelming majority of black students and parents didn't want their children to be in the minority in the school, and thus a target of teasing or harassment (what can be termed "the childhood cruelty rationale"). Second, because many Baltimore public school students are of a low-income background, middle-class parents feel that their children do not belong in an environment where the curriculum and student behavior might not reflect their own social class. Homeowners viewed these schools as having low performance scores and lacking the resources of other schools with middle-class student populations (see Maryland Report Card www.mdreportcard.org for student assessments in Baltimore City public schools).

The relationship between race and poverty in schools was clear to white homeowners, who knew that a mostly black school would not be well-funded. Orfield and Yun's study (1999) of resegregation in schools across the United States points to this problem: "A great many of the educational characteristics of schools attributed to race are actually related to poverty but the impacts are easily confused since in most metropolitan areas there are few if any concentrated poverty white schools while the vast majority of segregated black or Latino schools experience such poverty and the educational differences that are associated with it" (Orfield and Yun 1999:16). Village Heights parents were worried that any social capital that they could transfer to their children might be impeded by schools that were not academically rigorous. Parents perceived city public schools as lacking curricula geared towards independent thinking and critical analysis. They feared that public schools would not prepare their children for higher education. One white longtimer couple found that even a racially integrated public school outside of the neighborhood did not have the academic curriculum they were looking for, transferring their children from public to private school after a few years. Another longtimer mother worked at one of the most respected nonreligious private schools in Baltimore, where her children could take advantage of her tuition remission benefit.

Even though many of the parents I interviewed did not have the financial resources to pay the exorbitant tuition costs of the top private schools in the area, they were able to use other resources, such as job benefits and social connections, to send their children to schools they deemed academically appropriate. Otherwise, parents chose schools that had lower tuition, such as parochial schools. Other parents, who wanted to send their children to the more expensive elite private schools, relied on double-incomes. A 57-year-old white longtimer told me: "We did thirteen years of private school... (my daughter) was zoned for Francis Lowe, and she would have been the 43rd child in her kindergarten class with one teacher, one part-time aid. You can't do that to your own child if you have alternatives."

Almost all white homeowner-parents in this study used their racial and class privilege to avoid sending their children to schools that were deemed inappropriate. Montgomery (2006) termed these maneuvers of privilege "selective flight." According to interviewees, this avoidance occurred because the public school student body was mostly black and lower-income, or because the academic standards at the school were not at the level the parents required. This finding concurs with DeSena's research (2006) on gentry families in Greenpoint, Brooklyn, whose class privilege allows them to send their children to "better schools" outside the neighborhood. While Village Heights parents cannot be judged for not wanting to "risk" their child's future by sending them to local public schools, parental avoidance of these schools is antithetical to their views on the importance of racial integration, for themselves and their children. Many wished that their child's private school was more racially integrated, but it was a qualified version of racial integration: only integration within their own social class was acceptable. The fact that many middle class families have dual-earners means that most do not have the time or energy to become heavily involved in the local schools. Without a collective of middle-class parents (and particularly, mothers) involved with the schools, as with the Lewis-Lowe Education Corporation, it is unlikely that homeowner-parents will send their children to Village Heights public schools in the future. As a result, middle-class families exit the neighborhood for other school districts.

Conclusion

This article considered whether homeowners perceive influential social institutions as barriers or support systems to continued racial diversity in their neighborhood. As a *diversity by direction* neighborhood, it is imperative that these institutions remain strong to maintain stability in the community (Nyden, Lukehart, Maly, and Peterman 1998). I focused on two major social institutions: a special tax-based benefits program and the neighborhood public schools. From the Village Heights homeowner's perspective, both institutions exemplify the failure of local government to provide basic public services to its constituents. One institution, the Benefits District, was created by residents as a neoliberal project to address a lack of services, and the other institution, the public schools, are completely avoided by middle class white parents and perceived as a failed institution.

While the Benefits District was created to address a perceived failure of governance, I found that the VHBD was mostly viewed by homeowners as a stabilizing force for the neighborhood. The VHBD helped the neighborhood retain current residents and attract new ones over time. However, homeowners did not agree on how community organizations should be run or the role organizations should play in the community. While all agreed that community organizations should exist to address quality of life issues in the neighborhood, not all agreed on whether organizations should be volunteer-based or quasi-governmental bodies, such as the VHBD. Those longtimers who were involved in the Benefit District's inception argued that the neighborhood's problems (such as crime and vacant housing) were simply too endemic for an all-volunteer community association to handle. The fact that most of the newcomers I interviewed were not involved in community associations speaks to this fear, as the old guard of volunteer activists is not being replaced. Newcomers object to paying the VHBD surtax for extra benefits, but many also claim that they would rather pay someone to maintain the neighborhood than see it decline. (Some also argued that their professions did not allow them the time to volunteer in the neighborhood themselves.) A few very active homeowners (almost all longtimers) were against the Benefits District. Their arguments against the program did not rely on an anti-taxation perspective, rather that this neoliberal program created boundaries between Village Heights and other needy neighborhoods, threatening race and class diversity in the neighborhood (through its economic development efforts). It addition, an anti-consumerist stance was taken – that unpaid residents should work collectively to improve neighborhood quality, not paid employees from outside the neighborhood. The Benefits District faces reauthorization in 2010. If the VHBD's current reorganization is deemed a success by Village Heights residents and local politicians, it may become an organizational example for other cities to copy throughout the United States.[6]

In contrast to the perception of the Benefits District, homeowners uniformly perceived the local public schools as a major barrier to racial and class integration in the neighborhood. The overwhelmingly negative perception of Baltimore City public schools informed middle-class homeowners' decisions on whether to send their children to the local public schools. For those white homeowners who chose to stay and raise children in the neighborhood, very few enrolled their children in the local schools. Instead, most enrolled their children in public schools in wealthier city school districts, or sent them to private or parochial schools. Almost all homeowners were aware that families moved out of the neighborhood to send their children to different public schools. Newcomers (who for the most part, did not yet have children) said that they would not be willing to send their children to local schools and that local schools were a barrier to staying in the neighborhood.

As has been argued in other studies of integrated neighborhoods (see Ferman, Single-ton, and DeMarco 1998; Goodwin 1979; Saltman 1990), segregated public schools are problematic for maintaining stable, integrated neighborhoods. First, if middle-class fami-lies are not willing to send their children to local schools, the schools and the students attending them do not benefit from the resources brought by middle-class students and families. In Baltimore, this also means that majority low-income schools remain racially segregated. Second, if middle-class families avoid integrated neighborhoods because of the segregated public schools, then integrated neighborhoods will hold two extreme popu-lations: elite families, who can afford to send their children to private schools, and low-income families, who have no choice but to send their children to the local public schools. This creates more stratification in the neighborhood and squeezes middle-income people out of the community. Lastly, if white parents who value racial integration are not willing to "walk the walk" by sending their children to the local school, then others will follow, making it impossible to create the critical mass necessary to desegregate a school. Many white parents argued they wanted racially diverse schools for their children, but they did not want their children to be in the numerical minority, or to be in a school that held mostly children from low-income backgrounds. As shown in the larger Village Heights study, this belief is congruent with the homeowners' lack of tolerance for socioeconomic diversity, rather than coming from a simply racist perspective.

To sum, the failure of city government institutions to provide services forces residents in urban neighborhoods to create their own privatized institutions, furthering the neolib-eral trend in urban governance (Dávila 2004; Hackworth 2007; Smith 2002). My research shows that these projects can assist in maintaining racial and economic stability if they are perceived to be effective by residents. However, privatization of public services can be highly contested by fellow residents if viewed as a "gating program" for keeping lower class residents out of the neighborhood. In contrast to the VHBD, the extremely negative perception of the public schools, oftentimes based on race and class, continues to serve as a barrier to full racial integration in the neighborhood. Rather than responding to institu-tional failure through collective action, parents make individual decisions regarding exit (moving out of the neighborhood) or avoidance (sending their children to private school). In both institutional arenas, the failure of local government to address residents' quality of life concerns is a serious detriment to supporting the continuation of racially integrated and economically mixed stable neighborhoods.

Endnotes

[1]This is a pseudonym, as are the names of all neighborhoods, businesses, social institutions, and residents in this study, to protect the subjects' anonymity.

[2]The surtax has since been lowered to 12 cents per 100 dollars of property assessment.

[3]The Board of Directors of the VHBD consists of one voting member appointed by the Mayor, seven voting members from community organizations, six voting members from business organizations, five at-large voting members from the neighborhood, four non-voting members from neighborhood associations bordering the district, and two non-voting members from various non-profit organizations within the district.

[4]I use the term neoliberal for the VHBD because it is a quasi-public/private entity. It was not a term used by interviewees.

[5]When asked to list their top three concerns about the neighborhood, crime (personal and property), trash (or other lack of services), and local schools were mentioned most often by homeowners (in order of frequency).

[6]In 1996, Baltimore City approved the Midtown Benefits District. In 2004, San Francisco adopted a Community Benefit District (CBD) Ordinance, allowing communities within that city to form CBDs.

References

Abrahamson, Julia. 1959. *A Neighborhood Finds Itself*. New York: Harper & Brothers, Publishers.

Andersen, Elijah. 1990. *Streetwise: Race, Class, and Change in an Urban Community*. Chicago: University of Chicago Press.

Baltimore City Public Schools. 2007. *Baltimore City Public School System Comprehensive School Profile Report*. Retrieved February 20, 2007. (www.baltimorecityschools.org).

Berrey, Ellen C. 2005. "Divided over Diversity: Political Discourse in a Chicago Neighborhood." *City & Community* 4:143–70.

Dávila, Arlene. 2004. *Barrio Dreams: Puerto Ricans, Latinos, and the Neoliberal City*. Berkeley, CA: University of California Press.

DeSena, Judith N. 2006. "What's a Mother to Do?' Gentrification, School Selection, and the Consequences for Community Cohesion." *American Behavioral Scientist* 50: 241–57.

Ellen, Ingrid Gould. 2000. *Sharing America's Neighborhoods: The Prospects for Stable Racial Integration*. Cambridge, MA: Harvard University Press.

Ferman, Barbara, Theresa Singleton, and Don DeMarco. 1998. "West Mount Airy, Philadelphia." *Cityscape: A Journal of Policy Development and Research* 4: 29–59.

Goode, Judith. 2001. "Let's Get Our Act Together: How Racial Discourses Disrupt Neighborhood Activism." Pp. 364–92 in *The New Poverty Studies: The Ethnography of Power, Politics, and Impoverished People in the United States*, edited by Judith Goode and Jeff Maskovsky. New York, NY: New York University Press.

Goodwin, Carole. 1979. *The Oak Park Strategy: Community Control of Racial Change*. Chicago: University of Chicago Press.

Hackworth, Jason. 2007. *The Neoliberal City: Governance, Ideology, and Development in American Urbanism*. Ithaca, NY: Cornell University Press.

Harvey, David. 2005. *A Brief History of Neoliberalism*. Oxford, UK: Oxford University Press.

Hodge, David, C. 1980. "Inner-City Revitalization as a Challenge to Diversity?: Seattle." Pp. 187–203 in *Back to the City: Issues in Neighborhood Renovation*, edited by Shirley Bradway Laska and Daphne Spain. Elmsford, NY: Pergamon Press, Inc.

Johns Hopkins University. 2007. *Historical Census for Baltimore City*. Baltimore, MD: Government Public Library of Johns Hopkins University. Retrieved January 4, 2007. (http://webapps.jhu.edu/census).

Live Baltimore. 2007. *Home Center Home Sales Statistics*. Baltimore, MD. Retrieved January 4, 2007. (www.livebaltimore.com/nb/hs/).

Maryland State Department of Education. 2006. *Maryland Report Card*. Retrieved January 25, 2007. (http://www.mdreportcard.org/inidex.aspx).

Massey, Douglas and Nancy Denton. 1993. *American Apartheid: Segregation and the Making of the Underclass*. Cambridge, MA: Harvard University Press.

Molotch, Harvey Luskin. 1972. *Managed Integration: Dilemmas of Doing Good in the City*. Berkeley, CA: University of California Press.

Montgomery, Alesia F. 2006. "Living in Each Other's Pockets: The Navigation of Social Distances by Middle Class Families in Los Angeles." *City & Community* 5: 425–50.

Nyden, Philip, John Lukehart, Michael T. Maly, and William Peterman. 1998. "Neighborhood Racial and Ethnic Diversity in U.S. Cities." *Cityscape: A Journal of Policy Development and Research* 4: 1–269.

Orfield, Gary and John T. Yun. 1999. *Resegregation in American Schools*. Cambridge, MA: The Civil Rights Project, Harvard University.

Pattillo, Mary. 2007. *Black on the Block: The Politics of Race and Class in the City*. Chicago: University of Chicago Press.

Saltman, Juliet. 1990. *A Fragile Moment: The Struggle for Neighborhood Stabilization*. Westport, CT: Greenwood Press.

Smith, Neil. 2002. "New Globalism, New Urbanism: Gentrification as Global Urban Strategy." Pp. 80–103 in *Spaces of Neoliberalism: Urban Restructuring in North America and Western Europe*, edited by Neil Brenner and Nik Theodore. Oxford, UK: Blackwell Publishing.

Smith, Richard A. 1993. "Creating Stable Racially Integrated Communities: A Review." *Journal of Urban Affairs* 15: 115–40.

Stoecker, Randy. 1994. *Defending Community: The Struggle for Alternative Redevelopment in Cedar-Riverside*. Philadelphia, PA: Temple University Press.

Strauss, Anselm, and Juliet Corbin. 1998. *Basics of Qualitative Research: Techniques and Procedures for Developing Grounded Theory*, 2nd ed. Thousand Oaks, CA: Sage Press.

Taub, Richard P., D. Garth Taylor, and Jan D. Dunham. 1984. *Paths of Neighborhood Change: Race and Crime in Urban America*. Chicago: University of Chicago Press.

U.S. Census Bureau. 2000. *Census 2000 Summary Files*. Retrieved January 4, 2007. (www.census.gov).

APPENDIX

TABLE 1   Selected Demographic Information on Village Heights by Census Tract*

	Tract 1001 North Side of Village Heights and Ebett; ("the heart")	Tract 1002 East Side of Village Heights and Grantley	Tract 1003 West and South Village Heights
Total Population**	8,502	3,846	2,857
Race			
White (%)	64.4	26.7	37.5
Black (%)	12.4	68.3	47.0
Asian (%)	18.2	2.6	11.1
Median Family Income by Race			
MEI White	$51,563	$75,326	$63,000
MEI Black	$29,750	$27,902	$33,462
MEI Asian	$14,904	$22,344	$9,688
Home Ownership by Race			
White (%)	23.9	29.2	18.9
Black (%)	18.3	34.7	4.4
Asian (%)	8.5	1.8	8.0
Level of Education 25 yrs old+			
Less than HS (%)	3.8	30.2	36.9
HS Degree (%)	12.4	21.1	18.8
Some college to AA degree (%)	19.7	19.6	18.3
BA/BS Degree (%)	26.0	15.8	13.9
Graduate Degree (%)	38.1	13.3	12.2

*Tract numbers do not reflect the true census tract numbers for the Village Heights area.

**Because census tracts do not match VHBD boundaries, this table includes some population outside of Village Heights.

Source: *Census 2000 Summary File 1 and File 3*, U.S. Census Bureau (2000) (www.census.gov).

A Right to the City?
Race, Class, and Neoliberalism in
Post-Katrina New Orleans[*]

John Arena

*I think we have a clean sheet to start again. And with that clean sheet we have
some very big opportunities.*

—Real Estate Developer Joseph Canizaro, September 29, 2005

*Joe Canizaro, I don't know you, but I hate you. I'm going to suit up like I'm
going to Iraq and fight this.*

—Black Homeowner Harvey Bender, January 10, 2006

When rights conflict (as they inevitably do) force decides.

—Don Mitchell (2003:22)

Academics and political activists have increasingly, over the last decade, employed the
concept of a "right to the city," drawn from the work of the late French theorist Henri
Lefebvre (1968), to frame their critique of, and galvanize opposition to, the inequalities
and injustices of contemporary cities. In the academic world, for example, scores of recent
journal articles employ the concept in their title, and many more in their substantive analyses, while geographer Don Mitchell (2003) wrote a book by the same name. In 2007 a
collection of community organizations across the U.S. formed the *Right to the City* coalition—with advice and support from academics influenced by Lefebvre's work—to more
effectively fight against neoliberalism and "for housing, health care, public space... and
to build an alternative for our cities" (RTC 2009). A collective right to the city provision
was even included in the Brazilian Constitution in 2001 and out of the global Social Forum
movement a *World Charter for the Right to the City* has emerged (Harvey 2008).

The increasing use of this social scientific concept, and political slogan, coincides,
unsurprisingly, with the deepening of the neoliberal political and economic model that has

---

[*]John Arena, "A Right to the City?: Race, Class, and Neoliberalism in Post-Katrina New Orleans." Unpublished
2010. Printed with permission of the author.

effectively denied a right to the city to large segments of the working class. Neoliberalism, which emerges in the 1970s, is best understood as a response by ruling classes around the world to the increasing challenges to their rule that emerged in the post-World War II era, and that crystallized in the powerful labor, student, and guerrilla-insurgencies of the 1960s. As part of an effort to reassert their power and profits ruling classes, to various degrees, began, in the 1970s, abandoning the class-compromises embedded in the post-World War II Keynesian welfare state. While these reforms were unevenly applied across the world capitalist system, including within the core capitalist countries, they did provide some real material concessions and protections from the capitalist market. In place of the welfare state, or what Harvey (2005) has termed "embedded liberalism", the "neoliberal model" of privatizing public services, deregulating corporate activity, breaking the power of labor unions, and increasing the power of finance capital has taken hold over the last several decades. Urban communities, Neil Brenner and Nik Theodore argue, have been especially hard hit by this agenda, as cities have become "a key arena in which the everyday violence of neoliberalism has been unleashed" (2002: ix). In the U.S., the concrete manifestations of this violence—both structural and direct—have included the destruction of public housing and other forms of gentrification that displace low-income and minority communities from long established neighborhoods; the provision of government subsidies for high-end shopping centers and tourist attractions, while educational and social services are underfunded; to beefed up police forces and expanded use of confrontational, "zero-tolerance" policing techniques. Thus, urban neoliberalism represents, in effect, an effort by urban elites to reassert *their* right to the city, part of what Neil Smith (1996) calls the "revanchist" agenda of "taking back" the city from poor and working class communities, particularly racial minorities, immigrants and other vulnerable segments of the population. Thus, the right to the city is really about *class struggle and the city*; a struggle about who can and cannot be there, about who can and cannot shape and design the city; a struggle between contradictory, class-specific "human rights"—and, as Mitchell (2003) emphasizes, when rights conflict, force decides.

In this study I examine the competing and conflicting "right to the city" struggles that unfolded in a post-disaster context, that of post-Hurricane Katrina New Orleans. Before the storm struck on August 29, 2005, New Orleans was a city of approximately 465,000, with almost 70% of its residents being African-American. The city was run by what Adolph Reed (1999) calls a "black urban regime" form of government, in which a black political elite controlled the mayor and other top political positions, and ruled in alliance with largely white-controlled corporations. While having their differences, the city's political and economic elite were in general agreement over imposing a neoliberal development agenda that disadvantaged the city's black working class majority. At the same time, while supporting the regressive neoliberal agenda, the black political elite relied on the black working class for electoral support and legitimacy. The contradictory relationship at the heart of the black urban regime, and various grassroots, "right to the city" struggles that exposed these contradictions, such as the 1998 unionization campaign of city workers and the successful 2005 effort to block the privatization of New Orleans' Iberville Public Housing development, placed constraints and obstacles to fully imposing the neoliberal agenda. Hurricane Katrina, and the forced evacuation of the majority of the population, created a new "opportunity structure" for the city's white economic elite to reassert, to "reclaim" *their* city, and reassess their three decade long political sub-contracting relationship with the black political class. What follows is an examination of how the white corporate elite perceived and assessed these new political and demographic conditions, and what actions they took to place their imprint on the city. Conversely, I highlight how working class New Orleanians, particularly the city's black working class majority, worked to challenge this agenda and assert their right to the city. Two key expressions of this conflict examined below are the rebuilding of neighborhoods and reestablishing public services. The first case addresses how the *Bring New Orleans Back Commission*, an elite body appointed by the city's African-American Mayor, Ray Nagin, attempted to prevent the rebuilding of mainly black neighborhoods and "shrink the footprint" of the city. The second set of cases documents how political and economic elites were able to combine pre-storm privatization efforts, with post-storm political opportunities, to carry out a domestic version of "shock therapy" by rapidly dismantling and privatizing public schools, hospitals and housing. I conclude with an overview of the resistance to privatization and the weaknesses that prevented working class people from effectively asserting their right to the city.

Right to Return vs. Right to Exclude "Planning" and the Bring New Orleans Back Commission

The first key initiative taken by the local elite, following the forced evacuation and continuing displacement of most of the city's residents, was to have Mayor Ray Nagin create the "Bring New Orleans Back Commission" (BNOBC) in late September 2005. The origins of the BNOBC began in the post-Katrina conversations among forty or so powerful business leaders centered in the New Orleans Business Council, including investor James Reiss, and the city's wealthiest and most politically influential real estate developer, Joseph Canizaro (Cooper 2005; Cecil 2009: 44–47). In the immediate aftermath of the storm hundreds of thousands of New Orleanians and Gulf Coast residents were frantically looking for housing, tracking down loved ones, figuring out how to register for aid from FEMA, and dealing with psychological trauma. In contrast, many business, political, and civic elites were both celebrating the displacement—the "clean sheet"— wrought by the storm and forced evacuation, and assessing, as Canizaro termed it, the "big opportunities" now at hand. The celebratory mood is best captured by the comments of Baton Rouge Republican Congressmen Richard Baker, who exclaimed after the storm, "We couldn't clean up Public Housing in New Orleans. We couldn't do it, but God could", referring to the forced evacuation and closing of the city's Public Housing developments after Katrina (Cited in Babbington 2005: 4). In a host of other commentary, elites touted the opportunities created by the storm, while, at times, acknowledging its social costs. The thoughts shared by former New Orleans City Planning Director Kristina Ford graphically exemplified the thinly veiled attempts to mask the enthusiasm in which she and others greeted the effects of Katrina. Ford lamented that New Orleans was presented with a "*horrible opportunity* because of the destruction that caused it and the lives that are being blasted apart." Nonetheless, she emphasizes, the disruption wrought by the storm, "offers a chance to think about things that in the past were unthinkable".[1] In a similar vein, Judah Hertz, of the Hertz Investment Group, the largest owner of commercial real estate in the New Orleans Central Business District, acknowledged less than two weeks after the storm that there had been a "terrible tragedy", but that "it's a chance to rise like a Phoenix, and rebuild like never before…this is an urban planners' dream" (Thomas 2005).

In effect, political and economic elites were advocating and articulating, in their various public pronouncements, a theory of elite political intervention and urban change, what activist-writer Naomi Klein (2007) has termed, in her book by the same name, "the shock doctrine". That is, from the perspective of the politically active wing of the local—and national—capitalist class, and their organic intellectuals, the "window of opportunity" had to be seized. The natural and politically-produced destruction and forced evacuation of the majority of New Orleans residents, particularly poor and black working class communities, should be used to implement, or at least deepen, a "disaster capitalist," neoliberal agenda. In contrast to the free market ideology of neoliberalism,[2] the shock doctrine calls for employing state power to seize the opportunity of a physically displaced and disoriented working class to dramatically push forward the neoliberal agenda of "dismantle[ing]… assistance for labor and the poor and increase[ing]… assistance for capital" (Purcell 2008:15). A disaster creates the ideal opportunity to both "roll back" (Peck and Tidwell 2002), as part of the "destructive" (Brenner and Theodore 2002) phase of neoliberalism, any constraints or impediments on the exercise of a capitalist "right to the city", and to "roll out" the "creative" stage of the process where the ideal "neoliberal city", that embodies the freedom of capital, is constructed. Key BNOBC member James Reiss, in a pronouncement to the *Wall Street Journal* only nine days after Hurricane Katrina hit the city, underscores the need—and the right—of elites to envision, lead, and carry out this thoroughgoing reconstruction.

> Those who want to see this city rebuilt want to see it done in a completely different way: demographically, geographically and politically. I'm not just speaking for myself here. The way we've been living is not going to happen again, or we're out (Cooper 2005).

In a pivotal September 10th meeting Reiss, and a group of overwhelmingly wealthy white businessman associated with the New Orleans Business Council, met with Mayor Ray Nagin in Dallas, where he had moved his family, to explain to the city's titular head what needed to be done. While developer Joseph Canizaro, a personal friend of President Bush who attained the rank of "Ranger" in the 2004 Bush reelection campaign for having raised over $200,000, did not attend the Dallas meeting, he was clearly, as one prominent business leader observed, "the prime mover on this thing" (the creation of the BNOBC). Underscoring the critical power Canizaro wielded in the BNOBC's formation, the Mayor interrupted the September 10th meeting to take a call from the developer who was relaxing at his home in Utah. "It was an incredible thing to witness," one participant in the Dallas meeting commented, "The Mayor stood there on the phone nodding and jotting down notes, as if Joe were passing on bullet points directly for the President."[3] Shortly after this meeting, the Mayor announced, on September 30th, the formation of the Bring New Orleans Back Commission (BNOBC).

The BNOBC, composed of a 17-person commission, was, on the surface, a "diverse," racially representative body, with eight African-Americans, one Hispanic, and seven whites composing the board, while only two, including the co-chair, Barbara Major, were women, and no representative from organized labor was included.[4] Canizaro emphasized the need for racial inclusivity arguing that, "we in the business community must realize that we need to work with the balance of the community, particularly our African-American associates, to help develop a plan for the revival of the city" (Rivlin 2005). Canizaro had learned the value of these partnerships. In the 1990s, in collaboration with community organizer Barbara Major—who, unsurprisingly, was named the BNOBC's co-chair—Canizaro successfully gained the trust of the St. Thomas Public Housing development tenant leaders to agree to a privatization and downsizing plan developed by the a real estate think-tank, the Urban Land Institute, of which he had been a past president. This agreement, which eventually resulted in reducing the number of Public Housing apartments from 1500, to under 200, and fueled gentrification in the surrounding area, was crucial to increasing the value of his adjacent, riverfront property (Arena 2007a). The inter-racial alliance Canizaro forged helped traverse this potentially politically explosive endeavor—displacing a poor black community in a majority African-American city to increase the property value of land owned by a white developer. In 2002, Major and Canizaro built on their success at St. Thomas, by teaming up to help forge the *Committee for a Better New Orleans* (CBNO), a forerunner of the BNOBC, designed to bring black and white business and civic leaders together to develop plans and popular consensus for pro-business reforms in the city.

With the "opportunities" created by Katrina, Canizaro and the BNOBC set out to undertake a dramatic restructuring of the city that would have been impossible under the normal conditions within which the CBNO had operated. The backing the BNOBC received from President Bush, who dined with commission members in early October, and lauded their efforts, underscored the power they wielded and encouraged the body to undertake "bold" initiatives. Reflecting the ambitious aims of the BNOBC, which was incorporated as a non-profit, the commission's work was broken up into seven different committees (and subcommittees within them), with each-one headed by a BNOBC member: Education (Scott Cowen), Urban Planning (Joseph Canizaro), Infrastructure (James Reiss), Economic Development (Dan Packer), Social Services (Kim Boyle), Cultural (Cesar Burgos), Governmental Efficiency (Gary Solomon). The work of these committees would be brought together in a "Master Plan to advise, assist, and plan...the rebuilding of New Orleans", with the blueprint being presented to the Mayor for implementation in three months (BNOBC 2005). Thus, this non-elected group, which was not representative of the *class* make-up of the city, and in the context of most of the former 465,000 residents still displaced, was given considerable power to develop a blue-print for thoroughly restructuring New Orleans. In effect, the redevelopment plan was being privatized, awarded to a business-dominated, "public-private partnership," of non-elected officials, while the elected, deliberative, official bodies of American democracy, such as the city council, that allow for greater democratic input, were marginalized. These undemocratic features of post-Katrina planning are representative, David Harvey argues in his study of neoliberalism, of how neoliberal reform and restructuring are implemented. "Neoliberals", Harvey points out, tend to be "profoundly suspicious of democracy", and generally

> favor governance by experts and elites. A strong preference exists for government by executive order and by judicial decision rather than democratic and parliamentary decision-making. *Neoliberals tend to prefer to insulate key institutions... from democratic pressures* (2005: 66).

Indeed key leaders of the BNOBC placed upmost importance in protecting their deliberations from unwelcome, democratic, "populist" intrusions. The power bloc within the BNOBC, centered around the five white members of the New Orleans Business Council and, it appears, two black members, utility executive Dan Packer and banker Alden McDonald (see footnote #4), chafed that the "the open format of the meetings"—they were public hearings and broadcast on the local public access station—"discourages an honest debate over tough issues of race and class" (Rivlin 2005a). As Canizaro lamented, "if my fellow commissioners keep throwing out motions on the floor that we pass without any discussion, just to gain applause, it's just not going to work." In a similar vein Tulane University president Scott Cowen complained that "members of the commission are start-ing to use the meetings to cater to certain constituencies and stakeholder groups that they know are watching" (Rivlin 2005a). To contain the negative impact of "grandstanding", the commission's power bloc met regularly in private lunch meetings to develop a common position and project a united front at the BNOBC's meetings. The BNOBC's neoliberal modus operandi of creating "patterns of negotiations that incorporate business into gover-nance through closed and sometimes secretive negotiations" (Harvey 2005: 77), did face some challenges from elected officials, incensed over being locked out of secret meetings, such as the gathering in Dallas (Travis 2005). Nevertheless, as Mike Davis (2006) com-mented on the developments in the first few months after Katrina, "elected black officials protest[ed] impotently from the sidelines [while] a largely white elite has wrested control over the debate about how to rebuild the city." Rather than crusading legislators, it would take determined resistance of the displaced themselves to break through the anti-demo-cratic *cordon sanitaire* the BNOBC had constructed around its negotiations.

Downsizing the City

While all the BNOBC committees were dealing with issues central to the reconstruction of the city, the Urban Planning Committee, headed, unsurprisingly, by Canizaro, dealt with the immediate, and most politically volatile, issues of rebuilding flooded neighbor-hoods. "Whether all of the city's neighborhoods can or should be resettled... [was] the most contentious issue in play" in the immediate weeks and months after Katrina (Donze and Russell 2006). The position staked out and advocated by the BNOBC commission-ers, especially those within the power bloc, as well as important opinion makers, such as the *Times Picayune* newspaper, was that of "shrinking the footprint of the city," part of what New Orleans educator Lance Hill has called the racially and class-biased "exclu-sionary campaign." Proponents of downsizing presented various rationales—soil toxicity, continuing vulnerability to flooding, the three-decade long decline in the city's popula-tion, fiscal inability to support city services in sparsely re-settled neighborhoods, and/or lack of interest or financial ability for displaced residents to return—to justify eliminating "unviable" neighborhoods and converting them to other uses, such as flood plains to bet-ter protect the city. To further bolster the downsizing position, Canizaro and others cited studies by the Rand Corporation, and even those conducted by liberal, Brown University demographer and sociologist John Logan, that only 225,000 residents—about the half the pre-storm level—would be expected to return by August 2008, three years after the storm. Of course, any figure would be dependent on the type of government policies implemented to either facilitate or obstruct the return of the displaced. Nonetheless, the backers of the "smaller footprint" did not bother to contextualize these population assessments, but rather seized upon these "studies" to legitimate their position. A stream of articles in the local, and national press about the opportunities "under privileged" New Orleanians, particularly

African-Americans, were finding in the diaspora was used by "green space" advocates as further, sound, evidence of the need to downsize (Carr and Meitrodt 2005).

To receive "expert advice" on employing "best practices" in the reconstruction effort, the BNOBC contracted with the Urban Land Institute (ULI), the influential real estate industry think tank. The ULI was brought in, unsurprisingly, at the urging of Canizaro, who had been past president of the outfit, and contracted with them in 1993 to construct a redevelopment plan for the St. Thomas Public Housing project. These "land-use" experts came forward with a privatization and downsizing plan that—with help of community activist Barbara Major (and later BNOBC co-chair) —black public housing resident leaders supported as well (Arena 2007a). Thus, confident with their track record, in mid-October 2005, less than two weeks after the commissions' creation, the ULI agreed to assemble a fifty member consulting team, drawn from finance, government, real estate and planning, to advise the BNOBC.[5] On November 18, a little over a month after the ULI panel had been assembled, they delivered their preliminary recommendations. The committee's "most daring" proposal, according to *Times Picayune* reporter Martha Carr, called for "green spacing" a wide swath of the city, covering heavily flooded neighborhoods, and disproportionally black, such as New Orleans East and the Lower 9th ward. To carry out this agenda, the ULI called for the creation of a non-profit agency—the Crescent City Rebuilding Corporation—that would be in charge of all funds funneled to the city for rebuilding, with a primary responsibility being the buyout of properties in the green spaced areas. Furthermore, the agency would be awarded powers of eminent dominant to obtain properties of those that refused to voluntarily sell. Thus, far from the free-market principles of neoliberal theory, the ULI advocated the use of state power and funding to, like the BNOBC itself, create an unelected board, insulated from democratic pressure, to implement public policy.

The BNOBC members, and not only those from the Business Council, embraced these proposals as the type of "bold thinking" the city needed. BNOBC co-chair, and close Canizaro ally, Barbara Major lauded the ULI for their "bluntness" and "challenging us to make more difficult and controversial choices", such as blocking the return of people, disproportionally working class and black, to the city, a policy that violated international human rights accords the U.S. had signed (Carr 2005). In an interview with the magazine *Colorlines*, Major argued that policy makers must accept that many former residents would not return. In the context of efforts to green space the almost all-black 9th ward, and demolish public housing, Major lamented that "we fight to hold onto things that's no longer working" (Fernandez 2006). The "preliminary" report was an attempt by the BNOBC to test the political waters for the "smaller footprint" plan. City council members, and other elected officials, which although having a history of supporting pro-corporate neoliberal policies, were nonetheless more sensitive to democratic pressure, objected to preventing certain neighborhoods from rebuilding (Cecil 2009:71). Their opposition would stiffen as the public learned more about the BNOBC and ULI plans. Opponents included even BNOBC member, and city council president, Oliver Thomas, who weighed-in against the green spacing idea, by waving the bloody flag, announcing that "to fix this community, or that community, is not honoring the dead" (Russell and Donze 2006). Former Mayor, and National Urban League president, Marc Morial, also tapped into the growing outrage over the green spacing flooded neighborhoods by holding a mass meeting in New Orleans East in early January 2006, where he denounced the plan to overwhelming applause.

The smaller footprint plan did have its supporters. For example, the Bureau of Governmental Research (BGR), an outfit that emerged in the 1930s to oppose populist Huey Long under the guise of "good government", and whose leadership was drawn from the same demographic as the New Orleans Business Council, weighed-in for downsizing on the basis of fiscal constraints. The BGR position was provided with added academic gloss by Stephen Goldsmith, head of a major disseminator of neoliberal ideas—the Innovations in Government Program at Harvard University's Kennedy School of Government. Goldsmith, an advisor to the BNOBC's "governmental efficiency" committee, supported the ULI triage approach of focusing on only a few neighborhoods for rebuilding: "There's just no way for urban investment to work in city like New Orleans, even pre-Katrina, if you sprinkle investment everywhere…It's unfair to the community to pretend you can do everything, because you can't" (Russell and Donze 2006). The BGR and Harvard University positions are exemplary of the ideological tropes often introduced to justify neoliberal reforms; they fit within the "there is no alternative" genus of arguments popularized by the important neoliberal ideologue, former British Prime Minister, Margaret Thatcher. These experts presented their arguments for the racially and class discriminatory green spacing plan as, at best, "unfortunate," and yet inevitable and reasonable.

On January 11, 2006 over 500 people packed into a ballroom—while others had to stand in the hallway—at the Sheraton Hotel to hear the Joseph Canizaro-led Urban Planning committee present their proposals, which followed the general outline laid out by the ULI plan a month earlier. The city would place a moratorium on issuing building permits for four months during which time neighborhoods would have to demonstrate that at least half their pre-Katrina population planned to return. If neighborhoods did not reach the 50% threshold local authorities would designate them as "unviable" and slate them for green spacing. While neighborhoods would be given the opportunity to "prove their viability" the committee envisioned many would not. Indeed the commission issued a "green space map" where large green circles were placed on areas that were deemed unwise to rebuild. The six large green circles—representing future parks and other non-residential uses— were placed on the Lower 9th ward and other predominantly black neighborhoods while the white, upper—middle class, neighborhood of Lakeview, that was badly flooded, and actually had a lower elevation that the lower 9th ward, was not "green circled" and thus deemed viable. Finally, like the ULI plan, the committee proposed that a state created entity—now dubbed the Crescent City Recovery Corp.—"would oversee the expenditure of federal money…and the buying and selling and, in some cases, seizure of homes" (Cecil 2009:73; Russell and Donze 2006).

Opposition to the green spacing plans, which had been building, exploded as the BNOBC officially endorsed the idea. At the January 11th hearing a series of speakers rebuked the plan. The most memorable and forceful denunciation was from Harvey Bender, a black resident of New Orleans East and recently laid-off city worker—Mayor Nagin summarily fired 3,000, mostly black, city workers in October 2005. Bender shouted into the microphone, "Joe Canizaro, I don't know you, but I hate you. I'm going to suit up like I'm going to Iraq and fight this" (Rivlin 2006). A series of other speakers gave impassioned speeches against the committee's proposal to give neighborhoods four months to prove viability or face bulldozers. The growing movement against the green spacing plan was expressed three-days later at a special city council hearing—a body that came out against the BNOBC proposal a day after the raucous January 11 hearing. The budding movement was beginning to have an impact on Mayor Nagin, who until then had walked a middle line, neither endorsing nor opposing the plan. At the January 14 city council hearing a series of speakers, black and white, denounced the plan's violation of property rights, and some, as at the BNOBC hearing, raised threats of violence, such as white homeowner Alex Gerhold who warned that "I will sit in my front door with my shotgun," while others invoked the specter of civil unrest if they continued to face roadblocks to returning. Activist Malcolm Suber, with the Peoples' Hurricane Relief Fund, directed his ire at Canizaro, to overwhelming applause. Nagin who attended the meeting of over 500 people, began inching away from the BNOBC, explaining that he was "uncomfortable" with the four month moratorium, and that he would continue to issue building permits—although he did not rule out the idea of stopping construction (Donze 2006).

Popular pressure on the BNOBC and Mayor Nagin continued as a grass roots coalition organized to carry-on the tradition of starting the annual Martin Luther King (MLK) March, on January 16, from the overwhelmingly, black working class Lower 9th ward. The coalition, led by the public housing group C3/Hands Off Iberville, denounced the Mayor for abandoning the traditional route, arguing this was further evidence of his support for the BNOBC efforts to carry out what march organizer Mike Howells denounced as "ethnic and class cleansing"—the provocative concept that was increasingly being invoked to denounce the elite-led "reconstruction" plans.[6]

It was in this context of 1. growing grass roots opposition to the green spacing plan, and general discontent with the obstacles Katrina survivors, including homeowners, were facing, which was expressed at public forums; 2. competing political elites, such as the city council, and former Mayor Morial staking out positions against the BNOBC plan; 3. the grass roots-led MLK march, and others, condemning policies of "ethnic cleansing," that Mayor Nagin made his widely reported "Chocolate City" comment. At the city's official and truncated 2006 MLK march that culminated on the front-steps of City Hall, Nagin, after bashing black people for crime and out-of-wedlock childbirths, and invoking the standard conservative recipe of "self-help" solutions to social problems, exclaimed:

> We ask black people: it's time. It's time for us to come together. It's time for us to rebuild a New Orleans, the one that should be a chocolate New Orleans. And I don't care what people are saying Uptown or wherever they are. This city will be chocolate at the end of the day (Nagin 2006).

The call for a "chocolate New Orleans"—not his demeaning of black folks—generated widespread condemnation in the mainstream media as "reverse racism", as an effort to keep whites out of the city.[7] Yet, the significance of the speech was not the alleged expression of anti-white prejudice, but rather the window it provides for grasping the deep contradictions of the Nagin administration—and, more broadly, post-civil rights black urban politics— and how they are managed. The Mayor's rhetorical disregard for what "people are saying uptown" was a veiled reference to wealthy whites, and in particular, the BNOBC. It represented a politically inexpensive way to express his *independence*—even opposition—to his wealthy "governing coalition" partners that his electoral base was deeply suspicious of, but to which he was in fact closely associated. Conversely, his call for a "chocolate New Orleans" was to express *solidarity* with his black working and middle class "electoral coalition".[8] The speech was about appearing to serve his popular base, to help calm the political waters that had become even more unsettled following the BNOBC's endorsement of the green spacing plan, while still meeting the real needs of his governing partners. Nonetheless, while not yet opposing the green spacing idea, it was clear—following the outpouring of opposition to the plans indelibly connected to Joseph Canizaro—that he would have to deliver some real material concessions if he was to retain power and contain unrest. While not yet employing force to adjudicate between competing "rights", many were making clear they were prepared to defend their homes by any means.

At the same time Mayor Nagin was beginning to bend to mass pressure, there was a simultaneous stepped-up effort to generate support for the green spacing and other recommendations of the BNOBC; to portray them as "common sense", to construct what David Harvey (2005: 39) has called a "sense held in common". A key player in this effort was, unsurprisingly, the *Times Picayune* newspaper, a chief propagator of elite opinion.[9] The tenor of the paper's reporting had, since the storm, been sympathetic to the "smaller footprint" proposal, but its support became much more explicit following the announcement of the BNOBC's Urban Planning Committee's recommendations. Three of the papers most prominent columnists—Stephanie Grace, Jarvis Deberry, and James Gill—along with the paper's editorial board, came out in support of the buyout and green spacing plan. Grace's (2006) editorial was published January 12th—the day after the committee released its recommendations—while the other three appeared in the paper's Sunday, January 15th edition. The writers presented the proposals as "reasonable", with the editorial board (2006) arguing that "four months…should be long enough for citizens to determine whether they want to return to their neighborhoods and what they want their neighborhoods to include" while Deberry (2006) asserted that "many more people …would rather have money and an opportunity to locate to a less vulnerable spot." At the same time he dismissed as "sentimental attachment" the desire of those that wanted to rebuild their homes and communities, despite the flooding. Gill's (2006) venom was reserved, primarily, for the city council, who he lambasted as demagogic and irresponsible for opposing the plan, while portraying as delusional—clearly directed at African-American sentiment—those that argued the BNOBC plan was a "private land-grab scheme in the Lower 9th ward." Coverage over the ensuing weeks and months by the paper continued to portray the plan in a favorable light.

Professor Michael Cowan was another key "organic intellectual" in this textbook Gramscian attempt to construct the BNOBC downsizing plan as part of a hegemonic, widely accepted and internalized, "public opinion". Cowan, chairman of the City's Human Relations Commission, director of a literacy program at Loyola University, and advisor to Loyola's president, adhered to the "silver lining" interpretation of Katrina, seeing it as an opportunity to overcome the city's class and, particularly, racial divisions to forge a plan for the "common good". Emerging out of this analysis of New Orleans' [*black*] problem, Cowan formed a new post-Katrina organization, Common Good, which was designed to bring together civic, educational, religious, business, and even labor groups to cooperate in developing a new vision for the city. Critically, from Cowan's perspective, the new organization would help construct a more cordial, safe, public space where ideas could be discussed. In particular, Cowen criticized the "rage, suspicion, and polarization" that accompanied discussion of any public issue, in any public forum, from the school board debates on charter schools to his Human Relations Commission's hearings on police brutality (Nolan 2006a). He placed the blame on radicals that poisoned the environment and debate, and argued that those whose "views contribute to racial polarization" must be excluded from the discussions promoted by Common Good.[10]

On January 4, 2006, as part of the Common Good initiative, Cowan, along with Una Anderson, a school board member and major proponent of charter schools, and Ben Johnson of the Greater New Orleans Foundation, which funded Common Good, joined with twenty other non-profits in a press conference to express support for the BNOBC's all but announced plan to downsize the city. Cowan, and his Common Good outfit, also played a central role in organizing, along with BNOBC members Rev. Fred Luter and Archbishop Hughes, a group of religious leaders to also express their support for the BNOBC plans. The delegation employed a "there is no alternative argument" to justify support for the BNOBC initiatives, including the controversial green spacing plan, arguing that New Orleanians must "accept that much of the city is permanently gone" and encouraged "serious engagement with the proposed plan of Mayor Nagin's Bring New Orleans Back Commission" (Nolan 2006). Nonetheless, despite the best efforts of Common Good, and other outfits, such as the "good government" BGR, it was clear the tide was turning against the proposal. Popular mobilizations continued to denounce the plan. For example, when Governor Blanco and the newly formed, Louisiana Recovery Authority (LRA)—a state appointed agency which gained control of federal money distributed for recovery, especially rebuilding homes—made a tour of the city in early February, they were met by over 60 protestors in the lower 9th ward chanting "we're here to stay!" (Finch 2006). These and other protests forced Nagin to back off the green spacing plan and building moratorium. On January 22nd the Mayor publically rejected the moratorium on issuing building permits, and on March 21, in his official pronouncement on the BNOBC report, he discarded both the moratorium and the requirement that neighborhoods would have to show their viability, with at least 50% of the former residents prepared to return, before receiving city services (Filosa 2006; Eggler 2006).

The Silver Lining: Union Busting, Privatization, and Ethnic Cleansing

While popular protest defeated the BNOBC's "green spacing" plan, other efforts that effectively blocked the return of many people, disproportionally working class and African-American, did go through, effectively negating their right to the city. These measures included the $10 billion, primarily federally funded "Road Home" program, overseen through the State's Louisiana Recovery Authority (LRA), but which a private contractor, ICF International, administered (Hammer 2009; Road Home 2010). The program provided grants for *homeowners* to rebuild their dwellings, while providing no money for renters, who composed 53% of all pre-Katrina households, and 57% of African-American households (U.S. Census 2005). In addition, the formula used to make awards was based on the home's pre-Katrina assessed value, which did not take into consideration inflation since the last assessment, making it very difficult for the award to be sufficient enough to rebuild. Furthermore, due to historical and contemporary racist real estate and banking practices— such as red lining, predatory lending and "racial steering"—the value of black homes were undervalued compared to whites, presenting yet another layer of racial inequality embedded in the so-called Road Home program (Wise 2003).

In addition to the obstacles presented by the "Road Home" program, the systematic dismantling of public services—public schools, public health care, and public housing—represented a central method to deny a right to the city for a large section of the working class, particularly African-Americans. These three vital public services were all under attack pre-Katrina by local, state and national officials who pursued what Miller and Gleason (2008) call a similar "methodology" of privatization: "underfund public services, create an uproar and declare a crisis, claim that privatization can do the job better…break public control and divert public money to corporations and then raise prices." The displacement of the city's black working class majority removed a major political obstacle to a rapid and dramatic restructuring of public schools, hospitals and housing along privatized, neoliberal lines.

Before the storm the New Orleans' school system, like many urban schools, faced serious problems rooted in the racially and class-biased "uneven development" investment practices of corporations and governments and, in particular, the use of property taxes as the chief financing mechanism of public schools, which disadvantages poor urban and rural districts (Gotham 2003; Kozol 2005). With these deep structural problems, it is not surprising that enrollment in New Orleans schools plummeted, from 86,000 to 63,000 in the ten years prior to Hurricane Katrina, with a revolving door of 9 different interim or permanent superintendants during this same time period (AFT 2006). The system was also highly segregated by race and class, with most of the district's 3% of white students attending a handful of selective enrollment magnet schools, while many regular, open admission public schools were "failing,", albeit as measured by questionable standardized tests that the state and federal government were increasingly requiring districts to administer. The "solution" proffered and attempted by administrators, the state legislature, and local, corporate-run think tanks were neoliberal, "market friendly" reforms, such as school vouchers, charter schools, increased use of standardized tests as measures of success, and anti-democratic initiatives that took power away from elected school boards, increased those of state and school superintendants, and reduced public input at school board meetings. For example, in 2005, a year before the storm, the state superintendant imposed private contractors—Alvarez & Marsal, a New York "turnaround" firm whose track record included "cleaning up" the St. Louis system through cutting staff and closing schools—to take over the district's finances, and in 2004 the state legislature increased the power of the superintendent and drastically reduced that of the elected board (Rucker 2004; Thevenot 2005).

Therefore, when Hurricane Katrina hit, observers like *Wall Street Journal* columnist Brendan Miniter, saw it providing "A Silver Lining"—as he entitled his column a week after Katrina—to radically reform a "failing public school system". Miniter joined others, such as the Heritage Foundation, in demanding that state and federal authorities take advantage of the storm to convert the New Orleans public school system into a privately run charter system, which could then be rolled out as a model for the rest of the country. Federal, state, and most local officials largely agreed with the *Wall Street Journal*/Heritage Foundation analysis, and moved aggressively to institute a deeper neoliberal restructuring by building on the pre-Katrina foundation. On October 7th, 2005, after the U.S. Department of Education pledged $20 million to Louisiana solely for charter schools, Louisiana's Democratic Governor, Kathleen Blanco, issued an executive order eliminating the requirement that parents and faculty approve conversion of an existing public school, overseen by the local school board, to a privately-run charter school, as well as other impediments (AFT 2006). On the same day as the Governor signed the executive order, the New Orleans school board—after "weeks of high-level talks among officials in the offices of the governor, the state schools superintendent, the state board of education, and the Louisiana legislature", and under the direction of Alvarez & Marsal, the firm that controlled the district's

finances—voted to convert all 13 schools in the unflooded west bank of the city into charters, and abrogate the pre-existing union contract covering the entire workforce—teachers,
custodians and cafeteria workers (Gewertz 2005). While various conservative and liberals lauded these "reforms", attorney and public school activist Willie Zanders, expressing
widespread disapproval among the city's and district's African-American majority that had
been largely locked out of the debate, denounced the use of these disaster capitalism techniques, decrying that "While we're still counting bodies in New Orleans, you're giving
away the schools" (Ritea 2005).

The rapid transformation of the selective admission, magnet, Lusher elementary
school, which was located in a little-flooded section of uptown New Orleans, near Tulane
University, underscores how much of post-Katrina restructuring was built on infrastructure
laid before the storm. In 2004, the state legislature passed Act 193, which, among other
things, greatly increased the power of the superintendent vis-à-vis the elected school board.
The then superintendant, Anthony Amato, quickly took advantage of these powers to negotiate an agreement making Tulane University a "partner" with Lusher. This business-school
"partnering"—a form of privatization and key feature of neoliberal reform—was a long-
time goal of the university that would facilitate construction of a guaranteed admission policy for the children of faculty and administrators. As part of this new, formal partnership,
Tulane and Lusher principal Kathy Reidlinger, with the superintendant's support, pushed
to get board approval for the school's expansion to the junior and senior high school level.
Even before receiving the board's consent, they moved to appropriate an existing, open
admission, all-black school as its future site. Yet, these pre-Katrina Tulane-Lusher initiatives were stymied by the heated opposition of community activists that saw the expansion plan as only deepening the system's inegalitarian, neo-apartheid features (Bernofsky
2009a). The displacement of most of the city's 60,000-plus public school students and their
families, and the heading of the BNOBC education committee by Tulane President Scott
Cowen, placed the Tulane-Lusher team in a strategic position to push through their reform
plan that had become bogged down under the political encumbrances of pre-Katrina New
Orleans. In classic disaster capitalism form, Tulane-Lusher operatives quickly exploited the
opportunities created by a "clean slate". On September 14, while still meeting in the state-
capitol, Baton Rouge, the New Orleans school board approved Lusher's plan to reopen as
a charter school and partner with Tulane, and on October 28 the board gave the green light
to the school's commandeering of the almost all-black, low-income, Fortier High School
for its planned high school expansion, which would prioritize admission of children of full
time Tulane employees (later expanded to include Loyola, Xavier and Dillard Universities). As with the west bank schools, the charter conversion broke the existing collective
bargaining agreement with the United Teachers of New Orleans (UTNO) labor union, with
Tulane announcing that they would use non-union, uncertified, Teach for America Volunteers to work in the new school, rather than draw from the existing pool of existing
certified, but displaced, teachers.[11] With the 1,000 African-American Fortier students, and
many public school activists, displaced, the Lusher-Tulane consortium was able to avoid
the political obstacles that had blocked their expansion only a year before (AFT 2006: 26).

The most far reaching initiative in the remaking of New Orleans was taken by Democratic Governor Blanco in November 20005, when she signed Act 35, a sweeping measure
that led to the state takeover of 102 "failing" schools, out of a district total of 128 (Maggia
2005). Again, as with other measures, this move was not unprecedented: the rating system

to authorize a State takeover, and entity to administer the schools, had been erected before Katrina. Yet, after the storm, the Governor and state legislature dramatically expanded the number of schools that fit the "failing" category by employing a new formula, one that was targeted at large districts, that all but had New Orleans name on it.[12] The 102 schools—of which only a fraction were reopened—were to be run by the Recovery School District, an agency that the state board of education created in 2003 to take over "failing" schools, but which greatly expanded under the new legislation (RSD 2010). Like the above discussed charters, the RSD schools would not be "encumbered" by the New Orleans schools collective bargaining agreement with the United Teachers of New Orleans (UTNO), with the systems superintendant free to choose what teachers to hire, free of seniority rules (Maggi 2005a). The earlier decision to exclude RSD and Charter school workers from union representation culminated in a December 9th vote by the New Orleans schools board to fire the district's entire workforce of 7,500 teachers, nurses, custodians and cafeteria workers, which would take effect January 31, 2006.[13]

UTNO, and their president, Brenda Mitchell, had, like most teacher unions in the U.S., pursued a traditional business-unionism model of cooperation with management, and the Democratic Party. For example the union supported, in early 2005, before the storm, the privatization of the school board's finances by the Alvarez and Marsal firm—the same company that oversaw the dismantling of the school system and breaking the union contract (Thevenot 2005). Therefore UTNO was totally unprepared for the new post-Katrina political environment as their former "friends of labor" abandoned them. Underscoring the union bureaucracy's disorientation in the radically changed political environment, Mitchell (2010) lamented that "I could not believe what was going on. We had been working shoulder to shoulder with the State Superintendant [of schools, Cecil Picard]. We did not have an adversarial relationship [before the storm]." Yet, Mitchell soon realized that despite the union's willingness to do whatever was necessary to reopen the schools, including waiving provisions of the union contract, the state superintendent, Cecil Picard, the Democratic Governor, Kathleen Blanco, most of the state legislature, and the school board, made it clear that they no longer considered the union President and UTNO part of the team. As Mitchell ruefully acknowledged, "they had a plan in place, and they saw the union as an obstacle to that plan."

While unions were locked out and no-longer considered legitimate partners in the new, 21st century school system being blazed in post-Katrina New Orleans, a host of local and national foundations, non-profits and think tanks emerged to help fund and manage the new system. At the top of the chain are large foundations—Gates, Broad, Fisher Fund, and the Walton Family—who, as they have done nationally, provided financial, ideological, and political support, along with the locally-based Greater New Orleans Foundation, for a dramatic expansion of charter schools. Indeed, with the "remaking" of the school system, New Orleans had the largest percentage of students in charter schools of any district in the country (Simon 2007). At the mid-range level was the local "charter complex", a collection of privately run and funded organizations that oversee the new system, largely replacing the role of the former school board.[14] The final component of the system is a slew of for-profit and non-profit charter school operators. The non-profits include those established for a particular school, such as Lusher's, as well as national operators, including KIPP, Cosmos Foundation, and EdFutures, supported heavily by the Walton Foundation, while several for-profit companies, including Edison Schools, Mosaica, the Leona Group, have entered New Orleans' "emerging education market" (Ritea 2006; Simon 2007).

The top down formula used to restructure New Orleans schools after Katrina is a prime example of how the "stakeholders" of the former system—teachers, parents, and students—were denied their right to the city. That is, not only were they denied the right to access two basic human rights—education and work—but they were largely denied any democratic input in reorganizing that institution. As legal scholar, and social justice activist Bill Quigley (2007) observed, underscoring the undemocratic nature of the process, "a massive experiment [is] being performed on thousands of primarily African-American children in New Orleans," an experiment in which "no one asked the permission of the children. No one asked permission of their parents." The end product of this "experiment," as of the 2008–2009 school year, has been a two tiered, neo-apartheid "public" school system, one that includes only about two-thirds of the 128 schools, and half the students, that existed pre-Katrina. On one side are charter schools, most of which are selective admission, receive financial support from foundations, and enjoy, generally, newer facilities, more certified teachers, and smaller class sizes than the other half of the "experiment". In contrast, the second tier, RSD, open admission, "public" schools, made up almost entirely of low-income African-American students, do not receive supplemental funding from foundations, have many uncertified teachers, and operate out of sub-standard facilities, with some not even having working kitchens or water fountains. In a city where many students still suffer from psychological trauma associated with displacement, students at the John McDonogh High School protested, in 2007, against the school's "prison atmosphere," denouncing that there were more security guards than teachers.[15]

The post-Katrina closure of New Orleans' public hospital—Rev. Avery C. Alexander Charity Hospital—and the demolition 5,000 public housing apartments, across four developments, followed a pattern similar to the dismantlement of the public school system. New Orleans Charity hospital was part of the State's Charity system, established in the 1930s, and that by 2005 had 9 hospitals statewide. As with the public school system, the Governor and state legislature introduced several pieces of legislation in the decade before Katrina—with backing from the powerful health care industry lobby—that reduced the ability of the public to defend the system. For example, in 1997 the Governor and state legislature restructured the Charity Hospital system, placing it under the jurisdiction of Louisiana State University (LSU), and thereby ending its status as a self-standing agency with all major budgteing and programmatic decisions requiring approval by the state legislature. In 2003, Republican Governor Foster signed Act 906—based on recommendations of a 40-person commission dominated by private health care interests—further reducing democratic control over the Charity system by allowing LSU to discontinue various services, and make other budgetary and programmatic changes, without legislative approval. In addition, under the same measure, the ground breaking 1926 law making health care a right was "amended," allowing the Hospital to deny services to those that made over 200% of the poverty-line but had not paid for past services. These changes were part of making the hospital, "better able to compete in the marketplace," as State Senator Tom Schedler, sponsor of the legislation argued, further undermining and de-legitimating Charity's historic role of guaranteeing health care as a basic right. Between 2003 and 2005 Charity faced continued budget cuts and service reductions which threatened its ability to even pass accreditation (Moller 2003; 2003a; LSU 2003).

On September 4, 2005, five days after floodwaters inundated the basement of Charity Hospital, curtailing most back-up generator power, and the water and sanitation system, patients and most of the staff were evacuated. Over the next two weeks, from September 5–19, hospital staff, LSU and Tulane University residents, members of the Oklahoma National Guard and German engineers successfully drained floodwaters from the hospital's basement and cleaned debris and had mopped all the floors of the 21 story structure. Yet, on September 19, "with the first three floors ready for use, a half-dozen of the doctors said they were abruptly ordered out of Charity" by Donald Smithburg, the CEO of LSU's Health Care Division. With the full support of Governor Blanco, LSU moved to close Charity permanently, flouting the requirement that the state legislature must approve closure of any hospital in the Charity system, one of the few democratic controls that remained after the 2003 restructuring. At this point LSU and "CEO" Smithburg began arguing that the old building had to be abandoned, with their handpicked consulting firm arguing the hospital was 65% damaged, which was more than the 51% threshold set by the Federal Emergency Management Agency (FEMA) to fund a replacement.[16]

In place of outdated "Big Charity", with its quaint mission of serving the poor and uninsured, what was needed, according to CEO Smithburg, was a replacement hospital "with a new model, less reliant on public dollars", and a "new mission", focused on generating revenue. As a result of LSU's drive to establish a new "teaching" hospital, geared for research and not serving the poor, the agency even returned a $345 million advance grant from FEMA, money intended to reopen Charity (Maggi 2005). LSU then entered into a continuing legal battle with FEMA to get over $600 million, which authorities argue is needed to replace the hospital they claimed that was more than 50% damaged. The new, as of yet (2010) unbuilt hospital, would be part of a new "bio-medical complex" built away from the original site of Charity, and on a 67 acre residential neighborhood now occupied by many homeowners that returned and rebuilt their flood damaged homes (Save Charity Hospital 2010). The 67 acre site itself would be part of the larger Greater New Orleans BioSciences Economic Development District (GNOBEDD), established by the state legislature in 2005, with its own taxing and bonding power. Encompassing 1500 acres, the mission of GNOBEDD is "growing both the programmatic and physical development of the biosciences sector of the New Orleans economy." Instead of providing health care for the poor and uninsured, the new hospital would be part of a larger initiative to "encourage the bioscience industry to locate within the district… and build a globally competitive innovative economy" (New Orleans BioInnovations Center 2010). Thus, consistent with how neoliberal reforms operate, the State of Louisiana's role in health care did not disappear, but rather the mission changed, from meeting the needs of the poor and uninsured, to facilitating the profit-making ventures of the bio-medical industry. The neoliberal reform of the state denied not only the right to work for many Charity hospital employees—who were fired, like public school teachers—but also, with the closure of a public hospital that was the primary source of health care for 40% of the pre-Katrina population, a right to health care, and even life. Indeed, a study by City Health Director Dr. Kevin Stephens found that the New Orleans mortality rate for the first six months of 2006 was 47% higher than the pre-Katrina level, due, in great part, to the closure of Charity and the dearth of affordable health care (Stoddard 2007).

The third component of the post-Katrina assault on public services, and maybe the most well publicized, was the demolition of public housing, home to some 15,000 low-income New Orleanians, almost all African-Americans. The pre-Katrina downsizing of public housing (in New Orleans and across the country) was facilitated by the Clinton administration's (1992–2000) HOPE VI privatization program, and the ending, in 1995, of the "one for one" rule—embraced by then Mayor Marc Morial—that required the replacement of every demolished unit of public housing. With the "lifting" of this poor-peoples protection, and the elimination, in the same year, of a locally appointed board to oversee the city's Housing Authority of New Orleans (HANO), the structures were in place to massively downsize the system. Between 1995 and 2005 the number of units was cut in half, from over 14,000, to under 8,000 units. Following the storm, the Department of Housing and Urban Development (HUD)—having taken direct control of HANO in 2002—with the full support of the Nagin administration, closed five of the conventional developments, blocking the return of former residents. Authorities targeted the "projects"—sturdy brick structures built in the 1940s and 1950s—for immediate demolition even though they withstood the storm much better than most of the private housing stock, and served as hurricane protection for many poor, black families that could not evacuate. The dynamic public housing movement was able to force open the Iberville development, but four others—Laffite, C.J. Peete, St. Bernard, and most of B.W. Cooper—eventually met the wrecking ball. The use of force to adjudicate between competing rights was most dramatically expressed at the December 20, 2007 city council meeting where New Orleans police tasered, beat, pepper-sprayed and arrested demonstrators who attempted to register their opposition to demolition.[17]

Drawing Lessons from Post-Katrina New Orleans

The struggles unleashed in the aftermath of Katrina represent a dramatic case of the racialized— due to the way race is embedded in U.S. urban development—class struggle for the city. The ruling class, at a local, regional, and national level, carried out a concerted effort to exercise their right to the city, to restructure New Orleans along lines to advance their power and profits, a goal Harvey (20005) argues is the driving force behind the neoliberal restructuring agenda. The local ruling class, for example, through the BNOBC, pushed to create a whiter and wealthier New Orleans—to change the demographics, as James Reiss phrased it—that would better suit their needs. In another key terrain of the racialized class struggle, the ruling class, at all levels, moved aggressively to further the "neoliberalization" of public services. The dismantling of public schools, for example, *decreased* the power of workers, *increased* the power of corporations to shape how schools are organized and what type of labor power—future workers—is produced, and *expanded* areas of profit-making to sectors previously closed off.

Despite impressive gains, the ruling class initiative, as we saw, did not proceed unopposed. In fact, mass pressure, from homeowners and others, defeated the BNOBC's green spacing plan, designed to remake the demographics and politics of the city. Public Housing residents—the most stigmatized section of the New Orleans community—and their allies were able to mount a sustained social movement that reopened one development, kept the wrecking ball away from four others for over two years while they brought attention to the issue nationally and internationally, and effectively challenged the legitimacy of the "deconcentrating poverty" and other rationales invoked to legitimate demolishing public housing. The grassroots Committee to Reopen Charity Hospital has been the center of a campaign that has kept a powerful state and local-level "growth coalition" at bay for over four years in their effort to reopen Charity Hospital and stop the demolition of the lower mid-city neighborhood. Furthermore, the social movements have not simply been on the defensive but, like the ruling class, have used the storm to envision their own restructuring plan, to argue another city, country and world are possible. The deep racial and class inequality, and infrastructural decay, exposed by Katrina necessitates, "radical reconstructionists" argue, a "third reconstruction" (Morrison 2010). That is, racially and economically just reconstruction requires a massive, federally funded public works program—with direct government employment at prevailing wage—to rebuild public services and infrastructure in New Orleans, the entire Gulf Coast, and, eventually, throughout the entire country. A longer historical trajectory will be needed to assess whether the working class—such as Nicaragua and Mexico following earthquakes in 1972 and 1985, respectively, and even the Great flood of 1927 that devastated Louisiana and other states along the Mississippi River (see Barry 1997)—can fully exploit the political opportunities and mount a political challenge.

The findings of this study do indicate that to exploit the legitimacy crisis produced by ruling class' neoliberal reconstruction efforts, the radical reconstructionists will have to confront several ideological and organizational obstacles. The first impediment is what Howells and Arena (2009) call traditional or "neoliberal voluntarism." Foundations, non-profits and other components of what Jane Roelofs (2003: 22) terms the "protective layer of capitalism," captured and contained the genuine desire among many people, especially youth, to address the injustices Katrina unmasked. The idealism and energy of hundreds of thousands of volunteers that trekked to the region after Katrina was, largely, safely funneled into self-help non-profit projects that not only do not challenge, but in many ways abet the neoliberal agenda. What is needed, instead, is a "movement voluntarism" that connects volunteers with the social movements. A second trench that will need to be traversed is the business unionism "partnership" model, exemplified by, with some exceptions, the teacher union, as well as the "progressive" Service Employees International Union, AFL-CIO investors, and the building trade unions, who have all collaborated in the destruction of public services and communities in post-Katrina New Orleans, and hobbled any popular challenge (Arena 2007; Morrison 2010). Maybe most problematic are a variety of "radical", primarily post-Katrina, grassroots, non-profits, registered with the federal government as tax-exempt 501 (c) 3 organizations that subsist through grants from a variety of corporate foundations. These organizations, such as Safe Streets/Safe Communities, New Orleans Workers' Center for Racial Justice, Louisiana Justice Institute, ACORN, Common Ground Relief, Critical Resistance, and the disbanded Peoples Hurricane Relief Fund, often mouth radical discourse. Nonetheless, their funding from such entities as the Ford, Soros, and Rockefeller foundations, and government agencies like the Dept. of Housing and Urban Development (HUD), many of which are bankrolling neoliberal reform efforts, compromise these non-profits. For example, the well known community organization ACORN received millions of dollars from HUD after Katrina and, unsurprisingly, refused to particulate in the public housing movement (Howells 2009). The undemocratic, financially and politically compromised, non-profit model of organizing is a third critical obstacle that must be overcome before the working class in New Orleans, and across the country, can mount a challenge needed to reclaim their right to the city.

Endnotes

[1]Carr & Meitrodt 2005. The Carr and Meitrodt article includes other revealing comments, ranging from academics to developers. For an overview of celebratory comments, from U.S. Senator David Vitter to the American Enterprise Institute, see Arena 2007. For a searing critique of how liberal sociologists, and the Democratic Party-allied think tank, the Brookings Institution, framed and touted the "opportunities" created by Katrina, and how they could be exploited, see Reed and Steinberg 2006.

[2]See Harvey (2005: 70–81) and Brenner and Theodore (2002: 352) on the distinction between neoliberalism as an ideology and its actual implementation.

[3]Rivlin 2005. Reportedly there were three African-Americans who participated, Dan Packer, head of Entergy-New Orleans, renowned jazz musician Wynton Marsalis, who participated by speakerphone, and State Senator Derrick Shepherd, who was not invited, but had been tipped off about it by former Mayor Marc Morial's brother, Jacques, and encouraged to attend. For the most comprehensive analysis of the meeting to date, see Cecil 2009: 44–51.

[4]The African-American members included co-chair Barbara Major, head of a non-profit health clinic and close associate of Canizaro; Kim Boyle, an attorney with a powerful local law firm, Phelps Dunbar; Rev. Fred Luter, Pastor at Franklin Baptist Church; Wynton Marsalis, the renowned jazz musician; Aldon McDonald, President of the Black-owned Liberty Bank; Dan Packer, the head of the Entergy corporation's local utility operation; Anthony Patton, head of his own advertizing agency; David White, McDonald franchise owner and Nagin confidant; Oliver Thomas, city councilman; the Hispanic member was lawyer and real estate developer Cesar Burgos; the white members included Canizaro, a banker and developer, Boysie Bollinger, shipbuilder and major Republican donor, and Bush ally; Catholic Archbishop Alfred Hughes; James Reiss, an investor; Gary Solomon, CEO and Chairman of the Board of Crescent Bank and Trust, and "venture capitalist", involved in businesses, from daiquiri shops and restaurants to payday loan operations; Scott Cowen, President of Tulane University; co-chair Mel LaGarde, President and CEO of the Delta region of the Hospital Corporation of America. Canizaro, Solomon, Bollinger, Cowen, and Reiss were all members of the New Orleans Business Council, the most powerful business association in the city (BNOBC 2005).

[5]For more on the advisory committee's make-up, see Carr 2005; on funding, see ULI 2005.

[6]For evidence of the term's increasing use, and efforts to de-legitimate its application to describe—and denounce—developments in post-Katrina New Orleans, see Donze and Eggler 2005.

[7]For further critique of the "reverse racism" charge, and contextualization of the comments, see Arena 2006; Wise 2006; Cecil 2009: 79–94.

[8]In Nagin's first mayoral race he did not receive a majority of the black vote. Yet, with the changed demographics post-Katrina, and emerging white contenders, he would clearly need a majority of the black vote in the Spring 2006 election, especially as his former wealthy white backers began to abandon him (see Cecil 2009 on this latter development).

[9]For more on newspapers and other local media as central components of local, "pro-growth" coalitions, see Logan, Bridges, Crowder 1999.

[10]Contentious school board meetings raised particular resonance for Cowan, since his wife, Kathy Reidlinger—the principle of a selective admission elementary magnet school before the storm, that was, post-Katrina, converted into a semi-privatized charter school and expanded into a junior and high school—was a prime target of "polarizing" activists, such as Assata Olugbala and Albert "Chui" Clark.

[11]Tulane's central role in firing New Orleans public schools teachers and abrogating their union contract is consistent with how they treated their own workers in the wake of Katrina. The American Association of University Professors (AAUP) censored Tulane for lifting tenure, firing professors, and restructuring departments without faculty input—all of which violated the Faculty Handbook and other policy documents—as part of their post-Katrina restructuring plan, dubbed "Bold Renewal". The AAUP also castigated the University for failing to provide proof of "financial exigency" invoked by President Cowen and the board of trustees to justify layoffs and other "emergency measures" (Bernofsky 2009). In addition, the Belfor Corp., a politically connected firm contracted by the University for various repairs, was sued by the Southern Poverty Law Center for not paying workers, mostly immigrants, overtime pay while they labored at Tulane and other sites (SPLC 2006) . For further evidence of the Teach for America program displacing veteran teachers, see Toppo (2009).

[12]For a detailed outline of how the threshold of "failing schools" were lowered under the bill, and targeted the New Orleans district, see AFT 2006:13–15. Most of the African-American legislative delegation, except for State Senator Ann Duplessis, a Liberty Bank executive, whose boss was BNOBC member Alden McDonald, voted against the bill. Nonetheless, members of the delegation, such as Karen Carter and Edwin Murray, played key roles in passing pre-Katrina legislation enabling a state take-over of local schools.

[13]The firing was preceded by the board's placing of all workers on "disaster leave" without pay, on September 15. A lawsuit delayed the dismissal order until March 2006. The report by the Center for Community Change (2006) provides a detailed chronology of actions taken by state and local authorities to dismantle the New Orleans public schools.

[14]For an overview of the division of labor in the charter complex, including the central roles played by New Schools for New Orleans, New Leaders for New Schools, and The Cowen Institute for Public Education Initiatives, see New Schools for New Orleans 2010.

[15]New Schools New Leaders 2009; Quigley 2007. For more on the myriad of problems in the second tier RSD schools, see AFT 2006; Ritea 2007; Warner and Simon 2007. For evidence that Charter Schools perform better simply because they take the best students, and dump the rest into traditional public schools, see Van Lier 2009.

[16]Nossiter 2005; for a detailed chronology of events surrounding Charity Hospital, post-Katrina , see Ott 2007.

[17]For footage of the December 20, 2007 city council hearing, see YouTube 2007. Documentation on pre and post-Katrina Public Housing is taken from Arena 2010, 2007.

References

American Federation of Teachers (AFT). 2006. *National Model or Flawed Approach?: The Post-Katrina New Orleans Public Schools.* American Federation of Teachers. November.

Arena, J. 2006. "The Contradictions of Black Comprador Rule: Understanding Ray Nagin's Chocolate City Comment." *ZNET*. January.

_____. 2007. "Whose City Is It?: Public Housing, Public Sociology, and the Struggle for Social Justice in New Orleans Before and After Katrina," in *Through the Eye of Katrina: Social Justice in the United States*, Richelle Swan and Kristen Bates, eds. (Durham, NC: Carolina Academic Press).

_____. 2007a. *Winds of Change Before Katrina: New Orleans' Public Housing Struggles Within a Race, Class, and Gender Dialectic*. Ph.D. Dissertation, Tulane University.

_____2010. "Black and White, Unite and Fight?: Identity Politics and New Orleans Post-Katrina Public Housing Movement," in *Neoliberal Deluge: Hurricane Katrina, Late Capitalist Culture, and the Remaking of New Orleans*, Cedric Johnson, ed. (Minneapolis: University of Minnesota Press).

Babington, Charles. 2005. "Some GOP Legislators Hit Jarring Notes in Addressing Katrina." *Washington Post*. September 10, p. A4.

Barry, John. 1997. *Rising Tide* (New York: Simon and Shuster).

Bernofsky, Carl. 2009. "Tenure, Tulane Style." October. Available at: http://www.tulanelink.com/tulanelink/tenure_06a.htm.

_____. 2009a. "Lusher Charter Schools." October 6. Available at: http://www.tulanelink.com/tulanelink/decision_03d.htm#Lusher.

Brenner, Neil and Nik Theodore. 2002. *Spaces of Neoliberalism: Urban Restucturing in North America and Western Europe*. (Malden, MA: Blackwell).

Bring New Orleans Back Commission. 2005. "Commission Members." Available at: http://www.bringneworleansback.org/Commission_Members/.

Carr, Martha. 2005. "Experts to Give Ideas for New Orleans." *Times Picayune*. October 12.

Carr, Martha and Jeffrey Meitrodt. 2005. "What Will New Orleans Look like Five Years from Now?" *Times Picayune*. December 25, p. A1.

Cecil, Katherine. 2009. *Race, Representation, and Recovery: Documenting the 2006 New Orleans Mayoral Election*. Masters Thesis, University of New Orleans.

Center for Community Change. 2006. *Dismantling a Community*. Washington, D.C.

Cooper, C. 2005. "Old-line Families Plot the Future." *Wall Street Journal*. September 8, p. A1.

Davis, Mike. 2006. "Who is Killing New Orleans?" *The Nation*. April 10.

DeBerry, Jarvis. 2006. Buyout Offer Could Be Best Deal for Many." *Times Picayune*. January 15.

Donze, Frank and Gordon Russell. 2006. "Nagin Panel Says Hardest Hit Areas Must Prove Viability, City's Footprint May Shrink." *Times Picayune*. January 11, p. A1.

Donze, Frank and Bruce Eggler. 2005. "Nagin Not Ignited by Explosive Testimony." *Times Picayune*. December 17, P. B1.

Eggler, Bruce. 2006. "Nagin Accepts BNOB Blueprint; He, Panel in Tune Except on Land Use." *Times Picayune*, March 22, P. A1.

Fernandez, Daisey. 2006. "The Future of the Ninth Ward." *Colorlines*. Spring.

Filosa, Gwen. 2006. "Nagin Says He'll Oppose Building Moratorium." *Times Picayune*. January 22, p. A1.

Finch, Susan. 2006. 'Residents Rally in Lower 9." *Times Picayune*. February 7.

Gewertz, Catherine. 2005. "New Orleans Adopts Plan for Charters." *Education Week*. October 19.

Gill, James. 2006. "Twist and Pout." *Times Picayune*. January 15.

Gotham, Kevin. 2002. *Race, Real Estate, and Uneven Development: The Kansas City Experience, 1900–2000* (Albany: SUNY Press).

Grace, Stephanie. 2006. "Plan Is a Compromise, But It May Be Our Best Shot." *Times Picayune*. January 12.

Hammer, David. 2009. "Road Home Approves Rebuilding Extension." *Times Picayune*. August 21, p. A1.

Harvey, David. 2005. *A Brief History of Neoliberalism* (Oxford: Oxford University Press).

_____. 2008. "The Right to the City." *New Left Review* 53 (Sept-Oct): 23–40.

Howells, Mike. 2009. "ACORN, Public Housing, and Post-Katrina New Orleans: Defending Affordable Housing?" Available at: http://nyc.indymedia.org/en/2008/10/100672.html.

Howells, Mike and J. Arena. 2009. "Voluntarism Will Not Rebuild the Gulf Coast: Building a Political Movement Can." *Counterpunch*. July 30. Available at: http://www.counterpunch.org/howells07302009.html.

Klein, Naomi. 2007. *The Shock Doctrine. The Rise of Disaster Capitalism* (New York: Metropolitan Books).

Kozol, Jonathan. 2005. *Shame of the Nation: Restoration of Apartheid Schooling in America* (New York: Crown Publishers).

Lefebvre. Henri. 1968. *Le droit à la ville* (Paris: Anthopos).

Logan, John, Rachel Bridges Whaley, and Kyle Crowder. 1999. "The Character and Consequences of Growth Regimes: An Assessment of Twenty Years of Research," in *The Urban Growth Machine*, Andrew Jonas and David Wilson, eds. (Albany: SUNY Press).

LSU Health Sciences Center. 2003. *Annual Report*. Baton Rouge.

Maggi, Laura. 2005. "La. Agency Gives Back Much of FEMA Money." *Times Picayune*. September 27, p. A2.

_____. 2005a. "State to Run Orleans Schools; Local Board Loses Authority over 102." *Times Picayune*. November 23.

Miller, Steven and Jack Gerson. "The Corporate Surge Against Public Schools." *Universidad Publica*. Available at: http://firgoa.usc.es/drupal/node/39815.

Miniter, Brendan. 2005. "A Silver Lining?" *Wall Street Journal*. September 6.

Mitchell, Brenda. 2010. Interview by author. January 12.

Mitchell, Don. 2003. *The Right to the City: Social Justice and the Fight for Public Space* (New York: Guilford Press).

Moller, Jan. 2003."Charity Hospital Changes Approved." *Times Picayune*. May 29, p. A1.

_____. 2003a."Public Hospital Cuts Proposed." *Times Picayune*. July 30, p. A1.

Morrison, Derrick. 2010. "Post-Katrina New Orleans: A Third Reconstruction?" *Against the Current*. 144 (January-February).

Nagin, Ray. 2006. Transcript of Speech delivered at 2006 Martin Luther King Parade, New Orleans. Available at: http://www.nola.com/news/t-p/frontpage/index.ssf?/news/t-p/stories/011706_nagin_transcript.html.

New Orleans BioInnovation Center. 2010. "Greater New Orleans BioSciences Economic Development District." Available at: http://www.neworleansbio.com/gnobedd/index.html.

New Schools for New Orleans. 2009. "A Brief Overview of Public Education in New Orleans, 1995–2009." In possession of author.

_____. 2010. "Our Key Partners." Available at: http://www.newschoolsforneworleans.org/aboutus_keypartners.php#bes.

Nolan, Bruce. 2006. "Religious Leaders Urge Honest Talk on Recovery." *Times Picayune*. February 3, p. A1.

_____. 2006a. "Change is Mantra of Citizen Group." *Times Picayune*. February 12, p. A1.

Nossiter, Adam. 2005. "Dispute Over Historic Hospital for the Poor Pits Doctors Against the State. *New York Times*. December 17, p. A19.

Ott, Brad. 2007. "Avery C. Alexander Charity Hospital in New Orleans." In possession of author.

Peck, J. and A. Tickwell. (2002). "Neoliberalizing Space." *Antipode*, 34 (3): 380–404.

Powell, Alan. 2006. "New Charter Schools Get Help from Grant." *Times Picayune*. June 13.

Purcell, Mark. 2008. *Recapturing Democracy* (New York: Routledge).

Quigley, Bill. 2007. "New Orleans Children Fighting for the Right to Learn." *Truthout.* August 9, 2007. Available at: http://www.truthout.org/article/bill-quigley-part-i-new-orleanss-children-fighting-right-learn.

Recovery School District. 2010. "Frequently Asked Questions." Available at: http://www.rsdla.net/InfoGlance/FAQs.aspx.

Reed, Adolph. 1999. *Stirrings in the Jug: Black Politics in the Post-Segregation Era* (London: University of Minnesota Press).

Reed, A. and S. Steinberg, S. (2006). "Liberal Bad Faith in the Wake of Hurricane Katrina." *ZNET.* May 4. Available at: http://www.zmag.org/content/showarticle.cfm?ItemID=10205.

Right to the City (RTC). 2009. "Our History." Available at: http://www.righttothecity.org/our-history.html.

Ritea, Steve. 2005. "Orleans Board Makes 13 Schools Charters." *Times Picayune*. October 8, p. 1B.

_____. 2006. "Charter School Bids Flow In." *Times Picayune*. December 23, p. A1.

_____. 2007. Left Behind?" *Times Picayune*, April 30, p. A1.

Rivlin, Gary. 2005. "A Mogul Who Would Rebuild New Orleans." *New York Times*. September 28, p. A1.

_____. 2005a. "Divisions Appear within a Storm Recovery Commission." *New York Times*. October 30, p. A29.

_____. 2006. "Anger Meets New Orleans Renewal Plan." *New York Times*. January 12.

Road Home. 2010. "The Homeowners Assistance Program, Week 184 Situation & Pipeline Report." Road Home. January 1. Available at: http://www.road2la.org/.

Roelofs, Joan. 2003. *Foundations and Public Policy: The Mask of Pluralism* (Albany: State University of New York Press).

Rucker, Philip. 2004. "Bill Gives Schools Chief Uncommon Clout." *Times Picayune*. June 9, p.A1.

Russell, Gordon and Frank Donze. 2006. "Officials Tiptoe Around Footprint Issue." *Times Picayune*. January 8, p. A1.

_____. 2006a. "Rebuilding Proposal Gets Mixed Reception." *Times Picayune*. January 12, p. A1.

Save Charity Hospital. 2010. "Review the Plans." Available at: http://www.savecharityhospital.com/content/review-plans.

Simon, Darran. 2007. "Eight New Charters Endorsed for N.O." *Times Picayune*. December 4, p. A1.

Smith, Neil. 1996. *The New Urban Frontier: Gentrification and the Revanchist City* (New York: Routledge).

Stoddard, Ed. 2007. "Post Katrina Death Rate Shoots Up." *Reuters News Service*. June 22. Available at: http://www.reuters.com/article/idUSN2139658520070622.

Southern Poverty Law Center (SPLC). 2006. "Rodrigues et al. vs. Belfor USA Group Inc." February 1. Available at: http://www.splcenter.org/legal/docket/files.jsp?cdrID=53&sortID=4.

Thevenot, Brian. 2005. "La. Asks N.O. School Board to Cede Reins." *Times Picayune*. April 8, p. A1.

Thomas, Greg. 2005. "In Battered CBD, Some See Opportunity." *Times Picayune*. September 12, p. C1.

Times Picayune Editorial Board. 2006. "A Responsible Plan." January 15.

Toppo, Greg. 2009. "Teach for America" Elite Corps or Costing Older Teacher Jobs" *USA Today*. July 29.

Travis, Robert. 2005. "Turf Wars, Political Strife Threaten Plan to Rebuild; Racial Tension Mars Initial Discussions." *Times Picayune*. September 18, p. A1.

Urban Land Institute (ULI). 2005. "Bring New Orleans Back Commission to Work with Urban Land Institute on Developing Rebuilding Strategy for the City." Press Release, October 12. Available at: http://commerce.uli.org/AM/Template.cfm?section&CONTENTID=37 412&TEMPLATE=/CM/ContentDisplay.cfm.

Van Lier, Piet. 2009. "Ready to Learn: Ohio Assessment Shows Charters, Magnets Get Head Start." *Policy Matters*. October. Available at" Policymattersohio.org.

Warner, Coleman and Darran Simon. 2007. "Classroom Space Is in Crisis." *Times Picayune*. May 1, p. A1.

Wise, Tim. 2005. *Affirmative Action: Racial Preference in Black and White* (New York: Routledge).

_____. 2006. Chocolate City?" *ZNET*. Available at: http://www.zmag.org/znet/view/article/4518.

Youtube. 2007. "New Orleans City Council Shuts Down Public Housing Debate." December 20. Available at: http://www.youtube.com/watch?v=cMBWAXfGsc4.

Culture of Poverty?*

William Julius Wilson

Anyone who wishes to understand American society must be aware that explanations focusing on the cultural traits of inner-city residents are likely to draw far more attention from policy makers and the general public than structural explanations will. It is an unavoidable fact that Americans tend to deemphasize the structural origins and social significance of poverty and welfare. In other words, the popular view is that people are poor or on welfare because of their own personal shortcomings. Perhaps this tendency is rooted in our tradition of "rugged individualism." If, in America, you can grow up to be anything you want to be, then any destiny—even poverty—can be rightly viewed through the lens of personal achievement or failure. Certainly it's true that most Americans have little direct knowledge or understanding of the complex nature of race and poverty in the inner city, and therefore broadly based cultural explanations that focus on personal character are more likely to gain acceptance.

We can easily see that explanations focusing on the character and capabilities of the individual dominate American thinking. Consider studies of national public opinion. After analyzing national survey data collected in 1969 and 1980, James R. Kluegel and Eliot R. Smith concluded that "most Americans believe that opportunity for economic advancement is widely available, that economic outcomes are determined by individuals' efforts and talents (or their lack) and that in general economic inequality is fair."[1] Indeed, responses to questions in these two national American surveys revealed that individualistic explanations for poverty (e.g., lack of effort or ability, poor moral character, slack work skills) were overwhelmingly favored over structural explanations (e.g., lack of adequate schooling, low wages, lack of jobs). The most frequently selected items in the surveys were "lack of thrift or proper money management skills," "lack of effort," "lack of ability or talent" (attitudes from one's family background that impede social mobility), "failure of society to provide good schools" and "loose morals and drunkenness." Except for "failure of society to provide good schools," all of these phrases point to shortcomings on the part of individuals as the causes of poverty. The Americans who answered the survey considered structural factors, such as "low wages," "failure of industry to provide jobs," and "racial discrimination" least important of all. The rankings of these factors remained virtually unchanged between 1969 and 1980.

---

*Wilson, William Julius, *More than Race: Being Black and Poor in the Inner City* (New York: W. W. Norton, 2009). Reprinted with permission.

A 1990 survey using these same questions, reported by Lawrence Bobo and Ryan A. Smith, revealed a slight increase among those who associated poverty with institutional and structural causes, especially the "failure of industry to provide enough jobs."[2] Nonetheless, Americans remained strongly disposed to the idea that individuals are largely responsible for their economic situations. In the three times the survey was administrered—1969, 1980, and 1990—the most often selected explanation was "lack of effort by the poor themselves." In fact, across all three surveys, more than nine out of ten American adults felt that lack of effort was either very or somewhat important in terms of causing poverty. Fewer than 10 percent felt it was not important.

The weight Americans give to individualistic factors persists today. A 2007 survey by the Pew Research Center revealed that "fully two-thirds of all Americans believe personal factors, rather than racial discrimination, explain why many African-Americans have difficulty getting ahead in life; just 19% blame discrimination."[3] Nearly three-fourths of US whites (71 percent), a majority of Hispanics (59 percent), and even a slight majority of blacks (53 percent) "believe that blacks who have not gotten ahead in life are mainly responsible for their own situation."[4]

These findings on the importance of individualistic causes of poverty contrast sharply with those in a survey conducted in twelve European countries (England, Ireland, France, Belgium, Holland, Switzerland, Germany, Norway, Sweden, Luxembourg, Austria, and Italy) in 1990.[5] A substantial majority of the citizens in each of these countries favored structural over individual explanations for the causes of poverty and joblessness in their own nations. Given the rising ethnic and racial tensions between host populations and migrants of color from Asia, Africa, and the Middle East, we might have expected these attitudes to shift closer to those held by Americans. However, a 2007 survey of twenty-seven European Union member states revealed that only one in five European Union citizens supported the idea that people live in poverty because of "laziness and lack of will power." Thirty-seven percent viewed "injustice in society as the cause of poverty," 20 percent attributed the cause to "bad luck," and 13 percent found poverty "an inevitable part of progress."[6] The attitudes of ordinary European citizens and public rhetoric in the European Union focus much more on structural and social inequities at large, not on individual behavior, to explain the causes of poverty and joblessness. Obviously, citizens in other Western democracies do not share the American emphasis on individualistic explanations for the problems of poverty.

The strength of American cultural sentiment that individuals are primarily responsible for poverty presents a dilemma for anyone who seeks the most comprehensive explanation of outcomes for poor black Americans. Why? Simply because cultural arguments that focus on individual traits and behavior invariably draw more attention than do structural explanations in the United States. Accordingly, I feel that a social scientist has an obligation to try to make sure that the explanatory power of his or her structural argument is not lost to the reader and to provide a context for understanding cultural responses to chronic economic and racial subordination.

Let me pursue this idea by first considering the neighborhood-effects research that focuses on concentrated poverty. Hundreds of studies have been published on the effects of concentrated poverty in neighborhood environments since the late 1980s. The research suggests that concentrated poverty increases the likelihood of social isolation (from mainstream institutions), joblessness, dropping out of school, lower educational achievement, involvement in crime, unsuccessful behavioral development and delinquency among adolescents, nonmarital childbirth, and unsuccessful family management.[7] In general, the research reveals that concentrated poverty adversely affects one's chances in life, beginning in early childhood and adolescence.

Some scholars, however, have been concerned that these studies reached conclusions about neighborhood effects on the basis of data that do not address the problem of *self-selection bias*, a term used in research to describe the effect of people grouping themselves together according to common characteristics. Proponents of self-selection bias argue that the effects we attribute to poor neighborhoods may instead be caused by the characteristics of families and individuals who end up living there. In other words, they believe that disadvantaged neighborhoods might not be the cause of poor outcomes, but rather that families with the weakest job-related skills, with the lowest awareness of and concern for the effects of the local environment on their children's social development, with attitudes that hinder social mobility, and with the most burdensome personal problems are simply more likely to live in these types of neighborhoods.

For example, as John Quigley and Steven Raphael point out, "in interpreting cross-sectional data on the isolation of low-income workers from job concentrations, it is likely that those with weaker attachments to the labor force will have chosen to locate in places where employment access is low [e.g., inner-city ghetto neighborhoods]. This is simply because monthly rents are lower in these places."[8]

Indeed, some scholars maintain that neighborhood effects disappear when researchers use appropriate statistical techniques to account for self-selection bias.[9] Because the appropriateness of measures capturing neighborhood effects is not discussed as a major problem in such studies ... many readers will conclude that structural explanations of concentrated poverty and related problems like discrimination, segregation, and joblessness are less persuasive than those that focus on personal attributes. But, as I shall attempt to show, there is little basis for ignoring or downplaying neighborhood effects in favor of emphasizing personal attributes. Indeed, living in a ghetto neighborhood has both structural and cultural effects that compromise life chances above and beyond personal attributes.

Arguments about self-selection bias were not seen as seriously challenging conclusions about neighborhood effects until publication of the research on the Moving to Opportunity (MTO) experiment, a housing pilot program undertaken by the US Department of Housing and Urban Development (HUD) between 1994 and 1998. The MTO program was inspired by the Gautreaux program, an earlier effort to assist minorities who wished to leave the inner city. The Gautreaux program was created under a 1976 court order resulting from a judicial finding that the Chicago Housing Authority had deliberately segregated black families through its site selection and tenant selection policies and the US Department of Housing and Urban Development (HUD) had knowingly funded such violations of civil rights. Named for Dorothy Gautreaux, who initiated the original lawsuit, the program sought to remedy previous segregation by offering black public housing residents a chance to obtain subsidized housing throughout the greater Chicago area. By the time the Gautreaux program ended in 1998, it had placed 7,100 families, with over half relocating to white suburbs.

As the program unfolded, it allowed researchers to systematically compare the education and employment experiences of families who had been assigned to private subsidized housing in the suburbs with those of a comparison group with similar characteristics and history who had been assigned to private apartments in the city. Research on this program reveals that the families who were relocated to housing in the suburbs experienced significantly higher rates of employment, lower school dropout rates, and higher college attendance rates.[10]

Although some believed that the Gautreaux program removed the self-selection bias problem in a quasi-experimental way, "critics were not mollified," because the selection of participants and their placement in new neighborhoods were nonrandom.[11] That is, "the Gautreaux program was the result of a court-ordered desegregation ruling and not a research experiment,"[12] so some argued that self-selection was still a factor. After all, Gautreaux participants were persons struggling to leave poor, inner-city neighborhoods. Some might argue that perhaps they were successful in their new setting not because they were no longer defeated by structural factors, but because they had the gumption to fight their way out of the ghetto in the first place.

These criticisms were addressed in HUD's MTO demonstration program. More specifically, from 1994 to 1997 HUD conducted a lottery that awarded housing vouchers to families living in public housing developments in high-poverty neighborhoods in five cities: Boston, Baltimore. Chicago, Los Angeles, and New York. Families who entered the lottery, thus indicating their desire to move, were randomly assigned to one of three groups. One was awarded housing vouchers that could be used to rent in the private market in any area, one was awarded housing vouchers restricted to private rentals in low-poverty neighborhoods, and one did not receive either of the two vouchers and was therefore treated as a control group to be compared with the other two groups.

The MTO interim evaluation studies were considered superior to the research on the Gautreaux program—as well as other research on neighborhood effects—because they were based on data from a randomized experimental design that eliminated the self-selection bias "that had made it difficult to clearly determine the association between living in poor neighborhoods and individual outcomes."[13] The reports and publications on the interim evaluation, which was finalized in 2003, provided mixed evidence for neighborhood effects in comparisons between the group whose MTO vouchers were restricted to low-poverty areas and the group that did not receive vouchers. On the one hand, during the five-year period following random assignment, the MTO movers who had relocated to low-poverty areas were more likely to have experienced improvements in mental health and less likely to be obese, and girls experienced a significant reduction in "risky behavior" (drinking, taking drugs, engaging in sex, and so on). On the other hand, research investigators found no evidence of an impact on employment rates and earnings, or of any marked improvement on the educational or physical health outcomes of children and young men. These mixed results have led some, including reporters, to question whether there really are enduring negative effects of living in poor, segregated neighborhoods.

However, although the research on the MTO experiment is rigorous, serious problems with the design of the experiment limit the extent to which one can generalize about neighborhood effects. First of all, the treatment was weak. That is, the voucher was restricted for only one year, and the restrictions were based on neighborhood poverty, not racial composition. Indeed, many MTO movers relocated to neighborhoods that were not significantly different from the ones they had left. For example, three-fifths of MTO families entered highly segregated black neighborhoods. Such neighborhoods tend to be considerably less advantaged than integrated areas. Sociologist Robert Sampson analyzed the neighborhood attainment of all Chicago MTO Families and found that after approximately seven years, although the voucher winners resided in neighborhoods with poverty rates somewhat lower than in the neighborhoods of control families, both groups had clustered in segregated black neighborhoods that were still considerably poorer than what an overwhelming majority of Americans will ever experience (neighborhoods with poverty rates of roughly 30 percent).[14]

One of the major differences between Gautreaux and MTO was that many Gautreaux families with vouchers moved to *white* suburban areas that were *significantly less impoverished* than their previous neighborhoods. In addition, at the time of the experiment's interim evaluation, as many as 41 percent of the MTO families who had entered low-poverty neighborhoods subsequently moved back to more disadvantaged neighborhoods. Because of such extensive out-migration, these MTO families accumulated relatively little time in areas of low poverty, and correspondingly they did not have an extended opportunity to experience life in low-poverty neighborhoods that were racially integrated.[15]

Moreover, nearly three-fourths of the children in the MTO experiment remained in the same school district, often in the same schools, at the time of the interim evaluation. Stefanie Deluca's comment on these findings, based on her interviews of MTO parents in Baltimore, reveals that school choice was a low priority for some parents. "It is quite striking," she states, "how little some parents thought that school mattered for learning, relative to what the child contributed through hard work and a good attitude...."[16] Furthermore. as pointed out by Quigley and Raphael, the experiment had not improved accessibility to employment opportunities for MTO movers, because their new neighborhoods were no closer to areas of employment growth.[17] Finally, a number of the projects that had housed many participants prior to their MTO relocation were torn down during the time of the experiment, forcing individuals in the control groups to also move and thus making it difficult to determine differences between voucher families and those without vouchers.

Rather than concluding from this research that neighborhoods do not matter, it would be prudent to state simply that although the MTO research raises questions about the extent to which neighborhoods affect the social outcomes of children and adults, it certainly does not resolve these questions. The MTO is best viewed as a policy experiment rather than a measure of social processes. We learn a lot from the MTO regarding how helpful it would be to offer ghetto residents housing vouchers with restricted use based on neighborhood poverty for one year. What the MTO tells us little about is the effect of neighborhoods on the development of children and families.

I think that overall quantitative studies generate mixed or weak findings about the effects of living in poor, segregated neighborhoods because of crude or inadequate measures to capture neighborhood effects. If a random experiment or even a non-experimental study could be generated that would allow researchers to capture the impact of a range of factors distinguishing different neighborhoods, including identifying factors that are cumulative over time, there would be significantly different findings on the impact of living in inner-city ghetto neighborhoods. Allow me to elaborate briefly.

In an impressive study that analyzes data from the Panel Study of Income Dynamics (PSID), a national longitudinal survey with methods designed to measure intergenerational economic mobility, Patrick Sharkey found that "more than 70% of black children who are raised in the poorest quarter of American neighborhoods will continue to live in the poorest quarter of neighborhoods as adults."[18] He also found that since the 1970s, a majority of black families have resided in the poorest quarter of neighborhoods in *consecutive generations*, compared to only 7 percent of white families. Thus, he concludes that the disadvantages of living in poor, black neighborhoods, like the advantages of living in affluent, white neighborhoods, are in large measure inherited.

Accordingly, this persistence of neighborhood inequality raises serious questions about studies on neighborhood effects. Many of these studies substantially underestimate the racial inequality in neighborhood environments because they use a single-point-in-time, or a single-generation, measure of neighborhood poverty or income.[19] Whereas living in the most impoverished neighborhoods is a temporary state for white families, most black families who lived in the poorest neighborhoods in the 1970s continue to live in such neighborhoods today. Sharkey suggests, therefore, that the focus of the research on neighborhood effects might be shifted to an examination of how the effect of living in poor neighborhoods over two or more generations differs from the effect of short-term residence in such neighborhoods. This brings us back to another shortcoming of the MTO experiment. Sharkey states the following:

> The difficulty with interpreting the results from the MTO as estimates of "neighborhood effects" lies in the conceptualization of a move to a new neighborhood as a point-in-time "treatment." This perspective ignores the possibility that the social environments surrounding families over generations have any lagged or cumulative influence on family members, and it ignores the complex pathways by which this influence may occur. For instance, the neighborhood may have an influence on an individual's educational attainment in one generation, in turn influencing the individual's occupational status and income as an adult, the quality of the home environment in which that individual raises a child, and the developmental trajectory of that child. These indirect pathways are obscured in observational studies that control for a set of covariates such as education or the quality of the home environment, and they are impossible to assess in experimental approaches such as MTO.[20]
>
> …

Thus, in addition to structural influences, exposure to different cultural influences in the neighborhood environment over time must be taken into account if one is to really appreciate and explain the divergent social outcomes of human groups. But to repeat, in delivering this message we must make sure that the powerful influence of structural factors does not recede into the background.

Endnotes

[1]James R. Kluegel and Elliot R. Smith, "Affirmative Action Attitudes, Effects of Self-Interest, Racial Affect, and Stratification Beliefs on Whites' Views," *Social Forces* 61 (1983), 797–824. See also James R. Kluegel and Elliot R. Smith, *Beliefs about Inequality: Americans' Views of What Is and What Ought to Be* (New York: de Gruyter, 1986).

[2]Lawrence Bobo and Ryan A. Smith, "Antipoverty Politics, Affirmative Action, and Racial Attitudes," in *Confronting Poverty: Prescriptions for Change*, eds. Sheldon H. Danziger, Gary D. Sandefur, and Daniel H. Weinberg (Cambridge, MA: Harvard University Press, 1994), 365–95.

[3]*Blacks See Growing Values Gap between Poor and Middle Class: Optimism about Black Progress Declines* (Washington, DC: Pew Research Center, November 13, 2007), 33.

[4]Ibid.

[5]Commission of the European Communities, *The Perception of Poverty in Europe* (Brussels: European Commission, 1990).

[6]Commission of the European Communities, *Poverty and Exclusion* (Brussels: European Commission, 2007).

[7]For a summary of some of the important studies on neighborhood effects, see Mario L. Small and Kathryn K. Newman, "Urban Poverty after the Truly Disadvantaged: The Rediscovery of the Family, the Neighborhood, and Culture," *Annual Review of Sociology* 27 (2001), 23–45.

[8]John Quigley and Steven Raphael, "Neighborhoods, Economic Self-Sufficiency, and the MTO," *Brookings-Wharton Papers on Urban Affairs*, 2008, 3.

[9]See, for example, William N. Evans, Wallace E. Oates, and Robert M. Schwab, "Measuring Peer Group Effects: A Study of Teenage Behavior," *Journal of Political Economy* 100, 966–91; and Robert Plotnick and Saul Hoffman, "Using Sister Pairs to Estimate How Neighborhoods Affect Young Adult Outcomes," *Working Papers in Public Policy Analysis and Management*, No. 93–8 (Seattle, WA: Graduate School of Public Affairs, University of Washington, 1993). For a good discussion of the issue of self-selection bias, see Paul Jargowsky, *Poverty and Place: Ghettos, Barrios, and the American City* (New York: Sage Foundation, 1997).

[10]James E. Rosenbaum and Susan Popkin, "Employment and Earnings of Low-Income Blacks Who Move to Middle-Class Suburbs," in *The Urban Underclass,* eds. Christopher Jencks and Paul E. Peterson (Washington, DC: Brookings Institution, 1991), 342–56; James Rosenbaum, Stefanie DeLuca, and Tammy Tuck, *Moving and Changing: How Places Change People Who Move into Them*, Institute for Policy Research Working Paper, WP–02–09 (Evanston, IL: IPR, 2002); J. E. Kaufman and J. Rosenbaum, *The Education and Employment of Low-Income Black Youth in White Suburbs*, Institute for Policy Research Working Paper, WP–91–20 (Evanston, IL: IPR, 1991), published in *Educational Evaluation & Policy Analysis* 14 (1992), 229–40; James E. Rosenbaum, Susan J. Popkin, Julie E. Kaufman, and Jennifer Rusin, *Social Integration of Low-Income Black Adults in White Middle-Class Suburbs*, Institute for Policy Research Working Paper, WP–91–06 (Evanston, IL: IPR, 1991), published in *Social Problems* 38 (1991), 448–61; and J. Rosenbaum and S. Popkin, *Economic and Social Impacts of Housing Integration : A Report to the Charles Stewart Mott Foundation* (Evanston, IL: IPR, Northwestern University, 1990).

[11]Susan Clampet-Lundquist and Douglas S. Massey, "Neighborhood Effects on Economic Self-Sufficiency: A Reconstruction of the Moving to Opportunity Experiment," *American Journal of Sociology* 114 (2008), 109–45.

[12]Micere Keels, Greg J. Duncan, Stefanie DeLuca, Ruby Mendenhall, and James Rosenbaum, "Fifteen Years Later: Can Residential Mobility Programs Provide a Long

Term Escape from Neighborhood Segregation, Crime, and Poverty?" *Demography* 42 (2006), 51–73.

[13]Jeffrey R. Kling, Jeffrey B. Lieberman, Lawrence F. Katz, and Lisa Sanbonatsu, *Moving to Opportunities and Tranquility: Neighborhood Effects on Adult Economic Self-Sufficiency and Health from a Randomized Housing Voucher Experiment*, Princeton IRS Working Paper, No. 481 (Princeton, NJ : Princeton University, April 2004, revised October 2004), 31.

[14]Robert J. Sampson, "Moving to Inequality: Neighborhood Effects and Experiments Meet Social Structure," *American Journal of Sociology* 114 (July 2008), 191–233.

[15]Sampson, "Moving to Inequality"; Clampet-Lundquist and Massey, "Neighborhood Effects."

[16]Stefanie DeLuca, "All over the Map: Explaining Educational Outcomes of the Moving to Opportunity Program," *Education Next*, Fall 2007, 25, 17. Quigley and Raphael, "Neighborhoods, Economic Self-Sufficiency."

[17]Quigley and Raphael, "Neighborhoods, Economic Self-Sufficiency."

[18]Patrick Sharkey, "The Intergenerational Transmission of Context," *American Journal of Sociology* 113 (January 2008), 931–69.

[19]Ibid.

[20]Ibid., 963.

Business Elites Re-Claiming New York*

Kim Moody

Cities change. For its first two hundred years New York was a merchant city, a key port in the Atlantic economy, where goods were bought and sold domestically and internationally, but only occasionally made and those mostly for local consumption. In the nineteenth century New York saw work and residence separated and sorted out by class. As the century progressed, Manhattan rapidly filled in the grid plan drafted in 1811. Beginning in the 1840s or 1850s, New York, along with other cities in the Northeast, began the process of becoming a center of industry. It was not a city of big industry, but of many smaller, often specialized firms.

By the time of the Civil War, the city's commercial and financial faces turned west as well as seaward. As industry spread westward across the Great Lakes and down the Ohio Valley, meeting the Mississippi at St. Louis, and as western agriculture became mechanized, New York financed and shipped much of the swelling output of the new industrial power that was the United States. Reaching from the Great Plains to Europe, the city's role at the center of the Atlantic economy grew and its population exploded. From 1870 to 1910 the population of Manhattan alone grew by one and a half to reach 2.3 million.[1]

In the 1880s, immigrants began to arrive in waves and from farther away in eastern and southern Europe than the earlier migrant groups. In 1898, the city's geography changed dramatically as Brooklyn, Queens, and Staten Island united with Manhattan and the Bronx (which had been annexed piecemeal in 1873 and 1895), expanding its industry as well as its size and population, which reached almost 5 million by 1910 for the combined city. By the 1940s, it was the biggest manufacturing center in America. It was still, of course, a commercial city and already a financial center. Each phase of its development was a response to larger national and international economic change and each incorporated much of the last, but the central economic dynamic changed. In this way, it remained a diversified economy[2] While each of these changes was in line with general developments in the country and broader world, human agency was at play with each transition. All of these transformations were battlegrounds socially, economically, and politically.

Martin Shefter described the rhythm of these later battles as the "machine/reform dialectic." In the face of fiscal crises, usually the result of a combination of economic "panic" and the excesses of Democratic machine rule, the city's respectable elite would forge a fusion ticket to oust the crooks and re-establish fiscal responsibility. This scenario would be repeated in 1894, 1913, and 1933, each reform movement, whatever its unique features, under control of the city's business elite. After 1937, Shefter argues, the city's political regime became "pluralist," mainly because labor unions and sometime independent parties they organized (American Labor and Liberal) became important.[3] The regime that would begin to emerge following the fiscal crisis of 1975 we will call neoliberal.

Beneath and behind these political changes, however, were class forces, new and old, engaging in a tug of war over the city's space, resources, and wealth. The city's clubhouse system of machine politics that formed the core of Shefter's "machine/reform dialectic," as he shows, was largely a response by Tammany Hall to the emergence of an independent labor movement that made its mark on the 1886 mayoral election. He writes, "The defections Tammany had suffered to the United Labor Party in 1886 encouraged its leaders to strengthen their district organizations by establishing a network of clubs that involved the machine in the social lives of Democratic voters."[4] Both 1913 and 1933 were years of working-class upsurge in the city as in the nation. The last of these produced the administrations of Fiorello La Guardia, who implemented the New Deal in New York and also unleashed Robert Moses to reshape the city with public money. La Guardia and his successors presided over the acceleration of New York's unique "social democratic polity," or welfare state. This was economically supported by federal money and the city's industrial base, and politically pushed for by its industrial working class with its broad variety of organizations, as described in Joshua Freeman's *Working-Class New York*.[5]

The city, however, began to change once again after World War II. African-Americans from the South and Puerto Ricans from the island arrived in growing numbers. At the same time the manufacturing and transportation jobs they hoped for began leaving. Before there was white flight, there was industrial exodus. These goods-making and -moving industries were reduced by competition from more efficient facilities inland; driven or zoned out by bankers and developers who saw more valuable uses for the land they occupied; rendered obsolete by new technology; plowed under by Robert Moses's bulldozers; or swallowed up by what we call globalization. The city lost population, particularly white population, as more and more whites left for the suburbs and beyond. If Robert Moses drastically altered the built environment, migration, in and out, transformed who did the city's work and who filled its neighborhoods. With these changes and the rise of the United States as a world economic, political, and military superpower came new political currents: the civil rights struggles of the 1950s and 1960s; Black and Puerto Rican nationalism; the women's movement; the antiwar movement of the Vietnam era; and the upsurge and organization of the city's huge public-sector workforce, its hospital workers, and others. All of these forces expanded and deepened the city's public provision, adding to the "social democratic polity" shaped by earlier generations of working-class people. The city became the site of a complex web of class, race, gender, and anti-imperialist conflict, replicating in new form the old fight over space, resources, and wealth. This story has been told often in many different ways, sometimes as an explanation for the city's social problems, sometimes as a prelude to the fiscal crisis of 1975, frequently in an effort to blame the victims.[6] We will refer to it… but not attempt to retell it in detail. The focus… is on what happened during and after 1975.

Class and Race

A few years ago, a colleague of mine at Brooklyn College asked me if I thought class was still a meaningful framework in which to look at politics. It was an obvious question given that most attempts to analyze or untangle New York City politics do so in terms of race and ethnicity. New York was classically the American city of ethnic politics. After the demographic transformation mentioned above, it certainly could lay claim to be a prime example of the centrality of race in urban politics in the United States. Class seemed to have faded or been pushed into the background as the social struggles that began in the 1950s in the United States focused on racial and gender oppression. One need not make the whole leap to postmodernism to accept the reality of racial politics in urban America. Nor can one deny that even class oppression or exploitation is often experienced as racial oppression by working-class people of color. In New York City, as elsewhere, housing, education, employment, even entertainment, are allocated as much or more by race as by class. The interaction of the two in these fields of life is so intimate as to defy any strict delineation or separation. Race is central to American life—period. Why, then, insist on using class as an analytical framework as well as race?

My answer is: because class won't go away. It is imposed on politics and life by the actions, behavior, investment, and political priorities of capital and the incredibly powerful social class it reproduces globally, nationally, and in our cities. If the working class in the United States is fragmented, disorganized, in retreat, and bamboozled by business gurus, politicians of all stripes, religious demagogues, and often its own leaders, the ruling capitalist class has been on the organized offensive worldwide for three decades or more. Despite its own internal contradictions, capital has shaped and imposed the neoliberal agenda for the world. However complex the process by which capital gets its political act together, it seems rather obvious that nationally, and even globally, it has done so, and it has succeeded in imposing much of its agenda on the United States and a good deal of the rest of the world. The resistance to it takes many different forms, but it is usually the working and/or other subordinate classes that form the bulk of that resistance whether in their own name or not. So it is in New York City, the metropolis at the center of much of this global neoliberalism.

To impose its agenda in New York, the city's business elite had to reassert its influence over city affairs in the era of social movements. Exasperated by the cost of this "welfare state" in one city, by the apparent capitulation of the politicians to the new unions and social movements in the 1960s, and by the seemingly unquenchable demands of these new forces, the city's ruling class, its business elite, its "permanent government," reacted in a highly unified and organized way to establish more direct control of "their" city in the mid–1970s. So, although race remains central and ethnicity important, and though immigrant status adds another dimension to race and ethnicity, class won't go away.

Turning Points

In little more than a decade and a half the economy of New York was transformed from a diverse production site in which 45 percent of its workers made or moved tangible goods and structures to one in which only half that proportion did so. The city's economy had become more and more dependent on the export of financial and other producer services, which accounted for almost half the value produced in the city in the mid–1970s.[7] The shift was even clearer in New York's globally connected export sector. According to the Temporary Commission on City Finances, manufacturing lost 12,159 export-based jobs in 1965–69 and 41,987 in 1969–73—just before the big recession of 1974–75. Transportation saw slight gains in 1965–69 due to air transport, but a net loss in all transport of 10,226 in 1969–73. The financial sector gained 59,242 jobs in 1965–69, but 18,657 were lost in 1969–73. Over the whole period in the export sector, manufacturing had lost 54,146 jobs net, while finance picked up 40,585 and other services remained flat, losing only a few jobs.[8] In terms of the city's crucial export sector, New York became less economically diverse and more vulnerable to fluctuations in the world economy. The 1960s were a turning point in the New York economy against which the financial and fiscal problems and crisis of the 1970s must be understood.[9]

The early and mid–1970s were also a turning point in the world economy and international and domestic politics. In 1971 the Bretton Woods system of currency exchange was dismantled. By this time Germany and Japan were becoming serious competitors against U.S. industry. And the 1974–75 world recession set off a decade or more of economic stagnation among the major industrial nations.[10] The recession and the prolonged stagnation that followed discredited the Keynesian foundations of American liberalism and European social democracy in the eyes of many, leading to two important political shifts. The first was a general move to more centrist, even austere economic policies by the Democrats in the United States, and eventually by the European left. In the United States, at least, supply-side economics became a catch-phrase even before Ronald Reagan took office. Next was the rise of a new, harsh conservatism and its election to government in the United States, Britain, and much of continental Europe by the early 1980s.[11] This trend was prefigured in the United States by Nixon's New Federalism, which was continued by Ford and his treasury secretary, William Simon, although the thrust of this early policy direction was blunted by an uncooperative Democratic Congress and partly derailed by Watergate and its aftermath.[12] Nevertheless, neoliberal economic policy was taking shape.

In the United States in the early 1970s big business organized itself around a common political agenda. Thomas Byrne Edsall described this effort in his 1984 study of the forces underlying the Reagan revolution when he wrote:

> During the 1970s, business refined its ability to act as a class, submerging competitive instincts in favor of joint, cooperative action in the legislative arena… the dominant theme in the political strategy of business became a shared interest in the defeat of bills such as consumer protection and labor law reform, and the enactment of favorable tax, regulatory, and antitrust legislation.[13]

At the center of this development was the Business Roundtable, pushing what would become the Reagan economic policy agenda. The Roundtable, founded in 1972 by 125 of the nation's largest industrial, commercial, and financial corporations, aggressively lobbied the federal government for tax reductions on business, deregulation in transportation and finances, labor law "reform" designed to weaken unions and austere fiscal policies. The neoliberal agenda was given further definition and an organized social base. The Roundtable was supported by conservative think tanks such as the Heritage Foundation, founded in 1973, and by a variety of ad hoc business-based coalitions such as the Consumer Issues Working Group, which helped defeat the Consumer Protection Agency, and the National Action Committee on Labor Law Reform, which aided in the defeat of labor's attempt to improve labor law.[14] Many of the top corporate executives who founded the Roundtable and some of the other organizations lived or worked in the New York area. Directly or indirectly, their ideas provided a backdrop to the city's policy options just as they did in Washington, D.C.

These same global trends affected America's other ailing cities as well, causing widespread fiscal distress, but given New York's central place in the world economy, they hit New York harder and at a sharper angle. Furthermore, the forces of global recession hit a city already vulnerable to financial and fiscal crisis. By May 1975, New York edged up to default on its bloated short-term debt.

For New York's powerful business elite, this crisis offered an opportunity to roll back a decades-old tradition of social spending and provision far in advance of other American cities. In the 1930s, the city's welfare provision and public sector grew enormously under the fusion-reform regime of Fiorello La Guardia as a result of New Deal money that flowed into the city, first to pay for "home relief" the city could no longer afford. The federal Civil Works Administration, Public Works Administration, and later the Works Progress Administration provided millions to rehabilitate the city's parks and build bridges under the guidance of Robert Moses, as well as to build its first public housing project.[15] As Joshua Freeman has shown in his *Working-Class New York*, by the 1940s the city provided a unique cluster of urban social institutions that he characterizes as a "social democratic polity." This included a public hospital system that had twenty-two hospitals at its height, an expanding City University system, extensive public housing, significant union-provided cooperative housing, rent control long after it was eliminated in other cities, and civil rights legislation before most other cities. All of these were fought for and defended by the city's vibrant labor movement and left-wing parties.[16] To this was added the new or expanded social programs of the 1960s: Medicaid, Medicare, the War on Poverty with its community participation setup, and growing welfare rolls. Promising still more strains on the city's budgets were the social movements of that era and the new, initially militant municipal unions.

For New York's business elite the growing costs of the city's "social democratic polity" and Great Society programs had, with the changes in the city's economy and its place in the new global marketplace, come to clash with long-held priorities for city expenditures. Although some of New York's business elite had backed many of these more recent reforms and their major political champion, John Lindsay, their costs now seemed exorbitant and the corporate price tag too high. The whole experience of the late 1960s and early 1970s seemed to many in the business elite to be a threat to the city's position in the global economy as well as to their own economic priorities. In a 1971 report from Chase Manhattan Bank, David Rockefeller, a central actor in New York's and the nation's elite, wrote, "It is clear to me that the entire structure of our society is being challenged." In a closed-door meeting of top business executives in 1973, one concluded, "If we don't take action now, we will see our own demise. We will evolve into another social democracy."[17]

Business's "developmentalist" view of city finances had called for fiscal restraint on social programs and largesse on infrastructure projects and spending that underwrote the upward and outward expansion of the city's central business district. The social movements and the new programs that came in their wake had shifted the city's financial priorities even further from its own. The fiscal and financial troubles of the mid–1970s were the call to action and the opportunity to act. The city's fragmented politics, along with the decline of the social movements and the relative "maturity" of the municipal unions, cleared the way for a reversal of priorities via the establishment of a "crisis regime," a series of state-sponsored organizations and offices imposed on the financial governance of New York City.

As David Harvey has pointed out, New York City in the mid–1970s was a sort of rehearsal for the larger neoliberal reorganization of national priorities that would take place in the United States under Ronald Reagan and in the United Kingdom under Margaret Thatcher. Restraint on social spending, privatization, deregulation, and, most importantly, the reassertion of class power by the nation's capitalist class are at the center of the neoliberal project. The word was not yet in wide use in the mid–1970s, but the sense that the city's business elite, themselves at the center of the national and global capitalist class, had lost power and with it control of the city government's priorities was strong. The crisis regime shaped in 1975 would in many ways be an example of how government could be used to reassert class power and shift priorities toward both the traditional goals of business and the newer ideas that would be known as neoliberalism.[18]

Political Fragmentation, Interest Groups, Coalitions, and Elites

New York's style of "interest group governance" described long ago by Sayre and Kaufman was unique in several ways.[19] First, the political structure of the city undermined the "strong mayor model" many thought embodied in the city charter. The borough presidents, seated on the Board of Estimates, brought the demands of not one political machine but five, plus the minimachines of the Republican, Liberal, and Conservative parties. They competed for city jobs, judgeships, capital projects, vending and supplier contracts, zoning variances, etc., all of which bid up the budgets, while they simultaneously sought to keep taxes on their constituencies low. Unlike Chicago, with its unitary Daley machine, New York City had no central disciplining force other than the mayor and the two other citywide members of the Board of Estimate who still relied on the cooperation of the county organizations to get elected.[20]

While Tammany was alive and well, candidates for citywide office could be negotiated by county leaders. The fragility of this setup had already been demonstrated when the Brooklyn machine challenged Tammany candidate James Walker in the 1925 Democratic primary. Although the challenge failed, it was a warning shot. But after the defeat of Tammany's candidate in the 1961 Democratic primary, its position as first among equals declined terminally. Indeed, the county machines had lost power over the years. La Guardia's 1938 charter revision had strengthened the mayor by extending his appointment and dismissal authority over most department heads, and limited the patronage powers of the county organizations by centralizing much of the contract award system. Further charter revisions limited the role of the borough presidents, and first New Deal and then Great Society programs replaced some of the old functions of the machine with bureaucratically managed redistributive programs. Additionally, as Mollenkopf points out, the county organizations came to rest on taxpayer-supported legislators and their staffers more than the clubhouse. By the 1970s, the centrality of the media further weakened the role of the county organizations in mayoral elections.[21] Still, the regulars controlled most county organizations, which in turn controlled access to the ballot for locally elected city and state offices and could create a margin of victory in citywide elections as well as in each borough.[22]Even reformer Lindsay, with no real machine, was forced to distribute patronage largely on the recommendation of the county Democratic organizations.[23] As always, the county organizations expected something in return for their efforts beyond the depleted supply of patronage jobs, and that something had to do with suppliers, contractors, vendors, and consultants. Some of those were "earned" through the small banks, insurance companies, and law firms controlled by "regular" Democratic district and county leaders who fed off the capital and expense budgets.[24] Part of it came through the city agencies the county organizations still influenced and through which some of the supplies, equipment, fees, and contracts were purchased. With such a competitive dynamic, reining in spending in large parts of both the capital and expense budget seemed a task for Caesar, not clubhouse denizens or well-intentioned reformers. A city situated so deeply in the global economy—like a nation—is less able to shape its future the more decentered its government.

Then there were the interest groups. Sayre and Kaufman envisioned a city with countless interest groups competing with one another for resources and preventing the rule of an elite. A sort of ultrapluralism was said to contribute to the weakness of government, something analogous to neoclassical economists' view of the market as an infinite number of more or less equal players. As Fuchs, Bellush, and others have pointed out, however, all interest groups are not equal nor is the system of political and social conflict as unstructured and fluid as Sayre and Kaufman argued.[25]

As Fuchs put it: "Power is not evenly distributed in the fiscal policy arena, and even when a city has a high degree of interest group activity, like New York, groups do not have equal access to the process."[26]

Furthermore, most interest groups are embedded in deeper social class and race formations that determine the level and type of access, available resources, and the ability to build effective coalitions. The contention here is that at that time, particularly given the financial nature of the crisis, access to the policy process and the resources to impact it were highly uneven, the overwhelming advantage lying with New York's business elite. I say business rather than banker or financial because, as I will argue, the intervention that created the crisis regime involved major players from much of corporate New York. I say elite because the vast majority of the city's small businesses had no real access and because even big business tends to be represented by those activist leaders whose access to policy making is regular and influential.

The other potential actors, mainly the black and Latino communities and organized labor, failed to have decisive influence over the outcome because they failed even to contemplate, let alone undertake, the construction of a broad coalition based on some alternative resolution of the crisis more favorable to working-class New York. Because both the unions and New York's black and Latino community activists had some influence on the city's social and political priorities in the 1960s, there has been a tendency to exaggerate their actual political power in the 1970s.

The period of the mid-to late 1960s certainly produced some high-profile activities and movements, as they did throughout much of the country. Actual political representation of African-Americans in city politics proportionate to their share of the population, however, would come later. As Charles V. Hamilton argued, institutional gains from the period of the social movements in New York came largely through community corporations and the various agencies associated with the War on Poverty, rather than through gains in the electoral process or in representation in city and state government.[27] As late as 1989, when whites composed only 48 percent of the city's voting age population, they held three-quarters of the seats on the city council and 82 percent of the votes on the Board of Estimate. Such black and Latino representation as existed was mostly encased in the county organizations, which ultimately played little role in the formation of the crisis regime.[28] It was also a time in which community action and other antipoverty programs, where blacks and Latinos had made gains, were being cut back. The power of the black community had been in the streets and there the demands were more representational than redistributive: school integration, community control, construction jobs in Brooklyn and Harlem were among the major goals of the 1960s.[29] The notable exception was the welfare rights movement. In New York, however, this movement, which gained steam and organizational presence in 1966, peaked in 1968 and was all but dead by 1970.[30] In fact most of the radical organizations of the late 1960s, such as the Black Panther Party and the Young Lords, had declined or disappeared by the early 1970s. The most obvious institutional legacy of the more radical movements was open admissions and the expansion of the City University of New York (CUNY) and the system of community boards, which became law in its contemporary form in 1969.[31] The potential power of the black and Latino communities lay in coalition among themselves and with the municipal unions, many of which already contained significant numbers of African-Americans, including officials at the local level and, in some cases, higher. While there was resistance from the black and Latino communities, particularly against cuts in the city's public hospital system, the black and Latino communities did not have the access to shape the crisis regime. Other than some black politicians and union leaders, there was not the institutional power to have a decisive impact without a broader coalition.[32] This did not happen.

The New York labor movement was deeply divided over such questions as urban development, civil rights, the Vietnam war, and even, frequently, which candidates to support. Like the public-sector workers, those in the private sector followed the national pattern of militancy, the 117-day strike of New York Telephone workers in 1971–72 being a prime example.[33] Neither private-nor public-sector union leaders, however, were able to consolidate effective coalitions prior to the crisis. The role of labor in city politics was fragmented, contradictory, and largely reactive.

The municipal unions that arose in the 1960s, of course, played a large role in the resolution of the financial crisis, but not one that shaped the crisis regime. The explosion of public-sector unionism across the country in the 1960s had its epicenter in New York. The two powerhouses of municipal labor were District Council 37 of the American Federation of State, County, and Municipal Employees (DC 37) and the United Federation of Teachers (UFT). Also important, though it did not negotiate directly with the city, was the Transport Workers Union (TWU) Local 100. Important in bargaining directly with the city were the uniformed service unions, the Uniformed Sanitationmen's Association, the Police Benevolent Association, and the Uniformed Firemen's Association. For most of the period examined here, TWU Local 100, with almost 40,000 members, led the system of pattern bargaining established in the 1960s. DC 37 had grown from about 20,000 dues paying members in the 1950s to 79,000 in 1970 and 106,783 in 1974–75. The UFT went from 5,000 (out of 40,000 teachers) in 1961, when it called its first strike, to nearly 71,000 in mid–1974. By the eve of the crisis each of these two unions spent over $12.5 million a year.[34] District Council 37 and the UFT, in particular, were not only large but well organized with significant professional staff and a clear-cut hierarchy. In addition, in the 1960s DC 37 had developed an effective political operation headed by Norman Adler. It was certainly an exaggeration to say, as the Bellushes did, that DC 37's electoral machine was a replacement for the clubhouse, but it was a sign of the role unions played in bypassing and to some extent diminishing the centrality of the county organizations to electoral politics. Adler, his staff, and local union volunteers also lobbied both city hall and Albany.[35]

Although prior to the crisis the unions sat together in the Municipal Labor Committee, they did not bargain together or cooperate directly in Democratic primaries to push labor candidates. Victor Gotbaum, executive director of DC 37, and UFT president Albert Shanker were cool, sometimes hostile, toward one another. Shanker had from time to time raided some DC 37 jurisdictions. Gotbaum had disagreed with Shanker when the UFT struck the Ocean Hill-Brownsville experimental school district three times in the fall of 1968 in opposition to community control. Gotbaum had joined with a group of black and liberal union leaders to pressure Central Labor Council president Harry Van Arsdale to get Shanker to call off the strike, a strike which rendered any alliance between the city unions and the black community problematic, to say the least.[36] Thus, for all the power and organization of the municipal unions, they did not present a united front until the crisis was upon them. Then, as we will see, Gotbaum became the recognized leader who most others followed willingly, Shanker and the police and fire unions hesitantly. It was only after the crisis was well under way that the municipal unions engaged in coalition bargaining with the city, and in 1977 they established a statewide political coalition of public-sector unions, the Public Employees Conference.[37]

The municipal unions, like much of the black and Latino communities, were embedded in the city's huge working class and to a lesser extent among those middle-class professionals in the public sector. In this sense they shared certain common interests in the way the city spent money. Their priorities (schools, housing, health care, parks, sanitation, etc.) were different from and frequently in conflict with those generally ascribed to New York's business elite, who saw capital infrastructure improvements that improved land values, restricted spending on social programs, restrained city worker wages and benefits, low property and business taxes, and tax breaks on office and luxury apartment construction in the central business district as priorities.

New York's working class, however, like that of the nation, was badly divided along racial lines and frequently competed along those lines for housing, jobs, and city resources. Potentially breaching that division was a rising cadre of black union leaders in both the private and public sectors. This was particularly true of DC 37, where ascendant leaders like Lillian Roberts, Charles Hughes, Charles Ensley, Stanley Hill, and others had already made their mark.[38] Despite this, no broader coalition was ever sought for working-class New York.

A Special New York Interest: Its Business Elite

The most powerful interest groups were those based in New York City's unique business elite, itself the social and economic center of America's corporate capitalist class. While the members of this elite may have lived in the suburbs as much as in the city, they made their business homes within the confines of Manhattan from Sixtieth Street to the southern tip of the island, the core of the city's central business district (CBD). At the heart of this community in the mid–1970s were the corporate headquarters of 84 Fortune 500 firms (down from 140 at its height, to be sure), and the headquarters of over 450 national companies altogether, including the nation's largest financial institutions and other giant producer and business service firms that earned New York the title of global city.[39] According to Matthew Drennan's calculations, in 1976 New York was home to firms that accounted for 24 percent of the sales of the Fortune 500, 41 percent of the assets of the nation's largest commercial banks, 34 percent of those of the largest insurance companies, and 29 percent of the biggest diversified financial outfits.[40] The number, size, and concentration of these firms gave them and those who ran them an influence even when they did not appear to intervene. Through both their market leverage and permanent and occasional organizations, these large business interests and their representatives affected city fiscal and financial affairs day in and day out.[41]

Furthermore, this business elite possessed a number of resource-rich institutions that had permanent access to fifty fiscal, financial, and political power centers. Among these were the City Club; the Citizens Union; the Real Estate Board of New York; the Commerce and Industry Association; the Rockefeller-led Downtown-Lower Manhattan Association; the Regional Plan Association; and the Citizens Budget Commission (CBC). Most of these organizations had sizable professional staffs and the full backing of the business elite. When Sayre and Kaufman wrote about the CBC it had six hundred affiliated business corporations and cooperated with most of the above organizations.[42] Shefter outlined the policy agenda of these groups and its relationship to past crises:

> Generally, when New York has been faced with a fiscal crisis or demands for the construction of new transportation facilities, a substantial part of the downtown business community has united behind a program calling upon the municipal government to: (1) stop financing current expenditures with borrowed funds; (2) balance its budget by slashing current expenditures rather than by raising taxes; (3) use its borrowing power capacity to improve the city's transportation infrastructure rather than for other purposes (such as building new schools); and (4) cover, to the greatest extent possible, the debt service with user-charges (fares on subways, tolls on bridges) rather than with local tax revenues.[43]

Alongside this, of course, is the role of big money in city elections. Money became central in the 1960s. In 1969 John Lindsay and his two opponents spent $3 million. By 1977 the cost for both the primary and general election was $6.5 million, with Koch alone spending $2.1 million. In his race for a third term in 1985, Koch spent a whopping $7.2 million, most of it from real estate and financial interests.[44] In New York City, just about every major business is involved in real estate development and politics in one way or another.

Matthew Drennan, in the *Setting Municipal Priorities* series, has called the dense network of large businesses on which the city's business elite is based the corporate headquarters complex. This complex included "headquarters offices, firms servicing headquarters offices, and ancillary services provided to the individuals who perform the headquarters and corporate service activities."[45] According to his econometric model, this complex accounted for 46 percent of the city's private economy in 1975, measured in terms of value added. The biggest slice of the corporate headquarters complex in 1975 was in producer services, which accounted for 83 percent of the complex. The value added produced by the firms in this complex came above all from what the city exported to the rest of the country and the world, composing 68 percent of the value added produced in the city. Drennan's complex accounts for two-thirds of this exported value added.[46] Manuel Castells describes the economic dynamic this way:

> It is because Manhattan is the CBD of New York, and New York is the corporate center of the largest economy in the world, holding what is still the most important international currency, that capital flows tend to converge on the location of the leading financial institutions.[47]

In other words, the city rests not primarily on its local or regional economy, but on the world economy in which New York's business elite is a major player. Thus, the dependency of city officials on its business leaders goes far beyond campaign contributions. There is the power to take its export-created income, capital, and jobs elsewhere either in whole through relocation or in part through outsourcing—the twin Damoclean swords always hanging over the city's tax policies and practices.

Endnotes

[1]George I. Lankevich, *American Metropolis: A History of New York City* (New York: New York University Press, 1998), 259.

[2]Ira Katznelson, *City Trenches: Urban Politics and the Patterning of Class in the United States* (Chicago: University of Chicago Press, 1981), 45–49; Thomas Bender, *The Unfinished City: New York and the Metropolitan Idea (*New York: The New Press, 2001), *passim*; Lankevich, *American Metropolis*, 259.

[3]Martin Shefter, *Political Crisis/Fiscal Crisis: The Collapse and Revival of New York City* (New York: Columbia University Press, 1992), 13–37.

[4]Ibid., 20.

[5]Joshua Freeman, *Working-Class New York: Life and Labor Since World War II* (New York: The New Press, 2000), 55–71.

[6]See ibid., 179–255; Shefter, *Political Crisis/Fiscal Crisis*, 41–81; François Weil, *A History of New* York (New York: Columbia University Press, 2004), 259–85 for progressive accounts; Roger Starr, *The Rise and Fall of New York City* (New York: Basic Books, 1985), *passim*, for a conservative interpretation; Robert Fitch, *The Assassination of New York* (London: Verso, 1993), passim, for an account of how the city's elite pushed manufacturing out.

[7]Charles Brecher and Raymond D. Horton, with Robert A. Cropf, *Power Failure: New York City Politics and Policy Since 1960* (New York: Oxford University Press, 1993), 7; Matthew Drennan, "Local Economy and Local Revenues" in Charles Brecher and Raymond D. Horton, eds., *Setting Municipal Priorities, 1988* (New York: New York University Press (1984), 56–58.

[8]Temporary Commission on City Finances, *The City in Transition: Prospects and Policies for New York: The Final Report of the TCCF* (New York, June 1977), 148.

[9]Weil, *History of New York*, 262–63.

[10]Robert Brenner, *The Boom and the Bubble: The U.S. in the World Economy* (London: Verso, 2002), 7–49.

[11]Kim Moody, *Workers in a Lean World: Unions in the International Economy* (London: Verso, 1997), 119–23.

[12]Sidney M. Milkis and Michael Nelson, *The American Presidency: Origins and Development, 1776–2002*, 4th ed. (Washington, DC: CQ Press, 2003), 326–29.

[13]Thomas Byrne Edsall, *The New Politics of Inequality* (New York: W. W. Norton, 1984), 128–29.

[14]Thomas Ferguson and Joel Rogers, *Right Turn: The Decline of the Democrats and the Future of American Politics* (New York: Hill and Wang, 1986), 100–113; Kim Moody, *An Injury to All: The Decline of American Unionism* (London: Verso, 1988), 127–35; Edsall, *New Politics of Inequality*, 120–29.

[15]Robert Pecorella, *Community Power in a Postmodern City: Politics in New York City* (Armonk, NY: M.E. Sharpe, 1994), 54–55; Robert Caro, *The Power Broker: Robert Moses and the Fall of New York* (New York: Vintage Books, 1975), 361–63, 345–46, 451–54, *passim*.

[16]Freeman, *Working-Class New York*, 55–71, 104–42 (see intro., n. 5).

[17]Dan Clawson, *The Next Upsurge: Labor and the New Social Movements* (Ithaca, NY: ILR Press, 2003), 38.

[18]David Harvey, *Brief History of Neoliberalism* (New York: Oxford University Press, 2005), 44–48.

[19]Wallace S. Sayre and Herbert Kaufman, *Governing New York City: Politics in the Metropolis* (New York: W.W. Norton, 1965).

[20]Ester R. Fuchs, *Mayors and Money: Fiscal Policy in New York and Chicago* (Chicago: University of Chicago Press, 1992), 214–25.

[21]Richard Wade, "The Withering Away of the Party System," In *Urban Politics, New York Style*, ed. Jewel Bellush and Dick Netzer (Armonk, NY: M.E. Sharpe, 1990), 271–94; John H. Mollenkopf, *A Phoenix in the Ashes: The Rise and Fall of the Koch Coalition in New York City Politics* (Princeton, NJ: Princeton University Press, 1992), 80; Pecorella, *Community Power*, 32–34.

[22]Mollenkopf, *Phoenix in the Ashes*, 76–80.

[23]Shefter, *Political Crisis/Fiscal Crisis*, 99.

[24]Jack Newfield and Paul Du Brul, *The Abuse of Power: The Permanent Government and the Fall of New York* (New York: Viking Press, 1977), 206.

[25]Fuchs, *Mayors and Money*, 242–43; Jewel Bellush, "Clusters of Power: Interest Groups," in *Urban Politics*, 296–334.

[26]Fuchs, *Mayors and Money*, 242.

[27]Charles V. Hamilton, "Needed, More Foxes: The Black Experience," in *Urban Politics*, 359–83.

[28]Mollenkopf, *Phoenix in the Ashes*, 72–92.

[29]Freeman, *Working-Class New York*, 179–200.

[30]Frances Fox Piven and Richard Cloward, *Poor People's Movements: Why They Succeed, How They Fail* (New York: Vintage Books, 1979), 288–308.

[31]Katznelson, *City Trenches*, 143 (see intro., n. 2).

[32]Robert W. Bailey, *The Crisis Regime: The MAC, the EFCB, and the Political Impact of the New York City Financial Crisis* (Albany: State University of New York Press, 1984), 40 11, 110–11.

[33]Freeman, *Working-Class New York*, 255.

[34]Joan Weitzman, *City Workers and Fiscal Crisis: Cutbacks, Givebacks, and Survival* (New Brunswick, NJ: Institute of Management and Labor Relation, Rutgers, 1979), 26–31, 53–58; Jewel Bellush and Bernard Bellush, *Union Power and New York: Victor Gotbaum and District Council 37* (New York: Praeger, 1984), 227; Mark H. Maier, *City Unions: Managing Discontent in New York City* (New Brunswick, NJ: Rutgers University Press, 1987), 112.

[35]Bellush and Bellush, *Union Power*, 239–67.

[36]Freeman, *Working-Class New York*, 225.

[37]Bellush and Bellush, *Union Power*, 266–68, 438–46.

[38]Freeman, *Working-Class New York*, 206–98; Bellush and Bellush, *Union Power*, 225–34.

[39]Sassen, *The Global City*, 90–125; Manuel Castells, *The Information City: Information Technology, Economic Restructuring, and the Urban Regional Process* (Oxford: Blackwell, 1989), 343.

[40]Drennan, "Local Economy" (1984), 48.

[41]Sanjek, *The Future of Us All*, 31–35.

[42]Sayre and Kaufman, *Governing New York City*, 503–8; Bellush, "Clusters of Power," 297–99.

[43]Shefter, *Political Crisis/ Fiscal Crisis*, 24.

[44]Mollenkopf, *Phoenix in the Ashes*, 92–94; Bellush, "Clusters of Power," 296–334.

[45]Drennan, "Local Economy" (1984), 45.

[46]Ibid., 44–58.

[47]Castells, *Information City*, 343.

Section V:
Other Institutional Implications

In this final section, we turn our attention to an array of other areas of sociological concern that have unfortunate institutional implications for life in urban America. Much of what we cover here also allows us to think about inadequate social conditions and whether they are emblematic of governmental negligence, willful manipulation by certain interested parties, an incompetence of public officials, or merely the unintended consequences of social policy. Sadly, recent news reports remind us of a need for continuing to inquire about a potential nexus between negative conditions and social policy. For example, the Department of Housing and Urban Development (HUD) announced in 2009 that homelessness is on the rise—not in large cities where we are accustomed to seeing increases, but in surrounding suburbs and rural areas.[1] Consequently, publicly funded shelters in the U.S. are struggling to accommodate the fastest growing population of homeless victims—families—as the number of dislocated families grew from about 473,000 to 517,000 between 2007 and 2008.

The *Christian Science Monitor* recently did a comparison of social policy in the United States and other countries.[2] According to the paper, a 2007 study looked at 173 countries where "a Harvard and McGill University research team found that 168 nations provide some form of paid income benefit for childbirth, leaving the United States in the company of four other countries—Lesotho, Liberia, Swaziland, and Papau New Guinea—that do not guarantee some form of paid maternity leave." In his book *Double Standard*, sociologist James Russell finds that Western Europeans enjoy roughly 10% higher levels of disposable income (on average) than U.S. residents because those countries rely far more heavily on progressive taxation and have more generous social welfare programs.[3] This raises questions about the effectiveness of U.S. social policy.

In this section we include studies that raise further questions about institutional arrangements and social policy in the U.S., particularly how urban dwellers are affected by an inactive and/or neglectful government. First, we consider the media, a social structure institutionally regulated by the Federal Communications Commission (FCC) since the early 1930s. Despite the media's ties to this agency of governance, many believe that media outlets operate irresponsibly, providing grossly inadequate coverage of diverse social events.[4] For example, studies suggest that media outlets negatively distort the level of group solidarity in U.S. cities regarding immigration conditions, often lack truthful reporting, exacerbate racial hostilities whenever new families move into certain areas of a city, and promote uncritical readership—which often fosters tacit support for public dollars to be spent for potentially wasteful city projects. [5]

In the opening article of the section, Peter Dreier discusses the impact of the media on U.S. cities. He argues that the media's lack of journalistic leadership on social issues nega-tively targets cities and, helps to compound urban problems by distorting or ignoring the effectiveness of government programs, intensifing race divisions, exaggerating news about crime, and rendering advocacy groups virtually invisible unless special circumstances exist. The shame of governance here is that the FCC appears to offer little in the way of progressive stewardship of the public's interest, but instead gives way to other influences that advance and construct unproductive public sentiments about cities.

In the next article, we include a study that deals with mass transit, as public transporta-tion is a major issue for urban areas. The question of mass transit is also connected to the federal government, as the Department of Transportation was formed in 1966 to oversee highway construction, railroads, civilian aviation, ports, and, of course, urban mass tran-sit. Today, sociologists and other social scientists evaluate mass transit as an important infrastructural resource in cities and discuss how it affects individuals and families. For example, one study on mass transit examines the relationship between family structure and the labor markets and finds that black and Latina women are more likely to rely on mass transit for employment purposes than white women. Unfortunately, scholars note that over the years there has been a decline in the public's commitment to mass transit, and a debate has ensued regarding causes for this decline.

One school of thought regarding the decline is based on a public choice thesis. It posits that the rise of middle-class incomes in the U.S. led to an increase in automobile purchases, which essentially decreased the demand for mass transit. Another school of thought was advanced in the 1970s by Bradford Snell, counsel to the U.S. Senate Subcommittee on Antitrust and Monopoly. Snell argued that the demise of mass transit was due to corporate and government manipulation of the supply of transportation.[6] The second article in this section is more sympathetic with Snell's thesis. Accordingly, Joe Feagin and Robert Parker argue that as cities have become "multinucleated," and the needs and desires for automo-biles have been used by certain actors to thwart the rationale for mass transit. They hold that collusion between allied public officials and business elites in the Auto-Oil-Rubber industrial complex was instrumental in forwarding an anti-mass transit agenda.

The last two articles in the section deal with issues that are in some ways interrelated: health and the environment. Both of these concerns have roots in the responsibilities of gov-ernment through two federal agencies that were formed to insure the safety of the public: the Environmental Protection Agency in 1970 and the Department of Health and Human Services, established in 1953. Despite the efforts of these agencies, researchers examine inconsistencies regarding the level of protection received by urban dwellers, and find, for example, a high incidence of diseases in African-American communities that are linked to toxic waste; and higher Hispanic residency rates in more polluted urban areas. The third piece in this section deals with claims of environmental racism and classism in the U.S. Specifically, Robert D. Bullard in his book *Dumping in Dixie* argues that growing empiri-cal evidence shows that toxic-waste dumps are not randomly scattered across the American landscape, but targeted for placement in low income neighborhoods that are disproportion-ately minority. Bullard provides examples of dumping in Houston and Dallas and discusses the complicity of public officials as well as the communities' response to the events.

The final article comes from a chapter in *Sick* by Jonathan Cohn. In this book, Cohn describes what he calls the untold story of America's health care crises and the people who pay the price. The chapter from *Sick* that we include here deals with various health dilemmas in Los Angeles. Cohn highlights, for example, the plight of poor LA residents and links inadequate health care to the overall economic climate in the state of California. His account of unfortunate health care conditions is essentially an indictment on the heath care delivery system. For example, he argues that programs like Medi-Cal are administratively deficient and replete with obscure guidelines that result in a lack of care for less well-off populations in the city.

Endnotes

[1]HUD report in the news about increase in suburban/rural homelessness: http://www. usatoday.com/news/nation/2009-07-09-homeless_N.htm.

[2]*Christian Science Monitor* <http://www.csmonitor.com/Commentary/Opinion/2010/ 0216/Is-Canada-more-pro-family-than-America>.

[3]James Russell. *Double Standard: Social Policy in Europe and the U.S.* (Lanham, MD: Rowman and Littlefield, 2006), pp. 73–74.

[4]Levon Chorbajian and Larry Beeferman. "Selling Supreme Court Nominees: The Case of Ruth Bader Ginsburg." *Critical Sociology*, 23 3, 1997: 3–32.

[5] Matt A. Barreto, Sylvia Manzano, Ricardo Ramirez, Kathy Rim. "Mobilization, Participation, and Solidaridad: Latino Participation in the 2006 Immigration Protest Rallies" *Urban Affairs Review* 44 5, 2009: 736–764; Gordana Rabrenovic. "When Hate Comes to Town" *American Behavioral Scientist*. 51 2, 2008: 349–360; Kevin Delaney and Rick Eckstein. "Local Media Coverage of Sports Stadium Initiatives" *Journal of Sport and Social Issues* 32 1, 2008: 72–93.

[6]Thomas Gregory. "Conspiracy or Consumer Choice," review of *Mass Motorization and Mass Transit: An American History and Policy Analysis* by David W. Jones. *Society for the History of Technology* 50, 2009: 673–676.

The Media Bad-Mouthing the City*

Peter Dreier

Many community activists, big-city mayors, and even urban scholars have spent much of the past several decades focusing on what is wrong with America's urban areas. "Our cities are burning," they seem to be crying. Then they demand action from the federal government: "Please help us put out the fire." The United States has many serious problems that are disproportionately located in urban areas. But our perceptions of the magnitude of these problems, their underlying causes, and most important, the capacity of society to find solutions to these problems is significantly shaped by how the major news media cover our cities.

In general, the way the major news media frame coverage of our cities reinforces an overwhelmingly negative and misleading view of urban America. The images from the nightly news, newsweeklies, and daily newspapers are an unrelenting story of social pathology—mounting crime, gangs, drug wars, racial tension, homelessness, teenage pregnancy, AIDS, inadequate schools, and slum housing.

Moreover, this perspective on our cities is compounded by news coverage of government efforts to address these problems. Government programs are typically covered as well-intentioned but misguided, plagued by mismanagement, inefficiency, and, in some cases, corruption. A standard news story focuses on one policy initiative (i.e., federal enterprise zones, welfare, community policing, subsidized housing) and proclaims that, despite government's best efforts, poverty and crime persist.

This is not to say that the media completely ignore good news about cities. For example. Grogan and Proscio's (2000) book, *Comeback Cities*, heralding a revival of America's inner cities through the work of community development corporations, received considerable media attention. The release of the 2000 Census data triggered a small flood of news reports about how, during the 1990s, poverty and crime rates declined in most central cities while population and homeownership rates increased. When the Brookings Institution released a report in early 2003 about the "dramatic" decline of concentrated poverty in the 1990s (Jargowsky, 2003), many major newspapers published stories about this trend, focusing on both the national data and local conditions.

Despite these examples, however, the day-to-day coverage of America's cities is overwhelmingly negative. More important, the drumbeat of negativism has its political consequences. Many Americans have concluded that problems such as poverty and crime may be intractable. Media coverage of our cities contributes to public cynicism about government in general and about society's capacity to solve urban problems. This undermines the

---

*Peter Dreier, "How the Media Compound Urban Problems." *Journal of Urban Affairs* 27 2, 2005: 193–201. Reprinted with permission.

311

public's trust in government, and thus has an overall conservative impact, regardless of whether editors and reporters consider themselves liberals, moderates, conservatives, or apolitical. Would you invest your hard-earned dollars in a company that has been failing for 40 years? The way the media frames urban issues compounds the obstacles to building a majoritarian coalition for metropolitan reform.

Crime News

Media coverage of urban crime is a good example. The public's beliefs about crime are based less on personal experience and more on what they see and read in the news media (Alderman, 1994). This is particularly important in terms of how suburbanites view the condition of nearby central cities. Americans are bombarded with news about crime, particularly violent crime. Crime news accounts for a significant share of daily news coverage. The phrase "if it bleeds, it leads" characterizes the disproportionate attention paid to crime and other threats to public safety, not only on local evening television news, but also on network television news and in daily newspapers. A study of news programming in 56 US cities found that violent crime accounted for two-thirds of all local news (Klite, Bardwell, & Salzmann, 1997). Murder accounts for less than 1% of all crime in Los Angeles but makes up 20% of all local news reports on crime (Iyengar, 1998). The extent of news coverage of crime typically has little to do with actual crime rates. The decline in urban violent crime rates in the 1990s did not result in a proportional decline in news coverage.

In addition, news coverage over-represents minorities as violent criminals (Alderman, 1994; Entman & Rojecki. 2000; Freeman, 1994). Elias' (1994) study of news magazines found that "criminals are conceptualized as black people, and crime as the violence they do to whites" (p. 6). In his study of local television news, Entman (1990, 1992) found black suspects were typically shown in handcuffs and in the custody of police officers while white suspects were typically shown with their attorneys (see also Dixon & Linz, 2000). Likewise, news reporting of the crack epidemic, starting in the 1980s, was heavily biased against urban African-Americans compared with the coverage of suburban white use of cocaine (Dreier & Reiman, 1996; Reeves & Campbell, 1994a, 1994b; Reinarman, 1994; Reinarman & Levine. 1997).

It comes as no surprise that even people who live in communities with little crime or drug problems think that they are the middle of a crime wave perpetrated primarily by black males (Liska & Baccaglina, 1990). As a result, "exposure to local news will strengthen public support for punitive approaches to crime and encourage the expression of racist attitudes" (Iyengar, 1998, p. 2; Valentino, 1999). Overall, local TV news programs "feed racial stereotypes, encouraging white hostility and fear of African-Americans" (Entman, 1994, p. 29). They portrays blacks as "violent and threatening toward whites, self-interested and demanding toward the body politic—continually causing problems for the law-abiding tax-paying majority" (Entman, 1994, p. 29).

Race and Poverty

Media portrayals of the urban poor overemphasize the so-called non-deserving poor and contribute to misleading racial stereotypes about the poor. Gilens (1999) found that news stories about poverty (in weekly news magazines and network nightly news shows) disproportionately focus on people who are on welfare or unemployed rather than those who are working. The stories about welfare recipients and the jobless are generally more negative in tone than stories about the working poor. The news media also exaggerates the extent to which African-Americans comprise the poor, a trend that began in the early 1960s and has since intensified. Between 1992 and 1998, the majority of people described as poor in weekly newsmagazines and television network news were black, even though the majority of poor Americans are white. Blacks comprised 29% of the nation's poor but accounted for 62% of the photographs accompanying news magazine stories about poverty.

Moreover, negative stories about poverty are disproportionately associated with photographs of African-Americans, while sympathetic portrayals of the poor (for example, connecting poverty to national economic conditions rather than personal characteristics, or stories about the working poor) are illustrated with photographs of whites. These trends contribute to a distorted view of the urban poor (Edy & Lawrence, 1999; Gilens, 1999).

Media coverage of urban blacks is typically framed as bad news. For example, news coverage of urban neighborhoods, particularly low-income black neighborhoods, focuses on problems rather than strengths, institutions, and assets (Kretzman & McKnight, 1993). Ettema and Peer (1996) analyzed news stories about two Chicago neighborhoods, Austin (a predominantly black neighborhood with a median household income of $24,877) and Lincoln Park (an overwhelmingly white neighborhood with a median income of $41,016) in the *Chicago Sun-Times* and *Chicago Tribune*. They found that "newspaper coverage of the lower income Austin neighborhood is largely a discourse of urban pathology" (p. 839). More than two-thirds of the stories about Austin were framed in terms of social problems compared with one-quarter of the stories about Lincoln Park. Stories about Austin viewed the community as crime-ridden and drug-infested. Both papers did, in fact, report good news, primarily efforts by individuals and community groups to respond to the symptoms of urban pathology, but stories about citizens and community groups organizing effectively to improve their communities were still rare.

The news media also distorts and racializes politics in its coverage of local elections. A study of local daily newspapers reporting on recent mayoral elections in Chicago, Los Angeles, and New York (each featured a white mayor succeeding an African-American mayor) found that news coverage focused primarily on the *horse race* aspects of elections, poll standings, endorsements, campaign strategies, contributions, and personalities rather than on such issues as urban development, education, crime, and city administration. In the Chicago papers' coverage of the 1989 and 1991 mayoral contests, for example, three out of every five paragraphs focused on horse race reporting. The newspapers also injected race into these election campaigns even when the candidates did not do so. News stories emphasized the racial horse race, assuming that the election was primarily about candidates seeking to consolidate their respective racial voting blocs. The media treated candidates' claims that they were seeking votes among all racial groups as mere rhetoric (Peer & Ettema, 1998; Sylvie, 1995). Such reporting undermines efforts to build cross-racial coalitions and address urban problems in class rather than racial terms.

Politics, Government, and Public Policy

Even after the elections are over, media coverage of local, state, and federal government pays more attention to politics (the ongoing horse race among public officials vying for attention) than to government (the distribution of public services and the effectiveness of government programs in our metropolitan areas). Indeed, newspapers allocate more space to sports than to local government and urban issues. They pay more attention to sports "box scores" than to "keeping score" of how well public officials and government agencies carry out public policies, or of the economic and social conditions in urban and suburban neighborhoods (Burd, 1986; Ernst, 1972).

Overall, the local newspaper (even those owned by national chains or conglomerates) is part of the urban growth coalition (Dreier, 1982; Mollenkopf, 1983; Molotch, 1976). Local news media, particularly newspapers, tend to be boosters, advocating economic growth in general and development projects intended to revitalize central business districts in particular. In the 1950s and 1960s, local newspapers eagerly promoted the federal urban renewal program as a tool to rebuild city downtowns. In recent decades, daily papers have generally supported construction of private sports stadiums, convention complexes, and large-scale transportation projects (such as Boston's Central Artery project and Los Angeles' Alameda Corridor project) as ways to promote civic pride, boost downtown land values, and make their cities more competitive. Occasionally the local press will oppose specific projects on environmental grounds or in response to significant community protest, but these are rare exceptions.

Part of the media's bias is due to the way it defines what is newsworthy, how it allocates its resources to identify news, and what kinds of people and organizations routinely become sources of information and, thus, news. For example, daily newspapers assign reporters to beats based on editors' views of where news is most likely to happen, such as city hall, the police department, and the courthouse. This leads, of course, to a self-fulfilling prophecy.

Because few newspapers (much less news magazines or TV stations) have regular beat reporters assigned to poor neighborhoods, stories about these areas are typically about breaking news (crime, fires, conflict) written by reporters with little familiarity with the community. Business-backed organizations (such as the chamber of commerce, foundations, or policy groups) have the resources (staff, reports, blue-ribbon task forces, social connections) to get their concerns into the media's line of vision, while low-income groups often have to resort to protest. As a result, local newspapers devote greater resources to official news (news initiated by government officials and agencies) and central business district concerns than to the concerns of low-income neighborhoods or to broad regional issues that require reporters to cover concerns that cross municipal boundaries. (Indeed, few newspapers have a regional beat designed to look at metropolitan-wide issues.) The media do not always take the public officials' perspective (indeed, they often seek to uncover mismanagement and misconduct) but they typically allow politicians and government officials to set the agenda regarding the issues that are covered (Gans, 1980; Sigal, 1973, 1986).

The national and local media often portray public policies addressing urban poverty and other problems as inefficient or mismanaged. The Aid to Families with Dependent Children program, for example, was often described as the *welfare mess* or *welfare abuse*. Stories focused on people who received benefits for which they were not eligible or who traded food stamps for drugs or alcohol, even though such abuses were exceptionally rare. Much less attention was paid to the fact that benefit levels were below the poverty line and that for many poor women it was a preferable alternative to low-wage work without health insurance (Edy & Lawrence, 1999).

Similarly, while the public housing program was generally reported sympathetically from the 1950s through the mid–1960s, since 1965 media coverage has been consistently negative, focusing on the anti-social behaviors (crime, drug use, gang membership) of its residents and presenting a misleading portrayal of public housing developments as high rise slums (Reed, 1999). The public still has misleading and stereotyped views about government-subsidized housing (the *projects*) despite the fact that, since the 1980s, most subsidized housing developments have been sponsored by community-based organizations, are designed as mid-rise or low-rise style buildings, and are well-managed.

Hardly ever do the media explain our urban condition as a consequence of federal policies that promote suburbanization and urban disinvestment. They generally do not acknowledge that efforts to revitalize cities (such as enterprise zones, community development block grants, subsidized housing, and others) have been counter to most federal policy. In effect, they are "swimming against the tide," trying to clean up the problems created by more powerful public policies that have promoted urban disinvestment (Dreier, Mollenkopf, & Swanstrom, 2005; O'Connor, 1999).

Even the recent upsurge of media interest in smart growth and suburban sprawl fails to examine these issues as the flip side of urban disinvestment. They are viewed primarily as reflecting consumer preferences for cars and single-family homes, not trends driven by federal transportation and housing policies. Suburban sprawl is framed by the media primarily as an environmental problem (pollution, traffic congestion, and loss of green space) and not as a problem of economic segregation.

The media frequently report on cities engaging in bidding wars to entice a particular company or shopping mall, but they rarely explain that this competition is fueled by federal and state zoning and tax policies that undermine the economic health of all the bidders (Cart, 1999; Chawkins, 1999; Egan, 1996; Firestone, 1999; Pedersen, Smith, & Adler, 1999; Purdum, 1999; Sanchez, 1999).

Everyday Problems and Collective Organizing

News coverage of the lives of ordinary people living in metropolitan areas focuses on the exceptional and unusual. The day-to-day concerns about making a living, health care, housing, neighboring, public services, and schools are typically out of the media's line of vision unless they feature drama and conflict. Everyday relations between different racial groups (including cooperation toward common goals or people simply getting along without rancor) are rarely newsworthy, while racial tensions and violence are staples of the news.

The daily realities of urban life become newsworthy when they are defined as problems, often a result of the findings of a study sponsored by a think tank, a government agency, a foundation, or a community group, or if a group resorts to protest to dramatize an issue. In the 1960s, for example, the New York City media paid little attention to slum housing, slum landlords, or the city's failure to enforce housing codes until tenant groups organized rent strikes and engaged in civil disobedience (Lipsky, 1970). Similarly, in the 1990s, Los Angeles media ignored slum housing problems until a blue-ribbon citizens' task force released a report documenting that one out of eight apartments in the city was substandard. Once the *Los Angeles Times* published a front-page article summarizing the report, public officials and tenant groups maneuvering to address the problem kept the issue alive (Tobar, 1997). Yet in the seven years after the public controversy occurred, the *Los Angeles Times* did not publish one follow-up news story to assess whether, or how well, the municipal government was implementing the code enforcement reforms it adopted in 1997 in response to the blue-ribbon report.

Rarely do the media report about solutions to problems, compounding popular cynicism that such problems are intractable. Rather, the media cover cities primarily as sites of social and economic problems. There are, of course, exceptions to this pattern. The news media run stories that show individual success stories, e.g., mothers who get off welfare and find a job. Their success is typically attributed to their individual character, not public policy. Occasionally the news media report community-level success stories, e.g., a well-run, low-income housing development sponsored by a church or community group. These examples are typically framed as "islands of success in a sea of failure."

Even rarer are stories that highlight systemic policy solutions or that reveal that government policies in other countries have made their cities more livable. Americans who rely primarily on mainstream media for information would hardly know that no other major industrial nation (including Canada) has allowed its cities to face the type of fiscal and social troubles confronting America's cities. Other democratic industrial nations do not permit the level of sheer destitution and decay found in America's cities (Dreier & Bernard, 1992). In terms of such indicators as violent crime, infant mortality, homelessness, poverty, and others, the US is the outlier among OECD nations (Rainwater & Smeeding, 2003). Such stories would demonstrate that our urban problems are neither inevitable nor intractable, but rather a matter of political priorities.

The efforts of poor and working class families to collectively solve problems through grassroots organizing are virtually invisible in the mainstream media unless it involves drama and conflict. Stories about unions, for example, appear primarily during strikes or other episodes of conflict, particularly if they include violence (Martin, 2004; Puette, 1992; Tasini, 1990; Witt, 1999). The work of community organizations like ACORN and the Industrial Areas Foundation network, and their many counterparts in cities around the country, are likewise virtually off the media radar screen unless they engage in dramatic public protests to draw attention to the problems they are organizing around (Putnam & Feldstein, 2003; Reynolds, 2002, 2004).

Reading or viewing the nation's mainstream press over the past decade, for example, you would hardly know that there has been growing momentum at the local level for progressive urban policies. One dramatic example is the growing number of cities (now more than 100) that have adopted living wage laws, a tribute to the alliances between unions, community organizations, and faith-based groups that have emerged in the past decade (Pollin & Luce, 1998; Reynolds, 2002). Local newspapers and TV stations will report on specific living wage battles in their cities but rarely put them in the context of a growing national movement for urban reform and for lifting the working poor out of poverty. Similarly, with a few exceptions, all urban daily newspapers have business pages that report on the ups and downs of financial corporations (interest rates, mergers, new branch openings), but they do not routinely report on the persistent problem of bank redlining (mortgage discrimination) in major cities and metropolitan areas unless local community groups are engaged in public protest. Even then the media frame these protests as specific battles between a community organization and a particular lender rather than as part of a broader national movement for community reinvestment that has made significant progress since the 1980s in changing national laws and corporate banking practices (Dreier, 2003).

Grassroots organizing is seldom dramatic. The news media rarely pay attention to the small miracles that happen when ordinary people join together to channel their frustration and anger into solid organizations that win improvements in workplaces, neighborhoods, and schools. The media are generally more interested in political theater and confrontation—when workers strike, when community activists protest, or when hopeless people resort to rioting. As a result, much of the best organizing work during the last decade has been unheralded in the mainstream press. This silence contributes to public cynicism by failing to show how urban conditions can improve when people organize effectively to pressure business and government to reform institutional practices and policies.

Conclusion

Entman (1994) argues that the ways the news media frame urban and regional matters may be "making urban America less governable, by deepening the chasm of misunderstanding and distrust between blacks and whites" (p. 29). Indeed, in our increasingly diverse metropolitan areas the tendency of the media to frame social issues in primarily racial terms undermines efforts at building bridges across racial and geographic boundaries.

More broadly, the media give their audience of readers and viewers little reason for optimism that ordinary people working together effectively can make a difference, that solutions are within reach, and that public policies can make a significant difference. As a result, what the media report as the public's apathy or indifference may simply reflect their resignation about the potential for changing the status quo. As Fallows (1997) observes, news coverage of urban affairs conveys the message that "the world being described is inexplicably and uncontrollably perilous" and that "the individual citizen can do nothing at all about the dangers except to avoid any entanglement in them" (p. 199). This kind of reporting is a recipe for public distrust of government and suspicion of policies to improve economic, social, and environmental conditions in our metropolitan areas.

References

Alderman, J. D. (1994). "Leading the Public: The Media's Focus on Crime Shaped Sentiment." *The Public Perspective,* 5, 26–27.

Burd, G. (1986). "Reporting an Urban "Box Score": The Journalistic 'Sports' Record to Measure Local Urban Performance." *Journal of Urban Affairs,* 8(2), 85–98.

Cart, J. (1999, September 7). "Rapidly Growing Phoenix Finds Dust Unsettling." *Los Angeles Times,* p. 1.

Chawkins, S. (1999, February 7). "Homes Sprouting, Farms Dying." *Los Angeles Times,* p. 1.

Dixon, T., & Linz, D. (2000). "Overrepresentation and Underrepresentation of African-Americans and Latinos as Lawbreakers on Television News." *Journal of Communication,* 50(2), 131–154.

Dreier, P. (1982). "The Position of the Press in the U.S. Power Structure." *Social Problems,* 29(3), 298–310.

Dreier, P. (2003). "The Future of Community Reinvestment: Challenges and Opportunities." *Journal of the American Planning Association,* 69(4), 341–353.

Dreier, P., & Bernard, E. (1992). "Kinder, Gentler Canada." *The American Prospect*, Winter, 85–88.

Dreier, P., & Reiman, J. (1996). "Prisoners of Misleading Facts." *Dissent*, Spring, 8–9.

Dreier, P., Mollenkopf, J., & Swanstrom, T. *Place Matters: Metropolitics for the 21st Century* (2nd ed.). Lawrence, KS: University Press of Kansas, 2005.

Edy, J., & Lawrence, R. (1999). Inventing Poverty: Popular Images of the Poor and U.S. Welfare Policy, 1930–1996. Paper presented at the American Political Science Association meetings, Atlanta.

Egan, T. (1996, December 29). "Urban Sprawl Strains Western States." *New York Times*, p. 1.1.

Elias, R. (1994b). "Official Stories: Media Coverage of American Crime Policy." *Humanist*, 54, 3–8.

Entman, R. (1990). "Racism and Local TV News." *Critical Studies in Mass Communication*, 7, 329–343.

Entman, R. (1992). "Blacks in the News: Television, Modern Racism and Cultural Change." *Journalism Quarterly*, 69, 341–361.

Entman, R. (1994). "African-Americans According to TV News." *Media Studies Journal*, 8(3), 29–38.

Entman, R., & Rojecki, A. *The Black Image in the White Mind: Media and Race in America*. Chicago: University of Chicago Press, 2000.

Ernst. S. W. (1972). "Baseball or Brickbats: A Content Analysis of Community Development." *Journalism Quarterly*, 49(1), 86–90.

Ettema, J. , & Peer, L. (1996). "Good News from a Bad Neighborhood: Toward an Alternative to the Discourse of Urban Pathology." *Journalism & Mass Communication Quarterly*, 73(4), 835–856.

Fallows, J. *Breaking News: How the Media Undermine American Democracy*. New York: Random House, 1997.

Firestone, D. (1999, November 21). "Suburban Comforts Thwart Atlanta's Plans to Limit Sprawl." *New York Times*, p. 1.1.

Freeman, M. (1994). "Networks Doubled Crime Coverage in '93 Despite Flat Violence Levels in US Society." *Mediaweek*, 4, 3–4.

Gans. H. *Deciding What's News*. New York: Vintage, 1980.

Gilens, M. *Why Americans Hate Welfare: Race, Media, and the Politics of Antipoverty Policy*. Chicago: University of Chicago Press, 1999.

Grogan, P., & Proscio, T. *Comeback Cities: A Blueprint for Urban Neighborhood Revival*. Boulder, Colorado: Westview Press, 2000.

Iyengar, S. (1998). *"Media Efect" Paradigms for the Analysis of Local Television News*. Paper presented at the Annie E. Casey Foundation Planning Meeting, September.

Klite, P., Bardwell, R. A., & Salzmann, 1. (1997). "Local Television News: Getting Away with Murder." *Harvard International Journal of Press/Politics* 2, 102–12.

Kretzman, J. P., & McKnight. J. L. *Building Communities from the Inside Out*. Evanston, IL: Northwestern University Center for Urban Affairs and Policy Research, 1993.

Largowsky, P. *Stunning Progress, Hidden Problems: The Dramatic Decline of Concentrated Poverty in the 1990s*. Washington, DC: Brookings Institution, Center on Urban and Metropolitan Policy, 2003.

Lipsky, M. *Protest in City Politics*. Chicago: Rand McNally, 1970.

Liska, A., & Baccaglini. W. (1990). "Feeling Safe by Comparison: Crime in the Newspapers." *Social Problems,* 37(3), 360–374.

Martin, C. *Framed! Labor and the Corporate Media.* Ithaca, NY: ILR Press, 2004.

Mollenkopf, J. *The Contested City.* Princeton: Princeton University Press, 1983.

Molotch, H. (1976). "The City as a Growth Machine." *American Journal of Sociology,* 82(2), 309–332.

O'Connor, A. (1999). "Swimming Against the Tide: A Brief History of Federal Policy in Poor Communities." In R. Ferguson & W. Dickens (eds.), *Urban Problems and Community Development* (pp. 77–121). Washington, DC: Brookings Institution Press.

Pedersen, D., Smith, V., & Adler, J. (1999, July 19). "Sprawling, Sprawling." *Newsweek,* p. 22.

Peer, L.. & Ettema, J. S. (1998). "The Mayor's Race: Campaign Coverage and the Discourse of Race in America's Three Largest Cities." *Critical Studies in Mass Communication,* 15(3), 255–278.

Pollin, R., & Luce, S. *The Living Wage: Building a Fair Economy.* New York: The New Press, 1998.

Puette, W. *Through Jaundiced Eyes: How the Media View Organized Labor.* Ithaca. NY: ILR Press, 1992.

Purdum, T. (1999, February 6). "Suburban Sprawl Takes its Place on the Political Landscape." *New York Times,* p. A24.

Putnam, R., & Feldstein, L. *Better Together: Restoring the American Community.* New York: Simon & Schuster, 2003.

Rainwater, L., & Smeeding, T. *Poor Kids in a Rich Country: America's Children in Comparative Perspective.* New York: Russell Sage Foundation, 2003.

Reed, M. (1999). "Representing the Projects: Race, Class, and Poverty in National Media Representations of Public Housing in the U.S., 1950–1997." Paper presented at American Sociological Association meetings, Chicago.

Reeves, J. L., & Campbell, R. *Cracked Coverage: Television News, the Anti-Cocaine Crusade, and the Reagan Legacy.* Durham, NC: Duke University Press, 1994.

Reeves, J. L., & Campbell, R. (1994). "Coloring the Crack Crisis." *Media Studies Journal,* 8(3), 71–80.

Reinarman, C. (1994). "The Social Construction of Drug Scares." In P. A. Adler & P. Adler (eds.), *Construction of Deviance.* Belmont, CA: Wadsworth Publishing Company.

Reinarman, c., & Levine, H. G. (1997). "The Crack Attack: Politics and Media in the Crack Scare." In C. Reinannan, & H. G. Levine (eds.), *Crack in America* (pp. 18–51). Berkeley: University of California Press.

Reynolds, D. B. *Taking the High Road: Communities Organize for Economic Change.* Armonk. NY: M .E. Sharpe, 2002.

Reynolds, D. B. (ed.). *Partnering for Change: Unions and Community Groups Build Coalitions for Economic Justice.* Armonk, NY: M.E. Sharpe, 2004.

Sanchez, J. (1999, November 23). "LA County's Growth Spurt Pushes North." *Los Angeles Times,* p. 1.

Sigal, L. *Reporters and Officials.* Lexington, MA: DC Heath Co., 1973.

Sigal. L. (1986). "Sources Make the News." In R. Manoff, & M. Schudson (eds.), *Reading the News* (pp. 9–37). New York: Pantheon.

Sylvie, G . (1995). "Black Mayoral Candidates and the Press: Running for Coverage." *Howard Journal of Communications,* 6(1–2), 89–101.

Tasini, J. (1990)." Lost in the Margins: Labor and the Media." *Extra!,* 3, 2–10.

Tobar, H. (1997, July 20). "Housing Laws No Cure for Slums' Ills." *Los Angeles Times,* p. 1.

Valentino, N. (1999). "Crime News and the Priming of Racial Attitudes During Evaluations of the President." *Public Opinion Quarterly,* 63(3), 293–320.

Witt, M. (1999, August 30). "Missing in Action: Media Images of Real Workers." *Los Angeles Times,* p. 1.

Downing Mass Transit*

Joe Feagin and Robert Parker

[M]ost U.S. cities have become *multinucleated*, with major commercial, industrial, and residential areas no longer closely linked to or dependent upon the downtown center. Decentralization has become characteristic of our cities from coast to coast. Essential to decentralization has been the development and regular extension of an automobile-dominated transportation system serving businesses and the general citizenry, but mostly paid for by rank-and-file taxpayers. With and without citizen consent, corporate capitalists, industrialists and developers, and allied political officials have made key decisions fundamentally shaping the type of transportation system upon which all Americans now depend.

The Auto-Oil-Rubber Industrial Complex

The auto-oil-rubber industrial complex has long been central to both the general economy and the urban transportation system in the United States. Automobile and auto-related industries provide a large proportion, sometimes estimated at one-sixth, of all jobs, although this proportion may be decreasing with the decline and stagnation in the auto industry over the last two decades. An estimated one-quarter to one-half of the land in central cities is used for the movement, storage, selling, and parking of automobiles, trucks, and buses. The expanding production of automobiles and trucks has been coordinated with the expansion of highways and freeways and has facilitated the bulging suburbanization around today's cities.

Because of the dominance of autos and trucks in the U.S. transportation system, the traditional social scientists… have typically viewed that transportation system as preordained by the American "love" for the automobile. For example, in a recent book on Los Angeles, historian Scott Bottles argues that "America's present urban transportation system largely reflects choices made by the public itself"; the public freely chose the automobile as a "liberating and democratic technology."[1] Conventional explanations for auto-centered patterns focus on the response of a market system to these consumers. Auto-linked technologies are discussed as though they force human decisions: Thus "the city dweller, especially in recent times, has been a victim of the technological changes that have been wrought in transportation systems…."[2] [T]raditional ecologists and other social scientists view the

---

*Joe R. Feagin and Robert E. Parker, *Building American Cities: The Urban Real Estate Game* (Frederick, MD: Beard Books, 2002). Reprinted with permission.

complexity and shape of cities as largely determined by technological developments in transportation—a reasonable view—but these technologies are not carefully examined in terms of their economic contexts, histories, and possible technological alternatives. For example, unlike the United States, numerous capitalist countries in Europe, including prosperous West Germany, have a mixed rail transit/automobile transport system. Their interurban and intraurban rail transit remains very important. For this reason, the U.S. system cannot be assumed to be simply the result of "free" consumer choices in a market context. The capitalistic history and decision-making contexts that resulted in the positioning of automobiles at the heart of the U.S. transportation system must be examined.

Early Mass Rail Transit

Rural and urban Americans have not always been so dependent on automobiles for interurban and intraurban transport. In the years between the 1880s and the 1940s many cities had significant mass transit systems. By 1890 electric trolleys were in general use. Indeed, electric trolley routes, elevated railroads, and subways facilitated the first urban expansion and decentralization. Some investor-owned rail transit companies extended their trolley lines beyond existing urbanized areas out into the countryside in an attempt to profit from the land speculation along the rail lines. Glenn Yago has documented how transit owners and real estate speculators worked together to ensure the spatial and economic development of cities by private enterprise. Transit companies were a significant force in urban sprawl. The suburban spread of Los Angeles, for example, got its initial push from the expansion of trolley rail lines. Not initially laid out as an automobile city, this sprawling metropolis developed along streetcar tracks; only later was the streetcar network displaced by automobiles.[3]

The reorganization and disruption of mass rail transit that took place in the early 1900s did not result just from the challenge of improved automobile technology. Rather, capitalist entrepreneurs and private corporations seeking profits reorganized and consolidated existing rail transit systems. Electrification of horse-drawn streetcars increased investment costs and stimulated concentration of ownership in larger "transit trusts" of landowning, finance, and utility entrepreneurs. Mergers of old transit firms and the assembly of new companies were commonplace, and there was much speculation in transit company stock. Yago has provided evidence on the corrupt accounting practices, over-extension of lines for real estate speculation, and overcapitalization which led to the bankruptcy of more than one-third of the private urban transit companies during the period 1916–1923.[4] Sometimes the capitalists involved in the transit companies were too eager for profits. "These actions in turn," Charles Cheape notes, "drained funds, discouraged additional investment, and contributed significantly to the collapse and reorganization of many transit systems shortly after World War I and again in the 1930s."[5]

Ironically, one consequence of the so-called "progressive" political reform movement in cities in the first decades of the twentieth century was that supervision of rail transit systems was often placed in the hands of business-dominated regulatory commissions, many of whose members were committed to the interests of corporate America (for example, transit stock manipulation for profit), rather than to the welfare of the general public. In numerous cases the extraordinary profits made by rail transit entrepreneurs, together with their ties to corrupt politicians, created a negative public image—which in turn made the public less enthusiastic about new tax-supported subsidies and fare hikes for the troubled rail transit systems. Moreover, as the profits of many of the private transit firms declined, public authorities in some cities, including Boston and New York, were forced to take over the transit lines from the poorly managed private companies in response to citizen pressure for mass transportation. This fact suggests that there has long been popular *demand* for publicly owned rail transit that is reliable, convenient, and inexpensive. Indeed, during the period 1910–1930 a *majority* of Americans either could not afford, because of modest incomes, or could not use, because of age or handicap, an automobile.[6]

A Corporate Plan to Kill Mass Transit?

By the late 1910s and 1920s the ascension of the U.S. auto-oil-rubber industrial complex brought new corporate strategies to expand automobile markets and secure government subsidies for road infrastructure. Mass rail transit hindered the profit-oriented interests of this car-centered industrial complex, whose executives became involved not only in pressuring governments to subsidize roads but also in the buying up of mass transit lines. For example, in the early 1920s, Los Angeles had the largest and most effective trolley car system in the United States. Utilizing more than a thousand miles of track, the system transported millions of people yearly. During World War II, the streetcars ran 2,800 scheduled runs a day.[7] But by the end of that war, the trolleys were disappearing. And their demise had little to do with consumer choice. As news analyst Harry Reasoner has observed, it "was largely a result of a criminal conspiracy":

> The way it worked was that General Motors, Firestone Tire and Standard Oil of California and some other companies, depending on the location of the target, would arrange financing for an outfit called National City Lines, which cozied up to city councils and county commissioners and bought up transit systems like L.A.'s. Then they would junk or sell the electric cars and pry up the rails for scrap and beautiful, modern buses would be substituted, buses made by General Motors and running on Firestone Tires and burning Standard's gas.[8]

Within a month after the trolley system in Los Angeles was purchased, 237 new buses arrived. It is important to realize that, for all the financial and management problems created by the private owners or the rail transit firms, the old transit systems were still popular. In the year prior to the takeover, the Los Angeles electric lines made $1.5 million in profits and carried more than 200 million passengers. The logic behind the corporate takeover plan was clear. The auto-related firms acted because a trolley car can carry the passengers of several dozen automobiles.

During the 1930s GM created a holding company through which it and other auto-related companies channeled money to buy up electric transit systems in 45 cities from New York to Los Angeles. As researcher Bradford Snell has outlined it, the process had three stages. First, General Motors (GM) helped the Greyhound corporation displace long-distance passenger transportation from railroads to buses. Then GM and other auto-related companies bought up and dismantled numerous local electric transit systems, replacing them with the GM-built buses. Moreover, in the late 1940s, GM was convicted in a Chicago federal court of having conspired to destroy electric transit and to convert trolley systems to diesel buses, whose production GM monopolized. William Dixon, the man who put together the criminal conspiracy case for the federal government, argued that individual corporate executives should be sent to jail. Instead, each received a trivial $1 fine. The corporations were assessed a modest $5,000 penalty, the maximum under the law.[9] In spite of this conviction, GM continued to play a role in converting electric transit systems to diesel buses. And these diesel buses provided more expensive mass transit: "The diesel bus, as engineered by GM, has a shorter life expectancy, higher operating costs, and lower overall productivity than electric buses. GM has thus made the bus economically noncompetitive with the car also."[10] One source of public discontent with mass transit was this inferiority of the new diesel buses compared to the rail transit cars that had been displaced without any consultation with consumers. Not surprisingly, between 1936 and 1955 the number of operating trolley cars in the United States dropped from about 40,000 to 5,000.

In a lengthy report GM officials have argued that electric transit systems were already in trouble when GM began intervening. As noted above, some poorly managed transit systems were declining already, and some had begun to convert partially to buses before GM's vigorous action. So from GM's viewpoint, the corporation's direct intervention only accelerated the process. This point has been accented by Bottles, who shows that GM did not single-handedly destroy the streetcar systems in Los Angeles.[11] These privately controlled systems were providing a lesser quality of service before GM became involved. The profit milking and corruption of the private streetcar firms in Los Angeles were not idiosyncratic but were common for privately owned mass transport in numerous cities.

Also important in destroying mass transit was the new and aggressive multimillion-dollar marketing of automobiles and trucks by General Motors and other automobile companies across the United States. And the automobile companies and their advertisers were not the only powerful actors involved in killing off numerous mass transit systems. Bankers and public officials also played a role. Yago notes that "after World War II, banks sold bankrupt and obsolete transit systems throughout the country at prices that bore no relation to the systems' real values."[12] Often favoring the auto interests, local banks and other financial institutions tried to limit government bond issues that could be used to finance new equipment and refurbish the remaining rail transit systems.

Because of successful lobbying by executives from the auto-oil-rubber complex, and their own acceptance of a motorization perspective, most government officials increasingly backed street and highway construction. They cooperated with the auto industry in eliminating many mass transit systems. Increased governmental support for auto and truck transportation systems has meant systematic disinvestment in mass transit systems. Over the several decades since World War II, governmental mass transit subsidies have been small compared with highway subsidies. This decline has hurt low-and moderate-income people the most. Less public transit since World War II has meant increased commuting time in large cities where people are dependent on the automobile, which is especially troublesome for moderate-income workers who may not be able to afford a reliable car; less mass transit has also meant increased consumer expenditures for automobiles and gasoline. Auto expansion has frustrated the development of much mass transit because growing street congestion slows down buses and trolleys, further reducing their ridership. As a result, governmental funding for public rail transit has been cut, again chasing away riders who dislike poorly maintained equipment. And fares have been increased. Riders who can use automobiles do so. And the downward spiral has continued to the point of extinction of most public rail transit systems.[13]

Mass transit was allowed to decline by the business-oriented government officials in most cities. Consumer desires were only partly responsible for this. Consumers did discover the freedom of movement of autos, and even in cities with excellent rail transit systems many prefer the auto for at least some types of travel. But consumers make their choices *from the alternatives available*. With no real rail transportation alternative to the automobile in most urban areas, consumers turned to it as a necessity. Ironically, as the auto and truck congestion of the cities has mounted between the 1950s and the 1980s, more and more citizens, and not a few business leaders, have called for new mass transit systems for their cities.[14]

...

Mass Transit in Other Capitalistic Countries

Comparative research on U.S. and German transportation systems by Yago has demonstrated the importance of looking at corporate power and economic structure. Mass rail transport developed in Germany before 1900. In the 1870s and 1880s the German national and local governments became interested in mass transit; at that time the coal, steel, iron, chemical, and electrical manufacturing companies were dominant in German capitalism. Interestingly, corporate executives in these industries supported the development of rail transportation; by 1900 the national and local governments had subsidized and institutionalized intraurban and interurban rail transport systems, which served the transport needs not only of the citizenry but also of the dominant coal, steel, chemical, and electrical industries. These industries also supplied equipment and supplies for the rail networks. In contrast, in the United States early transport companies were involved in manipulation and land speculation; transit service was rarely the central goal of the early rail transit firms. In contrast to Germany, dominance of U.S. industry by a major economic concentration did not come to the United States until after 1900, and when it did come, the auto-oil-rubber industrial complex was dominant. There was no other integrated industrial complex to contest this dominance of the auto-related firms, and governmental intervention was directed at support of motorization and the automobile. In Germany governmental intervention for mass rail transit had preceded this dominance of the motorization lobby. This suggests that the timing of the implementation of technological innovations in relation to corporate development is critical to their dominance, or lack of dominance, in cities and societies.[15]

Interestingly, it was the Nazi interest in motorization and militarization in the 1930s that sharply increased the role of auto and truck transport in Germany. Adolf Hitler worked hard to motorize the military and the society. After World War II, the German auto lobby increased in power, and an auto transport system was placed alongside the rail transport system. However, the West German government and people have maintained a strong commitment to both systems; and the OPEC-generated oil crisis of the 1970s brought an unparalleled revival of mass transit in Germany, whereas in the United States there was a more modest revival. The reason for the dramatic contrast between the two countries was that Germany had retained a rail passenger transport system, one that is still viable and energy conserving to the present day.

Endnotes

[1]Scott L. Bottles, *Los Angeles and the Automobile: The Making of the Modern City* (Berkeley: University of California Press, 1987), p. 249.

[2]Delbert A. Taebel and John V. Cornehls, *The Political Economy of Urban Transportation* (Port Washington, NY: Kennikat Press, 1977), pp. 6–7.

[3]Glenn Yago, *The Decline of Transit* (Cambridge: Cambridge University Press, 1984).

[4]Ibid.

[5]Charles W. Cheape, *Moving the Masses* (Cambridge, MA: Harvard Univeresity Press, 1980), p. 215.

[6]Glenn Yago, "The Coming Crisis of U.S. Transportation," paper presented at the Conference on New Perspectives on Urban Political Economy, American University, Washington, D.C., May 1981, p. 9.

[7]CBS News, *60 Minutes*, "Clang, Clang, Clang Went the Trolley!" *60 Minutes* Program Transcript, December 6, 1987.

[8]Ibid.

[9]Bradford C. Snell, "American Ground Transport," in *The Urban Scene*, edited by Joe R. Feagin (New York: Random House, 1979), pp. 239–266.

[10]Ibid., pp. 239–266.

[11]Bottles, *Los Angeles and the Automobile: The Making of the Modern City*.

[12]Yago, "The Coming Crisis of U.S. Transportation," p. 10.

[13]Ibid., pp. 6–7.

[14]Helen Leavitt, *Superhighway-Superhoax* (Garden City, NY: Doubleday, 1970), p. 9.

[15]Yago, *The Decline of Transit*, pp. 179–183.

Environmental Dumping in Dallas/Houston*

Robert Bullard

Growing empirical evidence shows that toxic-waste dumps, municipal landfills, garbage incinerators, and similar noxious facilities are not randomly scattered across the American landscape. The siting process has resulted in minority neighborhoods (regardless of class) carrying a greater burden of localized costs than either affluent or poor white neighborhoods. Differential access to power and decision making found among black and white communities also institutionalized siting disparities.

Toxic-waste facilities are often located in communities that have high percentages of poor, elderly, young, and minority residents.[1] An inordinate concentration of uncontrolled toxic-waste sites is found in black and Hispanic urban communities.[2] For example, when Atlanta's ninety-four uncontrolled toxic-waste sites are plotted by zip code areas, more than 82.8 percent of the city's black population compared with 60.2 percent of its white population were found living in waste site areas. Despite its image as the "capital of the New South," Atlanta is the most segregated big city in the region. More than 86 percent of the city's blacks live in mostly black neighborhoods. As is the case for other cities, residential segregation and housing discrimination limit mobility options available to black Atlantans.

Siting disparities also hold true for other minorities and in areas outside the southern United States. Los Angeles, the nation's second largest city, has a total of sixty uncontrolled toxic waste sites. More than 60 percent of the city's Hispanics live in waste-site areas compared with 35.3 percent of Los Angeles's white population. Although Hispanics are less segregated than the black population, more than half of them live in mostly Hispanic neighborhoods. The city's Hispanic community is concentrated in the eastern half of the city where the bulk of the uncontrolled toxic-waste sites are found.

On the other hand, large commercial hazardous-waste landfills and disposal facilities are more likely to be found in rural communities in the southern blackbelt.[3] Many of these facilities that are located in black communities are invisible toxic time bombs waiting for a disaster to occur.

Finally, the burden, or negative side, of industrial development has not been equally distributed across all segments of the population. Living conditions in many communities have not improved very much with new growth. Black communities became the dumping grounds for various types of unpopular facilities, including toxic wastes, dangerous chemicals, paper mills, and other polluting industries.

---

*Robert D. Bullard, *Dumping in Dixie: Race, Class and Environmental Quality* (Boulder, CO: Westview Press, 1990). Reprinted with permission.

The path out of this environmental quagmire is clearly one that involves more communities in activities designed to reclaim the basic right of all Americans—the right to live and work in a healthy environment. A political strategy is also needed that can draw from a wide cross-section of individuals and groups who share a common interest in preservation of environmental standards.

...

Most Americans encounter some type of unwanted land uses in or near where they live. Decisions surrounding the placement of needed (but unwanted) public facilities such as sewage treatment plants or municipal landfills, for example, have been hotly debated in community forums, planning boards, and city government. The usual consensus of these meetings is that few people want noxious facilities near their homes. Locational conflict involving unwanted land uses is inevitable. The question is, How will such conflicts be resolved? Unwanted land uses engender a sense of unfairness because they "gravitate to disadvantaged areas: poor, minority, sparsely populated, or politically underrepresented communities that cannot fight them off and become worse places to live after they arrive."[4]

Houston's Northwood Manor Neighborhood

In the 1970s, Houston was dubbed the "golden buckle" of the Sunbelt and the "petrochemical capital" of the world. The city experienced unparalleled economic expansion and population growth during the 1970s. By 1982, Houston emerged as the nation's fourth largest city with a population of 1.7 million persons spread over more than 585 square miles.[5] In 1980, the city's black community was made up of nearly a half million residents, or 28 percent of the city's total population. Black Houston, however, remained residentially segregated from the larger community. More than 81 percent of the city's blacks lived in mostly black areas with major concentrations in northeast and southeast sections of the city.

Houston is the only major city in the United States that does not have zoning. The city's landscape has been shaped by haphazard and irrational land-use planning, a pattern characterized by excessive infrastructure chaos.[6] In the absence of zoning, developers have used renewable deed restrictions as a means of land-use control within subdivisions. Lower-income, minority, and older neighborhoods have had difficulty enforcing and renewing deed restrictions. Deed restrictions in these areas are often allowed to lapse because individuals may be preoccupied with making a living and may not have the time, energy, or faith in government to get the needed signatures of neighborhood residents to keep their deed restrictions in force. Moreover, the high occupancy turnover and large renter population in many inner-city neighborhoods further weaken the efficacy of deed restrictions as a protectionist device.

Ineffective land-use regulations have created a nightmare for many of Houston's neighborhoods—especially the ones that are ill equipped to fend off industrial encroachment. Black Houston, for example, has had to contend with a disproportionately large share of garbage dumps, landfills, salvage yards, automobile "chop" shops, and a host of other locally unwanted land uses. The siting of nonresidential facilities has heightened animosities between the black community and the local government. This is especially true in the case of solid-waste disposal facility siting.

Public officials learn fast that solid-waste management can become a volatile political issue. Generally, controversy centers around charges that disposal sites are not equitably spread in quadrants of the city; equitable siting would distribute the burden and lessen the opposition. Finding suitable sites for sanitary landfills has become a critical problem mainly because no one wants to have a waste facility as a neighbor. Who wants to live next to a place where household waste—some of which is highly toxic—is legally dumped and where hazardous wastes may be illegally dumped?

The burden of having a municipal landfill, incinerator, transfer station, or some other type of waste disposal facility near one's home has not been equally borne by Houston's neighborhoods. Black Houston has become the dumping grounds for the city's household garbage.[7] Over the past fifty years, the city has used two basic methods of disposing of its solid waste: incineration and landfill. The data in Table 1 show the location of the city-owned waste disposal facilities. Thirteen disposal facilities were operated by the city from the late 1920s to the mid–1970s. The city operated eight garbage incinerators (five large units and three mini-units), six of which were located in mostly black neighborhoods, one of which was located in a Hispanic neighborhood, and one site was operated in a mostly white area.

All five of the large garbage incinerators were located in minority neighborhoods—four black and one Hispanic. All five of the city-owned landfills were found in black neighborhoods. Although black neighborhoods composed just over one-fourth of the city's population, more than three-fourths of Houston's solid-waste facilities were found in these neighborhoods. Moreover, lower-income areas, or "pockets of poverty," have a large share—twelve out of thirteen—garbage dumps and incinerators.

These environmental stressors compound the myriad of social ills (e.g., crowding, crime, poverty, drugs, unemployment, congestion, infrastructure deterioration, etc.) that exist in Houston's Community Development Block Grant (CDBG) target area neighborhoods.

The Texas Department of Health (TDH) is the state agency that grants permits for standard sanitary landfills. From 1970 to 1978, TDH issued four sanitary landfill permits for the disposal of Houston's solid waste. The data in Table 2 illustrate that siting of privately

TABLE 1   City of Houston Garbage Incinerators and Municipal Landfills

Neighborhood	Location	Incinerator	Landfill	Target Area[a]	Ethnicity of Neighborhood[b]
Fourth Ward	Southwest	1	1	Yes	Black
Cottage Grove	Northwest	1	-	Yes	Black
Kashmere Gardens	Northeast	2	-	Yes	Black
Sunnyside	Southeast	1	2	Yes	Black
Navigation	Southeast	1	-	Yes	Hispanic
Larchmont	Southwest	1	-	No	White
Carverdale	Northwest	1	-	Yes	Black
Trinity Gardens	Northeast	-	1	Yes	Black
Acres Homes	Northwest	-	1	Yes	Black

[a]Target areas are designated neighborhoods under Houston's Community Development Block Grant (CDBG) program.

[b]Ethnicity of neighborhood represents the racial/ethnic group that constitutes a numerical majority in the census tracts that make up the neighborhood.

TABLE 2   Privately Owned Houston Sanitary Landfills Permitted by the Texas Department of Health, 1970–1978

Site	Location	Year Permitted	Neighborhood	Ethnicity of Neighborhood
Holmes Road	Southeast	1970	Almeda Plaza	Black
McCarty	Northeast	1971	Chattwood[a]	White
Holmes Road	Southeast	1978	Almeda Plaza	Black
Whispering Pines	Northeast	1978	Northwood Manor	Black

[a]This predominantly white neighborhood is located just north of the McCarty landfill. The Chattwood neighborhood lies within Houston's Settegast Target Area. The Settegast Target Area had undergone a dramatic racial transition from 40 percent black in 1970 to more than 70 percent black in 1980.

owned sanitary landfills in Houston followed the pattern established by the city. That is, disposal sites were located in mostly black areas of the city. Three of the four privately owned landfill sites are located in black neighborhoods.

Controversy surrounding landfill siting peaked in the late 1970s with the proposal to build the Whispering Pines landfill in Houston's Northwood Manor neighborhood. In 1980, the suburban neighborhood had a population of 8,449 residents, of whom 82.4 percent were black. The subdivision consists primarily of single-family home owners. It also sits in the midst of the predominately black North Forest Independent School District—one of the poorest suburban districts in the Houston area.

Northwood Manor residents thought they were getting a shopping center or new homes in their subdivision when construction on the landfill site commenced. When they learned the truth, they began to organize their efforts to stop the dump. It is ironic that many of the residents who were fighting the construction of the waste facility had moved to Northwood Manor in an effort to escape landfills in their former Houston neighborhoods.

Local residents formed the Northeast Community Action Group (NECAG)—a spin-off organization from the local neighborhood civic association to halt construction of the facility. They later filed a lawsuit in federal court to stop the siting of the landfill in their neighborhood. The residents and their black attorney, Linda McKeever Bullard, charged the Texas Department of Health and the private disposal company (Browning-Ferris Industries) with racial discrimination in the selection of the Whispering Pines landfill site.[8] Residents were upset because the proposed site was not only near their homes but within 1,400 feet of their high school. Smiley High School was not equipped with air conditioning—not an insignificant point in the hot and humid Houston climate. Windows are usually left open while school is in session. Moreover, seven North Forest Schools—also without air conditioning—can be found in Northwood Manor and contiguous neighborhoods.

The lawsuit that was filed in 1979 finally went to trial in 1984. The federal district judge in Houston ruled against the residents and the landfill was built. The class-action lawsuit, however, did produce some changes in the way environmental issues were dealt with in the city's black community. First, the Houston city council, acting under intense political pressure from local residents, passed a resolution in 1980 that prohibited city-owned trucks carrying solid waste from dumping at the controversial landfill. Second, the Houston city council passed an ordinance restricting the construction of solid-waste sites near public facilities such as schools. This action was nothing less than a form of zoning. Third, the Texas Department of Health updated its requirements of landfill permit applicants to include detailed land-use, economic, and socio-demographic data on areas where they proposed to site standard sanitary landfills. Fourth, and probably most important, black residents sent a clear signal to the Texas Department of Health, city government, and private disposal companies that they would fight any future attempts to place waste disposal facilities in their neighborhoods. The landfill question appears to have galvanized and politicized a part of the Houston community, the black community, which for years had been inactive on environmental issues.

West Dallas (Texas)

Dallas is the seventh largest city in the nation with a population of 904,078 in 1980. The 265,594 blacks who live in Dallas represent 29.4 percent of the city's population. Dallas remains a racially segregated city with more than eight of every ten blacks living in majority black areas. West Dallas is just one of these segregated enclaves. The population of the West Dallas study area is 13,161 of whom more than 85 percent are black.[9] The neighborhood developed primarily as a rural black settlement on the fringe of the city. The area was one of the early dumping grounds for the city's solid waste. For years, West Dallas residents lived in squalor and had few basic services because they were outside of the city boundaries.

One of the oldest institutions in the neighborhood is the Thomas A. Edison School built in 1909. One of the oldest industries in the neighborhood is the 63-acre Murph Metals secondary lead smelter (later known as RSR Corporation). The company began operations in the neighborhood in 1934 near the Thomas Edison School. West Dallas was annexed by the city in 1954. Two years later, a 3,500-unit public housing project covering more than 500 acres opened just north of the smelter. Many of the residents' homes were torn down as a "slum clearance" effort to make way for the massive public housing development.

The Dallas Housing Authority is the chief landlord in the West Dallas neighborhood. Most of the privately owned housing near the public housing project is absentee-owned. Less than one-third of the housing in the area is owner-occupied. In the census tracts where the barracks-like public housing units are located, families are typically black, female-headed, and poor. More than two-thirds of the households have incomes below the poverty level.[10] The demand for privately owned housing in this low-income area that lies some four miles west of the sparkling "Big D" (as Dallas is affectionately tagged) skyline has been dampened by the concentration of public housing, systematic neglect by city government, deteriorating infrastructure, and industrial pollution from the nearby RSR lead smelter.

The housing project, which was built in the mid–1950s, was located just fifty feet from the sprawling West Dallas RSR lead smelter's property line and in a direct path of the prevailing southerly winds. The secondary smelter recovered lead from used automobile batteries and other materials. During peak operation in the mid–1960s, the plant employed more than 400 persons. However, it pumped more than 269 tons of lead particles each year into the West Dallas air.[11] Lead particles were blown by prevailing winds through the doors and windows of nearby residents and onto the West Dallas streets, sidewalks, ballparks, and children's playgrounds. Few West Dallas residents can afford the luxury of air conditioners to contend with the long and hot Texas summers. People usually leave their windows open, sit underneath shade trees, or socialize outside on their porches to keep cool.

The toxicity of lead has been known at least since the Roman era when the metal was widely used and lead poisoning cases were first documented. However, West Dallas residents were exposed to this environmental poison for five decades. Moreover, several generations of young children were subjected to unnecessary health risks associated with lead poisoning. In 1968 the city of Dallas enacted one of the strongest lead ordinances in the country. The ordinance prohibited the emission of lead compounds in excess of 5 μg/m^3 (micrograms per cubic meter) over any thirty-day period, and prohibited any particulate concentration greater than 100 μg/m^3. The ordinance, however, proved to be a worthless piece of legislation because city officials systematically refused to enforce its lead emission standards.

Dallas officials were informed as early as 1972 that lead was finding its way into the bloodstreams of the children who lived in two minority neighborhoods (West Dallas and East Oak Cliff) near lead smelters.[12] The Dallas Health Department study found that living near the smelters was associated with a 36 percent increase in blood lead level. Children near the smelters were exposed to elevated levels of lead in the soil, air, and households. The city was urged to restrict the emissions of lead to the atmosphere and to undertake a large screening program to determine the extent of the public health problem. The city failed to take immediate action on this matter.

After repeated violations of the lead ordinance, the city in 1974 sued the local smelters to force compliance. The suits were settled a year later after the firms agreed to pay fines of $35,000 and install pollution equipment. The city later amended its lead ordinance in 1976. The amended ordinance, however, was a much weaker version than its 1968 predecessor. The new ordinance—like the old version—was not enforced consistently, while lead companies in Dallas chronically and repeatedly violated the law. The Dallas Alliance Environmental Task Force, a citizen group appointed by the Dallas City Council in 1983 to address the health concerns of West Dallas, highlighted this point in its study:

> We believe that the City has missed many opportunities to serve and protect the community-at-large and two neighborhoods in particular in relation to the lead problem we now address. It is clear that the State and Federal governments have also failed in their opportunities to regulate an industry of this type with regard to the general welfare of citizens.[13]

The United States Environmental Protection Agency (EPA) in 1978 established the National Ambient Air Quality Standard, limiting airborne lead—an average of 1.5 micrograms per cubic meter of air averaged over a ninety-day period. Two years later the EPA—concerned about health risks associated with the Dallas lead smelters—commissioned another lead screening program. The 1981 study confirmed what was basically found a decade earlier: Children living near the lead smelters were likely to have greater lead concentrations in their blood than children who did not live near smelters. Soil-lead concentrations near the RSR smelter in West Dallas, for example, averaged nine times that in the control area, while the average near the Dixie Metals smelter in East Oak Cliff was thirteen times the norm.

Federal officials received the report in February 1981. The city and companies had the report three months later. West Dallas and East Oak Cliff residents, however, did not receive formal notification of the health risks associated with living so close to the lead smelters. It was not until June 1981 that the *Dallas Morning News* broke the headline-grabbing story of the "potentially dangerous" lead levels discovered by EPA researchers. The series of lead-related articles presented in the local newspapers triggered widespread concern, public outrage, several class-action lawsuits, and legal action by the city of Dallas and the state of Texas against the smelter operators.

Soil levels found around the West Dallas Boys Club—located just a short distance from the 300-foot smokestack of the RSR smelter—forced the directors to suspend outdoor activities. The first city-sponsored tests of soil at the Boys Club showed one sample that was sixty times the level considered potentially dangerous to children.

RSR voluntarily removed and replaced the soil at the Boys Club and at the nearby school. The West Dallas Boys Club, a program that enrolled more than 1,200 youths between ages 6 and 28, and the Maro Booth Day Care Center, a facility that served children from seventy-five low-income families, were later forced to close in 1983 because of the lead problem.[14]

After all of the publicity exposed the health threat, no immediate action was forthcoming by the EPA or the city to alleviate the lead contamination problem in West Dallas. Local opposition mounted against the company. At one meeting in the spring of 1983 more than 150 angry citizens packed a room in the George Loving Place public housing project to voice their opposition to a plan to move them out rather than close the lead smelter. Residents felt their plight was being ignored because they were poor, black, and politically powerless. Patricia Spears, a home owner, community leader, and operator of a West Dallas funeral home, summed up her community's dilemma: "If we lived in Highland Park or Northeast Dallas [affluent white areas], the lead plant would have been closed in 1981. Instead of them moving us, why don't they pull together and shut the lead plant down?"[15]

It was later revealed in the March 1983 hearings conducted by U.S. Representative Elliott H. Levitas (D-Ga.) that former EPA Deputy Administrator John Hernandez needlessly scrapped a voluntary plan by RSR to clean-up the lead-contaminated "hot spots" in West Dallas. But Hernandez blocked the cleanup and called for yet another round of tests to be designed and conducted by the federal Center for Disease Control (CDC) with the EPA and Dallas Health Department. The results of this study were available in February 1983. Although the new study showed a lower percentage of children affected than the earlier study had shown, it established the smelter as the dominant source of elevated lead in the children's blood.[16]

EPA officials from the Dallas regional office were especially critical of Hernandez's handling of the local lead issue and the general design of the 1983 Dallas lead study. The testimony of Dr. Norman Dyer, regional EPA chief of toxic substances, and Dr. William McAnalley, a former EPA toxicologist who resigned over the mismanagement of the Dallas lead problem, at the Levitas hearing sent shock waves through the federal EPA. They characterized the study findings as misleading and encompassing too large a study area. Moreover, the study did not look at blood levels of the children who lived downwind from the smelters, where the highly contaminated soil was found. This design was proposed by Dr. Dyer, but was turned down by the EPA in Washington as not "cost effective." In May 1983, the *Dallas Times-Herald* conducted this very analysis in West Dallas. The newspaper found that 34 percent of the children living in the areas where soil levels were above 1,000 parts per million (ppm) had elevated blood lead levels. More than 18 percent of the children who lived in areas where soil levels were above 300 ppm had elevated blood lead levels.[17] Hernandez's delay of cleanup actions in West Dallas was tantamount to "waiting for a body count."[18]

The Levitas hearings and the subsequent departure of EPA's top administrators thrust the handling of the Dallas lead problem into the national limelight. In March 1983, the Texas Air Control Board staff recommended that the state sue RSR for violating lead emission standards. One month later, the city of Dallas joined Texas Attorney General Jim Mattox in suing RSR in state district court in Dallas. The lawsuit did not seek to close the smelter but only sought the removal of tainted soil and reduced airborne lead emissions.

The lawsuit was settled out of court in June 1983 with RSR agreeing to a soil cleanup in West Dallas, a blood-testing program for children and pregnant women, and the installation of new antipollution equipment. The pollution control equipment, however, was never installed. In May 1984, the Dallas Board of Adjustments—an agency responsible for monitoring land-use violations—requested the city attorney to order the smelter permanently closed for violating the zoning code. Four months later, the Dallas Board of Adjustments ordered the West Dallas smelter permanently closed.[19] Although the smelter is now closed, much of the contaminated soil removed from "hot spots" remains on the site along with the contaminated equipment. West Dallas residents still have questions about the contaminated site itself and future land use in their neighborhood.

It is ironic that in its fifty years of operation the smelter had not obtained all of the necessary use permits for operating in the West Dallas residential neighborhood. The city not only had the legal means of forcing the company to comply with its lead emission ordinance but also had the legal power to close the smelter for violating its zoning ordinance. Slowly, it became apparent that the Dallas "secondary lead smelters are incompatible with residential neighborhoods."[20] It is unfortunate that many of the local residents had to pay a high health price for the city's ineptness in dealing with its black citizenry.

If nothing else, the plant closure was a tribute to the tenacity of the low-income black neighborhood to withstand the assaults of pollution, inept government officials, and institutionalized discrimination. D.W. Nauss, a *Dallas Times-Herald* reporter, captured the change in West Dallas residents:

> Once united only by poverty and powerlessness, the community has been brought together by the shared trauma of living with the lead smelter and the need to save what little they have. The pollution problem also has awakened the community to other concerns, such as industrial development and housing redevelopment, and has made many residents for the first time cast a hard, distrusting eye toward city plans for the area.[21]

One of the long and bitter legal battles of the West Dallas residents who have lived in the shadow of the RSR lead smelter was finally resolved in an out-of-court settlement in the summer of 1985. The settlement, estimated at $20 million, was reached between RSR and Dallas attorney Frederick M. Baron who sued on behalf of 370 children—almost all of whom were poor and black residents of West Dallas public housing—and 40 property owners. The agreement is one of the largest community lead-contamination settlements ever awarded. The settlement (with interest accruing over a thirty-year period) will funnel nearly $45 million to the children in periodic payments. Although no amount of money can ever repay the harm caused by lead poisoning of several generations of West Dallas children, the settlement does reveal that poor black communities are no longer willing to accept other people's pollution.

Another class-action lawsuit, *Annie Young et al. v. RSR Corp. et al.*, by residents of West Dallas and East Oak Cliff neighborhoods has not been resolved. Residents of these two mostly black Dallas neighborhoods are charging the city and the lead smelter companies with discrimination in the placement of the plants and in enforcing local environmental standards. As in the case of Houston's Northwood Manor residents, the Dallas residents may discover that environmental discrimination is easier to document empirically than it is to prove in a court of law.

Endnotes

[1]Michael R. Greenberg and Richard F. Anderson, *Hazardous Waste Sites: The Credibility Gap* (New Brunswick, NJ: Rutgers University Center for Urban Policy Research, 1984), p. 158.

[2]Commission for Racial Justice, *Toxic Wastes and Race*, p. 3.

[3]U.S. General Accounting Office, *Siting of Hazardous Waste Landfills*, p. 2; Samuel S. Epstein, Lester O. Brown, and Carl Pope, *Hazardous Waste in America* (San Francisco: Sierra Club Books, 1983), pp. 33–39; See Adeline Levine, *Love Canal: Science, Politics, and People* (Lexington, Mass.: Lexington Books, 1982), Chapter 1; Office of Technology Assessment, *Technologies and Management Strategies for Hazardous Waste Control* (Washington, D.C.: U.S. Government Printing Office, 1983), p. 3. Epstein et al., *Hazardous Waste in America*, pp. 6–11. Michael H. Brown, *Laying Waste: The Poisoning of America by Toxic Chemicals* (New York: Pantheon Books, 1980), p. 267.

[4]Quoted in the *New York Times*, November 19, 1983.

[5]Robert D. Bullard, *Invisible Houston: The Black Experience in Boom and Bust* (College Station: Texas A & M University Press, 1987), Chapter 2.

[6]See Robert D. Bullard, "Endangered Environs: The Price of Unplanned Growth in Boomtown Houston," *California Sociologist* 7 (Summer 1984): 84–112; Richard Babcock, "Houston: Unzoned, Unfettered, and Mostly Unrepentant," *Planning* 48 (1982): 21–33; Joe R. Feagin, "The Global Context of Metropolitan Growth: Houston and the Oil Industry," *American Journal of Sociology* 90 (May 1985): 1204–1230.

[7]Robert D. Bullard, "Solid Waste Sites and the Black Houston Community," *Sociological Inquiry* 53 (Spring 1983): 273–288.

[8]For a detailed account of this dispute, see Bullard, *Invisible Houston*, Chapter 6: *Houston Chronicle*, November 8, 11, 15, 22, 1979, December 15, 22, 1979, June 19, 1980; *Houston Post*, December 15, 1981.

[9]City of Dallas, *1987 Census Tract Book* (Dallas: Dallas Department of Housing and Neighborhood Services, 1987), pp. 4–10.

[10]The Enterprise Foundation, *Dallas: A Survey of Poverty and Housing* (Dallas: Meadows Foundation, 1983), pp. 43–45.

[11]*Dallas Morning News*, December 8, 1986, p. 1A.

[12]Ibid. Dallas Alliance Environmental Task Force, *Final Report*, (Dallas: Dallas Alliance, June 29, 1983), p. 6; *Dallas Morning News*, June 1, 1981; K. W. Brown, J. W. Mullins, E. P. Richitt, G. T. Flatman, and S. C. Black, "Assessing Soil Lead Contamination in Dallas, Texas," *Environmental Monitoring and Assessment* 5 (1985): 137–154.

[13]Dallas Alliance Environmental Task Force, *Final Report*, p. 3.

[14]*Dallas Morning News*, October 2, 1981, p. 1A.

[15]Quoted in *Dallas Morning News*, April 27, 1983, p. 1A. Interviews conducted on May 27, 1988, with Mattie Nash, a West Dallas neighborhood representative to the Dallas Alliance Environmental Task Force, and Reverend R. T. Conley, a West Dallas minister, yielded views similar to those of Patricia Spears. Local community leaders expressed the opinion that the government was dragging its feet because West Dallas was a poor black neighborhood.

[16]U. S. Environmental Protection Agency, "Report of the Dallas Area Lead Assessment Study," (Dallas: U.S. Environmental Protection Agency Region VI, 1983), p. 8.

[17]See Jonatha Lash, Katherine Gillman, and David Sheridan, *A Season of Spoils: The Reagan Administration's Attack on the Environment* (New York: Pantheon Books, 1984), pp. 135–136.

[18]Ibid., p. 131.

[19]See *Dallas Morning News*, October 18, 1983, p. 1A; December 7, 1986, p. 31A.

[20]Dallas Alliance Environmental Task Force, *Final Report*, p. i.

[21]*Dallas Times-Herald*, July 17, 1983.

Unhealthy and Sick in Los Angeles*

Jonathan Cohn

The drive from West 190th Street to Vernon Boulevard is a straight shot up the Harbor Free-way, right through the heart of South Central Los Angeles.[1] Although it can take forty-five minutes at rush hour, the traffic has usually thinned out by one o'clock in the morning—the time when a security guard named Jose Antonio Montenegro used to commute home from his job at an electronics factory. It was an easy drive he had come to know well and, on clear nights when he could glimpse the twinkling lights of the skyscrapers downtown, it was even vaguely picturesque.

But on a July evening in 2005, Tony, as he called himself, never saw the lights of down-town. In fact, the only lights he could see were the red and white ones on the backs of cars in front of him—and even they were a blur. Tony had started feeling woozy and disoriented a few minutes before, while he was finishing his shift. By the time he had pulled his pickup truck onto the highway, his vision started to go, too. He thought about pulling over, but even for somebody who lived in a relatively rough part of town, this was no place to stop in the middle of the night. So he pressed on, slowing his car to well below the speed limit, relying on his knowledge of the route to guide him home.

Somehow he made it, parking his truck on the street and stumbling his way into bed, not bothering to wake his wife or young son—hoping, apparently, that with a good night's sleep he'd feel right again. When he woke up the next morning, however, his vision had deteriorated even further. The blur was gone; now he could see nothing but darkness. Tony's wife, Gloria, promptly took him to a local clinic, where it didn't take a doctor long to deduce what had happened. For years Tony had battled diabetes. Now he had suffered one of the well-known complications of the condition: he'd had a stroke.

Tony was still relatively young at the time, just fifty, with a thick, muscular build. That made him a relatively unlikely victim of stroke, even with the diabetes, just so long as he got the regular medical care the condition requires. But regular medical care is exactly what Tony had lacked for most of his adult life. Although he'd been working full-time almost con-tinuously since arriving in the United States from El Salvador nearly twenty years before, he'd had health insurance only sporadically. On the income he and his wife made, medical care had become a luxury item and luxuries were not something they could generally afford. So Tony did not get his regular checkups or keep track of his blood sugar or take the medica-tions that had been prescribed for him. Medically, he was a walking time bomb.

Tony's situation was not unusual. In fact, it was—and is—entirely typical for its time and place. The urban poor face more health hazards than most Americans, for such reasons as the toxic dust of slum housing and the destructive effects of drug abuse. Yet the urban poor also have less access to medical care—because the jobs available to them frequently don't provide decent insurance and because the safety net facilities on which they depend simply aren't up to the task. Although this is hardly a new problem, it has gotten demonstrably worse as the strains on private and public health insurance have grown in the last twenty to thirty years. And nowhere is this more true than in Los Angeles, which by the end of the 1990s had come to resemble health care's version of the apocalypse. It had the nation's single largest concentration of people without insurance—nearly 2 million, or about one out of every three adults.[2] It also had what was, arguably, the single most overmatched network of publicly financed clinics and hospitals.

For the uninsured and underinsured of the inner city in Los Angeles, the lack of adequate medical care was just one of many routine hardships—not so different, really, from the difficulty of finding a job that would pay a decent wage, a car that would start in the morning, or a neighborhood where kids could play safely on the sidewalks. And in a perverse sense, this baseline of everyday struggle spared them the financial crises that had, over the years, affected middle-class families like the Rotzlers, the Hilsabecks, and the Sampsons.* If you lived in an economically depressed part of Los Angeles, or any other major American city, you probably didn't own a house to lose and hadn't accumulated savings to deplete once illness struck. Medical bills couldn't ruin you financially, simply because, to be ruined, you had to have amassed some wealth in the first place.

Still, even in the bleakest corners of South Central Los Angeles, some families clung to one precious asset: hope. It was the hope that they could break out of poverty and, eventually, put their children on a path to a better, more secure life—the same hope that had first lured Tony and Gloria Montenegro to the United States many years before. But for them and for millions of other families in America's sprawling ghettos, hope required health. And when the latter deteriorated, so did the former.

Like much of America, Los Angeles has undergone a dramatic economic transformation in the last 25 to 30 years. For most of the postwar period, the city was a center of industrial might—a hub of manufacturing activity as prosperous and vital to the country's well-being as Detroit or Pittsburgh.[3] But instead of turning out cars or steel, Los Angeles made airplanes. Rockwell, Lockheed, McDonnell Douglas—all of them had major operations in the city, where they produced not just glimmering flying machines but an affluent existence for the working and middle classes.

The decline of the cold war changed all that. Cuts in national defense spending devastated the aerospace industry—and, with it, the area's base of stable, decent-paying jobs. Although manufacturing in Los Angeles didn't completely die, it changed forever, shifting more to nonunionized industries such as garment making and upholstery, where the work paid far less. Meanwhile, the largest sources of new jobs were the service industries, which also had less generous wages and benefits. For a while, the number of Americans moving out of southern California actually exceeded the number coming in. But the state's population continued to balloon anyway, because of a constant influx of foreigners, pre-

---

*Editors' Note: These are middle-class families devastated by catastrophic medical bills and described in earlier sections of Cohn's book.

dominantly Latino and Asian. Along with the area's African-American community, the immigrants provided the bulk of the new low-wage workforce.

Tony was part of this wave.[4] As a child growing up in Santa Ana, a medium-size city in the north of El Salvador, he had worked on construction projects with his father, with whom he lived. (His father and mother had separated.) But from an early age Tony had aspirations for a professional life; he studied hard in grade school and was accepted by a university, where he had started to learn accounting. Tony says he was a good student—that is, until the political unrest began. It was the late 1970s, and El Salvador was descending into a civil war between the American-backed government and Marxist guerrillas. Although most of the actual fighting took place in the countryside, violence seeped into the cities as well. With the economy grinding to a halt and the university stopping classes, Tony decided to get out—partly because it was the only way to get ahead and partly, he admits because he was young and leaving seemed like an adventure. With a group of friends, he made his way to Mexico and then, driving in an old Ford Mustang, over the border to Texas. Another two days of driving brought him to Los Angeles, where some fellow refugees from El Salvador introduced him to a man who owned a garment factory and was looking for workers.

The factory was typical of the new economy in Los Angeles. It was an early twentieth-century cinder-block building that had been subdivided into large rooms scattered over ten floors, each room filled with immigrants from Asia and Latin America—most of them without official papers—who made clothing, shoes, or upholstery. (Tony got his working papers a few years later and eventually became a full U.S. citizen.) With only windows and fans to cool many parts of the building, it was literally a sweatshop. But for workers like Tony, it was also a home. By day, he sat hunched over a sewing machine, stitching together fabric covers for couches and being paid a few dollars for each new piece he produced. By night, he slept in a living area he and some of the other workers shared in the cavernous basement, two floors below ground level. There, the men cooked with hot plates and toasters, using stray cinder blocks to mark off their personal space, which they shared with the occasional mouse. Just one bathroom was available to them, a few stories up in a part of the factory that made shoes. Otherwise, the only plumbing consisted of a water hose snaked in from outside and a huge, empty oil tank underneath that the workers used as a drain and gradually filled over time.

Tony was OK with the living conditions. In fact, he says, he was happy to have the job—and a base from which to explore his new world. Like that of many other recently transplanted foreigners, his English was still very poor. But even when he was living in El Salvador, Tony had developed a passion for American and British music, from Sinatra to the Rolling Stones. One night, a man who was renting some space for himself in the factory—one of the few Anglos there—played an old album that Tony recognized. Tony used the opportunity to introduce himself by pointing at the record player and using one of the few English words he knew: "Beatles." He and the man, named Richard Berghendahl, became fast friends.

Eventually, the management changed and the new managers decided to renovate the building. Fortunately for Tony, he'd recently begun dating Gloria, who was also an immigrant from El Salvador and whom he'd first met at a party. Gloria had come from the countryside, fleeing the violence there. (She would later tell stories of waking up and walking out her front door to find dead soldiers lying at her feet.) Tony liked the fact that she was serious and mature, the type of woman who talked openly about her plans for the future—

somebody, in other words, with whom he could imagine spending his life. So the two soon married, in a storefront marriage parlor, and moved together into a house they found on the northern edge of South Central, just a mile or so from the Coliseum sports arena. It was a relatively small place—a stand-alone dwelling behind a larger home, with just two bedrooms, a kitchen, and a bathroom. But with Tony between jobs and Gloria making not a lot of money doing domestic work at a rest home, the $350 monthly rent was still more than they could afford on their own. They offered to split the house with Richard, who gladly accepted (since he had been living at the factory, too, and the alternative was sleeping in his old Volkswagen van).

It was 1986 when Tony and Gloria moved there, near the peak of the nation's crack cocaine epidemic that had turned Los Angeles—like most American cities—into a virtual war zone. The Montenegros were on the front lines, because across the street from their next-door neighbor's home was a liquor store with an outdoor pay phone. This phone was a magnet for drug dealers, and violence was common. One sunny afternoon, according to Tony, a crowd approached a young man standing in front of the liquor store. A minute later, the crowd had dispersed and the man was lying splayed on the sidewalk, blood streaming from a fresh bullet wound in his head.

At the time, the Montenegros' neighborhood, like most of south-central, was predominantly African-American. One day in 1992, while driving home from an English class he was taking, Tony heard that verdicts had been issued in the case of Rodney King, exonerating the policemen who had been accused of beating King—a young African-American man—during an arrest a year before. By the time Tony turned onto Martin Luther King Boulevard, the main thoroughfare that ran closest to his house, unrest over the verdict had already broken out. When he got to his cross street, he saw rioters torching the gas station on the corner and looters ransacking a nearby grocery store. Another group had broken into the liquor store across the street from Tony's home, so he quickly went inside and took Gloria up to the second floor. There, the two spent the night listening to rifles firing into the air and glass crashing onto the sidewalk, while the glow of their burning city lit up the sky.

Tony says he would have liked to move elsewhere—to Culver City or La Brea or anywhere that was a little less dicey. But, like his dream of resuming his business studies, that hope would have to remain on hold, given the limited income on which he and Gloria lived. After a stint working for a commercial printer, Tony had begun working as a security guard. The jobs paid modestly, at or just above the minimum wage. And although Tony had insurance while he worked for the printer, he didn't when he moved to security work. The first company that employed him didn't offer coverage. The second apparently did, but Tony says he didn't find out about it until after he'd been working there for several weeks—past the official enrollment period during which new workers were allowed to apply for coverage.

To this day, Tony says he's not certain whether or not the company informed him of the option. Given his still limited English, it's possible that he was told and simply didn't understand; it's also possible that nobody bothered to inform him. (Such confusion is common in immigrant communities.) But it wasn't something about which he had thought to inquire, since the previous job didn't offer benefits and he didn't expect them. Nor was it something he pondered particularly hard. After all, he'd always been healthy anyway.

Every year, the World Health Organization (WHO) publishes information from countries around the globe, tabulating statistics such as the number of children who receive all their recommended vaccinations and the number of people who die from various types of cancer. Every year, the Department of Public Health of Los Angeles County goes through a similar exercise, compiling statistics about the county's eight geographical districts. The Montenegros lived on the edge of what was called Service Planning Area 6 (SPA–6), which stretched from downtown Los Angeles in the north all the way to the city of Compton in the south. And by global standards, this area didn't stack up particularly well. The death rate from cervical cancer in the Montenegros' district was more than twice the average for the rest of the United States.[5] It was also higher than the average in most of the developed world and even in medical backwaters like rural China. Another set of data showed that the children of families in the Montenegros' section of Los Angeles were far more likely than their counterparts in the industrialized world to be born at dangerously low weights—and, afterward, to develop asthma or diabetes during childhood.[6] Going down the list of measures reveals the same story over and over again. According to virtually all meaningful statistics, the health of people living in and around South Central was substandard—and in a few instances, it bordered on what many would consider third-world conditions.

Service Planning Area 6 included South Central, which had become predominantly Latino; and Watts, which remained largely African-American. The two communities had distinct health profiles, for reasons of both genetics and culture.[7] (Among other things, Latinos overall seemed to benefit from a traditional diet rich in legumes.) But at least in this part of Los Angeles, the two groups did share one characteristic that helped explain the overall poor health outcomes: poverty. More than one-third of the residents had incomes below the federal poverty level of around $20,000 in yearly income for a family of four.[8] And many more residents had incomes hovering just above that level. Amid these economic conditions, drug use, unprotected sex, and other forms of destructive behavior were common—which was why, for example, the infection rate for AIDS in South Central Los Angeles was climbing even as the nation as a whole was bringing the epidemic under control.

The link between behavior and poor health undoubtedly reinforced public antipathy toward government spending on health programs in the inner city; if the people living in and around the Montenegros were shooting themselves up with drugs or shooting each other with bullets, just how much money was everybody else supposed to spend on bringing them back to health? But destructive conduct had a way of visiting consequences on people who had nothing to do with it, such as toddlers growing up in homes filled with secondhand smoke or teenagers catching stray bullets in drive-by shootings. And sometimes the people who chose to engage in unhealthy habits did so for legitimate reasons. Eating a proper diet wasn't easy in neighborhoods that lacked large grocery stores with affordable fresh produce.[9] (Not surprisingly, consumption of fruits and vegetables in SPA–6 was the lowest in Los Angeles.) And in particularly blighted sections of town, parents who returned from work late had to weigh the benefits of outdoor exercise for their children against the risk of violence. At one point, a housekeeper at a local hotel who lived about a mile and a half from the Montenegros explained that she kept her children inside, watching television, lest they get caught in cross fire while playing outside.[10] She wasn't paranoid: two weeks before the interview, a shootout outside her window had crippled a teenager.

In any event, behavior was not exclusively responsible for the health problems of the inner city.[11] Far from it. Living in South Central Los Angeles meant living in close proximity to the region's smog-producing freeways and soot-belching factories. All too frequently, it also meant living in substandard housing with old, chipped paint and decaying insulation. Community activists repeatedly claimed that these environmental hazards were part of the reason for the region's high rates of mortality from cancer. And while studies generally weren't able to substantiate the link with cancer, they did tie environmental hazards to at least two other problems that were reaching epidemic proportions, particularly among children: lead poisoning and asthma. On the opposite side of the Harbor Freeway from the Montenegros' house, a neighborhood adjacent to a group of metals factories had acquired the nickname Asthma Town. At Saint John's Well Child Center, one of several clinics that provided discounted and free pediatric service to the community, the majority of children who received care had dangerously high blood levels of lead, most likely from deteriorating house paint.[12] Doctors there had also become accustomed to dealing with less harmful, but no less disturbing, medical issues arising from substandard housing—such as treating rat bites and removing cockroaches from children's ears.

The other critical way economic hardship affected the health of people living in South Central Los Angeles was by cutting them off from routine medical care. Nearly half of the working-age adults in the area had no health insurance at all—a situation that reflected not only a lack of private, job-based coverage but also a confusing array of public insurance programs that supposedly existed to fill in the gaps. Together, the county, state, and federal government ran what were really a dozen separate health insurance plans, each one targeting a narrowly defined group of low-income people. There was Medi-Cal, California's version of Medicaid, which covered children, pregnant women, adults, families, and those who needed long-term care—but with different income thresholds for each group. Healthy Families, which was California's version of S-CHIP, also had varying income guidelines and its own registration process. The county ran its own insurance programs, based on ability to pay, but only for people who didn't qualify for the other programs.

Residents who were technically eligible for these programs frequently didn't know about them—or couldn't figure how to apply.[13] The programs also required continual renewals, requiring recipients to reaffirm their low-income status with extensive documentation; as a result, people frequently complained that they had been unexpectedly thrown off the rolls, sometimes because they'd failed to submit paperwork a second time and sometimes, they said, for no good reason at all.[14] The stringent requirements for enrolling in these programs ostensibly reflected a desire by the county and state to weed out people trying to defraud the system—a legitimate concern, to be sure. And, of course, not all those who told a journalist that they had filed paperwork on time had actually done so. On the other hand, it was an open secret that officials in California—and many other states—used these requirements as a way of trimming program rolls without attracting negative attention in the media.[15]

All this went a long way toward explaining why one-fourth of the adults in South Central Los Angeles had no regular source of medical care—a category that included Tony Montenegro. Although Gloria had gone onto Medi-Cal when she was pregnant, and although the program covered their son, Antonio, when he was born, Tony as an employed man was not eligible for these programs.[16] So he simply didn't bother with medical care. In fact, he can't remember going to the doctor even a single time in the early 1990s—not until one day when he noticed that his toe was starting to hurt.

As it turned red and swollen, it became too painful for walking and Tony decided he would have to get it checked out. He knew of a local storefront clinic, one of many in the area that provided cheap, á la carte medical care to immigrants on a cash business. For a $25 office visit fee, a doctor examined the toe, took a history, and decided that Tony should get tested for diabetes. Tony had a hard time believing that this could be the problem; except for the toe, he says, he felt absolutely fine, with no fatigue, no dryness of the mouth, none of the classic symptoms. But he got the test anyway and, indeed, it came back positive.

Now Tony had a serious problem. He was supposed to test his blood sugar daily, more often if he was under stress or had eaten badly. He was also supposed to take pills to control the sugar—and if those didn't work—inject insulin. But Tony figured that if he followed those orders to the letter, the test strips plus the medications would cost a few hundred dollars a month. And that was not money he and Gloria had lying around. Gloria was doing domestic work at a rest home for the elderly, making pretty much what Tony did: close to the minimum wage. That put their household income at around $25,000—and their expenses had increased since Antonio came into their lives. In addition to the extra food and children's supplies, the couple had decided to move into the main house on the same lot, a slightly larger apartment that had a living room. Between rent, food, utilities, clothing, gas, and the minimum required insurance for the car, they didn't have much at the end of the month.

So sometimes Tony got his supplies and medicine.[17] And sometimes he didn't. He hoped for the best and, for a while, he seemed to be getting by—until that night on the freeway when he had the stroke.

Endnotes

[1]Based on author interviews with Gloria Montenegro, Jose Antonio Montenegro, and Richard Berghendahl.

[2]The State of Health Insurance in California: Findings from the 2001 California Health Interview Survey (Los Angeles: UCLA Center for Health Policy Research), June 2002. Available at www.healthpolicy.ucla.edu. See also Julie Marquis, "Many in County Remain Uninsured, Survey Finds," *LAT*, October 17, 2000.

[3]As Harold Meyerson, one of the area's best-known writers, famously put it, after the cold war the bottom didn't fall out of the Los Angeles economy. The middle did. Harold Meyerson, "California's Progressive Mosaic," *American Prospect*, Vol. 12, No. 11, June 18, 2001; and Jonathan Peterson, "Industrial Blues in the Southland," *LAT*, July 27, 1991.

[4]G. Montenegro, J. A. Montenegro, and R. Berghendahl, interviews with author.

[5]In 1999, the age-adjusted mortality rate from cervical cancer in SPA–6 was 5.8; for the United States as a whole it was 2.2, and for rural China it was 4.17. Los Angeles County Department of Public Health, *Key Indicators of Public Health*, 1999/2000; World Health Organization, Worldwide Cancer Mortality Statistics.

[6]For comparisons, see Organization of Economic Cooperation and Development, *Health at a Glance: OECD Indicators 2005* (Paris, France), 2005, p. 33.

[7]See KFF, "Race, Ethnicity and Medical Care," Washington, D.C., October 1999.

[8]Los Angeles County Department of Public Health, *Key Indicators*.

[9]See also California Department of Health Services, "Nutrition and Health Barriers Facing California Latinos," *Issue Brief*, September 2005.

[10]Mariya Moratoya, interviews with author.

[11]Hector Becerra, "BP Settles Lawsuit for $81 Million," *LAT*, March 18, 2005; Deborah Schoch, "Study Links Freeways to Asthma Risk," *LAT*, September 21, 2005; and Ben Ehrenreich, "Goo and Gunk," *LA Weekly*, October 19, 2001.

[12]Jim Manja, Richard Morgan, and Paul Giboney, interviews with author. Manja is president of Saint John's; Morgan is an outreach worker there; Giboney is a physician at the Clinica Monseñor Oscar A. Romero. For more background on the area's lead poisoning problem, see S. J. Rothenberg, E. A. Williams Jr., S. Delrahim, E. Kahn, M. Lu, M. Manalo, M. Sanchez, D.J. Wooten, "Blood Levels in Children in South Central Los Angeles," *Archives of Environmental Health*, Vol. 51, No. 5, September-October 1995, pp. 383–388.

[13]Perhaps nothing better illustrated the confusion than a "decision chart" published by the state, designed to help residents of Los Angeles figure out whether they were eligible for public insurance and if so for which program. It was a ten-step flowchart with thirteen boxes, difficult for even a native English-speaking, Ivy League educated health care journalist to decipher. The sheet, published by the California Department of Public Social Services in July 2002, was available four years later at a URL on the department's website: http://www. ladpss.orgldpss/ health_care/healthcare_access_manual_pdffileslpdflHealth%2OCare%20 Decisio n%20Chart%202002.pdf.

[14]During interviews with uninsured residents of Los Angeles County in 2004, 2005, and 2006, these residents repeatedly raised this issue. For a systematic study of so-called churning in Medi-Cal and its effects, see Gerry Fairbrother, *How Much Does Churning in Medi-Cal Cost?* (Woodland Hills: California Endowment), April 2005. As the report notes, churning can end up wasting money, simply by fostering so much additional paperwork and communication.

[15]Barbara Lyons, interview with author.

[16]G. Montenegro and J. A. Montenegro, interviews with author.

[17]A study published in 2006 confirmed that because uninsured Latinos in Los Angeles were less likely to get routine physical examinations, they were more likely to develop blindness. Sylvia H. Paz, Rohit Varma, Ronald Klein, Joanne Wu, and Staley Azen, "Non-Compliance with Vision Care Guidelines in Latinos with Type 2 Diabetes Mellitus," *Ophthalmology*, Vol. 113, No. 8, August 2006, pp. 1372–1377.

Afterword

At a time when "big government" is again targetted by conservatives as the source of social ills, we present a different kind of government culpability narrative. The articles in this volume suggest that people living in urban areas are often disproportionately burdened by conditions associated with a lack of government action and/or oversight. For example, do some government culpability narratives help us indict criminal justice systems that brush aside or ignore the disparate impact of their practices on certain populations? Or, is it the absence of sound public policy that embraces a "right to housing" agenda[1] so that the benefits associated with living in stable communities do not accrue to certain groups based on class or race? Or would government culpability narratives help focus more attention on academic policies that are frequently rooted in complicated, contrived, and sometimes false notions of meritocracy? Sadly, the answer to these questions leads us to make arguments about a shame of governance, as we suggest that an improper stewarding of the public's interest often occurs. Thus, it is not necessarily government that ails us but government that consistently fails to address human needs while it allies itself with powerful commercial interests.

In the cases before us, we insist that the public's interest should be larger than immediate gratification for selected groups in society, or for those who we can characterize as having cumulative advantages. At the same time, however, some have suggested that the public's interests have been manipulated by neoliberal forces that undermine social policy in favor of private interests. A number of scholars are sympathetic to this assertion, and this volume provides a forum for this perspective. But, we also note that while we understand and argue that a shame of governance is a primary condition, we can take a few moments to be less abstract in our assertions.

If we contemplate that a shame of governance has dampened the life chances of many urban dwellers, we should be able to recognize that governments often reflect the values, norms, and acquiescence of majorities of the population they govern. Therefore, if large and scattered segments of the population are inwardly willing to adopt public choice theory arguments that are rooted in a market logic and remain silent about social arrangements that afford them a comfortable life *at the expense of others*, then it may be useful for us to be more vocal in pointing out *how* a shame of governance has come about.

For example, scholars and professionals at colleges and universities are often cognizant of the historical legacy of the U.S. and how institutions have helped to create, reproduce, and complicate classism, racism, and sexism in our society, all of which continue to hamper urban residents disproportionately today. Yet, many who are comfortably situated within the academy are ill-prepared or aloof and fail to engage solutions to race, class, and gender oppression. Instead, constructed variations of meritocracy conveniently shroud possible paths to resolution. Unfortunately, we argue that this posture contributes to anchoring unhealthy practices, while inspiring individually-oriented groups toward simple self-satisfaction and in the process discouraging the value of government culpability narratives.

Urban Society: The Shame of Governance is a reminder for us to recognize that practices of the past have not dissipated in their effects on many inner-city residents today. This, despite some researchers who suggest that we might remove ourselves from the rear-view mirror because *happier days are ahead*—as we celebrate the successes of those who have managed to avoid the wreckage around us. We used to have a name for these celebrations—*the survival of the fittest*. Once upon a time (*and at every possible turn*), staunchly capable scholars everywhere would handily pick apart and expose ideologies behind the cryptic promotion of these celebrations. Unfortunately, today, the energies associated with these festivities have been tacitly adopted by ever widening circles to the extent that—unsurprisingly—a shame of governance has become harder and harder for most to detect.

Endnote

[1]Bratt, Rachael G., Michael E. Stone and Chester Hartman. 2006. *A Right to Housing: Foundation for a New Social Agenda*. Philadelphia: Temple University Press.